Faithful Reason

D1553768

'The breadth of Haldane's reading in philosophy and theology...is astounding.'
Observer

'*Faithful Reason* is not merely readable, but elegant....The essays in this book are learned, clear and suggestive....The result is a book that is a pleasure to read.' *Paul Weithman, University of Notre Dame*

'*Faithful Reason* confirms my impression of the author as one of the most prolific, knowledgeable and wide-ranging analytical philosophers working today.' *Piers Benn, Imperial College, London*

In *Faithful Reason*, the noted Catholic philosopher John Haldane explores various aspects of intellectual and practical life from a perspective inspired by Catholic thought and informed by his distinctive philosophical approach: 'Analytical Thomism'. Haldane's discussions of ethics, politics, education, art, social philosophy and other themes explain why Catholic thought is still relevant in today's world, and show how the legacy of Thomas Aquinas can benefit modern philosophy in its efforts to answer fundamental questions about humanity and its place within nature. Drawing on a Catholic philosophical tradition that is committed to concepts of the world's intrinsic intelligibility and the objectivity of truth, *Faithful Reason*'s bold and insightful perspectives provide rich matter for debate, and food for further thought.

John Haldane is Professor of Philosophy and Director of the Centre for Ethics, Philosophy and Public Affairs at the University of St Andrews. His books include *An Intelligent Person's Guide to Religion* (2003), *Atheism and Theism*, second edition with J.J.C. Smart (2003) and *Modern Writings on Thomism* (2003).

Faithful Reason

Essays Catholic and philosophical

John Haldane

Routledge
Taylor & Francis Group

LONDON AND NEW YORK

First published 2004
by Routledge
11 New Fetter Lane, London EC4P 4EE

Simultaneously published in the USA and Canada
by Routledge
29 West 35th Street, New York, NY 10001

Routledge is an imprint of the Taylor & Francis Group

Typeset in Galliard by Graphicraft Limited, Hong Kong
Printed and bound in Great Britain by Antony Rowe Ltd, Chippenham, Wiltshire

British Library Cataloguing in Publication Data
A catalogue record for this book is available from the British Library

Library of Congress Cataloging in Publication Data
Haldane, John.
  Faithful reason : essays Catholic and philosophical / John Haldane.
    p. cm.
  Includes bibliographical references and index.
  1. Catholic Church and philosophy. 2. Thomists. I. Title.
  BX1795.P47H35 2004
  149'.91—dc22

                                                2003069348

ISBN 0–415–20702–9 (hbk)
ISBN 0–415–20703–7 (pbk)

Contents

Preface

The idea for this collection goes back some while, and since first being conceived the scheme of contents has undergone some revision. Such is the dynamism of even the dullest mind that what was thought one day may come to be replaced by a different, if not better, thought the next. That said, as minds mature they take definite shape, and this impresses itself on every mental product, so that within the diversity of a writer's output one may discern recurrent features. So it is in my own case, and a reader may quickly become familiar with the particular style and substance of my thinking. I am inclined to regard this as no bad thing as it establishes something of the order of a deep acquaintance, and sometimes even an approximation to friendship.

Agreeable as it should be, that is, of course, quite different to agreement. If readers feel themselves to be at odds with what I write I hope that they will at least judge that the disagreement is one between minds united by their common interests. In addition, while the limitations of the essay as a mode of intellectual inquiry are evident, so too should be its virtues: brevity, concision, and encouragement to readers to think directly for themselves. I can only hope that the present collection has enough of these features.

I am very grateful to the staff at Routledge, who have shown great patience in awaiting delivery of this collection. It is an old saying that 'man proposes and God disposes'; in the period since this collection was first contracted I have come to see the wisdom in this and in the corresponding saying that 'if you want to make God laugh tell him your plans'. My plans have several times been disrupted, and were it not for the patience of Clare Johnson and her colleagues this book might well have fallen by the wayside. I am also indebted to my family: my wife Hilda, and my children Kirsty, James, Alice and John, who have shown great fortitude in enduring my frequent distraction. It is to Hilda, without whom the children would not be, and without whom I would not be a professional philosopher, that this book is dedicated in loving friendship.

John Haldane
St Andrews

Acknowledgements

The chapters appearing below derive from the following sources and are reprinted with the permission of the original publishers.

1 'Thomism and the Future of Catholic Philosophy', from *New Blackfriars* 80 (1999), pp. 158–71. Reprinted with permission from *New Blackfriars*.
2 'MacIntyre's Thomist Revival: What Next?' from J. Horton and S. Mendus (eds), *After MacIntyre* (Cambridge: Polity Press, 1994), pp. 91–107. Reprinted with permission from Blackwell Publishing.
3 'The Diversity of Philosophy and the Unity of its Vocation: Some Philosophical Reflections on *Fides et Ratio*', from T.L. Smith (ed.), *Faith and Reason* (South Bend, Ind.: St Augustine's Press, 2001), pp. 141–52. Reprinted with permission from St Augustine's Press.
4 'Critical Orthodoxy', from *Louvain Studies* 14 (1989), pp. 188–204. Reprinted with permission from *Louvain Studies*.
5 'Infallibility, Authority and Faith', from *Heythrop Journal* 38 (1997), pp. 265–82. Reprinted with permission from Blackwell Publishing.
6 'Incarnational Anthropology', from D. Cockburn (ed.), *Human Beings* (Cambridge: Cambridge University Press, 1991), pp. 191–211. Reprinted with permission from the Royal Institute of Philosophy and Cambridge University Press.
7 'Examining the Assumption', from *Heythrop Journal* 43 (2002), pp. 411–29. Reprinted with permission from Blackwell Publishing.
8 'Medieval and Renaissance Ethics', from P. Singer (ed.), *A Companion to Ethics* (Oxford: Blackwell, 1991), pp. 133–46. Reprinted with permission from Blackwell Publishing.
9 'Natural Law and Ethical Pluralism', from R. Madsen and T. Strong (eds), *The Many and the One: Perspectives on Ethical Pluralism*, pp. 89–114. Copyright © 2003 by Princeton University Press. Reprinted by permission of Princeton University Press.
10 'From Law to Virtue and Back Again: On *Veritatis Splendor*', from J.W. Rogerson, M. Davies and M.D. Carroll (eds), *The Bible in Ethics* (Sheffield:

Sheffield University Press), 1995, pp. 27–40. Reprinted with permission from T & T Clark International.

11 'Can a Catholic Be a Liberal?' from *Melita Theologica* 43 (1992), pp. 44–57. Reprinted with permission from *Melita Theologica*.

12 'Religious Toleration', from *Filozofska Istrazivanja* 9 (1996), pp. 21–6. Reprinted with permission from *Filozofska Istrazivanja*.

13 'Chesterton's Philosophy of Education', from *Philosophy* 65 (1990), pp. 65–80. Reprinted with permission from the Royal Institute of Philosophy and Cambridge University Press.

14 'Religion in Education: In Defence of a Tradition', from *Oxford Review of Education* 14 (1988), pp. 227–37. Reprinted with permission from Taylor & Francis.

15 'Catholic Education and Catholic Identity', from T. McLaughlin, J. O'Keefe and B. O'Keefe (eds), *The Contemporary Catholic School* (London: Falmer Press, 1996), pp. 126–35. Reprinted with permission from Thompson Publishing.

16 'The Need of Spirituality in Catholic Education', from J. Conroy (ed.), *Catholic Education: Inside-Out; Outside-In* (Dublin: Veritas, 1999), pp. 188–206. Reprinted with permission from Veritas Publications.

17 'Medieval and Renaissance Aesthetics', from D. Cooper (ed.), *A Companion to Aesthetics* (Oxford: Blackwell, 1992), pp. 279–83. Reprinted with permission from Blackwell Publishing.

18 'Form, Meaning and Value: A History of the Philosophy of Architecture', from *Journal of Architecture* 4 (1999), pp. 9–21. Reprinted with permission from Taylor & Francis Ltd.

19 'Admiring the High Mountains: The Aesthetics of Environment', from *Environmental Values* 3 (1994), pp. 97–106. Reprinted with permission from White Horse Press.

20 *De Consolatione Philosophiae*, from M. McGhee (ed.), *Philosophy, Religion and the Spiritual Life* (Cambridge: Cambridge University Press, 1992), pp. 31–45. Reprinted with permission from the Royal Institute of Philosophy and Cambridge University Press.

Analytical Thomism and faithful reason

The essays that compose this book are interrelated both as regards the themes they explore and in respect of the broad intellectual approach they represent. Some years ago I gave the general title of 'Analytical Thomism' to a pair of lectures delivered at the University of Notre Dame.[1] The lectures concerned certain fundamental issues in metaphysics, epistemology and the philosophy of mind, and presented in outline the form of a unified account of these. The central element in this account was the idea of a *nature*, i.e. the *what-it-is-ness* of a thing; and I argued that the natures of the kinds of things that compose the world and the natures of our thoughts about those things are, in a sense, formally identical. What makes something to be a horse and what makes something to be a thought of a horse is the same structuring principle, viz. *horseness.* That being the case one might then say that the things of the world are reconceived in our thoughts of them. (The idea of a nature so understood also has a role to play, I believe, in reasoning about the mind/body question, about issues of value and practice, and about the origins and destiny of the world.)

Those familiar with medieval metaphysics will already recognize that the account I was offering is drawn from the work of Thomas Aquinas (particularly from the *Summa Theologiae* and the *Commentary on the De Anima* [of Aristotle]). Both prior and subsequent to those 1992 lectures I have explored aspects of this account in various writings,[2] as have others, and this has been part of a broader development of interest in Aquinas as a thinker from whom we can learn in our efforts to answer speculative questions about the nature of the mind and of the world.[3] Although those efforts have been pursued by people working in different intellectual traditions, that to which I belong, and hence that with which I have sought some synthesis with Aquinian thought, is analytical philosophy: thus the expression 'Analytical Thomism'.

In the dozen or so years since I coined the phrase it has entered into wider circulation, and ideas associated with it have attracted a certain amount of discussion. Elements of this have been critical, in part because the introduction of the expression has been viewed by some historically trained Thomists as part of an effort to claim superiority for a particular approach to Aquinas's thought;[4] and in part because others who, by contrast, are quite unsympathetic to Thomism have worried that an alliance between the ideas of Aquinas and the styles and methods of analytical philosophy is threatening to their own efforts to direct Catholic thinkers towards the postmodernist philosophies of Derrida and other Continental contemporaries. As one author has recently put it:

> We have recently witnessed a turn to analytic philosophy among American Catholics, who take the view that the legitimate heir of Thomas Aquinas, of the tightly argued and precisely formulated demonstrations of the *Summa Theologiae*, is the analytic tradition, and not what many see as the exotic and indecipherable texts of Derrida or the dissolution of human subjectivity in Foucault. The recent appearance of *Fides et Ratio* and its conception of 'reason' can and has been read as lending support to this view, the result of which could be to give new support to a more modernist analytic version of Aquinas.
>
> ...I am concerned that the possibility of a Catholic postmodernity and with it a serious interest in prophetic postmodernism will be eclipsed or even waylaid by a turn toward analytic thought among Catholic philosophers.[5]

In reply to the first (Thomist) group I am inclined to invoke the idea of complementarity in diversity, suggesting that where analytical and traditional approaches differ (more than stylistically), it may well be that what each provides is something that the other lacks. Thus, for example, analytical approaches to truth and reference, and to logic, recognize distinctions and possibilities that are generally absent from traditional Thomist accounts. On the other hand Thomistic treatments of moral psychology, of philosophical theology and of ontology invoke ideas not present in the thinking of most analytical philosophers.

So far as the second (postmodernist) group is concerned I recognize, as they do, an affinity between the broadly realist and rationalist orientations of both Thomistic and analytical philosophy; but whereas they see this as problematic I welcome it. Moreover, I take their own opposition to raise questions about the compatibility of their general outlook and particular views with traditional Catholic theology as that finds expression in documents as diverse (but continuous) as the Nicene Creed, the decrees of the Councils, and the major encyclicals of the Bishops of Rome, including the aforementioned *Fides et Ratio* (discussed in Chapter 3). Admittedly this further response may beg the question as to the status (and meaning) of these documents, and I would accept that there are genuine questions about the value of some late medieval and modern rationalist theology, and that the existential and aesthetic orientations of Continental thinkers is both a corrective to scientistic strains in analytical philosophy and a recovery of aspects of older religious thought. Indeed I argue as much in some of the following chapters. All of that said, however, there is at the heart of Catholic theology a commitment to the idea that the world is not of our making, that it is intrinsically intelligible, that truth is absolute and not relative, and that reason has the power to establish these facts; and these ideas receive a warmer reception within the world of analytical philosophy than they do within that of post-structuralist postmodernism.

We inhabit an intellectual culture in which there is a premium on novelty, not always accompanied by a concern for the intrinsic merits of the new view. As is well known, the scholastics of the Middle Ages had a rather different sense of what it meant to contribute to an intellectual project. In large part they saw themselves as interpreters of established truths or servers of causes whose virtue they presupposed. That is a viewpoint which I share and which is operative in the work presented here. 'Analytical Thomism' is, of course, a term of art and I should explain further what I meant by it and what its use is intended to recommend. Sometimes writers use the term 'Thomism', at other times they favour 'Thomistic'. It would have been useful if one of these were reserved for the ascription of ideas to St Thomas himself, and the other for ways of thinking that are in the spirit of Aquinas, or develop what he has to say; but it is far too late in the day to try to stipulate general uses. Let me just say that as I am using the term I mean by it ideas and styles of thought that derive from St Thomas but which are not necessarily employed by him and which he might even have difficulty comprehending. That would be likely to be so in respect of some ideas introduced by some of the Thomist commentators mentioned in Chapter 1.

By 'analytical' I mean to refer to a range of related features that have characterized English-speaking philosophy since Russell and Moore began the attack on post-Kantian idealism at the turn of the twentieth century; and also to a set of problems and styles of treatment of them. Analytical philosophy is not the same as 'linguistic philosophy', though in the middle of the twentieth century it included it. Analytical thought pursues answers to a range of questions by examination of intelligible structures, concepts or propositions. Thus, analytical Thomism involves the bringing into mutual relationship of the styles and pre-occupations of recent English-speaking philosophy and the ideas and concerns shared by St Thomas and his followers.

An obvious question which arises from this is why one should want to practise this kind of philosophy. In answer, it may be helpful if I say a little about my route thus far. The question might not arise for someone brought up in such a tradition, or for someone educated into a more familiar variety of Thomism who then became interested in analytical philosophy. My circumstance corresponds to neither of those. Coming from Britain it could hardly be a case of the first, since although there have been one or two writers (the late Elizabeth Anscombe and her husband Peter Geach are evident examples) part of whose work could, at a fair stretch, be described as instances of analytical Thomism, their influence in this respect has been limited and does not constitute any kind of tradition. Nor have I, like Sir Anthony Kenny, for example, been educated in Thomism and then moved towards analytical philosophy.

My journey has, for the most part, been in the other direction ('for the most part' because I did have a Jesuit schooling, and perhaps having been given the boy these scholastically trained teachers made the man in their likeness). Early on in my university studies I was introduced by my then teacher, David Hamlyn, to the thought of the pre-Socratics and was hooked. Many people, including experienced philosophers, think of these early figures only as proto-chemists-cum-physicists who had the misfortune to be about as ignorant of the material world as it is possible for anyone to be, who is also capable of asking the question: 'What is the nature of things?' I did not feel that then, and I am even less disposed to think it now. On the contrary, I felt, more or less straight off, that they hit the nail right on the head. If knowledge is to be possible, indeed, if anything is to be thought or said, that of which the knower has knowledge, or of which the speaker speaks, must have an intelligible structure. If there is no structure and articulation in the phenomenon, then there can be no description or explanation of it. In particular I was very taken by the ancient philosophical formulation involving the imposition of limit (*peras*) on the unlimited (*apeiron*) to produce the limited (*peperasmenon*).

Prior to taking up philosophy I had spent half a decade as an art student and I am quite sure that what persuaded me of the importance and veracity of these ancient ideas was my art school education. For art-making is all about discerning and creating structures. When later, as a philosophy student, I read Wittgenstein's instruction to attend to the differences, I heard an echo of the art teacher's command to look at the gaps between objects and draw them also. What I went on to study in Plato and Aristotle seemed to be elaborations, corrections and refinements of the pre-Socratic doctrine but not alternatives to it. Philosophy begins with the recognition of an ontological precondition of the possibility of knowledge: intelligible structure in the phenomena, a precondition that historically has been problematic for nominalism and which currently poses a challenge to postmodernist relativism.

In the same philosophy classes I encountered references to later medieval ideas, particularly those concerning the 'aboutness' or intentionality of thought, but when I asked my teachers what exactly the schoolmen or their successors believed about this issue no one seemed to know. Not content to leave matters there I started looking around in college and university libraries for material. Eventually I came across some volumes and journals of twentieth-century neo-Thomism which in those settings had rarely, if ever, been read. These sources were welcome, but I am sorry to say that as I looked at relevant chapters or articles they seemed too often to exhibit two characteristics which I subsequently found to be common features of modern neo-scholastic writings (though certainly not invariable ones).[6] Either they just reproduced medieval and scholastic terms and phrases whose meaning and significance had already puzzled me, or they were, even to my limited competence, rather poor philosophy. Although things have certainly improved due to reinvigoration of the Thomist tradition in North America and to the development of interest in medieval philosophy outwith Catholic circles,[7] I think there is still an important deficiency in much neo-scholasticism that calls for further changes to the philosophical diet provided to students in institutions where that tradition persists.

I came to think, and still believe, that what is wanted in philosophical thought, and what Thomas Aquinas provides the resources for, is a clear description of the intelligible structure of reality and of the appropriate principles of action (including issues in ethics, social philosophy and aesthetics) and that this is a matter of placing these phenomena in their true relationships. The provision of clear philosophical descriptions, or in Wittgenstein's phrase 'perspicuous representations', is an important part of the project of analytical Thomism.

As was said by H.H. Price, however, in criticism of English linguistic philosophy, 'clarity is not enough'. As well as understanding the nature of possibilities we need to determine which of them is true or desirable. In other writings I have pursued metaphysical questions about the nature of the mind and of reality, and engaged in the traditional Thomist task of trying to show how reflection upon the nature of things gives reason to believe in the existence of God.[8] Here, by contrast, I presume the truth of a broadly realist philosophy and the reasonability of religious belief, in particular that of Catholic Christianity, and consider its implications for faith itself, and for the conduct of human affairs. The chapters are organized into five sections: 'Catholicism and philosophy'; 'Faith and reason'; 'Ethics and politics'; 'Education and spirituality'; and 'Beauty and contemplation'. I have included a number of pieces which survey relevant aspects of the history of thought in the broad areas of my concern. I hope these prove informative and that they also serve to situate the non-historical discussions. Some of the chapters were written with philosophers in mind, others were directed also to theologians or to educationalists. In all cases, however, I have tried to write clearly so that anyone who is interested, and is prepared to read and think again, should be able to follow along. If someone should read all that is contained herein I would hope that, whatever he or she might feel about the inadequacies of my presentation, at least a sense of the comprehensiveness of the Catholic philosophical outlook might have been communicated.

Intellectually and theologically my approach is orthodox rather than radical. Thus far at any rate, I have been more concerned to understand old truths than to issue new challenges. But, of course, as anyone who has thought long and hard knows, the greatest challenge is to understand things as they are. According to Aquinas the point of speculative reason is to discern the true, and that of practical reason to achieve the good. These doctrines have still more ancient origins in the Greeks and they continue to define the broad structure of philosophical inquiry. What the Judaeo-Christian tradition adds to the efforts of rationality is a revelation of God to humankind. Some people, including some religious believers, feel a deep and general tension between faith and reason. For what it is worth, I can say, without qualification, that I have *never* felt this. That could be a failure suggesting a lack of one or other disposition, or perhaps of imagination; but I take some comfort from the fact that Aquinas, a great thinker and a great Catholic Christian, seems to have been similarly untroubled. There are many things I do not begin to understand and many I have only a weak grasp of, but nothing in what I understand on the basis of reason appears to contradict what I believe as a matter of faith. In that respect my faith seems reasonable and my reason faithful. It is for others to judge whether this is in fact the case.

Notes

1 The lectures were given in 1992 at the invitation of Alasdair MacIntyre. I am grateful for the opportunity they provided me to organize ideas that were then still in development. In subsequent years I have returned to Notre Dame many times, always benefiting from discussions with people there. In addition to Alasdair MacIntyre I must also express particular thanks to Ralph McInerny, director of the Maritain Center which supported that first visit as well as those later ones that were for the purpose of participating in the Center's summer Thomistic Institute – an important forum for the development of Thomistic thought.

2 See, for example, 'Mind–Word Identity Theory and the Anti-Realist Challenge', in John Haldane and Crispin Wright (eds), *Reality, Representation and Projection* (New York: Oxford University Press, 1993), pp. 15–37; 'Forms of Thought', in L.E. Hahn (ed.), *The Philosophy of Roderick Chisholm* (La Salle, Ill.: Open Court, 1997), pp. 149–70; 'Realism with a Metaphysical Skull' (with response by Putnam), in J. Conant and Urszula Zeglen (eds), *Hilary Putnam: Pragmatism and Realism* (London: Routledge, 2002), pp. 97–104; and 'A Thomist Metaphysics', in R. Gale (ed.), *Blackwell Guide to Metaphysics* (Oxford: Blackwell, 2002), pp. 89–109.

3 See Anthony Kenny, *Aquinas on Mind* (London: Routledge, 1993); John Haldane (ed.), *Mind, Metaphysics and Value in the Thomistic and Analytical Traditions* (Notre Dame, Ind.: University of Notre Dame Press, 2002); Robert Pasnau, *Thomas Aquinas on Human Nature* (Cambridge: Cambridge University Press, 2002); and Eleonore Stump, *Aquinas* (London: Routledge, 2003).

4 In this connection see Brian Shanley, 'Analytical Thomism', *The Thomist* 63, 1999, pp. 125–37. This is a review of an issue of the *Monist* that I edited under the same title: 'Analytical Thomism', *The Monist* 80.4, 1997.

5 See John D. Caputo, 'Philosophy and Prophetic Postmodernism: Towards a Catholic Postmodernity', *American Catholic Philosophical Quarterly* 64, 2000, pp. 549–67. A footnote to the quoted passage indicates that Caputo is referring in part to a debate initiated by my essay 'What Future Has Catholic Philosophy?' *Proceedings of the American Catholic Philosophical Association*, 1997, pp. 79–90. This is related in content to Chapter 1 below.

6 It is worth emphasizing that many good Thomistic teaching texts were produced in the first half of the twentieth century; for a sampling of these see *Modern Writings on Thomism* (Bristol: Thoemmes, 2003) selected and introduced by John Haldane – a set comprising reprints of the following texts: R.P. Phillips, *Modern Thomistic Philosophy* (1935); J. Peifer, *The Concept in Thomism* (1952); G. Klubertanz, *The Philosophy of Human Nature* (1953); J. Oesterle, *Ethics: The Introduction to Moral Science* (1958); and E. Simmons, *The Scientific Art of Logic* (1961).

7 For some account of this interest see P.J. Fitzpatrick and John Haldane, 'Medieval Philosophy in Later Thought', in A.S. McGrade (ed.), *The Cambridge Companion to Medieval Philosophy* (Cambridge: Cambridge University Press, 2003), pp. 300–27.

8 See in this latter regard J.J.C. Smart and J.J. Haldane, *Atheism and Theism*, 2nd edn (Oxford: Blackwell, 2003).

Part I

Catholicism and philosophy

Chapter 1

Thomism and the future of Catholic philosophy[1]

Introduction

When one takes account of the scale and range of Aquinas's achievements it becomes clear why he deserves to be described as the greatest of the medieval philosopher–theologians, for he was the first thinker of the high medieval period to work out in detail the new synthesis between Catholicism and philosophy. It is sometimes supposed that this just meant 'Christianizing' Aristotle. Even were that the limit of his achievement it would have been considerable, but in fact he went further. For while he opposed unquestioning appeals to authority, he believed in the idea of cumulative philosophical and religious wisdom and sought to integrate Neoplatonist, Augustinian and Anselmian ideas, as well as Aristotelian ones, with scripture, patristic teaching and evolving Catholic doctrine.

St Thomas inspired a tradition that bears his name; and just as he was a great thinker, so too is Thomism a great movement. It is rare, and not just among pre-modern systems of thought, in having lasted from the period of its birth to the present day. Platonism and Aristotelianism are more ancient, but neither has enjoyed the same degree of cultural continuity. Marxism has had enormous influence, but it is now all but abandoned, and while there may be positive reassessments of aspects of Marx's thought it is difficult to believe that it will ever again be widely adopted as ideology. Existentialism appears even more ephemeral, like a short-lived literary fashion. Notwithstanding its faltering emergence, and periods of decline or of marginalization, Thomism has been a feature of Catholic thought during seven centuries.

Here I will offer a short history of the movement and consider its present state and possible future development. While I hope that this history will be of some general interest, I am more concerned that readers draw lessons from it. As will emerge, those who have associated themselves with the thought of Aquinas have tended to move in one or other of two directions: towards the goal of faithful interpretation of the original system, or towards that of effective application to contemporary issues. Set at right angles to these movements is another pattern of variation: the rise and fall of Thomistic thought. One lesson, I suggest, is that Thomism has declined when it has ignored, or turned its back on, leading rival philosophies; and a second is that its revivals have generally been the result of engagement with other traditions. A third lesson is that the task of synthesis is promising but difficult. Thomism began as a synthesis of philosophy and theology and versions of it have ended in the tangled wreckage of unworkable combinations. A fourth lesson, following upon these others, is that in there is pressing need for a systematic re-articulation of neo-Thomist thought.

Aquinas and the first Thomism

Aquinas was born (in 1224) into a religious culture whose dominant intellectual tradition was a form of Christian Neoplatonism. The main source of this was St Augustine mediated via later Latin thinkers such as St Anselm. Early in his life, however, and under the direction of Albert the Great, Aquinas developed an intense interest in the more naturalistic philosophy of Aristotle. Works of 'the philosopher' were then being translated into Latin for the first time, having been rediscovered through contact with the Arab world where they had been preserved.

To Albert and Aquinas, Aristotle offered a more promising resource for the articulation of Christian doctrine than did the Augustinianism current in the cathedral schools and universities. Yet this new synthesis met with considerable opposition, for it seemed to be at odds with orthodoxy. In fact, St Thomas found himself in dispute with two groups. To one side were the Augustinians represented by the secular teachers and the Franciscans; and to the other were radical Aristotelian naturalists who held doctrines that are indeed difficult to reconcile with Christian orthodoxy. Aquinas sought to tread a middle path directing writings against each group in turn: *On the Eternity of the World* against Bonaventure and other Augustinian Franciscans, and *On the Unity of the Intellect* against Siger of Brabant and other Latin Averroists.

Although Aquinas's Christian Aristotelianism was later to be judged the 'most perfect' reconciliation of philosophy and faith, its immediate fate was to be attacked and subjected to ecclesiastical denunciation. In 1270 Bishop Tempier of Paris condemned several propositions associated with Aristotelianism, and in 1277, three years after St Thomas's death, he issued a further denunciation in which Thomistic claims were specified, though Aquinas was not named. In the same year Robert Kilwardby, Archbishop of Canterbury and a fellow Dominican, issued a similar condemnation and the following month the Pope endorsed Tempier's decree. Two years later a Franciscan, William de la Mare, produced a work 'correcting' the error of Aquinas's ways.

The Dominican response was to defend their master against these attacks. The general chapter appointed a committee to investigate the English Dominican disloyalty, and in the meantime they set about promoting the cause of Thomas as a thinker and as a saint. In 1282 William of Macclesfield responded to de la Mare countering his charges, and around the same time John of Paris produced a similar response. By 1286 the Parisian Dominicans commanded the study of Aquinas and this instruction was repeated elsewhere: in Saragossa (1309), in London (1314) and in Bologna (1315). Defence gave way to counter-attack and on 18 July 1323, within fifty years of his death, Aquinas was declared a saint by Pope John XXII. Two years later Bishop Bourret of Paris revoked Tempier's condemnation.

Ecclesiastical approval removed one obstacle to acceptance of Thomistic thought and his ideas began to spread and gain influence. Apart from their merit, an important factor in this development was the increasing number of colleges and universities. Each approved place of study would have houses belonging to the main teaching orders, and by this means the Dominicans ensured that their master's voice could be heard throughout Europe.

Early in the fifteenth century Aquinas found a powerful follower in the person of John Capreolus (1380–1444). In the late scholastic period the ideas of St Thomas had to compete with those of two other medieval figures, namely Duns Scotus and William of Ockham. Capreolus challenged various views of Scotus to such good effect that he earned the title 'foremost Thomist'. More common than dialectical defences, however, were informed commentaries on Aquinas's works, in particular the *Summa Theologiae*. These commentaries were important in transmitting Thomist doctrines, yet in themselves they did little to combat the rising tide of Ockhamist nominalism.

The second Thomism

The next century was the most troubled in the history of post-medieval Christendom. The Reformation divided Europe into Catholic and Protestant states. It would be wrong to suppose that Aquinas was only read by Catholics, for in England the Anglican Richard Hooker (1553–1600), and in Holland the Calvinist Hugo Grotius (1583–1645), were both influenced by studying his work. However, it was within Catholic regions that the next phase of Thomism developed. In particular, Spain and Italy gave rise to new theologically and metaphysically oriented presentations of Thomas's thought. In Protestant Europe reformers drove their axe to the roots of Catholic belief, and in response the Church of Rome set about renewing its intellectual resources. Thus was born the 'Counter-Reformation'.

The Council of Trent (1545–63) aimed to systematize Catholic doctrine producing a definitive Catechism in 1566 in which the thought of Aquinas had a major influence. Contrary to an oft-repeated tale, however, the *Summa Theologiae* was not placed on the altar alongside the Bible during meetings of the Council. Trent also encouraged the study of philosophy and theology in all Catholic colleges, seminaries and universities. This created a need for appropriate textbooks, which was met with a new style of manual setting out Thomistic thought. A further response to the reformers was the development of new religious orders. In founding the Society of Jesus, St Ignatius explicitly encouraged the study of Aquinas and Aristotle, and expressed the hope that interpretations of their ideas adapted to the needs of the time would be forthcoming.

In this he was drawing upon the earlier pre-Tridentine tradition of Thomistic teaching and commentary in which the major figures were Dominicans. In the first decade of the century Peter Crockaert (died 1514), a Belgian working in Paris, had substituted the *Summa Theologiae* for what had previously been the standard text for theological instruction, the *Sentences* of Peter Lombard. Likewise in Italy, Thomas de Vio Cajetan (1469–1534) was lecturing on the *Summa* and producing a major commentary later to be published alongside the works of Aquinas. In Spain Francisco de Vitoria (1485–1546) also made the *Summa* the basis of theological education, and he was followed in this by his disciple Domingo de Soto (1494–1560).

Early Jesuit Thomists included students of de Soto. But the full Jesuit appropriation of Thomas came later with Luis de Molina (1535–1600) and, most famously, Francisco Suarez (1548–1617). Starting from the need to produce theology adequate to meet that of the reformers, Suarez was led to the conclusion that it was not appropriate just to invoke the philosophy of Aristotle; instead fundamental issues needed to be addressed afresh. The result was a mix of Thomistic and non-Thomistic metaphysics. In fact, Suarez anticipates much of the thinking about essence, existence and identity of late twentieth-century analytical metaphysicians.

The Dominicans meanwhile had stayed closer to the detail of Aquinas's philosophy, in part out of loyalty to a brother who had long been misrepresented and maligned. Their need to evangelize and to educate also led them to produce a line of philosophical and theological textbooks, the most famous of which (still in use into the twentieth century) were those of John of St Thomas (John Poinsot, 1589–1644).

In 1568 Aquinas was named a 'Doctor of the Church', only the ninth person to be so honoured, and this led to the familiar title of 'Angelic Doctor'. By the end of that century there were two main schools of Thomism. The first had its strongest base in Italy, was associated with Dominican textual interpretation, and remained close to the historical doctrines of St Thomas. The second was rooted in Spain, centred around the Jesuit appropriation of Aquinas, and gave rise to treatises on particular philosophical themes.

Inevitably there was competition between these traditions; but the most heated conflict was doctrinal, not interpretative. It ran from around 1590 to 1610 and continued intermittently thereafter. The subject was grace, free will and divine foreknowledge. On the one side the Jesuit Molina argued that God's total omniscience is compatible with human liberty, because God knows what each person would freely do in every possible circumstance of choice, and distributes grace accordingly. In opposition the Dominicans, of whom the most prominent was Dominic Banez (1528–1604), contended that God knows who will be saved and who will be damned because he has distributed fully effective grace to some but not all. The Jesuits accused the Dominicans of Calvinist predestinarianism, while the Dominicans charged the Jesuits with Pelagianism.

This 'heresy-calling' led the popes to try and tame the debate, though without much success. Meanwhile the energies of Thomists had been largely distracted from the important task of developing the general system so as to take account of the rise of modern science and the new philosophies of rationalism and empiricism. The trial of Galileo (1564–1642) and the replies of Descartes (1596–1660) to his critics show the Thomists to have fallen behind their times. Indeed it was their ill-preparedness to engage modern thought rather than weaknesses within Thomism itself that led to the marginalization of the tradition in the seventeenth and eighteenth centuries.

The fate of Thomism in the latter period also reflected the general situation of the Catholic Church. The century featured many social disruptions and much ecclesiastical infighting. In 1772 the Jesuits were suppressed on the order of the Pope, and in the next decade Catholicism itself was battered by the French Revolution and by the rise of secularism. The new political thinking was anti-theocratic, anti-clerical, broadly democratic, and at best deistic, though often atheist. It is hardly surprising, therefore, that a system of thought born of medieval Catholicism did not flourish in these circumstances. The Dominicans went on producing new editions of St Thomas's writings but it is doubtful whether many other than Dominicans read them. Even in Rome ecclesiastics had lost interest in Thomism.

Neo-Thomism

As in the past, however, a process of revitalization led to a renaissance. Following the French Revolution, Catholic thought in France, Belgium and Italy divided between two movements: one that emphasized the centrality of faith and sought to deal with the threat from rationalism by side-stepping it; and a philosophical approach which maintained, along lines first suggested by Christian Neoplatonists, that the intellect directly intuits God in all its acts of knowledge. These two approaches came to be known as 'traditionalism' and 'ontologism'; their main proponents being Lamennais (1782–1854) and de Maistre (1752–1821), and Gioberti (1801–52) and Rosmini (1797–1855), respectively.

Elsewhere in Italy and in Spain, the Dominicans maintained loyalty to St Thomas. The Italian Tommaso Zigliara (1833–93) found favour with Bishop Pecci of Perugia (later to become Leo XIII), and in 1873 he was appointed Regent of Studies in the Dominican College in Rome where he was joined by Alberto Lepidi (1838–1922). Both men were critical of the traditionalists and the ontologists; and through their writings, teachings and administration did much to encourage members of their order in Italy and France to develop neo-Thomistic responses to these movements, as well as to the empiricism and rationalism to which they had been reactions. The revival of Thomism was much encouraged by the papacy. In 1846 Pius IX argued that reason and faith are compatible and that lapses into fideism and intellectual intuitionism are both to be avoided. Versions of traditionalism and ontologism were condemned and a return to the scholastic approaches was openly favoured. An important figure in this revival was Joseph Kleutgen (1811–83), a German Jesuit. Kleutgen identified the weaknesses in Catholic intellectual responses to modern thought. He argued that only Aristotelian metaphysics could provide a sure foundation for Catholic theology and expounded his own version of neo-Aristotelianism. Like St Thomas, Kleutgen and his colleagues affirmed the unity of the human person. Also while upholding the epistemological primacy of experience they maintained the possibility of establishing, by abstract reflection, various necessary truths about reality, principally that it is the creation of God. Although the thought of Aquinas featured in this movement it was more generally a revival of scholasticism rather than of Thomism as such.

In 1878 Gioacchino Pecci was crowned Leo XIII and the following year he published the famous encyclical *Aeterni Patris* in which Aquinas is commended as providing the surest intellectual foundation for, and articulation of, Catholic doctrine. Kleutgen is reputed to have contributed to the draft of the encyclical and certainly his scholastic stance was vindicated by it. Leo also appointed neo-scholastics to important posts in Rome. Once again, then, through the edict of a pope, Thomism became the orthodox system of thought for Roman Catholicism.

Neo-Thomism now looked in two directions. On the one hand it was commanded to address contemporary philosophical issues; and on the other it drew its inspiration from the past. These orientations gave rise to two lines of development, one 'problematic', the other historical. At the University of Louvain in Belgium a new school of scholastic scholarship emerged to which important contributions were made by Cardinal Mercier (1851–1926), Maurice de Wulf (1867–1947) and Martin Grabmann (1875–1959).

The problematic strand was first developed in response to the challenges of modern philosophy. Traditional Thomism assumed that the mind was in direct engagement with reality through experience. According to Aquinas both perception and intellection involve openness to the external world. After Descartes, Locke, Hume and Kant, the new orthodoxy was that the starting-point of all philosophy is consciousness. From this we need somehow to argue to the existence of external reality. Awed by this doctrine several neo-Thomists maintained that no philosophy could be credible that did not accept the new starting-point of immanent consciousness. The philosopher Joseph Maréchal (1878–1944), and the theologians Karl Rahner (1904–84) and Bernard Lonergan (1904–84) – all of whom were Jesuits – tried to show that it was possible to combine Kant's critical philosophy with the transcendental realism and theism of Aquinas. The result, 'Transcendental Thomism', though widespread in its influence among theologians, was never taken very seriously by philosophers.

Another attempt to synthesize Thomism with a modern philosophy is represented by the Polish 'Lublin school'. Here the sources have been several: Thomism as represented by French interpreters; phenomenology as advocated by Roman Ingarden (1893–1970), who had been a student of Husserl (1859–1938); and logic and philosophy of science. The best-known member of the school was Karol Wojtyla (1920–), who drew on the value theory of Max Scheler (1874–1928), Husserlian phenomenology and the anthropology of Aquinas, to devise a form of Thomist personalism articulated in his work *The Acting Person*. Wojtyla's time at Lublin was short, however, being promoted to the see of Cracow in 1958, and elected Pope in 1978. John Paul II was not the first, nor probably the last, pope to favour Thomism.

Two of the most important twentieth-century neo-Thomists were French laymen. Both were critics of transcendental Thomism and both had great influence in North America as well as in Europe. They were Jacques Maritain (1882–1973) and Etienne Gilson (1884–1978). Maritain was raised in a comfortable, politically liberal, Protestant family. Despairing of the materialism and secularism characteristic of Paris university and intellectual life, he and his wife made a provisional suicide pact but revoked this after attending lectures by Henri Bergson. While Bergson's 'vitalist' philosophy lifted their despair, it was not until they converted to Roman Catholicism and then discovered the philosophy of Aquinas that the Maritains felt they had found a wholly adequate worldview combining humanism with transcendence.

Maritain lectured and published widely in most areas of philosophy, and was a dominant influence in Catholic thought from the 1920s to the Second Vatican Council (1962–65). He approached the ideas of Aquinas somewhat ahistorically rather than as a medieval revivalist and drew from it a metaphysics, epistemology and value theory. In his most important work of speculative philosophy, *The Degrees of Knowledge*, he argues that we have knowledge of objective reality. Likewise, he insists that the natural order has an objective structure and that this is the proper concern of science. His value theory is similarly keyed to external realities, but value is seen as directed towards participation in the life of God. Maritain's social and political philosophy emphasized the irreducibility of community and of the common good, notions which have featured prominently in Catholic social teaching throughout the twentieth century and for which Maritain is often regarded as a primary source.

Gilson was also taught by Bergson, but his own interests lay in the history of ideas, in particular the relationship between modern philosophy and pre-modern scholasticism. His influence on the neo-Thomist revival was as much through his teaching and academic leadership as through his writings. He lectured in north America, and co-founded the Pontifical Institute of Mediaeval Studies in Toronto. Like Maritain, he deplored the subjective turn introduced by modern philosophy. However, he believed that attempts to invoke medieval thinking must be mindful of the variety of views held during the Middle Ages and, even more importantly, of the fact that they were developed primarily in theological contexts. Whereas Maritain presented Thomism as if it were a set of timeless ideas, Gilson distinguished between the teachings of Aquinas and those of later commentators who sometimes imported their own views or sought to synthesize Thomism with approaches current in their own day. Similarly, he argued that while St Thomas drew heavily on the work of Aristotle he often used Aristotelian notions for different purposes, generally to defend Christian theology, and added ideas of his own; the most important being the claim that God is necessary existence and the source of the being of other things.

The present day

Gilson's contextualist approach has been most widely followed among Catholic historians of the medieval period, but its influence is also apparent in the account of traditions of inquiry advanced by Alasdair MacIntyre (1929–). A convert, like so many other English-speaking Catholic philosophers, MacIntyre's understanding and use of Aquinas have been shaped not by a Thomistic education but by personal study and in response to the views of others. For some years he has taught at the University of Notre Dame where the Medieval Institute and the Jacques Maritain Center have each engaged scholastic thought. The second of these is directed by Ralph McInerny, himself one of the leading representatives of neo-Thomism in North America and for many years editor of the *New Scholasticism* (now the *American Catholic Philosophical Quarterly*), which together with the *Modern Schoolman* and *The Thomist* comprise the main English-language fora for the presentation of essays in neo-scholastic historical and problematic traditions.

Thus we have arrived at the present day. Contemporary historical scholarship in the area of Thomistic philosophy is of a high standard. This is largely a consequence of the efforts of Gilson and his followers. Aquinas and other medieval and scholastic figures have also benefited from a rise of interest in the history of philosophy, and by no means all who now study Christian medieval thought are themselves Catholics or even theists. At the same time it is natural that, as with Hooker and Grotius, those who avow a Christian worldview should look with intense interest at the work of the individual who is beyond question the greatest Christian philosopher–theologian.

In the future it is likely that the tide of interest in Aquinas will rise and fall as before. As in the past, this will partly reflect the intellectual condition of the Catholic Church and that of the colleges, seminaries and universities established to serve it. However, Aquinas and Thomism are not the preserve of Catholics only, or of those engaged in theology or avowedly religious thought. There is a growing interest in his ideas among philosophers trained wholly or partly in the analytical school. Drawing on the example of the British philosophers Elizabeth Anscombe, Peter Geach and Anthony Kenny, some younger writers have used Thomistic resources to deal with contemporary philosophical problems. Recent examples of this may be found in the 'Analytical Thomism' issue of *The Monist* (October 1997), one of the leading American philosophy journals. Others have turned to Aquinas as an important figure in the history of philosophy to be studied as one might any other thinker from the past.

Thus is repeated a pattern of previous centuries. Like Capreolus, Suarez, Kleutgen and Maritain, some wish to mine Thomas's work as a source of interesting ideas. Like Crockaert, Banez, Mercier and Gilson, others devote their efforts to giving an accurate representation of his thought. A precious few try to combine both tasks. Of course there is merit in each approach; but if the history of Thomism suggests that when its practitioners stray far from Thomas's central doctrines they are liable to fall into confusion, it also indicates the great cost of confining one's attention to the interpretative task. For Thomists the point of trying to understand Aquinas must be to see more clearly how best to formulate and answer perennial philosophical and theological questions.

Thomism and the analytical tradition

With that thought in mind I wish to consider further the role that Thomistic ideas might have in a Catholic engagement with the dominant mode of English-language philosophy, namely the analytical tradition, which I am here construing sufficiently broadly to embrace those, such as Jürgen Habermas, who now seek to be part of it.

Recently a colleague at a major Catholic university in the United States related an exchange between him and a postgraduate student at a secular university. The student's previous education had been at a traditionally minded Catholic institution, but now he found himself in a programme where he was expected to read and appreciate work by leading secular philosophers. The student reported how he found that he could not even enter into a reasonable dialogue with these thinkers or with his fellow students. The disagreement, he supposed, was over first principles which, by definition, could not be proven. He was intensely frustrated and was inclined, given his view of the current situation of academia and the impossibility of reasonable argument, to abandon his studies – though he was also disposed to try to fight back.

The advice given by my colleague was of exactly the right sort. First, he pointed out that engagement need not be on questions of first principles. Instead one may attempt an 'immanent' or internal critique, showing that a position is not consistent or defensible even on its own terms; and second one may try to show that a doctrine is contrary to observable facts or widely accepted views. He also noted that the ideas against which the student railed would not have become dominant if there were nothing to them, for they have been judged to be persuasive by people who are clearly neither fools nor knaves. The message to the student, then, was that he should learn how to expose conflicts in opposing views and to show that his own position could account for what is right in them while also accounting for more besides. The alternative to this policy (which has been practised to good effect in recent work by Alasdair Macintyre) is to abandon philosophy to those whom one believes to be in error.

Here I think my colleague had encountered a problem that has bedevilled Catholic philosophy at least in the US, for in Britain it has neither a collective identity nor an institutional base. Among those trained in the various branches of neo-scholasticism it is commonly supposed that analytical philosophy is something to be avoided as a serious threat to one's grasp of God, goodness and truth. This view derives from the belief that mainstream English-language philosophy is Logical Positivism. It is not just Catholic philosophers who are so affected, however; for the same thing is true of most Christian theologians of all denominations in the West. In this latter connection it is interesting to note an observation made by Fergus Kerr, OP, reporting on the creation of a database listing research projects in theology in British and Irish institutes of higher education from 1994 to 1998. Kerr writes that of the 4,000 items registered 'surprisingly few projects show much acquaintance with contemporary Anglo-American analytical philosophy, which (one might think) exerts considerable influence, for better or worse, on neighbouring disciplines and the general intellectual climate in our culture' ('Theological Research Initiative', *New Blackfriars*, February 1998).

The common belief is that from seeds sown in the early modern period a weed grew and took hold in the garden of philosophy. The lineage and flowerings are familiar: Hobbes, Locke, Hume, Russell, early-Wittgenstein, A.J. Ayer, and so on to contemporary scientific materialism. While this belief is not without foundation it is fragmentary and seriously and dangerously distorted. No-one who reads Locke, Mill or Russell could doubt that they held metaphysical views. One may be 'anti' their positions; but it is a mistake to suppose that they are anti-metaphysical positivists. Similarly, the practice of careful analysis and argument that they inspired has produced, and continues to produce, insightful and inspiring philosophy.

Wittgenstein's *Philosophical Investigations* is a work the depth of which will be celebrated for so long as philosophy is practised. Less exaltedly, in Oxford in the late 1950s and '60s very good philosophers such as Gilbert Ryle and J.L. Austin deployed broadly Aristotelian categories in connection with important issues in the philosophy of mind and moral psychology. Similarly, the work of Oxford-trained Catholics such as Elizabeth Anscombe and Peter Geach may be characterized as largely ahistorical, analytical Aristotelianism. Subsequently the centre of the philosophical world crossed the Atlantic. If anything, however, that strengthened the subject, and in the last thirty years some of the most important work of the second half of the century has emerged from North America.

Viewed as a group, analytical writers certainly have their own deficiencies. Among these is a lack of historical sense. It is not uncommon to find quite able philosophers writing as if the subject began in the twentieth century. This outlook is particularly marked among graduate students in the best analytical departments, who commonly speak as if not only currently favoured solutions but the problems they address were both newly minted. The story is told, often with appreciation, of one prominent analytical philosopher teaching at a leading institution who would wear a tee-shirt bearing a slogan derived from the anti-drug campaign: 'Just say "no" to history of philosophy.'

A further deficiency commonly to be found among analytical writers is a lack of love of wisdom (*philosophia*). By this I mean that one too rarely encounters individuals whose clear motivation is to achieve a form of understanding that may bring warranted peace of mind. Notable exceptions to this are thinkers influenced by a certain interpretation of the goal of Wittgenstein's later philosophy. For them the task is 'to let the fly out of the fly bottle' and to see it pass from agitation to regular flight. Significantly, however, this view of philosophy as therapy for the soul is sometimes ridiculed and generally ignored by analytical philosophers. These defects admitted, it remains a serious mistake to represent analytical philosophy as anti-metaphysical, sceptical and nihilistic. Indeed, for all that it stands in need of improvement, I believe it has a claim to be the prime continuant of Western philosophical rationalism.

The effects of neo-scholastic hostility to analytical thought have generally been bad ones. Without open and informed exchange between conflicting positions there is no growth, and in the life of the intellect without growth there is stagnation. For its own self-definition and benefit a philosophy needs to test itself against rivals; but any activity ordered towards truth also has a responsibility to respect the same search when it is evidently pursued by others. Avowedly Catholic philosophers in general, and neo-Thomists among them, are largely isolated from the mainstream. In consequence, their intellectual standards are often lower, and they are still not sufficiently learning from nor contributing to the main debates pursued in the wider world. This latter failing is particularly ironic since some of the central themes of contemporary analytical philosophy, such as intentionality, normativity, causality and explanation, holism and reductionism, and realism and anti-realism, have also been prominent in Thomistic and neo-scholastic thought from the Middle Ages onwards. Opportunities for productive engagement have been missed too often and for too long.

With its understanding of philosophy as a partly spiritual activity ordered to a supernatural end, Thomist thought can also help others appreciate the possibility of engaging in philosophy as something more than conceptual geography. Earlier I listed some characteristic deficiencies of analytical philosophy. It is arguable that these derive from its lack of a unifying *telos*. For the Catholic, by contrast, philosophy is an intellectual high road to speculative and practical truth. St Thomas was committed to such an understanding, and because of it he drew upon the best thought of his day and of the past. For him, the rediscovered philosophy of Aristotle provided the basis for a new synthesis of faith and reason. So today, Catholic philosophers should be setting about the task of refining and developing the Thomist synthesis by drawing into it the methods and insights of analytical thought – not to mention those of other philosophical movements. The tradition needs to engage in one of its periodic reassessments. As in the past that can be expected to lead to revitalization and renaissance.

Let me end by saying that it is not my view that a philosopher who is a Catholic must be a Thomist, or even that he or she must aim to be an avowedly 'Catholic philosopher' in the sense of being one who always seeks to bring Catholic solutions to philosophical problems. Indeed, I am conscious that the very phrase 'Catholic philosophy' will fill some readers with dread. This reaction may be prompted by the thought of the triumphalism of the ghetto, in which an isolated minority views the wider world through narrowed eyes and thereby sees it as a place of darkness.

It should be clear that this is neither my perspective nor my condition. For what it is worth my admiration of Aquinas, and of aspects of the Thomistic tradition, is the product not of a neo-scholastic philosophical education but of personal study and reflection. My teachers were, and my colleagues are, thoroughly analytical and I am a fully subscribing member of the same community. Indeed, in my experience those who react most strongly to the phrase 'Catholic philosophy' are those who have not had the advantages of an analytical upbringing but are refugees from seminary scholasticism. Had their teachers practised the engagement I am recommending the reactions of their students might have been otherwise. A Catholic may be a good philosopher without being a Thomist and without practising 'Catholic philosophy'; but it is worth such a person considering why they would wish to resist the possibility of harnessing their reason to their faith. For Aquinas, this possibility established an imperative: to try to achieve a synthesis of Christian revelation and philosophical insight. His achievement in this respect is part of the intellectual inheritance of every philosopher who is a Catholic. For that reason alone we owe his Thomism our attention.

Note

1 The following is the text of the Aquinas Lecture delivered in Oxford on 12 February 1998. I am grateful to the Dominicans of Blackfriars for the invitation to give the lecture and for their hospitality. I have drawn material from two other essays: 'Thomism', in E. Craig (ed.), *Routledge Encyclopedia of Philosophy* (London: Routledge, 1998) and 'What Future Has Catholic Philosophy?' in *Virtue and Virtue Theories, Proceedings of the American Catholic Philosophical Association* 72, 1998.

Chapter 2

MacIntyre's Thomist revival
What next?

> It has ever been a cause of deep and heartfelt sorrow to honest folk, and
> above all to good loyal sons of the Church, that the judgments of mankind in
> the sphere of religion and morals should be so variable, and so apt to stray
> from the truth...
>
> [F]alse evolutionary notions, with their denial of all that is absolute or fixed
> or abiding in human experience, have paved the way for a new philosophy of
> error. Idealism, immanentism, pragmatism, have now a rival in what is called
> 'existentialism'. Its method, as the name implies, is to leave the unchanging
> essences of things out of sight, and concentrate all its attention on particular
> existences.
>
> There is, too, a false use of the historical method, which confines its observa-
> tions to the actual happenings of human life, and in doing so contrives to
> undermine all absolute truth, all absolute laws, whether it is dealing with the
> problems of philosophy or with the doctrines of the Christian religion.
>
> Pope Pius XII, *Humani Generis* (1950)

Introduction

Alasdair MacIntyre is a welcome presence within a philosophical community
that is becoming increasingly scholastic in its theoretical inquiries and superficial
in its practical applications. He combines conceptual creativity with broad scholarship, in a form shaped by a Celtic sensibility and appetite for constructive
debate. No-one who has read MacIntyre's works can fail to feel challenged by
them. Indeed, even sympathizers are apt to find that just as they thought the
argument was running their way, there is a quick twist or turn and some thesis
is being vigorously defended which they took to be at odds with their cherished
position.

This raises the question of whether MacIntyre's many twists and turns may
even lead *him* in a direction counter to that in which he is claiming to be
moving. And the thought of this unsettling possibility suggests a further question of where, if a course correction is necessary, MacIntyre may go next. Such
speculations might have arisen in response to reading *After Virtue*[1] and *Whose
Justice? Which Rationality?*,[2] but whatever the response to those books, they can

hardly fail to arise in the mind of a thoughtful reader of *Three Rival Versions of Moral Inquiry*.[3] In this important volume, MacIntyre makes explicit his commitment to Roman Catholicism and to Thomistic Aristotelianism. Of themselves, these attachments are likely to prove uncongenial to many who have hitherto been fellow travellers along the road away from 'modernity'. But it will now seem that this road quickly divides, and that whereas one branch leads forward into postmodernity, the other – now walked by MacIntyre – doubles back towards pre-modern ideas. Indeed it remains to be seen how many of those who cited MacIntyre (along with Sandel and Taylor) in criticism of 'deontological liberalism', 'enlightenment rationalism' and 'the project of modernity' are likely to feel comfortable when presented with papal encyclicals and mentions of original sin. But there is also a question, I believe, of whether those who are sympathetic to Thomism should feel happy about MacIntyre's historicist version of it. Here I shall only be concerned with this second issue.

In what follows, I first recall the origins of MacIntyre's central themes in the work of Elizabeth Anscombe, recount something of the development of MacIntyre's view through the three books mentioned above and register some worries about what I take to be the relativist tendency of this. Next I look at the characterization of Thomism presented in the second and, especially, the third volume. Then I reflect upon further worries about the coherence of MacIntyre's present position and consider the question of where, if these worries are well founded, he might go next in his continuing enquiry. Needless to say there are many interesting aspects of these impressive writings which I shall not even mention. Also when I spoke above of 'worries' I chose my word deliberately. I should not be surprised to learn that I have misread aspects of his view, but if so it would be good to have that misreading corrected.

By implication, I shall be arguing that what has so far been a *trilogy* needs to be, at least, a *tetralogy*. MacIntyre ended *After Virtue* acknowledging the need to provide an account of practical reason. This led to *Whose Justice? Which Rationality?*, which itself ended with the thought that competing traditions need to demonstrate their explanatory resources. There then followed *Three Rival Versions*, which ends with the injunction to devise institutions within which Nietzschean and neo-Thomist critics of modernism might be heard. My suggestion, however, is that what is next required is a clearer statement than has so far been offered of what distinctive ideas the Thomist tradition might be able to contribute, and I shall argue that this must be a matter of developing certain metaphysical claims – perhaps under the title *The Truth in Thomism*, or more generally *The Requirements of Truth*.

A history of ethics

MacIntyre's dominant idea is, as he acknowledges, not a new one. In 'Modern Moral Philosophy',[4] Elizabeth Anscombe presented three theses: first, that moral philosophy should be shelved until we have an adequate philosophy of psychology;

second, that the distinctively moral vocabulary of deontological terms and uses is a surviving remnant of an outlook that has largely been abandoned; and third, that English-speaking moral philosophy has a single general character.

The substance of Anscombe's argument is that we find ourselves educated in the use of a range of terms and tones, for the evaluation and direction of character and of conduct, which derive principally from a legalistic view of morality – more precisely, from a Judaeo-Christian Divine Law ethics. Since the philosophical and theological presuppositions of this way of speaking have long since ceased to hold sway, the vocabulary is devoid of meaningful content – notwithstanding that, psychologically, it retains a commandatory force. Having mistaken force for content, modern moral philosophers set about trying to explain how the use of this moral vocabulary might be warranted. Unsurprisingly, one of the possibilities that soon occurred was that its purpose and warrant are not the stating of facts but the expression of preferences. All of this being so, the enterprise of moral philosophy needs to rid itself of the old legalistic terms and start afresh to think about how the evaluation and guidance of action might be rationally warranted. At this point Anscombe reintroduces Aristotle and suggests that questions of conduct might be approached via consideration of the habits of action and avoidance it is necessary to cultivate if one is to lead a good life. What a good life is might itself be determined by investigating the natural teleology of human kind. To know what a good X is one considers the kind of existence naturally characteristic of Xs and projects forwards into an idea of what flourishing for that kind of entity would consist in. This is a matter of developing an account of a natural form of life, or equivalently of a kind of animating principle *psuche* – hence the need for an 'adequate philosophy of psychology'.

It has often been supposed that Anscombe was encouraging the complete abandonment of a deontological vocabulary of absolute requirements and prohibitions, but this is a mistake. Her point, I take it, is that, *pace* Kant (and, by implication, latter-day neo-Kantians), pure prescriptive deontology only makes sense on the assumption that there is a transcendent legislative authority – God or (perhaps) Cosmic Order – and that unless one believes this, one should abandon that kind of moral thinking. Like MacIntyre, however, Anscombe was a traditionally minded Roman Catholic and *did* believe in the Law of God. Consequently she could find a place for absolutist language, *but not*, I think, as the kind of talk whose use might be warranted simply by a neo-Aristotelian theory of virtue. Better then not to use the term 'moral' in connection with both natural virtue and ordained law; or if one does, then it is essential to remember that these uses are not univocal but only analogous.[5]

I have set out Anscombe's theses in part as a reminder of the extent to which MacIntyre has been carrying on a project already begun, and in part to serve as a relevant basis for comparison and contrast between members of a class of philosophers, viz. Roman Catholic neo-Aristotelians, who might be thought to hold very similar views.[6] Clearly, anyone who wanted to follow Anscombe's suggestions and work out a broadly Aristotelian theory of virtue while retaining a Divine Law account of moral absolutes would have to make intelligible and defend two sets of controversial assumptions: one set *metaphysical*, having to do with human nature; the other *theological*, concerning God, His commands and the means of their reception.

Given that MacIntyre begins with something very close to Anscombe's analysis of modern moral philosophy, it is interesting to see how he places himself with respect to these two sets of assumptions. However, since his commitment to Christianity is only made explicit in the second and third volumes of the trilogy, the question of theological presuppositions is best delayed. Beginning with *After Virtue*, then, we are given a similar account of the separation of our moral vocabulary from the historical sources of its life. The account differs from Anscombe's discussion both in wealth of detail and in presenting Aristotelianism itself as one of those major sources. Furthermore, whereas Anscombe refers to a 'philosophy of psychology' and offers certain parallels involving the life of non-sentient organisms, MacIntyre sides with the critics of Aristotle's naturalistic philosophical anthropology, speaking of it as involving an untenable 'metaphysical biology'.[7] What is retained, however, is the Aristotelian idea that an ethics of virtue *requires* a teleology of agency. If certain act-dispositions are rationally to be encouraged (and others discouraged) then it must be possible to specify an end of action towards which these dispositions will lead us. Disavowing the effort to identify a natural *telos* for man as such, MacIntyre introduces the idea of a historically developed social nature, and within this the notion of a narrative history and a life of self-definition.

Later, he emphasizes that the rationality of cultivating a particular set of virtues in relation to a given end, and the rationality of that end's being prescribed, is not to be thought of as determinable from outwith the tradition of socially constituted norms and broadly moral practices in which the agent finds himself. On one interpretation of this suggestion, it seems to introduce an element of relativism. This will be worrying to those who saw the appeal to Aristotle as marking the adoption of a kind of naturalism that would begin with an empirical-cum-philosophical anthropology and move from this to an account of the virtues as rational habits which it is necessary to possess always and everywhere – variation only appearing at the level of their application in diverse circumstances.

The general question of relativism will be returned to, but for now the interest attaches to MacIntyre's internalist account of rationality. The supposed failure of liberalism has been due not to any accident of history – such as the existence within the political community of groups who are antagonistic to its neutralism or, more specifically, to its toleration of what they regard as intolerable. Rather, it was doomed to fail by virtue of its philosophical presuppositions. In MacIntyre's analysis, liberalism rests on an incoherent account of rational agents, that is, one which sees them as constituted as persons independently of their social context and which takes their deliberations to be answerable to ahistorical, transcendent norms of reasoning. Since these presuppositions are incoherent[8] it follows that reliance on them must lead to further incoherencies – including the disintegration of social practice. What is offered by way of fundamental reconstruction is the idea of practical rationality as emerging and developing through forms of social exchange. But of course there is not just one community, there are many. Similarly any given community has a history through which it has developed. Thus there will be as many forms of rationality as there are distinct communities, where the latter are individuated by reference to the forms and norms of social life.

Although I cannot pursue the point here, it is important to note that there are difficulties facing the idea of radically distinct communities. What exactly, for example, are the criteria of identity for cultures and societies? Where do *we* stop and *others* begin? Certainly, geography and time may separate communities but this empirical fact is, in itself, philosophically trivial. What has to be shown is that there are points of separation beyond these spatio-temporal ones which constitute incommensurable differences. A line of reasoning familiar from Wittgenstein and Davidson suggests that this may not be possible.[9] MacIntyre is dismissive of Davidson's interpretative argument but yet invokes a linguistic criterion of cultural difference: roughly, a culture is distinct from one's own to the extent that understanding what speakers belonging to it are saying involves learning the meaning of their words as terms in a second language. But this suggestion invites a reapplication of the Davidsonian argument: either such learning involves translation of terms from one language into those of another or it does not. If it does, then in what sense did the foreign language represent an incommensurable cultural difference, as opposed to an interesting variant of a common human culture? If it does not, then how does one know what one is saying, or indeed that one is saying anything coherent at all? It is worth adding that, in fact, MacIntyre manages to say a good deal about the meaning of the terms of the languages, and *ipso facto* about the concepts and practices of supposedly alien cultures and traditions.

Suspicions of relativism

Even allowing the thesis of the plurality of rationalities, questions arise as to what forms of practical rationality are or have been operative, of how cognitive progress within any given form occurs and, most importantly, of how any socially constituted rational order can be judged superior to any other. Here I say 'most importantly', not only for the special interest that question has for philosophical theorists, but because MacIntyre himself makes clear that the account of rationality as tradition-dependent is being developed for a practical purpose:

> [W]e must first return to the situation of the person to whom, after all, this book [*Whose Justice? Which Rationality?*] is primarily addressed, someone

who, not as yet having given their allegiance to some coherent tradition of
enquiry, is besieged by disputes over what is just and about how it is
reasonable to act, both at the level of particular immediate issues...and at
the level at which rival systematic tradition-informed conceptions contend.[10]

In a moment I shall consider what MacIntyre has to say about the way in
which proponents of one tradition may come to judge another to be superior.
But it is worth dwelling on the situation envisaged in the quoted passage. Here
we are to imagine someone who has not yet subscribed to 'a coherent tradition
of enquiry'. That immediately raises the question of how such a person can
choose between rival suitors for his or her mind and conscience. It would seem
that his or her choice must either be rooted in reason or else be non-rational.
But the former is excluded if rational norms are only available to a participant
within a coherent tradition, for, *ex hypothesi*, the addressee is a complete outsider. If the latter, however, then one may be hesitant to speak of a 'choice' as
having been made, and certainly it could not be seen as other than arbitrary
viewed from *all* rational perspectives. In *Three Rival Versions*, MacIntyre draws
upon Aquinas's account of the metaphysical preconditions of learning in order
to resolve a paradox of knowledge arising with respect to the introduction of a
tyro to the craft of moral inquiry.[11] But the present difficulty concerns someone
who is supposed to understand what he hears presented to him but does not
know how or whether to commit himself. Given the other assumptions it is
doubtful that the envisaged situation is even intelligible. But if it is, then it
seems to imply that MacIntyre's position on the present case is either contradictory or else lends support to a relativist conclusion. We are prohibited from
saying that the rootless addressee can choose on the basis of transcendent
norms of practical reason, so that excludes a realist resolution. This returns us to
the thought that all choosing is from within a tradition, but if so there is after
all nothing to be said by or to such a person, and *a fortiori* he cannot make a
rational choice. Indeed, earlier in *Whose Justice? Which Rationality?* MacIntyre
says as much himself:

> The person outside all traditions lacks sufficient rational resources for
> enquiry and *a fortiori* for enquiry into what tradition is to be rationally
> preferred. He or she has no adequate relevant means of rational evaluation
> and hence can come to no well-grounded conclusion, including the conclu-
> sion that no tradition can vindicate itself against any other. To be outside
> all traditions is to be a stranger to enquiry; it is to be in a state of intellec-
> tual and moral destitution.[12]

But this contradicts the suggestion that such a person stands to be helped by
what MacIntyre has to say. One might suppose, however, that the addressee's
deficiency is not in respect of reason *as a whole* but only in regard to moral
rationality. This would make intelligible the idea that he can understand

something of what is being urged upon him without yet being able to assess the rival specific and general claims. But if that is so then he, the outsider to moral traditions, has reason to regard the disagreement between the rival suitors as being, for him, rationally undecidable. Of course, from *within* the competing traditions, rival, purportedly conclusive, demonstrations may be advanced. But nothing can be made of these either from a perspective of transcendent moral rationality – for there is none – or from the perspective of speculative or scientific reasoning, not because the latter does not exist but because, *ex hypothesi*, its concepts and criteria of rationality find no place for moral notions and reasoning. Viewed from this second perspective, the situation of competing traditions seems precisely that which invites a relativist description. A rational inquirer finds himself confronted by rival accounts of *moral* reasoning between which it is said to be impossible for him to make a rational choice. This suggests either that the rival accounts lack any kind of rationality, or that their rationality is internal to them. Thus we arrive at either non-rationalism or relativism.

MacIntyre discusses relativism, not in connection with the case of the outsider (generally conceived of as the disinherited product of Enlightenment individualism) but as it seems to arise directly from the claim that rationality is only constituted within traditions of inquiry. Ironically, indeed, the second of the passages just quoted occurs in this discussion. His strategy for dealing with relativism is twofold. First, he considers how participants in different traditions might come to recognize the superiority of a rival through experiencing an epistemological crisis which the rival has more effective means of diagnosing and treating. (This becomes the central theme of *Three Rival Versions* – the victor being Thomism.) But since he allows that events might not take this course and traditions could persist in irresoluble conflict he turns to a second consideration. This takes the form of the earlier dilemma which he uses to confront someone who moves from the claims he, MacIntyre, accepts, that is, *that norms and requirements pertaining to morality are always tradition-dependent and that there are rival (and incommensurable) traditions*, to the claims that he rejects, that is, *that one's own evaluative deliberations are rationally undermined by these facts and that truth is shown to be, at best, relative to a system of inquiry*. The dilemma is intended to reveal the incoherence of the presupposition of these latter claims. Given the immanence of practical reasoning, someone must either be within a tradition and hence operating with its standards and so committed to their correctness, or else outside it and hence not equipped to take a view one way or the other.

The point of my previous remarks was to suggest, first, that the second disjunct defeats MacIntyre's educational aim and so he must either abandon it or this disjunct; and, second, that the very composition of the disjunction overlooks a possibility implied by MacIntyre's own characterization of the outsider. Since he hears and understands he is possessed of reason, even though he is a moral alien. And what this reason tells him is that the matters placed before him are not ones that his or any other 'external' rationality can investigate. A further worry now arises concerning the structure of MacIntyre's defence against relativism. Although he begins by considering this as the challenge that his position is relativistic, he proceeds to treat it as if it were a challenge made *by* a relativist who regards MacIntyre as holding back from relativism.

For convenience, let me speak of the Cartesian-cum-Kantian view of reason as *universalism*, of MacIntyre's tradition-constituted rationality as *immanentism* and of the idea that is now under consideration as *relativism*. (These correspond to the Encyclopaedist, Thomist and Genealogical conceptions explored in *Three Rival Versions*.) Employing these terms, the present charge is that immanentism, as MacIntyre presents it, either is, or implies some version of, relativism. It is curious, therefore, that his defence is concerned with demonstrating the incoherence of relativist claims. For that is not likely to be an issue between MacIntyre and his present critic, be he a universalist or some other sort of immanentist. What is actually needed is a demonstration that immanentism neither is nor implies relativism. Certainly one indirect way of going about this would be to start by deriving a contradiction from relativism and tracing its roots to assumptions which are demonstrably absent from immanentism. But MacIntyre's argument falls short of that. The dilemma he presents to the relativist invites two responses. One is to argue that it does not refute relativism, and so cannot serve the role in the defence of immanentism mentioned above. The other response is to observe that even if it does refute it, the task of showing that MacIntyre's immanentism is not incoherent remains incomplete until it has been established that it is not itself a version of relativism or a position that leads to it. One way of developing my previous argument would be to say that while the dilemma may prevent a participant in a moral tradition from simultaneously affirming its norms and denying them any special authority, that is compatible with occupying a theoretical stance from which they are seen relativistically. Whatever we think about that, however, there remains the question of the philosophical status of immanentism and this issue leads me to MacIntyre's revival of Thomism.

MacIntyre and Thomism

MacIntyre has many very interesting things to say about the structure of traditions of inquiry, about how an individual might make his way through these and extend them, and about how rival traditions can engage with one another and what it would mean for one of them to emerge from such engagement as recognizably superior. Here I can only consider the last of these aspects as it bears on the way in which MacIntyre discusses Thomism.

In *Whose Justice? Which Rationality?* and in *Three Rival Versions* it is argued that the absence of transcendent norms of inquiry does not exclude the possibility of one tradition being judged better than another. *Ex hypothesi*, that judgement cannot be made from outwith the competing traditions and hence it can only be rooted within one or more of them. However, it is neither likely nor ultimately intelligible that anyone involved in moral inquiry would take the claims to superiority on behalf of a rival at their own estimate. How then can the proponent of one position possessed of its own criteria of rationality defer to the superior rationality of another view? MacIntyre's answer involves the idea of a tradition running into difficulties and finding that it lacks the means to understand those difficulties and/or to resolve them. A rival may then offer a historical-cum-philosophical analysis and solution – both, of course, couched in terms generated from within itself. Real progress comes when the tradition in crisis recognizes *by its own lights* that the rival has the conceptual and argumentative resources it lacks. In *Whose Justice?* MacIntyre develops a history of such engagement and victory, leading from Homer to Aristotle to Augustine to Aquinas, and in *Three Rival Versions* this process is explored more fully in relation to competing nineteenth-century conceptions and their contemporary descendants. Besides saying more about the logical character of relations between these rivals, the latter book also devotes much space to characterizing what MacIntyre takes to be the most successful tradition of inquiry, viz. *Thomism*. For many readers, myself included, this will be its point of greatest interest and innovation.

Earlier I named several philosophers who are both Roman Catholics and, in a broad sense, neo-Aristotelians. These are distinguished figures but they are few in number, and fewer yet would be willing to be described as Thomists. Indeed in Great Britain I doubt that there are sufficient Thomists to constitute a football team (even assuming age and infirmity were not disqualifications). In the United States matters are certainly different, mainly because of large-scale immigration from Catholic countries and the existence of seminaries, colleges and universities established in consequence. Even so, Thomism has been in decline throughout the twentieth century as younger Catholics lost either their faith, or the traditional taste for philosophy – or having retained it took to a diet of Continental thought ranging from existentialism to deconstructionism and beyond. Ironically, these French, German and Italian-inspired schools are major participants in one of MacIntyre's rivals to Thomism, viz. the *genealogical* tradition. This might be dismissed as a sociological curiosity, but given MacIntyre's historicism he needs to explain why Thomism has lost out to Nietzsche in North American Catholic institutions of learning (or equivalently, why Gilson, Maritain and Simon have been neglected while Gadamer, Levinas and Derrida have been taken up with enthusiasm). The same is true on the Continent itself. In Louvain, for example, the site of the nineteenth-century Thomist revival, Thomism has largely given way to phenomenology and critical theory. At one point MacIntyre speaks with admiration of Grabmann, Mandonnet, Gilson, Van Steenberghen and Weisheipl. But these are dead authors whose influence is confined to the most scholarly members of the neo-scholastic community, and though I share something of MacIntyre's admiration for such men they could hardly be said to have produced a renaissance of Thomistic philosophy. For good or ill (very much the latter, I think) in those places where Thomism can be found, the *zeitgeist* would suggest that if any conception has emerged victorious from an engagement of rival conceptions it is postmodernity rather than pre-modernity.

There are 'neo-Thomist' viewpoints from which this might not seem a bad thing, such as those which reinterpret Aquinas through the methodologies of postmodern thought. In his *Le Point de départ de la métaphysique* (1926), for example, Joseph Maréchal argued that if the Thomist synthesis was to have any chance of being 'revalidated' in the context of modern philosophy it would have to develop its methodology of inquiry. So while the metaphysical and epistemological realism of St Thomas need not be departed from, it was necessary to adopt the Kantian method of transcendental deduction in order to address the new epistemological 'problematic'. This tradition of 'Transcendental Thomism' has continued and been developed in North America by Bernard Lonergan and others,[13] and on the Continent by its most distinguished proponent Emerich Coreth. Moreover, Coreth's major work *Metaphysik* has been abridged and translated for North American college students by Joseph Donceel, another proponent of this continuation of Thomism.[14] What should come as no surprise, however, is that the content of this philosophy stands in direct opposition to the realism of Aquinas himself. So this 'revalidation' of the perennial philosophy has resulted in its transformation into one of the many anti-realisms of post-Cartesian thought. MacIntyre makes a similar point about the revival of Thomas via Kant attempted by Rosmini in the nineteenth century. Subsequently he also mentions Maréchal, but not the later figures whose influence is still active, and continues:

> And if this were the whole story of Thomism it would at least appear as, and perhaps be, a story of defeat. But happily *Aeterni Patris* [Pope Leo XIII's encyclical commending the study of Aquinas] also generated a quite different set of intellectual enterprises, those which, in retrieving stage by scholarly stage the historical understanding of what Aquinas himself said, wrote, and did, recovered for us an understanding of what is distinctive about the mode of enquiry elaborated in its classical and most adequate form by Aquinas.[15]

The 'different set of intellectual enterprises' is that associated with the historians of Thomism quoted earlier. As I remarked, however, their work – like that of English historians of philosophy writing about Lockean empiricism, for example – has produced exegetical and interpretative insights but not generated a living philosophy generally acknowledged to be able to engage with and be proven superior to Davidsonian philosophy of action, Nagelian moral psychology or Parfitian moral theory.

I also suggested, however, that the growing dominance within academic philosophy of 'postmodern' ideas and methods might not be universally unwelcome among some of those with an interest in Aquinas, for they might see in it a way to reinterpret what is at any rate not a modernist philosophy and thereby give added historical weight to the case against universalist rationalism.[16] A further example of this is suggested by MacIntyre's own discussion of the fourteenth-century fate of Aquinas's reinterpretation and synthesis of earlier traditions. He mentions Meister Eckhart and describes his mystical theology as a repudiation of the Thomist achievement but allows that it may not have been seen as such:

> Eckhart may well have believed that he was only carrying certain strands of Aquinas's thought further. When in 1325 he was accused of heresy, he claimed to be a Thomist. But it is precisely because and insofar as he was not that he has exerted such influence on a variety of later non-Thomistic and anti-Thomistic thinkers, most notably on Hegel and Heidegger.[17]

Several aspects of this discussion are of interest. MacIntyre goes on to quote John Caputo's interpretation of Eckhart as a kind of mystical existentialist, but charges none the less that he (Eckhart) was guilty of an erroneous appropriation of the Thomist language of 'being' for irrationalist purposes, and that Heidegger's interest in Eckhart was precisely because of this anti-Thomist stance. In an earlier book which, however, MacIntyre does not mention (entitled *Heidegger and Aquinas*) Caputo seeks 'to undertake a confrontation of the thought of Heidegger and of Thomas Aquinas on the question of Being and the problem of metaphysics', and offers a MacIntyrean-sounding rationale for doing so: 'The cutting edge of this confrontation lies in the fact that each thinker is included in the other's history of the oblivion of Being.'[18] The conclusion of this study is a thesis about what lies at the heart of Aquinas's work: '[B]ehind the discursive arguments, the conceptual distinctions, the whole impressive display of *ratio*... there lies the experience of Being...a profound, if implicit mysticism. In the end, St Thomas is properly understood only by converting the coin of his metaphysical theology into its religious and alethiological equivalent.'[19]

In short, Aquinas is not so far from Eckhart and Heidegger. Clearly this conclusion is at odds with MacIntyre's interpretation, and it is a further reminder that to the extent that Aquinas is discussed by those among whom a revival might be expected he is often seen in quite different historical and philosophical terms from those presented in *Three Rival Versions*. This fact also raises a general methodological question. According to MacIntyre, the superiority of Thomism consists in its ability to construct a rational narrative within which the advances and crises of other traditions can be described and transcended. But the construction of such a narrative – of self and other – is liable to be controversial. In *Whose Justice?*, MacIntyre invokes something like the theory-ladenness of observation:

> There are no preconceptual or even pretheoretical data, and this entails that no set of examples of action, no matter how comprehensive, can provide a neutral court of appeal for decision between rival theories.... To put the

same point another way: each theory of practical reasoning is, among other things, a theory as to how examples are to be described, and how we describe any particular example will depend, therefore, upon which theory we have adopted.[20]

Applying this thesis to the present issue suggests that the competition between the Genealogist, the Encylopaedist and the Thomist, and the disputes between different proclaimed continuations of Thomism itself, such as the Kantian, the Heideggerian and the Rationalist, cannot be resolved by reference to empirical histories. In relating the sort of narrative with which MacIntyre is concerned, at least two kinds of theoretical formation will feature (perhaps inseparably intertwined). First, events will be related historically (I do not say causally); and second, history will be articulated into passages of ascent and descent, of progression, retrogression and stagnation, etc. Clearly it is a matter of contention whether the work of an author represents advance or confusion in the development of an inquiry, and such matters are not resolvable without reference to a *philosophical* investigation of the issues and arguments. But that casts doubt on the very idea that history or narrative can, of themselves, play a major part in determining the standing of a tradition. MacIntyre writes:

> The standards of achievement within any craft are justified historically. They have emerged from the criticism of their predecessors and they are justified because and in so far as they have remedied the defects and transcended the limitations of those predecessors as guides to excellent achievement within that particular craft.... So it is within forms of intellectual enquiry, whether theoretical or practical...because at any particular moment the rationality of a craft is justified by its history so far, which has made it what it is in that specific time, place, and set of historical circumstances, such rationality is inseparable from the tradition through which it was achieved.[21]

What need to be assessed, however, are arguments and concepts considered in their own right and largely independently of their role in any recorded sequence of debates. This thought prompts worries about the historical conception and methods of enquiry which constitute the framework of MacIntyre's project, but it also directs attention on to the philosophical character of the Thomism he favours.

Given MacIntyre's criticism of Rosmini and others, it would be ironic if he were guilty of a similar revisionist tendency. But as I read his trilogy I find myself worrying about this, and the main worry is related to the earlier concern about relativism. There is not the opportunity here to enter into detailed debate about the interpretation of Aquinas or the status of the arguments and theses MacIntyre advances. But perhaps I may register a doubt about the general character of the position. In several places in *Whose Justice?* and *Three Rival Versions*, MacIntyre sets out elements of the Thomist view. This is done in ways which contribute to the establishment of that view as a *via media* between the radical relativism of the genealogist and the universal rationalism of the encyclopaedist.

One way of viewing this third tradition is as a mode of thinking that recognizes the truth in each of its rivals while rejecting the false. The genealogist insists on the historically situated and open-ended character of inquiry and concludes that its objects are similarly immanent – that they are, in some sense, constructions or projections of thought rather than independent features detected by it. The encyclopaedist, by contrast, takes the objects of reason to be transcendent and assumes that the means of engagement with them are likewise independent of historical conditions of inquiry. In response to these opposing assertions one might try to construct a *via media* by combining the idea of the immanence and open-endedness of the means of inquiry with that of the transcendence of its objects. In places MacIntyre seems to offer just this view of the Thomism he espouses. That is to say, he presents it as a form of theistic philosophical realism committed to a view of the objects of reason as mind-independent, but a realism which maintains that reason itself is shaped and advanced through traditions of inquiry.

At least four questions now arise in my mind. First, whether this is an accurate description of MacIntyre's view. Second, whether it is faithful to the character of Aquinas's epistemology and metaphysics. Third, whether this combination of ideas is a coherent one. And fourth, whether, if it is coherent, it does not trivialize, or at least diminish the philosophical interest of, the historical-tradition model of the circumstances of inquiry. Needless to say, these questions are related to one another. As regards its accuracy on MacIntyre's intentions, consider the following:

> The temporal reference of reasoning within a craft thus differs strikingly from that of either encyclopaedic or genealogical reasoning. The encyclopaedist aims at providing timeless, universal, and objective truths as his or her conclusions, but aspires to do so by reasoning which has from the outset the same properties. From the outset all reasoning must be such as would be compelling to any fully rational person whatsoever. Rationality, like truth, is independent of time, place, and historical circumstances....[For the genealogist] to treat tradition as a resource is one more way of allowing the past to subjugate the present. And the central symptom of the sickness of this type of social existence, from the genealogical standpoint, is that, despite its historical recognition of the historical situatedness of all reason-giving and reason-offering, it understands the truth to which it aspires as timeless. Hence the rationality of craft-tradition is as alien and hostile to the genealogical enterprise as is the encyclopaedist's to either.[22]

This sounds like the *via media* I described, incorporating a realist metaphysics, and certainly MacIntyre cites Aquinas in terms which affirm both writers as realists. Elsewhere, however, truth is characterized in ways that suggest a pragmatist version of anti-realism: 'The mind is adequate to its objects [i.e. attains to truth] in so far as the expectations which it frames on the basis of [its] activities are not liable to disappointment and the remembering which it engages in enables it to return to and recover what it had encountered previously, whether the objects themselves are still present or not.'[23]

Subsequently he explicitly criticizes the identification of the concept of truth with that of warranted assertability on the grounds that what is warranted at one stage of inquiry may not be so later: 'The concept of truth, however, is timeless.'[24] But two points are relevant to this. First, an anti-realist need not seek to identify truth with warranted assertability. He may not be looking for conceptual analyses, anyhow; but even if he were, the relevant notion would be something like Hilary Putnam's 'idealized rational acceptability'[25] and that looks to be what MacIntyre's inquiry-based account suggests. Second, given the conceptual connections between rationality and truth, and the claim that the former is immanent within, and constituted by, traditions of inquiry, it is difficult to see how truth itself can be tradition-transcendent, which is what metaphysical realism requires.

The latter issue concerns the coherence of the combination offered by the *via media*. No such question would arise if the claim that practical and theoretical inquiries are tradition-immanent were to be interpreted as saying no more than that the forms and progress of inquiries are shaped by history. This removes a philosophical worry but at the price of turning the major thesis of MacIntyre's trilogy into a commonplace of humane learning. And certainly he is claiming something more: 'It is no trivial matter that all claims to knowledge are the claims of some particular person, developed out of the claims of other particular persons. Knowledge is possessed only in and through participation of dialectical encounters.'[26]

My persistent worry is that any interpretation of this claim which makes it out to be more than a version of the commonplace of scholarship must lead to a relativism quite at odds with what I take to be the philosophy of Aquinas. Like MacIntyre, I view the work of St Thomas with interest and admiration and look to it as a source for the articulation of a credible form of philosophical realism.[27] I very much hope, therefore, that we will see a future volume by MacIntyre setting out the truth in Thomism – in ways which make clear why such worries as I have presented here are unfounded.

Notes

Work on the essay was done during the period of a Visiting Fellowship at the Institute for Advanced Studies in the Humanities, University of Edinburgh. I am grateful to the then Director (Professor Peter Jones), staff and co-fellows of the Institute for making my time there agreeable and educative. I am also indebted to the Carnegie Trust for the Universities of Scotland for financial support.

Epigraph from the introduction to Pope Puis XII, *Humani Generis* (1950), paras 1, 6, 7; translated under the title *False Trends in Modern Teaching: False Opinions which Threaten to Sap the Foundations of Catholic Teaching* (rev. edn, London: Catholic Truth Society, 1959).

1 *After Virtue* (London: Duckworth, 1981).
2 *Whose Justice? Which Rationality?* (London: Duckworth, 1988).
3 *Three Rival Versions of Moral Inquiry* (London: Duckworth, 1990).
4 G.E.M. Anscombe, 'Modern Moral Philosophy', *Philosophy* 33 (1958); reprinted in *Ethics, Religion and Politics: The Collected Philosophical Papers of G.E.M. Anscombe*, vol. 3 (Oxford: Blackwell, 1981).
5 In fact her view may be more complicated than this, see 'Authority in Morals', in Anscombe, *Ethics, Religion and Politics*, vol. 3: *Contraception and Chastity* (London: Catholic Truth Society, 1977); and 'Morality', in *Pro Ecclesia et Pontifice* (London, 1982).
6 It is interesting to note in passing how many of those associated with an influential cognitivist movement within moral philosophy belong within this broad grouping: Elizabeth Anscombe, John Finnis, Peter Geach, Germain Grisez, Alasdair MacIntyre, Charles Taylor and Henry Veatch.
7 *After Virtue*, ch. 12. I try to defend the appeal to naturalistic philosophical anthropology in support of normative inquiry in 'Metaphysics in the Philosophy of Education', *Journal of Philosophy of Education* 23 (1989).
8 I cannot discuss this aspect of MacIntyre's work here but I believe that the radical case against individualism is overstated by MacIntyre and its other well-known critics, viz. Charles Taylor and Michael Sandel. I discuss something of this in 'Individuals and the Theory of Justice', *Ratio* 27 (1985), and in 'Political Theory and the Nature of Persons: An Ineliminable Metaphysical Presupposition', *Philosophical Papers* 6 (1992). By the same token, a modest communitarian conclusion seems warranted by consideration of the conditions of reflective agency. This is explored in 'Identity, Community and the Limits of Multiculture', *Public Affairs Quarterly* 7 (1993).
9 See Donald Davidson, 'On the Very Idea of a Conceptual Scheme', in *Inquiries into Truth and Interpretation* (Oxford: Clarendon, 1984).
10 *Whose Justice? Which Rationality?* p. 393.
11 *Three Rival Versions,* ch. 3, p. 63; ch. 6, p. 130. I discuss the same issue from an avowedly realist interpretation of Aquinas in 'Chesterton's Philosophy of Education', Chapter 13, below.
12 *Whose Justice? Which Rationality?* p. 367.
13 See B. Lonergan, *Insight: A Study of Human Understanding* (London: Longman, 1957). For an appreciative analytical account of Lonergan see Hugo Meynell, *An Introduction to the Philosophy of Bernard Lonergan* (London: Macmillan, 1976).
14 *Metaphysics*, ed. and trans. J. Donceel (New York: Herder & Herder, 1968).
15 *Three Rival Versions*, p. 77. For the text of *Aeterni Patris* and interesting discussions of the development of Thomism since its publication, see V. Brezik (ed.), *One Hundred Years of Thomism* (Houston, Tex.: Center for Thomistic Studies, 1981).
16 I should note my considerable reservations about the use of such terms and expressions as 'postmodernism', 'the project of modernity' and so on. My own use of them is broadly quotational. For a development of these reservations see 'Cultural Theory, Philosophy and the Study of Human Affairs', in J. Doherty, E. Graham, M. Malek and D. Riches (eds), *Postmodernism in the Social Sciences* (London: Macmillan, 1991).
17 *Three Rival Versions*, pp. 165–6.
18 See John D. Caputo, *Heidegger and Aquinas: An Essay on Overcoming Metaphysics* (New York: Fordham University Press, 1982), pp. 1–2.
19 Ibid., p. 283.

20 *Whose Justice? Which Rationality?* p. 333.
21 *Three Rival Versions*, pp. 64–5.
22 Ibid., pp. 64–6.
23 *Whose Justice? Which Rationality?* p. 356.
24 Ibid., p. 363.
25 I think there are interesting resemblances between MacIntyre's position and the subtle ideas developed by Putnam. See the latter's *Representation and Reality* (Cambridge, Mass.: MIT Press, 1988), 'Internal Realism as an Alternative Picture', pp. 113–16; and 'Realism with a Human Face', in *Realism with a Human Face* (Cambridge, Mass.: Harvard University Press, 1990).
26 *Three Rival Versions*, p. 202.
27 I try to develop some of the elements of this in 'Brentano's Problem', *Grazer Philosophische Studien* 35 (1989), and in 'Mind/World Identity Theory and the Anti-Realist Challenge', in J. Haldane and C. Wright (eds), *Reality, Representation and Projection* (New York: Oxford University Press, 1993). For further discussion of MacIntyre's position see 'Natural Law and Ethical Pluralism', Chapter 9, this volume, pp. 137–9.

Chapter 3

The diversity of philosophy and the unity of its vocation

Some philosophical reflections on *Fides et Ratio*

Introduction

In the ordinary run of things Roman documents offer little in the way of philosophical interest. The present pontificate, by contrast, has been distinguished by the number of occasions on which John Paul II has invoked philosophical considerations in the course of addressing the Church. Three encyclicals spring to mind: *Veritatis Splendor, Evangelium Vitae* and *Fides et Ratio*. In the first two, moral philosophy is in view, and certain contemporary normative theories are criticized.[1] Although the Pope makes efforts to limit himself to general considerations and to avoid affirming any specific philosophical position, it is unsurprising to find his own colours showing, and thus the potential for controversy is not altogether avoided. Consider, for example, the following passage from *Veritatis Splendor*:

> [O]ne has to consider carefully the correct relationship between freedom and human nature, and in particular *the place of the human body in questions of natural law*. A freedom which claims to be absolute ends up treating the human body as a raw datum, devoid of any meaning and moral values until freedom has shaped it in accordance with its design. Consequently, human nature and the body appear as presuppositions or preambles, materially necessary for freedom to make its choice, yet extrinsic to the person, the subject and the human act.... *A doctrine which dissociates the moral act from the bodily dimensions of its exercise is contrary to the teaching of Scripture and Tradition*.[2]

The concluding reference to the teaching of scripture might suggest that the requirement to consider the body is a religious or theological one, and in that sense something extra-philosophical. Mention of the 'tradition' is more ambiguous: on the one hand it might be taken to mean the Church's moral teaching as that derives from Catholic moral theology; or it may be interpreted as referring to the philosophical tradition of natural law ethics. But this disambiguation involves a contentious if not false disjunction. For until quite recently Catholic moral theology (understood as theory and not as casuistry) has largely consisted in a synthesis of natural law and scriptural interpretation.

Quite apart from the attitude of dissenters opposed to particular first-order claims such as those concerning sexuality, the avowal of a particular form of rational justification of morality is somewhat controversial. It will not be enough, so far as *Veritatis Splendor* is concerned, to affirm some or other form of moral objectivism; one is expected (or is it required?) to subscribe to natural law. Moreover, while the insistence upon the relationship between right action and 'human nature' may seem a formal point satisfiable in indefinitely many ways; what is said – about the human body – suggests that some styles of reasoning that describe themselves as 'natural law ethics' will not do. Consider, for example, someone who argues that certain types of action are prohibited because they violate norms concerning the attainment of goods whose value is determinable by the practical rationality that we possess in virtue of our rational nature. Such a person will not yet have met the requirement set out in the quoted passage. For the 'natural' in natural law refers not only to the *source* of practical rationality but to its subject matter. In the Pope's account of things ethics is essentially *about* the lives of rational animals, and our embodiment is not a further feature to which pure practical reason might then attend. If I have him aright, for John Paul II philosophical anthropology is not something to which moral rationality might turn for empirical premises, rather it is the source and precondition of morality.

Indeed, the quoted passage expresses a yet more determinate philosophical conception: that of Thomistic anti-Cartesian personalism; Christian-Aristotelianism filtered through Husserl. For my own part, I find this *committed-voice* rather more congenial than the *committee-speak* of other church documents. Even so, I suggest that a question arises as to the appropriateness of such a level of philosophical specificity in a document addressed to the universal Church, given that Catholic moral philosophers and moral theologians who are evidently cognitivists or objectivists nevertheless differ quite widely on the nature of moral reasoning and thus on the grounding of moral prescriptions and requirements.

I raise this matter at the outset because the third of the encyclicals, *Fides et Ratio*, is largely and not incidentally concerned with the nature and role of philosophy, and while the Pope repeatedly assures readers that he is not seeking to accord priority to any single philosophical system – writing that 'The Church has no philosophy of her own nor does she canonize any one particular philosophy in preference to others' (§49) – the suspicion arises that in truth he believes that only one approach (or family of approaches) will do.[3]

Since the text is directed to a range of constituencies beyond the formal addressees (the bishops), it is difficult to be altogether sure about this however; and in face of that uncertainty one might not think it profitable or respectful to pursue the issue. Yet for those committed to the philosophical tradition which has the best claim to be *the* philosophy of Catholicism, viz. Thomistic

Aristotelianism, and for those interested in the development of Catholic philosophy and in the potential for engagement with philosophers outside the Church, these matters are critical. They concern nothing less than the limits of acceptable philosophical pluralism and thus bear heavily upon the prospects for such enterprises as *ARCIC* (*Analytical Roman Catholic Inter-Philosophical Conversation*).[4] For it could be that like the other *ARCIC* (*Anglican–Roman Catholic International Commission*) this exchange may run into difficulty over the authority of 'the Bishop of Rome', that description now being used *de re*, and in connection with John Paul's metaphilosophical doctrine about the nature of true philosophy, or his theology of speculative and practical reason.[5]

Requirements and tasks

The focus of my discussion is on issues raised in sections 80 to 91 of Chapter VII, 'Current Requirements and Tasks'. In the course of this – the penultimate chapter of *Fides et Ratio* – the Pope identifies three obligations for contemporary philosophy:

(i)   to recover the sapiential dimension of the discipline (§81);
(ii) to establish and maintain epistemological realism (§82); and
(iii) to achieve genuinely metaphysical range (§83).

It is tempting to partition these tasks into two; grouping the second and third as aspects of a single speculative enterprise – *the establishment of realism* – and taking up the first as an exercise for practical philosophy. But that would run counter to the view of their relationship expressed in the text, and I believe counter to the proper need for an integrated conception of philosophy as dialectic and the practice of the love of wisdom.

So far as the wider philosophical world is concerned, my own feeling is that the recovery of the sapiential dimension is the place to concentrate one's efforts, and I shall make a first attempt on this task later. However, it is also necessary to say something about (ii) and (iii), since as the Pope observes: 'this sapiential function could not be performed by a philosophy which was not itself a true and authentic knowledge, addressed to ... [reality's] total and definitive truth, to the very being of the object which is known' (§82). So as to provide the required context for this discussion let me give a brief overview of the chapter.

Earlier in the encyclical we are introduced to the universality of the philosophical impulse and to the power of its influence in shaping culture. This establishes one point of interest for the Church, but a second lies in the ancient role of philosophy as handmaiden and messenger on behalf of faith. Precisely because he values the several traditional functions of philosophy John Paul II goes on to express concern at tendencies among philosophers and theologians to limit severely the function of philosophy as discerner of objective truth. These 'false trends', as one might term them (echoing the phraseology of Pius XII in

Human Generis), are discussed in Chapters IV, V and VI. This then sets the scene for the identification of current requirements and tasks listed above.

Thus, philosophy is to establish our capacity to '*know the truth*' (*adequatio rei et intellectus*) and to achieve 'genuine metaphysical range capable of transcending empirical data in order to attain something absolute, ultimate and foundational in its search for truth' (§82). These requirements exclude certain philosophical options: (i) *radical phenomenalism*; (ii) *relativism*; (iii) *eclecticism*; (iv) *historicism*; (v) *scientism*; (vi) *pragmatism*; and the more general vice to which he thinks these bad practices lead, viz. *nihilism*.

No doubt it would not have been appropriate for the Pope to give detailed descriptions of these erroneous perspectives, in part for reasons of space, but also so as to avoid needless controversy in what is a work of doctrinal instruction and not a philosophical monograph. Nevertheless, this list of errors deserves much more discussion than it receives. Both clarification and more precise characterization are needed. For one thing the syllabus includes stances that seem to be of logically different kinds, some epistemological (e.g. phenomenalism), some metaphysical (e.g. scientism) and others perhaps stylistic (such as eclecticism). More to the point, however, if Catholic philosophers are to engage with the wider world, they will need to start making distinctions within these categories and that, I think, will quickly return us to the issue of tolerable pluralism.

Identifying philosophical positions

Certainly not every way of going on is as good as any other, but there are differences within the broad range of those who would agree with the necessity of the second and third tasks. Let me illustrate by observing one way in which philosophers with motives akin to the Pope's own have shied away from one kind of metaphysical realism precisely because it seems to lead to *scientism*.

Before doing that, however, I think it is appropriate to offer a couple of remarks about the 'syllabus of errors' cited above. The first on the list is 'eclecticism: by which is meant the approach of those who, in research, teaching and argumentation, even in theology, tend to use individual ideas drawn from different philosophies without concern for their internal coherence, their place within a system, or their historical context' (§86). So described, this hardly qualifies as 'a current of thought' (§§86, 91) or as 'a position' (§90), at least as those expressions are generally used and understood. Rather it represents a form of intellectual incompetence or irresponsibility and certainly not something that one could imagine anyone seriously proposing as an alternative philosophical approach. No doubt such intellectual vice should be warned against, but it seems out of place in a catalogue of contrasting philosophical approaches. There is, however, a different notion of 'eclecticism' appropriately applied to certain 'currents' or 'positions'. This connotes syntheses or blends of ideas or methods drawn from different historical approaches. Whether particular cases of this are reasonable is dependent upon actual specifics, but it would ill behoove a Thomist to issue a blanket condemnation since Thomism is itself eclectic – and Karol Wojtyla's Lublin variant is highly so.

A second example of the need for 'fine-tuning' is provided by the inclusion of 'pragmatism' in the list of currents of thought. This might be apt were it not for the peculiar definition given of it: 'An attitude of mind which in making choices, precludes theoretical considerations or judgments based on ethical principles' (§89). Certainly there is a use of the term 'pragmatist' (lower case 'p') in which it contrasts with action based on principle; but once again this does not represent a philosophical position so much as the avoidance of one. On the other hand the current of thought known to philosophers by the title 'Pragmatism' (upper case 'P'), and which is the subject of an entry in every philosophical dictionary or encyclopaedia, is far from precluding theoretical considerations or ethical judgements. Whatever one's view of the thought of Pierce, James and Dewey, it is undoubtedly philosophical, and one of its distinctive features is the philosophical emphasis given to values and norms.

What these examples suggest is that those who wish to commend *Fides et Ratio* to a philosophically educated readership will need to provide clarifying, qualifying terminological glosses. More substantial, however, is the task of determining the range of philosophical positions compatible with the encyclicals committed to epistemological and metaphysical realism. I cannot attempt this here, but I would like to touch on the issue of philosophical realism since this is an unquestionable commitment of John Paul II and one of the main issues in contemporary secular philosophy.

First, then, realism is not an 'all or nothing' position. For example, one and the same philosopher might favour a realist position on causality but not on mathematics. That is to say, he or she might hold, in opposition to Hume, that causal relations obtain in nature prior to and independently of human thought, but also maintain that truth in mathematics is not a matter of correspondence with some mind-independent reality, but rather of provability in a constructive system, which is to say that mathematical facts are not discovered but created by thought. This raises the question of how realism either total or partial should be understood. A very common answer equates realism with facticity or truth, but a more metaphysical account would be in terms of mind-independent existence.

This is not the occasion to explore the details and difficulties of these options, but it needs to be pointed out that an exclusive and strict mind-independent criterion is liable to result in a position uncongenial to the orientation of the encyclical. The reason is that much of what we ordinarily take to be objective is not wholly mind-independent. Colours, tastes and other secondary qualities are partly constituted by subjective sensibility, and many common descriptions of the 'world' express schemes of classification that reflect our interests rather than mind-independent natures. The Vatican is extensively and exquisitely decorated in marbles of various types, but marble is not itself a natural kind. Much but not all that is classified as 'marble' is limestone in a crystalline or granular state; and limestone is an aggregate of calcium carbonate and other chemical compounds. Thus, what *from the point of nature* are importantly different substances are grouped together by us because of their appearances – ones which themselves depend upon the form of our sensibility. Some metaphysical realists take this to be reason to say that 'marble' does not really exist. Pressed repeatedly this restrictive 'natural substance' metaphysics becomes reductive scientific realism, which is only one step away from scientism. The Pope is right to reject the latter, but doing so coherently is liable to require relaxing the requirement on realism, or at least allowing that not everything that is objective is real (in the metaphysician's strict sense).

To repeat, my point is not to argue to a particular realist doctrine but only to suggest that when relaying the message of *Fides et Ratio* greater understanding must be shown in identifying philosophical positions for praise or criticism. Quite generally, much more work needs to be done on the issue of the range of tolerable 'realisms', and none of us can afford to be triumphant about the 'tradition' or dismissive of others' ways of going on. Indeed, the common necessity of philosophy to make progress on these issues provides an opportunity for dialogue between Catholic philosophers and others.[6]

The sapiential dimension

Let me turn now to task (i) and to John Paul's call to academic philosophy to return to the ancient concern with the pursuit of wisdom. He writes: 'To be consonant with the word of God, philosophy needs first of all to recover its sapiential dimension as a search for the ultimate and overarching meaning of life' (§81). I think this is perhaps the most valuable positive contribution of the encyclical and one that can and should be carried beyond the world of Catholic thought. With this in mind, I would like to explore the relationship between philosophy conceived of as the practice of wisdom and the idea of philosophical spirituality as a demeanour adopted in the face of reality as one's speculative metaphysics takes it to be.

There seems little difficulty in understanding the idea of spirituality and of the spiritual life within the context of religious thought. In Christianity especially these are given definite content by reference to the indwelling of the Holy Spirit and to practices of prayer, meditation and devotion by which the soul progressively partakes in the life of God – not substantially but relationally as an adopted child might increasingly partake in the life of a family.[7]

When we turn to (non-religious) philosophy, however, a question arises whether any form of spirituality can find a home there. Yet even the most cursory reflection upon human experience, and on the efforts of great writers and others to give expression to it, suggests that there is a domain of thought, feeling and action that is concerned with discerning the ultimate truth about the human condition and with cultivating an appropriate mode of being or demeanour in response to that truth. The phenomenology is compelling, the concerns are intelligible, and for some reason intelligent people persist in supposing that it must be a central part of philosophy to deal with these matters and therefore look to it to do so.

Philosophers themselves, at least academics in the dominant Anglo-American tradition, either ignore such appeals as one might the entreaties of a door-to-door evangelist; suggest they are confused in ways similar to those in which some metaphysicians suggest that people are mixed up when they ask about first or ultimate causes; or else, if they are inclined to grant something to the claim that questions of non-religious meaning and spirit do arise and call for attention, they point to moral theory or possibly to aesthetics as being the relevant departments to visit.

While this last option has the merit of recognizing that there is something to be catered for, it makes a mistake in consigning it to moral philosophy as this is now understood, for that is concerned essentially with rightness of conduct, and first and foremost with conduct bearing upon other moral subjects. Notwithstanding its welcome breadth, contemporary virtue ethics remains a version of moral theory and as such is concerned principally with action. Likewise, aesthetics is concerned principally with disinterested contemplation of objects of experience. Spirituality involves intellect, will and emotion and is essentially contemplative, but the process of discovering the nature of reality, evaluating its implications for the human condition and cultivating an appropriate demeanour in the face of these is not reducible to ethics, nor to aesthetics. Yet unless philosophers can show this enterprise to be confused or exclusively religious they are open to the charge of neglecting something of fundamental, indeed perhaps of ultimate, human importance.

The practice of wisdom

The French classical scholar and historian of philosophy Pierre Hadot has made a series of very interesting studies of the aims and methods of the six ancient schools of philosophy, viz. *Stoicism, Epicureanism, Platonism, Aristotelianism, Cynicism* and *Pyrrhonism*, arguing that each reflects and in turn seeks to develop a permanent possibility of the human spirit. These studies have been collected and translated into English under the title *Philosophy as a Way of Life*, and I strongly recommend them.[8] I shall not even attempt to summarize his many conclusions, but I do want to extract one or two points so as to advance my own discussion.

First, then, Hadot discerns in the various ancient traditions, but especially in the Stoics, a distinction between '*philosophy*' (*philo-sophia* conceived of as the formation of the soul, or the deep structure of character, with the addition of an orientation towards the good), and *discourse about philosophy* (understood as the investigation of the nature of things, and to a lesser extent our knowledge of them). This, of course, is related to the more familiar distinction between practical and speculative philosophy. But whereas modern, recent and contemporary thought has invested greatest effort and talent in the pursuit of speculation in the form of epistemology and metaphysics, the ancients, and again I am focusing on the Stoics, give priority to thinking about practice, and within that to the cultivation of wisdom and the development of the spiritual life. Epictetus observes that 'the lecture room of the philosopher is a hospital'[9] which is to say that his work is the cure of souls. Later he writes: 'How shall I free myself? have you not heard it taught that you ought to eliminate desire entirely?...give up everything...for if you once deviate from your course, you are a slave, you are a subject.'[10] Hadot's reading of such texts is both informed and imaginative. It also encourages him to make three claims of great interest. First, he construes much more of the writing of antiquity as belonging to philosophy, in the sense of the practice of wisdom, than has been common among historians of ancient philosophy. More precisely and more strikingly he argues that these texts concern and in some cases *are* spiritual exercises. Second, and in direct opposition to the assumption which I mentioned that the notion of spirituality is in origin a religious one, he claims that in fact Christianity appropriated this area of reflective practice from pre-existing philosophical traditions and even that it took over 'as its own certain techniques of spiritual exercises as they had already been practised in antiquity'.[11] Third, he implies that the historical interest of all of this is perhaps its least significant aspect. In an essay responding to Foucault's use of his earlier work Hadot writes:

> I think modern man can practice the spiritual exercises of antiquity, at the same time separating them from the philosophical [metaphysical] or mythic discourse which came along with them. The same spiritual exercises can, in fact, be justified by extremely diverse philosophical discourses. These latter are nothing but clumsy attempts, coming after the fact, to describe and justify inner experiences whose existential security is not, in the last analysis, susceptible of any attempts at theorization or systematization....It is therefore not necessary to believe in the Stoic's nature or universal reason. Rather, as one practices them, one lives concretely according to reason. In the words of Marcus Aurelius: 'Although everything happens at random, don't you, too, act at random.' In this way, we can accede concretely to the universality of the cosmic perspective, and the wonderful mystery of the presence of the universe.[12]

This passage is full of promise, but a few comments are called for. First, the exercises he refers to, what Foucault called '*pratiques de soi*' (practices of the self)[13] are designed to liberate one from (inappropriate) attachment to exterior objects and the pleasures deriving from them. By regular self-examination one keeps a check on the tendency to exteriority, and by contemplating the impermanence of things one seeks to master or to possess oneself, attaining happiness in interior formation. Writing-up this examination, or better, perhaps, examining through writing, is one form of spiritual exercise.

Where Hadot takes issue with Foucault is in claiming with the ancient authors (including Plotinus) that the movement toward interiorization is 'inseparably linked to another movement, whereby one rises to a higher psychic level, at which one encounters another kind of exteriorization, another relationship with the "exterior" – or what one might term the "real"'.[14] Without necessarily wishing to reject it, one may reasonably call for further specification of this transcendent movement. A major direction of development is likely to lead to the inexpressibility of the mystical encounter with the 'One', but other possibilities suggest themselves, including moderate versions of Platonist ontology and even naturalistic Aristotelianism. Rather than pursue this, however, let me voice a reservation about the claim that spiritual formation may proceed independently of the truth of the accompanying philosophical discourse (metaphysics).

Presumably, even Hadot thinks there are some limits to just how wrong one can be at the speculative level while keeping on track in the practice of wisdom. Also there is reason to tie the two together as constituent components of a single enterprise, such that the content of spiritual formation is dependent upon its metaphysical complement. The argument for this is quite straightforward. One reason for believing that the issue of spirituality arises within philosophy is reflection on a parallel relationship between religious belief and practice. Suppose someone was persuaded by philosophical or historical arguments that the God of Christian theism exists, but that he or she then seemed wholly unmoved by this acceptance. One would be inclined to say, I think, that religiously speaking the thing (conversion) has not yet begun. For *that* belief requires the formation of a demeanour appropriate to its content. Likewise, I wish to say that a reductive materialist who really believes that his philosophy gives the ultimate truth about reality should be moved (by reason) to ask how in the face of this immensely significant belief he or she should compose themselves. It seems unintelligible to suppose that *nothing* follows for the enquirer from arriving at a fundamental view of reality be it physicalist or theist. Not only does the question arise of how to compose one's spirit in the face of this, but the content of the metaphysical belief must condition the character of the resulting demeanour.

Conclusion

The believer in Christian theism will be moved towards familiar Christian religious practices, and the reductive physicalist whose metaphysics is after all not so very different from that of the Old Stoics may wish to explore their spirituality. I think, therefore, that Hadot is wrong to try to loosen the link between philosophy and philosophical discourse; spirituality and metaphysics go together as I believe the writers of antiquity would agree.

The example of the Stoics and of other figures in ancient philosophy gives some reason for thinking that a kind of philosophical spirituality can be fashioned on a non-theological worldview. Suppose, however, that this is an illusion. That raises the following question. If it should seem after all that the necessary condition for the possibility of spirituality is some religious truth, and if the need and possibility of spirituality should seem compelling, then might we have the beginnings of (a new version of) an (old) argument for religion?

Academic philosophy has travelled far from the concern of its founding fathers to provide a guide to life. Along the way it has lost sight of the very idea of spiritual values, and in its current phase it may have difficulty recovering or refashioning this idea. This very fact deserves to be examined, and that examination might itself mark the beginning of a form of philosophical-*cum*-spiritual exercise: nothing less than an assessment of the value of what most academic philosophers currently practise in the name of their discipline.

Put another way and in the prophetic voice of John Paul II:

> [P]hilosophy needs first of all to recover its sapiential dimension as a search for the ultimate and over-arching meaning of life. This first requirement is in fact most helpful in stimulating philosophy to conform to its proper nature....In doing so it will be not only the decisive and critical factor which determines the foundations and limits of the different fields of scientific learning, but will also take its place as the ultimate framework of the unity of human knowledge and action, leading them to converge towards a final goal and meaning.
>
> (§81)

Notes

1 For contrasting philosophical commentaries see A. MacIntyre, 'How Can We Learn What *Veritatis Splendor* Has to Teach?' *The Thomist* 58.2 (1994), pp. 171–95; and 'From Law to Virtue and Back Again: On *Veritatis Splendor*', Chapter 10, below.

2 *Veritatis Splendor* (London: Catholic Truth Society, 1997), pp. 75–7.

3 Given that it treats of philosophy in general while *Veritatis Splendor* treats of moral philosophy (and theology) in particular, one might have expected that *Fides et Ratio* would have appeared first. It is of interest, therefore, that the latter was embarked upon first in the mid-1980s.

4 See J. Haldane, 'Theism', in *Atheism and Theism*, ed. J.J.C. Smart and J.J. Haldane (Oxford: Blackwell, 1996) 2nd edition 2003, 'Analytical Thomism', *The Monist* 80 (1997), pp. 485–6; and 'Thomism and the Future of Catholic Philosophy', Chapter 1, above.

5 For reservations about whether the Pope's conception of the autonomy of philosophy fully recognizes its self-governance, as operating by reason according to its own methods and principles, see Anthony Kenny, 'The Pope as Philosopher', *The Tablet*, 26 June 1999, pp. 874–5; and Jean Porter, 'Letting Down the Drawbridge', *The Tablet*, 3 July 1999, pp. 922–4.

6 In this connection see H. Putnam, 'Aristotle After Wittgenstein', in *Words and Life*, ed. H. Putnam (Cambridge, Mass.: Harvard University Press, 1994), pp. 62–81; and J. Haldane 'On Coming Home to (Metaphysical) Realism', *Philosophy* 71 (1996), pp. 287–96.

7 I use the analogy of participation in the life of a family rather than that of a parent given that in Christian mystical theology partaking in the life of God involves entering into the mutual divine life of three Persons.

8 See P. Hadot, *Philosophy as a Way of Life: Spiritual Exercises from Socrates to Foucault*, ed. A.I. Davidson (Oxford: Blackwell, 1995).

9 *The Discourses of Epictetus*, ed. C. Gill (London: Everyman, 1995), pp. 3, 23, 30.

10 *Discourses*, pp. 4, 4, 33.

11 Hadot, *Philosophy*, p. 206.

12 'Reflections on the Idea of the "Cultivation of the Self"', in Hadot, *Philosophy*, p. 21.

13 See M. Foucault, *History of Sexuality*, trans. R. Hurley, 4 vols (New York, 1984), vol. 3.

14 Hadot, *Philosophy*, p. 211.

Part II

Faith and reason

Chapter 4

Critical orthodoxy

Introduction

It is appropriate that the following discussion should be headed by a title that has about it a ring of Chestertonian paradox. For the issues I wish to consider involve ideas that were of paramount interest to Chesterton and, perhaps more importantly, the conclusion to which I shall proceed is one which may be seen to follow from reflection upon a striking claim of which he himself made much, namely, that theory is necessary for action. As will become clear in due course one formulation of this principle is especially well-suited to the present context. At the outset of one of his polemical works of common sense Chesterton writes:

> It is the whole definition of man that in social matters we must actually find the cure before we find the disease.[1]

Before returning to the themes of politics and social ethics, however, I must first deal with my main topic which is that of religious orthodoxy within Roman Catholicism. A topic which will be of primary interest to Catholics – and my discussion is largely addressed to them – but which may also interest others given its topicality, and the fact that conservation in the different departments of life is now a matter of lively debate.

Conflicting tendencies

In recent times there has been much discussion of the position of several well-known doctrinal and moral theologians, including Hans Küng, Edward Schillebeeckx and Charles Curran, whose published views have brought them into conflict with church authorities and in particular with the Roman Sacred Congregation for the Doctrine of the Faith under the Prefectship of Cardinal Ratzinger. During the same period in which these figures came to prominence there has been a parallel development among conservative Catholics writing and organizing in opposition to what they regard as the excessive liberalization within the Church since the Second Vatican Council. These two tendencies (conveniently, if not always accurately, characterized as *progressivism* and *traditionalism*) seem now to be locked into what threatens to be a long-running and damaging dispute leading, at best, to confusion and scandal among the faithful and, at worst, to the fragmentation of the Church into schismatic sectarianism.

Commentary on disputes always risks adding fuel to the fire. It should be clear, however, that given the depth and extent of current disagreements it is not likely that the cause of intra-Catholic unity, and thereby of inter-Christian ecumenism, will be served by remaining silent and hoping for the best. All too often rival opinions have been expressed in a spirit of suspicion and resentment. There is pressing need, therefore, to set out clearly the central points of disagreement between opposing groups and to put to one side (perhaps for future discussion) those which do not bear upon matters of faith but are expressions of personal taste and temperament or of social outlook. Only by shared reflection on the nature and content of Roman Catholicism can there be the common understanding that is a necessary condition of progress. This reflection, I suggest, might best begin by considering what it means to be a Roman Catholic.

My concern here is quite limited. I do not intend to assess in full the merits of the various conflicting positions nor even to detail the entire range of their disagreements. Rather I propose, first, to consider some formal features of the Catholic faith and to suggest that these establish logical limits to the development of doctrine; and, second, to indicate the extent to which proponents of both progressive and traditional tendencies sometimes confuse theological and other claims. Concerning the former issue, it seems that there are those who transgress these limits in their writings, teachings and practice. In such cases I suggest that logic demands that their revisions be clearly recognized for what they are, namely, doctrinal dissent. First, however, it is necessary to present a rough sketch (though not, I hope, a caricature) of the views which traditionalists and progressives have of one another.

Terms of opposition

The former thinks of his opponent as espousing a demythologized, morally consequentialist, pastoral theology in which Christ is characterized as being principally concerned to deliver a radical social message. The unit of salvation in this scheme is not the individual sinner but the group. The evil which binds men is not an essential feature of their embodied human nature but is a product of environmental, social and psychological forces. A condition of Christ's delivering this teaching with moral authority was that he should share fully in the common lot of humankind. It is held to be inconsistent with such sharing, however, that Christ could have been conceived other than by the means ordained for all human beings. Likewise, the elevation of Mary to the status of *Theotokos* and the insistence upon her Immaculate Conception and Bodily Assumption are rejected as alienating the human from God by removing the circumstances of Christ's life from the natural order in which all humankind is embedded and through which any progress (and, ultimately, any salvation) must be accomplished. In short, Christ's commission was to free his fellow humans from the bondage of history and not to bind them further with myth, doctrine and ritual.

The progressive, meanwhile, takes his conservative co-religionist to be concerned with perpetuating a basically anti-egalitarian and hierarchical view by appeal to a theology preoccupied with transcendence, mystery and magic and expressed in ungrounded obscurantist language. In this conception Christ and the human being are as Sovereign and subject. And while the former is infinitely good the latter are, by their very nature, fallen and given to evil. No matter how people strive to overcome their innate defects they are perverse in their wills and always relapse into sin. Thus the Incarnation is as much a *moral* mystery as a *metaphysical* one. In becoming man and dying on the cross God saved his subjects from the otherwise certain disaster to which they are impelled by their corrupt natures.

Given this understanding of Christ's life and death it was inevitable that believers should surround these events with various myths so as to emphasize the supernatural character of the Saviour. Accordingly, one finds successive generations insisting upon the miraculous and the extraordinary in all aspects of the faith. On the progressive's account of it, then, contemporary traditionalism is another manifestation of familiar reactionary attitudes: a reliance upon the structure of institutions, customs and laws to substitute blind, fearful compliance for inquiring thought, and a general preference for the supposed certainties of the past over the open-minded pursuit of truth.

The scope of disagreement

One could develop these accounts more fully and also distinguish different positions on either side. However, the general outlines are clear enough. According to the traditionalist the progressive seeks to naturalize the life and message of Christ so to force him into the mould of moral and social radical and in so doing renders him barely divine. Meanwhile the progressive charges his opponent with presenting Christ as hardly human – a transcendent being concerned principally with a future point in history when this world has passed away and its population been consigned either to everlasting damnation or to worship of their Sovereign Master.

This is to present the conflict in terms of fundamental theology but it is perhaps as familiar from its expressions at other levels, for example, in disputes about the proper form of the liturgy, the language of the eucharistic prayers, communion in the hand, general absolution, and so forth; in controversy over matters of morals and religious teaching; and in disagreement concerning relations with other churches. One might gather these various issues under four headings: *liturgy, morality, catechetics* and *ecumenism*. Generally, however, such particular concerns stem from, and lead back to, the kind of basic opposition of views outlined above.

At this point, however, two objections may be raised to the foregoing. First, that the contrast I have drawn represents the dispute at its most extreme; that it hardly ever takes this acute form and hence that most of those involved would reject the pictures presented of their views. Second, that the representation of their opposition connects theological beliefs with socio-political ones. As regards the former complaint it is true that I have sketched the contrast at its strongest, but this is to the good, for it highlights the relevant areas of difference which undoubtedly exist and any weaker version of either view represents a move towards agreement. Concerning the latter point, I think it is undeniable that in very many cases there is such an association of the religious with the political, but later I shall claim that this connection is to some extent detachable. Indeed, the failure to recognize the largely contingent nature of the connection between theology and politics is a major and widespread error committed by both sides and is a source of a good deal of irrelevant argument.

Theories and identity

Before considering the latter point it will be useful to examine some formal aspects of the nature of the Catholic faith. Quite generally an institutional, highly theologically informed religion commits its members to the truth of certain claims and to the validity of a set of practices. One may reflect upon these features in the abstract, without examining their content, and to do this I shall invoke the idea of a *theory*, not as a specialized term of art, but in the familiar sense of an account or explanatory scheme which purports to describe and interpret some phenomena and which may also prescribe certain activities with respect to them. Given this very broad use of the idea, it follows that physics, domestic science and Roman Catholicism are all types of theory.

Suppose, then, that one is introduced to a particular system of thought and practice. One may ask of all the beliefs and modes of behaviour associated with it whether or not they are essential. Characteristically, the result of this inquiry will be to show that some are so, that others are suggested by the theory but are not necessary to it, while others still are neither necessary nor suggested but are merely historical accretions. No doubt the marginal and inessential elements contribute to its interest, but they need not be preserved for the theory to retain its identity. Should one of the necessary features be abandoned, however, it follows directly that the theory has been rejected. This logical fact is not always obvious since the product of a change may appear to differ only slightly from the original. Indeed, the difference may not even be noticeable to an untutored observer. Nonetheless, it is an important and inescapable truth that if any item ceases to have one of its essential properties what remains is something different.

In reply it could be objected that not everything has an essence. And, more particularly, that some theories can survive radical developments of all their elements. I suspect that this response rests on two confusions. First, a failure to maintain the distinction between a *theory* and what it is of – its *subject matter*. And second, a failure to distinguish between a *particular* theory of a general type and the *kind* to which it belongs. As regards the former, the error lies in identifying the persistence of a phenomenon through the development of theories about it with the survival of a theory itself. For example, the heavenly bodies remained the same even though the angelic explanation of their motion was replaced by a Newtonian account. The latter confusion is related to this and arises from the observation that, while one theory (of chemistry, say) gradually gave way to another, both are nonetheless (chemical) theories. Certainly successive distinct accounts may be of the same *subject type* but they are nevertheless different individual theories, as may emerge in their mutual incompatibility.

The bearing of this on present concerns is that Roman Catholicism is in the relevant *very broad sense* a kind of theory and has a structure of beliefs and practices which constitutes its essence. This should be clear enough. Yet sometimes when writing in the context of the development of doctrine, theologians and others argue in a way which suggests they are oblivious to the fact or wish to deny it. Any attempt to assert the latter usually involves one or both of the confusions I noted. For while reality survives our modifications of view about its nature and while changes in doctrinal commitments may be within the limits of *Christian* theories, neither consideration enables one to escape from the fact that, once one has rejected an essential element of Roman Catholicism, one is *ipso facto* no longer a Roman Catholic.

Nor is it to the point to stress the organic, living character of the faith and to argue that, as with all organisms, the life of the Church involves change and development. Of course it does. But the only changes that are compatible with the continuing identity of a thing are accidental ones, that is, ones that do not modify its essence. (In the terminology familiar from scholasticism, alteration in respect of an essential feature necessarily involves the loss of the *substantial form* of an individual. What emerges after such change is a distinct entity.)[2] Thus, the Church today is the same body as was established through Christ and grew through the Councils of Trent and of Nicaea, *if and only if it is the same in all essentials*.[3]

Admittedly, it is not always possible to say just what elements are essential to a theory and I suspect that this is the case with the Catholic faith. Perhaps the Creed tells us what core beliefs are necessary, but there may, for example, be other propositions that are entailed by these, though one may not be able to see clearly (or even to discern at all) this connection between them.[4] Be this as it may, the Nicene Creed articulates a set of essential claims such that to reject any one of them is to abandon the faith. The history of such rejections is familiar and need not be detailed save to note that the groups that emerged from the Reformation had the clarity of vision to recognize their status and to call themselves by different names.

Thus, while there are many non-Catholic Christian theories there could not be such a thing as non-Catholic Catholicism. Yet, as I remarked, it appears that there are some who lack the perception to recognize this or the honesty to admit it. For although they have rejected articles of faith they seek to maintain the identity of their new theories with historical Catholicism and also to teach in its name. Such claims are at best logically confused and are at worst deceitful. I assume that the former is by far the more common circumstance.

Evidence and interpretation

Consider next another formal feature of all theories, namely, that they are (to employ an expression familiar to logicians) under-determined by evidence. What this means is that any theory transcends the particular phenomena it serves to interpret and explain. Just as physics goes beyond what is given at a particular time and place by positing entities and forces to account for the nature and occurrence of an event, so Christian theology extrapolates from, and thereby adds to, the description of the historical episodes around which it was formed.

Generally the only resources one has in the work of developing an account of some phenomenon are the evidential record itself and a variety of methodological principles – such as that one should seek to explain the facts with the maximum of economy and simplicity. But even with the operation of these constraints there is slack in the connection between evidence and theory with the corollary that several conflicting explanations may be compatible with the same data. Many forms of Christianity are like this. They take their start from a common body of evidence (the scriptures) and then develop different theories based upon it. In this way they are vulnerable to criticism to the extent that any of their claims run counter to the evidence or offend against a methodological criterion, or do both.[5]

Having introduced this admittedly limited but nonetheless useful general way of thinking about religious belief, what emerges is that however it may be for other religions, and also for non-Catholic Christians, the position of Catholicism with respect to the development of essential doctrine is altogether different. For it claims that there are two main sources of truth about God – scripture *and* Church.

In recent years there has been a steady growth in the development of Catholic scriptural scholarship and in related studies. All of this is most welcome, particularly as these were for so long areas of shameful ignorance within Catholic thought. Yet whatever results are delivered by this work, and whatever insights are achieved through it, it is perfectly obvious that if one's *sole* source of information about God was scripture one would almost certainly not be a Roman Catholic. Anyone who accepts the Bible as God's Word and holds in addition that any 'theory' based upon it must answer to such demands as those of simplicity and economy will conclude that Catholicism is hopelessly extravagant. It makes many claims and enjoins several practices which by these and other criteria must be unwarranted. Further, and most importantly, the points at which it oversteps the evidential base are not all concerned with inessentials but include articles of faith.

That Catholicism fails this test does not, however, render it unacceptable. It claims to have further resources in the inspired activity of its Pontiff and Councils. Of course, one might well reject the monumental claims to authority of these latter. But to do so is once again to cease to be a Roman Catholic. Indeed, over the centuries many have come to the conclusion that the Church's claim to be an additional channel for the transmission and expansion of God's revelation (through which the disclosure recounted in scripture may be further understood) is untenable and they have acted accordingly. Today, however, and sadly, there are those who assert or consciously imply such a denial of the *Magisterium* and yet suppose that this is not a matter that renders them unsuitable to the holding of positions of authority and influence within the Church.

The fabric of the faith

At this point let it be quite clear that nothing in what I have said is either intended, or could reasonably be interpreted, as an attempt to drive anybody from Catholicism. I imagine that most reflective Catholics have some worries about the faith – either general ones concerning the reality at which it aims to be directed or more particular problems to do with the coherence of individual doctrines.[6] Moreover, such worries may not be due simply to ignorance or perplexity as to what a certain proposition means or as to how it could be true. It may be that what one does understand appears to contradict it. Even so there is as yet no reason to abandon the faith since it is no part of Catholicism to claim that every doctrine is demonstrable by sound deductive arguments, or even that it is perfectly intelligible. There are mysteries which resist every effort to make them plain. Accepting this, however, if one does arrive at the settled view that some essential belief or practice is simply false or invalid, it follows of necessity that one has ceased to be a Roman Catholic – no matter how close the resultant body of doctrines is to the original. And one has certainly forsaken any right to teach or preach in the name of this faith.

All of this should be clear and I hope it will be so to anyone who reflects on the considerations involved. Indeed, none of it would need pointing out were it not for the fact that there has been a good deal of clouding of the issues. So much so that at times it seems as if almost all matters of faith and morals are open questions to be resolved by theologians in whatever ways they find acceptable.[7] Perhaps the practice of analysis may prove effective in helping to disperse some of this mist, thereby revealing the existence of logical limits to doctrinal development. Unquestionably there is both room and need for theological investigation, but equally there is a clear sense in which the impossibility of non-Catholic Catholicism must make for theological conservatism.

This conclusion runs counter to tendencies in much progressive doctrinal thought which seek to reconstruct central ontological claims including the doctrines of the *Trinity*, the *Incarnation*, *Resurrection* and *Ascension*, the *Communion of Saints* and the *Real Presence* as expressions of moral, socio-political and spiritual commitment. It also runs counter to the currently fashionable trend to substitute for the largely deontological traditional Catholic moral theology various versions of (eudaimonistic) consequentialism. The motivation for these reformative tendencies has several springs, among which is an intelligible, though by no means undisputably virtuous, desire to try to incorporate the claims of contemporary philosophical, ethical, political and sociological theories so as to produce 'informed and relevant' theology.[8] In the light of the foregoing conclusion, however, two thoughts should now suggest themselves as corrections to overindulgence in this practice. First, the resources of scripture and the Church provide 'information' that cannot be outweighed without being rejected, and in respect of essentials this means abandoning the Catholic faith. Second, the Church's doctrinal teaching is guaranteed eternal 'relevance' by its source – the Word of God – and is not prey to changes of circumstance.

In addition, assuming if not complete doctrinal holism then at least credal 'molecularism', that is, the idea that no article of faith stands in isolation from others, it follows that reformation in respect of one produces distortions through-out the entire system of doctrine. Indeed, as history testifies, this may lead to the complete rejection of Christianity. One begins with some part of the whole and reinterprets it so as to render it generally acceptable by current standards of intelligibility. But then it emerges that in consequence another part needs corresponding adjustment and so on. The theology of the Mass is not separable from that of Calvary or of the Resurrection, and the latter connects with general eschatology and with the understanding of the Kingdom of God. Give up a single article and one ceases to be a Catholic, continue the process and one may end up no longer even a Christian.

There are those who having begun by reforming marginal beliefs and practices and ridding themselves of non-essential historical accretions are now at a point at which their Catholic faith is in danger if not already lost. This is a position at which any thinking person might one day arrive and no service is done either to the Church or to the individuals concerned by issuing premature charges of heresy. Understanding and support are what is required not con-demnation.[9] It must be equally plain, though, that it is quite wrong for such 'non-Catholic Catholics' to continue to preach and teach in the name of a faith to which they no longer subscribe. One has the right to state one's differences and to argue for them. And even, I think, to do so in Catholic *fora*. But one also has intellectual and religious obligations not to mislead others into thinking that a rejection of an essential doctrine is merely a sound reinterpretation of it. The warnings against such an offence have the authority of Christ Himself and will not be made more solemn or more serious by human repetition.[10]

Confusing attitudes

A good deal more might be written on these issues and I have no doubt that the pattern of future events will lead to further discussion and debate.[11] Rather than pursue them here, however, I want next to return to the theme introduced earlier, namely, the confusion of other theories (be they moral, political, philosophical or whatever else) with Catholic faith and practice.

There are those, of whom I am certainly not one, who believe that Christianity and politics have no possible connection. On the contrary, however, one's religious views of the nature of the world, of its origins and of the place of man within it do imply moral and other claims. An important part of the political realm is morality at a social level and I cannot imagine any Christian, let alone any Catholic, arguing that his faith has no moral implications.[12]

This said, there is a strong tendency for both traditionalists and progressives to import political viewpoints into areas in which they are inappropriate and where they can only provide distorted perceptions. One such impression is the thought of the Kingdom of God as a state of affairs in which men and women, having been brought to a new level of self-awareness by the gospel of liberation, will have achieved fulfilment by manipulating the environment through co-operative labour and under a basically collectivist organization of society.

On the other side, among some who claim to uphold traditional Catholic teachings, there is a willingness to tolerate grave social injustice and even tyranny in the belief that the fallen human is so disposed to evil that any system of laws and institutions that serves to keep a person in check, particularly a person who claims to be Christian, is better than the chaos which results from the free exercise of an innately perverse will. To this is sometimes added the claim that people cannot ever be made happy by any development of their empirical natures. Only when their spirits are freed from physical imprisonment and are given 'sight' of the divine is there the possibility of genuine satisfaction. In short, the world is a vale of tears to be endured and not attended to. Any programme aimed at intellectual enlightenment and material improvement is thus suspect. For it may proceed from a vain belief in the perfectibility of the human by natural means and lead to disaster, prompted and encouraged by the forces of darkness.

In his critical reflections on Dr Edward Norman's 1978 Reith Lectures, Professor Michael Dummett confronts these and other presumptions which are often deployed in reconciling Christian theology with non-opposition to illiberal and anti-egalitarian political systems.[13] Dummett's response is principally concerned with replying to a more moderate version of the view that Christians ought to refrain from pursuing political and social ideals, but his arguments are for the most part quite general and establish the inconsistencies implicit within such a position. It is not possible to detail those arguments here but I would strongly recommend a reading of Dummett's short study to anyone disposed to follow this line. What he reminds us of is that for the Christian there is an obligation to be alert and active in the service of God and of our fellows, and that this requirement draws us into the social realm and determines certain attitudes with respect to behaviour there. To engage in tyranny, persecution, aggression and exploitation, or to fail to condemn these when they occur, is incompatible with sincere discipleship of Christ.

Returning now to the theological expression of the opposition between traditionalist and progressive, it appears that just as there is a move on either side to emphasize one aspect of Christ's dual nature over and against the other, so each repeats his insistence on the supremacy of the spiritual over the physical, and *vice versa*, in respect of the human. On the one hand the advocate of humanist-inspired Catholic renewal makes Christ almost wholly human and the human being almost wholly matter; on the other, the Neoplatonist opponent stresses the transcendence of Christ and accordingly takes us to be essentially spiritual beings in exile from our natural environment.

It is not, I think, fanciful to suggest that there are echoes in this dispute of Arian, Pelagian and Manichean doctrines. Certainly both extremes would do well to reflect on Aquinas's account of the human as exhibiting both spiritual and physical characteristics essentially. Strict dualism and materialism are both at odds with the dominant scriptural tradition concerning human nature and run counter to much philosophical argument. One might avoid the pathways that lead to those positions by considering the implications of the historical teaching that Christ combined two natures in one Person, and that human beings are likewise unities exhibiting different aspects. These suggest that human fulfilment can only be achieved by the perfection of this unified nature and that this cause will not be furthered by neglecting either our physical or our spiritual aspects.[14]

These matters are proper topics for research and argument, subject to the qualifications drawn when considering the logical limits of doctrinal development. What cannot be disputed, however, is that while the truths of Catholicism imply certain moral claims and prescribe social ideals, the former are logically prior and cannot be reduced to the latter. Further, though belief in the Word of God as expressed through scripture and Church commits one to various standards, for example, of justice, benevolence, co-operation and so forth, it does not determine the political system through which these should be pursued. It does, though, exclude some as unacceptable. For example, employing evil means to a good end is forbidden.[15] There is, however, no *a priori* proof for the claim that state socialism is either better or worse suited to the realization of these ideals than is libertarianism. Consequently arguments directed at this issue must be distinguished from those concerning the content of the faith. Adam Smith, Burke and Marx all have something to teach us about the conditions required for human flourishing, but their insights are subsequent to, and independent of, the truths of the Catholic faith.

Failure to be clear about this point often underlies the hostility of traditionalists and progressives towards one another. It is indisputable that Catholics should be concerned with the oppressed and disadvantaged at home and abroad.

To deny this is to reject the faith no less than if one were to say there is no resurrection. Yet there is perhaps a more charitable explanation of the unsympathetic response of some traditionalists to the appeals by others for the Church to give assistance to those in need and for it to oppose oppressive governments. For in recent years there has been a steady proliferation of 'reformative theology' whose advocates sometimes appear more concerned with the secular world and with systems of thought born out of it than with the doctrinal teachings of the Church. It is not altogether surprising, therefore, that challenges to traditionalists' motives and concerns draw sharp responses, particularly when they are delivered in forms associated with a main theme of much progressive theology, that is, the insistence upon the priority of political action. One might suppose, then, that at least some of these unsympathetic reactions to the demand for social involvement are not directed against the literal content of this demand but against what is believed to lie behind it.

Be this as it may, such responses are inappropriate and unworthy. And if there is an explanation of them involving concern about the theology commonly connected with the politics of liberation there is also reason to believe that some traditionalists have their attitudes to the faith shaped by attachment to right-wing politics. Correspondingly, it is this fact that is sometimes the target of progressives' criticism. Such unhappy exchanges might be avoided if there were not widespread confusion of religious and political conservatism. Whatever may be the assessment of the latter in relation to the moral and social ideals implied by Catholicism I have suggested that conservatism with respect to doctrine is the only coherent theological attitude.

Conclusion

Finally, then, let me return briefly to the problem introduced at the outset in explanation of my title. I have argued above that for a Roman Catholic there can be no departure from doctrinal orthodoxy, that logic implies conservatism. Put another way, dogmatic belief implies belief in the immutability of dogma. But the implication of conservatism does not extend to political ideology or social and economic theory and thus the question arises of what stance to take towards those areas of life in which the task is to secure the social good. Some assert that a certain kind of political conservatism in the *Civitas Terrena* is simply a corollary of allegiance to the *Civitas Dei*. What supports this claim, however, is an appeal to a more or less 'Constantinian' conception of Christianity – the view which locates all true value and meaning outside of the natural order and so assigns responsibility for the conduct of wordly affairs to wordly philosophies, thereby arriving at the conclusion that in so far as religion has any influence to exert in the political realm it should side with existing structures and policies.

This is an untenable view and is open to objection on two counts. First, the *vale of tears* picture of the world is fundamentally at odds with historical

Judaeo-Christian teaching and derives from the kind of neo-Manichean views I mentioned previously. We are part of a created universe that is in itself intrinsically good and though men are often inclined to choose evil this perversity should not be identified with their physical embodiment. Correspondingly, the Christian has no right to set himself against the pursuit of material and social well-being. But equally, the concern with poverty, disease, oppression and other forms of human suffering must be informed by a vision of the proper state of humankind. Second, to the extent that one believes that the ways of the world are inevitably flawed this conviction provides reason for importing a higher conception of value in order to criticize and reform political structures and to shape social practice to the ideal prescribed by God through the prophets and revealed in Christ.[16]

These two lines of thought now come together to indicate the conclusion signposted by my title. In reply to the question: How may one remedy the ills apparent in the world?, the answer for the Roman Catholic is that one must combine a true understanding of the nature of the disease such as can only be provided by reference to the Word of God as this is embodied in scripture and Catholic doctrine, with a commitment to put that teaching into practice. To seek to do so will inevitably bring one into opposition to existing economic and social policies to the extent that these are grounded in a narrow humanism quite at odds with Christ's command 'to love one another as I have loved you'. That is to say, one must combine theological orthodoxy with a critical social outlook such as, for example, is to be found in the writings of Chesterton.[17]

Notes

1 *What's Wrong with the World* (London: Cassell, 1910), p. 3.
2 The references to essentialism and to scholasticism may prompt in some readers the response that the theoretical presuppositions of my argument are anachronistic and that the inadequacy of traditionalist theology to the contemporary context derives in part from its attachment to this outmoded and largely discredited philosophical system. Certainly it has been said that Catholic theology must accommodate itself to the central ideas of post-Enlightenment Continental philosophy. The grounds for the necessity of this accommodation are rarely explored and my impression is that the main reasons motivating such claims are ones of expediency – in particular the fear that otherwise theology will not be thought intellectually respectable. But this attitude, as well as being (ironically) intellectually corrupt, also misconceives the relationship between doctrinal theology and philosophy and neglects their disparate foundations and attachments: revelation and unaided reason, respectively. As regards the supposed inadequacy of scholasticism, the claimed superiority of modern Continental thought and the wish to harmonize theology with prevailing philosophical ideas, it is perhaps worth observing what many commentators appear quite remarkably not to have noticed, namely, that in contemporary English-speaking secular philosophy, the dominant themes and methods closely resemble those central to scholasticism, e.g., *essentialism* in metaphysics, *realism* in epistemology, *non-dualist immaterialism* in the philosophy of mind and *non-consequentialism* in ethics. An

exception to the general neglect of this congruence is Fergus Kerr, 'The Need for Philosophy in Theology Today', *New Blackfriars* 66 (1984), pp. 248–60.

3 For a clear discussion of the Catholic idea of the immutability of dogma, see A. Kenny, 'The Development of Ecclesiastical Doctrine', in *Reason and Religion* (Oxford: Blackwell, 1987).

4 This raises the possibility that one may unwittingly come to hold a set of beliefs incompatible with the true content of Catholicism. Given the limitations of human understanding such a prospect cannot be excluded. Nonetheless there is a clear and important difference between the following: (i) the rejection of a recognizably essential doctrine *D*; and (ii) believing, in addition to *D*, a proposition that is incompatible with it, though one is unaware of this inconsistency.

5 Let me say in passing that I am well aware that discussing belief in these terms may strike some readers as inappropriate. Certainly the technique is limited. Faith is not a form of natural science but is a response to the Word of God. This said, it should be clear that my purpose in employing these means is likewise limited.

6 A useful pastoral discussion addressed to those who have difficulties with their faith, but are sincere in their pursuit of truth, is contained in R. Butterworth, 'Is the Faith Worth Keeping?' *The Month* 240 (1979), pp. 400–6.

7 I am not proposing the contrary claim: that *all* matters of faith and morals are closed questions. There are areas of legitimate dispute.

8 For a recent attempt of this sort see Fergus Kerr, *Theology After Wittgenstein* (Oxford: Blackwell, 1986). The policy is at risk in so far as one may 'reinterpret' a doctrine out of existence. This is not the place to discuss it but it seems that Kerr's espousal of Wittgensteinean views about persons as natural objects threatens the intelligibility of such notions as the communion of saints and prayer to and for the dead. For further commentary on Kerr's useful book see my review of it in *The Philosophical Quarterly* 38 (1988).

9 See Butterworth, 'Is the Faith Worth Keeping?', p. 401.

10 Matthew 12.36–7; 18.6–7; Galatians 1.7–9.

11 Since first writing this essay there has developed a lively debate among some Catholic theologians, and other writers in Britain, on issues closely related to those discussed here. This debate was initiated by Michael Dummett in an essay titled: 'A Remarkable Consensus' published in *New Blackfriars* 69 (1987). There Dummett argues that a condition of membership of the Catholic Church is acceptance of what he titles the 'principle of the paramountcy of unity': 'the proposition that it is enjoined on Catholics, whatever the provocation, never to take any step to disrupt the unity of the Church' (p. 424). The debate continued in subsequent issues of *New Blackfriars* during 1987 and 1988 and was contributed to by Brian Davies, E. Duffy, J. Fitzpatrick, P. Gifford, Nicholas Lash and Timothy Radcliffe.

12 For further discussion of this issue see my 'Christianity and Politics: Another View', *Scottish Journal of Theology* 40 (1986), pp. 259–86.

13 *Catholicism and the World Order* (London: Catholic Institute for International Relations, 1979).

14 For some discussion of these issues in connection with recent attempts to support dualism as giving the true account of human nature, see my 'A Glimpse of Eternity: Near Death Experiences and the Hope of Future Life', *The Modern Churchman* 30 (1988), pp. 20–8. Contrary efforts to give a wholly naturalistic account of the human capacity for thought are subjected to extensive criticism in my 'Psychoanalysis, Cognitive Psychology and Self-Consciousness', in *Mind, Psychoanalysis and Science*, ed. P. Clark and C. Wright (Oxford: Blackwell, 1988), and in 'Naturalism and the Problem of Intentionality', *Inquiry* 32 (1989), pp. 305–22. The task of giving some positive account of human nature as that of rational animals is begun in 'Folk

Psychology and the Explanation of Human Behaviour', *Proceedings of the Aristotelian Society*, Supplementary Volume 62 (1988).

15   Romans 3.5–21.

16   There are, however, difficulties in seeking to combine religious values with political deliberation and practice. For some discussion of these see my 'Christianity and Politics: Another View'.

17   Among the multitude of Chesterton's writings the following are most relevant to the issue of religious orthodoxy and social criticism: *Orthodoxy* (London: Bodley Head, 1908); *What's Wrong with the World* (London: Cassell, 1910); *The Everlasting Man* (London: Hodder & Stoughton, 1925); *The Thing* (London: Sheed & Ward, 1929); and *St Thomas Aquinas* (London: Hodder & Stoughton, 1933).

Chapter 5

Infallibility, authority and faith

In recent years there has been a growth of reflective interest among Christians of all denominations in the role of the Papacy. This is due in part to liberalization within the institutions of Catholic theology which has encouraged members of the Church of Rome to examine critically the standard justifications of doctrine; and also to the recognition by other Christians of the need for a universal human leader of the faith, whose role transcends those of chairman, director or chief spokesman of a single denomination, or even of an association of these – such as is the President of the World Council of Churches. Particularly in an era in which the Christian religion has to compete with powerful rival religious and secular ideologies, it is widely held that the gospel message should be given authoritative expression through the mouth of one chosen (or at least recognized) by the whole Christian community to be its leader.

This conclusion is argued for in the famous *Final Report* of the Anglican–Roman Catholic International Commission (ARCIC) which goes so far as to associate it with the Papacy, and thereby to commend the primacy of the Roman see:

> According to Christian doctrine the unity in truth of the Christian community demands visible expression. We agree that such visible expression is the will of God and that the maintenance of visible unity at the universal level includes the *episcope* of a universal primate. This is a doctrinal statement.... Though it is possible to conceive a universal primacy located elsewhere than in the city of Rome, the original witness of Peter and Paul and the continuing exercise of a universal *episcope* by the see of Rome present a unique presumption in its favour.[1]

The achievement of such agreement between Anglican and Roman Catholic theologians in striking, even if, as the Sacred Congregation of the Doctrine of the Faith pointed out, the account given by ARCIC of the status of the chair of Peter falls short of that traditionally maintained in Catholic belief. At the same time, however, it is clear that not all Christians are presently prepared to move this far towards the Roman position, or even to agree to the doctrinal claim about the legitimacy of a universal primacy. Even the best efforts of the enthusiastic ecumenists of ARCIC were unable to resolve the issue of teaching authority, and in particular that attaching to a primate of the Christian community.[2]

The major stumbling-block is, of course, the idea of an *extraordinary magisterium* as maintained by Rome in the dogma of Papal Infallibility. This and the teaching on artificial contraception have for some years been the aspects of Roman Catholicism most frequently challenged by friends and opponents both within and outwith the Church. This gives good reason to devote attention to the claim to infallibility in order to see what place it has in the fabric of Catholic belief, considering whether it is essential to it, or if, given the growing though qualified sympathy towards the idea of a universal leader, this 'offending' thread might be removed so as to make the pattern with the figure of the Bishop of Rome woven prominent within it more generally acceptable.

In what follows, I begin with some historical observations and relate the question of papal infallibility to that of religious authority in general, indicating several reasons why this relationship is important. I then explore the concept of infallibility from a philosophical perspective considering certain challenges to its coherence.

The historical background

On Monday 18 July 1870, in the final public session of the First Vatican Council, four months after it had been presented with a draft document concerning the episcopal authority and infallibility of the Pope, a bishop of the Church received from the hand of Pius IX a final decree which he then read to the assembled Fathers:

> We teach and define as a divinely revealed dogma, that when the Roman pontiff speaks *ex cathedra* – that is, when he, using his office as pastor and teacher of all Christians, in virtue of his apostolic office, defines a doctrine on faith and morals to be held by the whole Church – he, by the Divine assistance promised to him in the blessed Peter, possesses the infallibility with which the Divine Redeemer was pleased to invest his Church in the definition of doctrine on faith and morals, and that therefore, such definitions of the Roman Pontiff are irreformable in their own nature and not because of the consent of the Church.[3]

Almost immediately afterwards the Council was dissolved as war broke out between France and Prussia. For those who had pressed hard to have the dogma defined, and who had seen the sole function of the gathering as the affirmation of the supremacy of the Papacy in ecclesiastical, credal and moral affairs, the Council had been a triumphant success. For others, however, it was a cause of disappointment. On behalf of the English, Lord Acton had cautioned against a definition, warning that it would give weight to the claims of those who viewed Rome as a bastion of illiberal, anti-democratic, procrustean and obscurantist Christianity.[4] Such claims appeared to derive support from Pius IX himself, for in an encyclical published six years earlier (*Quanta Cura*, in the appended *Syllabus of Errors*) he had condemned the proposal that 'the Roman Pontiff can, and should, reconcile and harmonize himself with progress, with liberalism, and with recent civilization'.

In Germany and Austria the reception was similarly cool. Professor Döllinger, a friend of Acton and leader of liberal Catholic opinion, remarked that 'as a Christian, as a theologian, as a historian and as a citizen, I cannot accept this doctrine', and so saying took his leave of the Church. Franz Brentano (now remembered chiefly as a philosopher and precursor of phenomenology but at the time a priest and university lecturer) had written a paper outlining the case against infallibility at the request of Bishop Ketteler of Mainz, and he received the news of the Council's decision as evidence of an irrational tendency within Catholicism which he could no longer accept.

Even moderate Church opinion within Germany was troubled by the definition, fearing that it would be read as signalling the beginning of a new form of papal tyranny in which the Pope would have absolute personal power to dictate all matters of Church organization and religious teaching, and thus could ignore the previously valued general consensus of Church opinion as expressed in the agreed views of the whole episcopate. To some extent their concern was justified since the received interpretation was that the Pope was now the one and only responsible authority. Indeed, by 1875 the German bishops found it necessary to issue a statement seeking to locate the special status of papal pronouncements within the context of the tradition of the magisterial infallibility of the whole Church – a statement the correctness of which was recognized by Pius IX who wrote in reply agreeing with its essential thesis that the Pope's authority is ultimately that of the divinely commissioned Apostolic Church.

In England the Protestant reaction was as predicted by Acton: horror among High Churchmen who had hoped for conciliatory gestures with a view to furthering the cause of reunion; and among the Low Church Evangelicals, and those outside the Church of England who expected the worst from Rome, a sense of satisfaction at having their prejudices confirmed. For the reaction of Catholic intellectuals other than those who followed Döllinger (out of the Church) and Brentano (out of Christianity), it is useful to look to Newman.

Since Salmon's celebrated attack upon the dogma,[5] many commentators have followed him in quoting from the writings of Newman as evidence of the opposition to the definition among educated Catholic opinion. Certainly Newman expresses deep concern in this connection, and in his letter (written in 1870) to Bishop Ullathorne at the Council, he attacks the definitionist party and voices his hope that their cause will fail:

What have we done to be treated as the Faithful have never been treated before?....Why should an aggressive faction be allowed to make the hearts of the just to mourn, whom the Lord hath not made sorrowful?....With these thoughts before me, I am continually asking myself whether I ought not to make my feelings public; but all I do is to pray those great early Doctors of the Church, whose intercession would decide the matters, – Augustine and the rest, – to avert so great a calamity. If it is God's Will that the Pope's Infallibility should be defined, then it is His Blessed Will to throw back 'the times and the moments' of the triumph He has destined for His Kingdom; and I shall feel I have but to bow my head to His Adorable Inscrutable Providence.[6]

As the final sentence implies, however, Newman's concern is not directed towards the *content* of the claim to an extraordinary teaching authority, but at the manner of those (ultramontane extremists) then urging a wide-ranging definition, and at the issue of whether the moment was appropriate for a declaration. In the event, the 'aggressive faction' failed to obtain a definition of unrestricted scope which, as Newman perceived, would have been scandalous, lacking any scriptural or historical foundation and being at odds with the idea of Christianity as a revealed religion. Concerning the text of the actual declaration he was happy enough, writing: 'I saw the new definition yesterday, and am pleased at its moderation....The terms are vague and comprehensive, and, personally, I have no difficulty in admitting it.'[7]

Since becoming a Roman Catholic, Newman had accepted papal infallibility but unlike many other converts of the period he was not an enthusiast for its definition. He held it 'not as a dogma, but as a theological opinion; that is, not as a certainty, but as a probability'.[8] None the less, while resisting the suggestion that it was *de fide*, he defended the idea of infallibility, and in the *Apologia* offers an argument in its favour deriving from belief in the Incarnation:

Supposing then it to be the Will of the Creator to interfere in human affairs, and to make provisions for retaining in the world a knowledge of Himself, so definite and distinct as to be proof against the energy of human scepticism, in such a case – I am far from saying that there was no other way – but there is nothing to surprise the mind if He should think fit to introduce a power into the world, invested with the prerogative of infallibility in religious matters. Such a provision would be a direct, immediate, active, and prompt means of withstanding the difficulty; it would be an instrument, suited to the need; and, when I find that this is the very claim of the Catholic Church, not only do I feel no difficulty in admitting the idea, but there is a fitness in it, which recommends it to my mind.[9]

Thus the position within Catholicism in the period leading up to and following Vatican I involved a mix of attitudes: *conservative* support for the dogma, motivated by a belief in the need for a powerful, supreme authority; *radical* dissent based on the same analysis of what papal infallibility means, and on commitment to liberal, consensus theology; and finally, *moderate* acceptance of it, but with concern about the scope of the definition and about its reception by non-Catholics. Outside the Roman Church the response was universally critical.

The current situation

A century or so later the state of things is more or less the same. Following a period of settlement and then general subscription to the dogma, the divisions within Catholicism are now somewhat greater; and notwithstanding the sympathy towards the idea of a universal primacy mentioned earlier, other Christians remain opposed to papal infallibility.

It is important for several reasons to keep in mind the fact that the issue is a (very) special case of religious authority. First, this explains why there has been so much controversy about the very idea of this extraordinary magisterium during the last one hundred and fifty years, i.e. during the period in which a belief in *individualism* has come to be held, almost universally, as the essential foundation of any acceptable moral, political, legal and social philosophy. Given enthusiastic assent to the proposition that each person is an autonomous agent whose beliefs, life-policies and decisions must be respected and who is, in consequence, alone responsible for his or her freely chosen actions; and given also a practical commitment to the realization of these moral ideas in the organization of society through the establishment of political democracy, acceptance of a charter of human rights, and the administration by a free and independent judiciary of a law before which all are equal, it is not at all surprising that there is both suspicion of, and a tendency to reject, any claim to final authority made on behalf of one person in respect of the essential religious beliefs of all mankind. In short, the dogma is judged to be offensive to the autonomy of the individual, whether standing alone, or as member of a community.

A second reason to retain sight of the real nature of the issue is that in many recent discussions of infallibility it seems that what is contested is not the theological propriety of this idea but its very coherence. There is a genuine question, to which I shall return, as to whether it makes any sense to suppose that someone's pronouncements could be infallible, and unless a positive answer is available all other considerations become merely academic. Unless it is possible for the Pope to be infallible it is idle to explore what part such authority has to play in the life of the Christian Church. Yet establishing its mere possibility is not enough. There is need to see how it connects with the ordinary teaching role accorded to other members of the Christian body, and this is a question about the priority and scope of different sources of authority.

Third, to the extent that someone finds infallibility unacceptable because restrictive of theological inquiry, he or she ought to ask themselves whether their real objection is to all forms of Church authority in matters of Christian belief. Clearly, for some this is the case, but if so it then raises a further critical question, viz., can there be such a thing as *Christian theology* in the absence of a source of doctrinal authority? If the answer is 'no', there arises an obligation to give account of where that authority resides.

The coherence of infallibility

There are three main aspects to the philosophical problem presented by the dogma. One is *conceptual*, another *metaphysical* and the third *epistemological*. What might it mean to speak of someone as being 'infallible'? What is the nature of the state that constitutes the making of an infallible pronouncement? And what sort of justification might be available for the dogma? Clearly, there is an order of logical priority among these questions. The second, for example, implies that infallibility is possible, while the first does not; and it is precisely the latter that has been the issue in recent attacks on the dogma. Reviewing the course of the extensive debate that followed the publication of his controversial book on the subject,[10] Hans Küng writes as follows:

> Are there perhaps pronouncements, definitions, dogmas or propositions which are not only true (this is not disputed), but also infallibly true, since certain office-bearers are unable, because of the special help they receive from the Holy Spirit, to err in a given situation. It was precisely to this that the question mark in the title of my book *Infallible?* pointed. Yet there is general agreement that, in the whole of the debate so far...not one theologian has been able to produce any proof of the *possibility* [my emphasis] that the Holy Spirit guarantees the infallibility of certain pronouncements.[11]

The interest of this quotation is twofold. First, it makes clear that Küng's own central challenge is to the very *possibility* of infallibility – a challenge which takes the form of arguing that the notion is senseless. Second, it indicates that this attack is itself confused in that it takes the bearers of the contested property of infallibility to be *statements*, or perhaps more precisely their propositional contents, when, as the logic of the concept demands and the words of the 1870 definition imply, the candidates for having this property are actions of the Pontiff (and, on other occasions, Church Councils), i.e. certain *declarations*.

The importance of the latter point is that while it may be meaningless to speak of a sentence as being infallible, it is not nonsense – though it may be false – to claim that a particular person or other authority is incapable of error, and therefore that what they say must be true. However, the underlying Küngian objection can be reformulated to take account of this correction; the point being that he is questioning the coherence of the claim that what someone says *must be true*. Some propositions, we suppose, are necessarily true, either because they express conceptual truths, e.g. 'No bachelor is married', or else truths of a kind which, though not conceptual, could not be otherwise, e.g. statements of identity, such as 'Pope John Paul II is Karol Wojytla'.[12] If someone makes a statement that is in one or other of these senses necessarily true, then it follows *ex hypothesi* that what he or she says *must* be true. It simply is not possible that their utterance be false.

The subject matter of actual and potential papal or conciliar definitions, i.e. matters of faith and morals, is rarely, if ever, of this sort. If the dogma of Infallibility holds that in certain circumstances the relevant authorities cannot err, it is not because they then utter only necessary truths, but rather because their utterances are guaranteed by divine power to be free from error. In short, infallibility is not a property of sentences but of persons' pronouncements.

There are, then, at least two distinct ways in which it might be held that what a person says *must* be true: (i) if what they utter is, in itself, a necessary truth, conceptual or otherwise; and (ii) if, by whatever power, they themselves are incapable of error. In the latter case it is not required that the content of their infallible pronouncements be *necessarily* true. Küng, however, offers an argument against this general conclusion and *ipso facto* against (ii). The arguments rest on a philosophical thesis about the nature of language, viz., 'every proposition can be both true and false, depending on its claim, circumstances, meaning'.[13] If every proposition can be both true and false, then it is not the case that some proposition cannot be false, and therefore it is not the case that some proposition must be true; and if there is no proposition that must be true, then no statement from whatever source can be supposed free from error. Thus, since every proposition can be false none can be the subject of an infallible pronouncement; therefore, infallibility is an incoherent notion.

The idea that the truth value of a proposition is not something fixed, and, more radically, that as circumstances alter it *must* change with them, is widely favoured by recent opponents of the dogma who associate the claim to infallibility with a scholastic absolutist conception of knowledge. Thus, in the same issue of *Concilium* as contains Küng's article, Irving Fetscher offers the following suggestion in response to what he describes as: '[the] historically conditioned proneness to error [of human judgement]':

> The Church could try to take history more seriously – in the past Catholic thought has been dominated too much by Aristotelian Thomism. The Church might also learn to accept the fact that *although pronouncements may have been free from error when they were made they cannot be absolutely valid for all time* [my emphasis].[14]

This passage offers a concise statement of themes prominent in post-Vatican II Catholic theology: dissatisfaction with the philosophical tradition in terms of which doctrine has been developed, usually coupled with rejection of the contemporary equivalent of the scholastic method, viz., conceptual analysis, and a declared preference for a Marxist-cum-existentialist-cum-phenomenologist synthesis; and subscription to the relativist principle that the truth of a proposition is always restricted by the time, place and source of its utterance.

Concerning the matter of philosophical methodology, it has been said against the old and new traditions of logical analysis that 'clarity is not enough'. This is true, but clarity is a necessary condition for understanding. Without it, what issues is confusion – as is evident in the present case. It is simply incoherent to suppose that what was true could now be false and thereby to conclude that nothing can be 'absolutely valid for all time'. The source of this error is a failure to make two related distinctions: first, that between a *propositional content* (what is said in the making of a statement) and a *propositional bearer* (the linguistic entity used to embody that content, e.g. a sentence of English); second, that between sentences (i.e. *bearers*) the truth value of whose contents are *dependent* upon the time and place of utterance, and sentences which are not thus *context-dependent*.

Consider the sentence 'The present Pope is John Paul II.' At the time of writing, what it says is true, but there is reason to suppose that at a future date someone who uttered another instance (*token*) of this sentence (*type*) would be saying the false, and certainly if someone gave voice to it a century ago what they said was then not true. Many sentences are such that even if their meaning remains constant one cannot determine whether or not the propositions they express are true or false without knowing when, where and by whom they were uttered. 'Today is Tuesday', 'It is raining', 'I am tired', are simple and obvious examples of this. Others, however, are not context-dependent for their truth. 'A square is a four-sided figure', 'A whole is not less than any of its parts', 'Nursing mothers are older than their children', 'God is the creator of all things visible and invisible', 'Lightning is a type of electrical discharge', are all instances of sentence types of which (provided there is no change in meaning) every token states the same propositional content and the same truth value.

Sometimes, however, it happens that a word changes its meaning, and then it may be that a sentence of the latter type which previously expressed a true proposition subsequently expressed a false one. If we came to use the word 'square' to mean what we presently mean by 'round' it would then be false to say that a square is a four-sided figure. In principle, we could overcome problems facing the determination of the truth or falsity of a sentence by regimenting language; for example, by adding spatio-temporal references. That we adopt this practice only very rarely is due to its inconvenience and to the fact that it is largely unnecessary since something close to it is implicit in actual usage. In all of this, however, it is important to keep sight of the fact that declarative utterances have determinate truth conditions.[15] While words may be used in a variety of ways, on a variety of occasions, with the same or different meanings, to express a range of propositional contents, it remains the case, *pace* Küng and Fetscher, that what is said in the making of a pronouncement (the *content*) is timelessly true or false, and this is so whether or not the sentence used to embody the proposition (the *bearer*) is context-dependent or ambiguous.

Our language and our knowledge develop; hence meanings and our beliefs about the truth of sentences alter accordingly, but truth itself is immutable, and theological statements are neither privileged nor deprived in this respect. The same sentence of English may be *used* to express different propositions whose truth values may also vary but it is not the case that 'every proposition can be both true and false depending on its aim, circumstances, meaning', or that 'pronouncements [which] may have been free from error when they were made...cannot be absolutely valid for all time'. The patent falsity of this latter claim is made more obvious by substituting 'true' for 'free from error', and again for 'valid'. Both opponents of the dogma offer arguments which trade on ambiguities in the terms used to describe declarations. 'Proposition' and 'pronouncement' are employed to refer to *what* is said in an utterance *and* to the *sentence used* to say it. The *propositional content* of a statement, which is what we are interested in, is always either true or false and cannot be both. Thus, nothing in the 'historical relativism' challenge presented by Küng and Fetscher casts doubt on the suggestion that in some cases *what someone says must be true.*

As was seen above, the previous italicized claim might be true for different reasons: either because *what* the speaker says, the proposition he expresses, is itself necessarily true; or else because the fact of *his* saying it somehow guarantees its truth. It will be generally agreed that the contested status of a given range of papal pronouncements does not depend upon whether or not they are necessary truths. For example, it could have been the case that at the end of Mary's life there was no Assumption. Here I am not contesting the dogma, only suggesting that it concerns a *contingent* matter. By contrast, it may be supposed that the statement that there are three divine Persons in one God may be metaphysically necessary.[16] Having rejected as confused the objection that no judgements can be infallible because no proposition is eternally true, I want next to consider if there is any other reason for thinking that the very idea of an infallible declaration is incoherent, and therefore that there is not even 'the possibility that the Holy Spirit guarantees the infallibility of certain pronouncements'.

Infallibility and knowledge

Two interesting arguments, apparently to this effect, need to be examined, though to my knowledge neither has been discussed in the theological literature challenging or defending the idea of infallibility within the Church. The first derives from Wittgenstein and connects the concept of judgement with the possibility of error, concluding that where it is impossible to be mistaken, judgement is absent and consequently claims to *knowledge* are out of place. In an important statement of these thoughts Wittgenstein writes the following:

> The question is what kind of proposition is 'I know I can't be mistaken about that' or again, 'I can't be mistaken about that'?
> This 'I know' seems to prescind from all grounds: I simply know it. But if there can be any question at all of being mistaken here, then it must be possible to test whether I know it.[17]

The final sentence links the idea of genuinely knowing something with having grounds or reasons for believing it, i.e. with the existence of considerations that could be produced in response to an expression of doubt that what one professes to know is in fact the case. But the claim to absolute certainty cited in the previous paragraph is meant, by its imagined author, to exclude even the possibility of doubt and hence to reject the request for justification. To this, Wittgenstein responds that *knowledge*, properly speaking, is not a matter of conviction, a kind of intense or vivid psychological state which one then reports by announcing 'I know it'. Rather it is an achievement behind which stand various supports, *reasons*, to which it is appropriate to refer when one's claim to knowledge is contested, and such claims are *essentially* contestable. On one reading of this argument, therefore, it may appear that the notion of an infallible pronouncement (an assertion) belonging to a class of statements *guaranteed* to be immune from error is simply contradictory.

This is clearly a more formidable objection than that considered above, for it derives from a profound analysis of the logic of epistemological concepts in which Wittgenstein presents a sustained attack upon long and widely held views. None the less, I believe that *a* conception of infallibility escapes this onslaught; one which there are independent reasons to favour as appropriate in any plausible account of an extraordinary magisterium.

The background to Wittgenstein's discussion in *On Certainty* is formed by a tradition of Cartesian scepticism and by G.E. Moore's attempt to refute this radical doubt by means of appeal to 'common-sense' propositions. Descartes considered which of his beliefs could not be doubted, assuming that if any were indubitable this would imply that one could not be wrong about them. Since sense-perception had proved fallible in the past, and one might presently be dreaming or suffering a series of delusions inflicted by a malign demon, beliefs in the existence of an external world (including one's own body) are not beyond doubt.[18] All that one can be certain of is that one is thinking and thereby knows the content and character of one's thoughts; and that one understands the meaning of the terms in which the sceptical doubts are expressed.

The challenge then is to show how certainty can be extended to embrace propositions concerning contingent matters of fact. Moore's well-known response consists in citing examples of ordinary basic beliefs, such as 'that mantelpiece is at present nearer to my body than that bookcase',[19] about which he claims we can be certain. Then, since its truth entails the metaphysical proposition: 'there is an external world', we can be certain of this also. For should anyone cast doubt on the first claim he must support it with evidence which will also be such as to entail the second proposition.

What Wittgenstein argues is that *both* the sceptic and the common-sense realist go wrong in thinking that the idea of achieving absolute certainty in the making of claims is a coherent one. He agrees with Moore that some propositions cannot be doubted but takes this to show precisely that the assertion of them is not an expression of *knowledge*. Equally he rejects the Cartesian assumption that if something is beyond doubt then one cannot be mistaken. First, the inference from indubitability to infallibility is simply invalid (*I cannot doubt that p*, does not entail: *I know that p*); but second, Wittgenstein maintains that where doubt is impossible and certainty obligatory, there we have not knowledge but the presupposed foundations of belief.

Why knowledge and doubt go together is because the former is not a self-intimating mental state. No matter how strongly convinced I am of the truth of a belief, it is possible that I am mistaken. Therefore in order to vindicate a claim to know that *p*, one needs to provide evidence for it. This in turn may perhaps be questioned and tested, and further grounds produced. However, this process must come to an end with a set of assumptions for which no further evidence can be provided. These propositions, therefore, are indubitable; not because we cannot be wrong about them but because of their place in the structure of thought. They are propositions which have 'a peculiar logical role in the system of our empirical propositions'. The certainty with which we affirm them is not (as Descartes and Moore in their different ways would wish) that arising from the recognition of truths that we can judge infallibly. 'This direct taking-hold corresponds to a sureness, not to a knowing.'[20] These foundational assumptions lie below the level of knowledge and constitute a 'world-picture' (*Weltbild*): 'the inherited background against which I distinguish between true and false'; 'Knowing only begins at a later level.' They can be both *true* and *believed*, but because of their basic character nothing can be evidenced from them, and accordingly they cannot enjoy the status of knowledge.

'A knowledge definite and distinct'

The claim for infallibility within the Church is presented as an answer to a sceptical problem (recall Newman's comment quoted earlier); a gift of certainty where otherwise there would be doubt. But Wittgenstein seems to show that the price of *certainty* is the loss of *knowledge*. Some propositions can be insulated from doubt by being accorded the logical status of foundations, but *ipso facto* they cannot then be presented as items of genuine knowledge. Some writers have not been slow to see implications for religious belief in this conclusion and have suggested that it provides a defence of religion against scepticism. If what lie at the bases of all conceptual schemes and bodies of belief are world-pictures providing ways of viewing life, which support but are not supported by further claims, then while a world-picture may be adopted or abandoned it cannot be refuted. Certainly, this may be a route along which some who favour a religious perspective on the world wish to pass but it is not one that is open to those committed to the non-fideistic and rationalist approach of traditional Catholic theology.

In the post-Enlightenment period, during which was developed much of the doctrinal theory that dominated the century and a half leading up to Vatican II, Roman Catholicism was deeply influenced by 'Cartesian scholasticism'. It is not surprising, therefore, to find some authors writing as if papal infallibility rested on the Roman Pontiff's having 'privileged access' to a body of truth and the capacity to know by introspection when one of his beliefs is immune from error. The relevant psychological mark being the formation of an intention that, other conditions being satisfied, the proclamation of this belief as a dogma be infallible. It is the prevalence of views of this sort that gives point to another of Küng's objections, viz., that the Pope is (absurdly) held to be infallible whenever he wants to be.[21]

The latter view is indeed worthless and makes it difficult to see how the Catholic claim that the Pope can fall into heresy, and thereby merit removal from office by a council of the Church, could be sustained (save perhaps in cases where he was so mentally incapacitated as to be unable to form the intention to pronounce infallibly – but how could this be determined, given the Cartesian conception of the mind as essentially private?). However, while something like the unacceptable interpretation may be suggested by the 1870 definition, its rejection is compatible with the affirmation of infallibility.

Descartes, Moore and certain theologians assume that immunity from error in judgement is indicated by indubitability. Hence they suppose that sceptical challenges are to be met by indicating propositions concerning which doubt is impossible: either because of their content, e.g. 'I am younger than the world', or because of their self-intimating character, e.g. 'I am experiencing a yellow after-image', or 'Mary, having completed the course of her earthly life, was assumed into heavenly glory' (as declared by Pius XII on 1 November 1950). And they think that the sense of certainty that accompanies the complete resistance to the pressure of doubt is a recognition of the infallibility of these beliefs. However, Wittgenstein both undermines the mentalistic model of infallibility (how could conviction guarantee the truth of a belief?) and demonstrates that the 'certainty' attaching to Moorean propositions is a function of their status as constituent assumptions of the language game. What he offers in their place *is* a rejection of scepticism but one implying the following conditional: *for any proposition, if it is genuinely indubitable then it is foundationally secure.* This presents the seeker after certainty with the choice of holding, with respect to some proposition p, either (i) that p is beyond rational doubt and thereby is not an item of knowledge, or (ii) belief that p is a proper candidate for the status of knowledge and thereby is not indubitable. In any event what must be abandoned is the idea that infallibility is entailed by the epistemic impossibility of supposing p to be false. Of course, if I *know* that p then I cannot be wrong in believing it, and if I know that I know it then I cannot doubt it; but from the fact that I cannot coherently doubt that p, knowledge and infallibility do not follow.

The defender of magisterial infallibility now has three options before him. First, he could make papal and conciliar pronouncements foundationally secure in the sense already introduced. This has the general disadvantage, mentioned above, of putting religious belief beyond reason and knowledge but also involves abandoning the historical claim that the security of dogmatic definitions is supported by evidence from a range of (a priori and a posteriori) sources. Second, he could try to adopt the less radical version of the Wittgensteinian position accepting that infallible declarations lack the status of evidentially justified true beliefs, and therefore do not constitute knowledge according to *this* traditional conception of its nature, but maintaining that nevertheless they are *true* and *believed*. Moreover, since his claim is that whenever the responsible authority defines matters of faith and doctrine it is immune from error, the relationship between the beliefs of this authority and their truth is not merely accidental. Rather, the position is that: if the authority A defines p, then p is true. This indicates a law-like relation best represented by a subjunctive conditional, i.e. if A were to define p (in the appropriate circumstances) then p would be true. Of course, the truth of p is independent of A's defining it in the sense that it is not A's definition that makes p true – rather, A defines p because it is true.

These considerations now suggest the following statement of the second position available to the 'infallibilist': A is an infallible authority within a given context if and only if, when A declares that p,

(1) p is true.
(2) If p had not been true A would not have declared it.

Since this account means to accommodate itself to the Wittgensteinian position no mention is made of grounds or evidence connecting A's belief that p with the truth of p. However, if, as many philosophers now favour, one takes it that *knowledge* itself requires no 'evidential-justification' link but merely the satisfaction of conditions similar to those given above, it may be claimed that infallible declarations do, after all, constitute the expression of knowledge and not merely of true belief.

The third and final response is the strongest, making no attempt to incorporate the Wittgensteinian account of cognitive security. This points out that infallibility in the sense of 'immunity from error' is not only not entailed by Cartesian introspective certainty, or Moorean common-sense indubitability, but equally does not entail them, i.e. it is logically independent of these features. Consequently, no argument meant to undermine appeal to them touches the claim that whatever someone says in certain circumstances must be true – so long as this assertion is not itself derived from claims about the introspective certainty or common-sense indubitability of the types of proposition he articulates.

The epistemological premise that indubitability is *sufficient for knowledge* is usually linked in the minds of those who maintain it with the thesis that it is *necessary for infallibility*. However, in claiming that there is a teaching authority in the Church that is free from error it need not be supposed that the contents

of the infallible declarations are indubitable in themselves. Indeed, it is precisely because dogmas do not commend themselves to all who consider them that a reliable religious authority is postulated. Typically, conciliar and papal definitions have emerged in circumstances of dispute about their subject matter, and if they succeed in commanding assent it is not because it has been pointed out that, after all, the truth of the matter is clear and intuitively obvious. If anything is patently evident in respect of Catholic doctrine it is that the truth of the claims that constitute it is not patently evident. Nor could it be seriously thought that in defining a dogma the Church takes its appointed task to be simply that of recasting a proposition which previously was maintained in an obscure form so as to make its truth unmistakable.

The dilemma forced upon the Cartesian-inspired seeker after certainty (of choosing between knowledge proper and foundational security) is escaped by the present response, since it makes no connection between infallibility and the epistemic impossibility of doubt. The proposal is simply that, concerning matters of doctrine and morals essential to the Faith, the appropriate authorities cannot err, and *not* that they are gifted with the capacity of rendering dogma indubitable to all rational enquiry. Furthermore, since it also rejects the Cartesian conception of the mechanism of infallibility which suggests that doctrinal truths signal their presence to the papal mind's eye, it is in order to ask what grounds support the declaration of a dogma.

The propriety of this request indicates that what are being presented are claims to *knowledge* as Wittgenstein characterizes them, i.e. evidenced beliefs. Earlier I suggested that this conception of knowledge may not be obligatory but the point to note here is that the present account of magisterial infallibility can grant all of the Wittgensteinian assumptions and emerge unscathed. The secure status of dogmatic definitions according to this view is not due to their being given the logical role of foundational presuppositions within a language game. For, as was seen, their contents are contestable (and *contested* by participants in this 'language game'). Instead, their status is simply that entailed by the claim that their author cannot err.

At this point someone may ask why one should believe that the Catholic Church is possessed of an infallible teaching authority. The only answer, I think, is that suggested by Newman.

> In proportion to the probability of true developments of doctrine and practice in the Divine Scheme, so is the probability also of the appointment in that scheme of an external authority to decide upon them, thereby separating them from the mass of mere human speculation, extravagance, corruption and error, in and out of which they grow. This is the doctrine of the infallibility of the Church.[22]

If something like the Christian revelation were true, then one would expect that God would have provided the means for its inerrant transmission across space and time. The Church of Rome proclaims itself to be possessed of such a gift and thus fulfils that expectation. Such reasoning is defeasible in as much as its premises may be contested and its mode of inference is not deductive. But my task has not been to prove the doctrine of infallibility – only to show, in the face of certain objections, that it is neither incoherent nor empty. To quote Newman again, but from another context, 'one step enough for me'. In a religious context, infallibility and authority are only important if they support and are supported by a faith rooted in scripture and in the teaching traditions of the Church.

Notes

1 Anglican–Roman Catholic International Commission, *The Final Report* (London: Catholic Truth Society/SPCK, 1982), Authority in the Church II, paras 6–9, pp. 83–5.
2 See ARCIC, *Final Report*, Authority in the Church I, para. 23, p. 64; and Authority in the Church II, paras 31–3, pp. 96–8.
3 Denzinger-Schönmetzer, *Enchiridion Symbolorum* (Freiburg: Herder, 1963), 3073–4.
4 See V. Conzemius, 'Lord Acton and the First Vatican Council', *Journal of Ecclesiastical History* 20 (1969), pp. 267–94.
5 G. Salmon, *The Infallibility of the Church* (London: Murray, 1952), revised edition.
6 *Letters and Diaries of John Henry Newman*, ed. C. Dessain and T. Gornall, SJ (Oxford: Oxford University Press, 1973), vol. 25, pp. 18–20.
7 Newman, Letter dated 23 July 1870, op. cit., p. 164.
8 Newman, Letter dated 21 June 1868, ibid.
9 Newman, *Apologia pro Vita Sua*, ed. Martin J. Svaglic (Oxford: Clarendon Press, 1967), pp. 219–20.
10 Hans Küng, *Infallible? An Enquiry*, trans. E. Mosbacher (London: Collins, 1971).
11 Hans Küng, 'A Short Balance Sheet on the Debate on Infallibility', *Concilium* 83 (1973), p. 63.
12 For a clear and stimulating discussion of these matters, see Saul Kripke, *Naming and Necessity* (Oxford: Blackwell, 1980).
13 Küng, *Infallible?*, p. 141.
14 I. Fetscher, 'Certainty, Truth and the Church's Teaching Office', *Concilium* 83 (1973), p. 63.
15 Here I ignore the challenge to this claim arising from vague contexts, as it is not relevant to the present issue.
16 That is to say if it is true it is necessarily true. It is an important question whether central Christian dogmas concern metaphysical necessities. After a long period of neglect this question is once again receiving attention, mostly from philosophers. Theologically trained writers tend still to accept the older view that all necessary truths are analytic and are knowable a priori. Thus Patrick McGrath who rightly accuses Küng of confusing propositions with 'propositional formulae', then goes on to concede to him that 'every proposition which is genuinely informative and not a mere tautology is capable of being either true or false': 'The Concept of Infallibility', *Concilium* 83 (1973), p. 69. Following Kripke, however, I take it that the 'non-analytic, a posteriori but necessary' is a legitimate category and that metaphysical necessities fall within it.
17 Wittgenstein, *On Certainty* (Oxford: Blackwell, 1969).

18 Descartes, 'Meditations on First Philosophy', 1 and 3, in E.S. Haldane and G.R.T. Ross (eds), *Philosophical Works* (Cambridge: Cambridge University Press, 1911).
19 G.E. Moore, 'A Defence of Common Sense' in *Philosophical Papers* (London: Allen & Unwin, 1959), pp. 32–59.
20 Wittgenstein, *On Certainty*, 511.
21 Küng, *Infallible?*, pp. 101ff.
22 Newman, *An Essay on the Development of Christian Doctrine* (London: Longmans, Green & Co., 1906), p. 78.

Chapter 6

Incarnational anthropology

Introduction

The renaissance of philosophy of mind within the analytical tradition owes a great deal to the intellectual midwifery of Ryle and Wittgenstein. It is ironic, therefore, that the current state of the subject should be one in which scientific and Cartesian models of mentality are so widely entertained. Clearly few if any of those who find depth, *and truth*, in the Wittgensteinian approach are likely to be sympathetic to much of what is most favoured in contemporary analytic philosophical psychology. Finding themselves in a minority, they might well look elsewhere for support, hoping to establish the idea that opposition to scientific and Cartesian ways of thinking is by no means philosophically eccentric. Perhaps this partly explains the increasing British and North American interest in 'Continental' thought, particularly as it bears (as most of it does) on the nature of human beings. Husserl, Heidegger, Merleau-Ponty and Sartre are obvious enough subjects for such attention.

In his interesting essay 'Getting the Subject Back into the World', Fergus Kerr joins a growing group of English-speaking writers attracted by the work of Heidegger.[1] Untypically, however, Kerr's attention has been caught by Heidegger's speculations about the involvement of *theological* ideas in the development of a view of persons as somehow set above, against or apart from the world of subjectless *things*. I am not a Heidegger scholar and I shall not raise any questions about Kerr's speculative interpretation of his subject. Indeed, I shall not be greatly concerned with Heidegger at all. I will, however, consider Heidegger's explicit claim that Christian theology has bequeathed to modern times an entirely misconceived account of human beings, and in connection with this suggestion I will discuss some issues in the area of theology and philosophy of mind. The latter conjunction of topics is now rarely encountered. I regard this as unfortunate, for there may lie within it the possibility of achieving a better understanding of what we are and how we differ from other things – be they *subjects* or *objects* – and how such differences are made possible. Before proceeding to Heidegger and theological anthropology, however, I need to review something of current philosophical psychology and to identify certain features of it.

Contemporary philosophy of mind

Anyone who reads extensively within contemporary philosophy of mind and reflects upon what they have been studying should feel the discomfort of intellectual claustrophobia. Notwithstanding that the subject is widely and actively pursued its content is remarkably confined. The boundaries of possibility are taken to stand close to one another and the available options are correspondingly few and, I believe, unappealing. They are, basically, one or another form of *physicalism*, reductive or not, and one or another form of dualism. Even this characterization suggests a wider range of possibilities than is actually favoured. Most contributors to contemporary discussions assume some version of *property dualism*, the main point of difference being over the question of how the relevant properties (and perhaps all properties) are to be regarded, i.e. projectively or detectively, reductively or non-reductively, nominalistically or realistically, and so on.

Recent times have seen a renaissance of realist versions of dualism, though the small, frail and uncertain offspring do not match the robust products of Platonic, Augustinian and Cartesian conceptions. For a large part, however, philosophy of mind has gone *anti-realist* – in various related senses of that term. Two such approaches are especially prominent and correspond to similar traditions in metaethics, viz., *relativism* and *error theory*. A commonly held version of the former, which again is easily described by way of its parallel application in ethics, is *projectivism*. According to this, we are (for whatever reason) disposed to ascribe to human beings, and to some other things, a range of characteristics which they do not in fact possess. As one might say, following Hume:[2] 'Take any bodily behaviour allowed to be an utterance, examine it and its causes in all lights, and see if you can find that matter of fact, or real existence, which you call *meaning*. In whichever way you take it, you find only bodily movements. There is no other matter of fact in the case. The meaning entirely escapes you, as long as you consider the object. You never can find it, till you turn your reflection into your own breast, and find a response, which arises in you, towards this behaviour.'

Many people who hold this sort of view, such as Dennett, are projectivists only in respect of certain classes of phenomena.[3] They advocate realism with regard to constitutive features of the ground upon which the response-dependent characteristics are imposed. Indeed, the very metaphor of *projection* seems to force realism at some level, for it does not seem possible that what faces us is simply layer upon layer of projections, images all the way through.[4] On the other hand, there are those, including Hilary Putnam, who think that the conjunction of projectivism and realism, with regard say to psychology and physiology respectively, fails to register the full implication of at least some of those considerations which might have moved one in the direction of projectivism in the first instance.[5] It is often supposed, for example, that no coherent account can be given of the idea that objects are possessed of properties independently of our conception or experience of them; or similarly that it makes no sense even to think of the world as delineated apart from particular theories or practices within which talk of things and their characteristics features. Thus, some hold that any *philosophical* distinction between the real and the projected is misconceived. For present purposes it will be sufficient (though not uncontroversial) to characterize views of this sort as instances of wholesale *conceptual relativism*. On this account one need not accord priority to one domain over another (though one is not necessarily prohibited from doing so). It is easy to see, therefore, why those who take everyday psychology seriously, but who are repelled by ontological dualism, are attracted to some version of this view.

By contrast with accounts which regard the subject matter of intentional psychology as partly (or wholly) constituted by our affective responses and practical interests, advocates of *error theories* consider psychological concepts as products of mistaken hypotheses and insist that there are simply no phenomena to which they are properly applicable. Quite literally *nothing* is an intentional state or process. In view of this conclusion one might suppose, with Paul Churchland for example, that *eliminativism* is the only reasonable option; but, in fact, one could allow that, notwithstanding the vacuity of everyday (and theoretical) psychology, we cannot or should not abandon our erroneous assumptions.

For various reasons which I have set out at length elsewhere and will not now repeat, I regard eliminativism and error theory as entirely misconceived and ultimately unintelligible.[6] I am in sympathy with their proponents to this extent, however, that if projectivism or total conceptual relativism are the best that can be hoped for by way of securing the position of our common view of ourselves as persons, then it would be better to say that our self-conception is a delusion – for all that it may be inescapable.

This is not the occasion to pursue the issue but it is appropriate for what follows to register my opposition to this form of anti-realism also. One reason for doing so is that such views involve a generalized version of *compatibilism* which suffers from the same weakness as the restricted versions introduced in connection with freedom and determinism. Given the metaphysics of the projectivist, for example, we are invited to believe that while an event may be wholly determined in its causes it may be conceived of in a fashion which allows it to be a free action. Certainly it is believable that what is determined may be *thought of* as being free, but thinking does not make it so and in the circumstances this belief would be false. Of course the projectivist may reply that on his view our taking something to have a psychological character may be sufficient for its possessing it, for responses *constitute* the phenomena. But then I think we would do better to view things as they really are and say that so far as what *occurred* is concerned it was determined, notwithstanding that we may regard it in ways that take no account of this.

Considering these rejections of *relativism* and *error theory*, one might expect enthusiasm for recent versions of *realist* property dualism. Once again, however,

I cannot see that these come close to being coherent, never mind convincing. Admittedly they accord reality where other views elevate delusion but they give no intelligible account of how mental properties are related to physical ones; more precisely, they give no adequate account of how the two sets of properties are *integrated*. Some authors take the view that the two sets cannot be brought together in any way that accords with such common assumptions as that thought may be causally efficacious, and so they retreat to some form of epiphenomenalism. It is difficult to see that this is anything other than a defeat so far as concerns the attempt to give account of ourselves in accord with the testimony of experience and reflection. If the existence of psychological phenomena makes no difference to the course of events, then we are more than half way in to the position occupied by the error theorist. But this conclusion, like that of the unrestricted error theory, is so far at odds with the evidence which continues to motivate philosophy of mind that it is barely intelligible as an answer to the question: What is our nature as thinkers and agents? Moreover, current versions of property dualism are wont to combine it with substance monism of a physicalist type. This encourages an emphasis on 'our' in the previous question, for reflection suggests that there is a continuing psychophysical subject of thought and action. The neo-dualist is apt to cite the human body or some part of it, i.e. the brain, as being that with which this subject is associated, but these suggestions are fraught with conceptual and epistemological difficulties and we are no nearer to understanding how subjectivity could be a characteristic of an entity whose sortal or substantial identity is given by its physical nature.

Heidegger, *Dasein* and the image of God

In the light of these difficulties it is appropriate to step back and consider how the current condition arose and also what options might be available beyond those already discussed. I presume that it is partly in this spirit that Fergus Kerr, having previously made a commendable study of Wittgenstein,[7] has turned to consider the historical analysis and philosophy of mind of Heidegger, and it is clear why some of what Heidegger has to say is likely to be received sympathetically by those already attracted by Wittgenstein's work on similar themes.

In *Sein und Zeit*,[8] Heidegger takes on the task of showing how being embedded in the world is a precondition of our mindedness in general (*Dasein*) and hence, ironically, of those concepts and thoughts which seem to suggest an independently constituted subjectivity, and so give rise to the familiar problems of modern philosophy; most obviously, external-world scepticism and solipsism. He writes as follows:

> From what we have been saying, it follows that Being-in is not a 'property' which Dasein sometimes has and sometimes does not have, and *without* which it could *be* just as well as it could with it. It is not the case that man

'is' and then has, by way of an extra, a relationship-of-Being towards the 'world' – a world with which he provides himself occasionally. Dasein is never 'proximally' an entity which is, so to speak, free from Being-in, but which sometimes has the inclination to take up a 'relationship' towards the world. Taking up relationships towards the world [whether cognitive or sceptical] is possible only *because* Dasein, as Being-in-the-world, is as it is.[9]

Later Heidegger applies this conclusion directly to the issue of scepticism and considers the idea of the subject as this has been developed within the Western philosophical tradition:

> We *must* presuppose truth. Dasein itself, as in each case my Dasein and this Dasein, *must* be; and in the same way the truth, as Dasein's disclosedness, *must* be. This belongs to Dasein's essential thrownness into the world... even when nobody *judges*, truth already gets presupposed in so far as Dasein is at all.
>
> A sceptic can no more be refuted than the Being of truth can be 'proved'. And if any sceptic of the kind who denies the truth, factically is, [*sic*] he does not even need to be refuted...
>
> [W]ith the question of the Being of truth and the necessity of presupposing it, just as with the question of the essence of knowledge, an 'ideal subject' has generally been posited....Is not such a subject *a fanciful idealization?* With such a subject have we not missed precisely the *a priori* character of that merely 'factual' subject, Dasein?[10]

Forgetting the unattractive pretension and self-indulgence that is characteristic of Heidegger's writing, there are easily identifiable parallels between the thoughts indicated above and Wittgenstein's central ideas with regard to human nature and knowledge,[11] and between both of these and the recent work by Davidson on subjectivity and cognition.[12] It is not altogether clear, however, what precise positive view, *if any*, Heidegger offers in place of those he dismisses. The expressions 'Dasein', 'Being-in-the-worldness', 'factual subjectivity', etc., are possibly suggestive of something congenial to those seeking to 'get the Subject back into the World', but they are terms of art whose meaning requires further articulation and whose application has to be shown to be illuminating. I am not myself confident that these tasks can be accomplished, or that if they were to be then anything genuinely novel would be revealed.

One might, nonetheless, find value in Heidegger's critical ideas about the origins of the supposedly false dualism of (worldless) subject and (subjectless) world. As Kerr observes, Heidegger claims to identify two central sources for this – located, as one might say, in Athens and in Jerusalem. The first is the idea that there is an important difference between Man (Subject) and the rest of nature (World) inasmuch as he possesses, and it lacks, rationality – *zoon logon ekhon*. The second is the Judaeo-Christian doctrine that man is made in the image of God – *imago Dei*. On the same page as the last of the passages quoted above Heidegger goes on to write as follows: 'Both the contention that there are eternal truths and the jumbling together of Dasein's phenomenally grounded "ideality" with an idealized absolute subject, belong to those residues of Christian theology within philosophical problematics which have not as yet been radically extruded.' However, the main locus of his case for identifying the supposedly pernicious influence of theological ideas comes in the section titled *How the Analytic of Dasein is to be Distinguished from Anthropology, Psychology, and Biology*.[13] It is there that he writes of the Christian idea of transcendence, according to which 'man is something that reaches beyond himself...[being] more than a mere something endowed with intelligence', and cites as specimen texts passages from Calvin and Zwingli. Setting aside questions of evidential support (seven lines of text from two authors both belonging to the Reformation), and questions of historical interpretation, an issue arises concerning Heidegger's philosophical competence.

Kerr quotes the following passage from *Metaphysische Anfangsgrunde der Logik*: 'The problem of the existence of the external world and whether it can be known is implicated in the problem of the knowledge of God and of the possibility of proving God's existence.'[14] The nature of this implication and of its direction is not adequately explained. At one point it looks as if the problem of the external world (*epistemological transcendence*) is taken to be the source for the idea of an ultimate object set against the plurality of cognitive subjects, but elsewhere it seems that it is the idea of an unconditioned absolute being outside the world (*theological transcendence*) which gives rise to the general notion of objects outwith the mind and then, by a further stage, to the idea that there is a problem as to how, if ever, the cognitive subject makes contact with the world.

Evidently Kerr is in some measure of agreement that Heidegger does not put up much of a show when it comes to substantiating the claim that Christian theology is the source of a troublesome conception of human beings from which philosophers must free us. But his interest is caught by the idea that elsewhere Heidegger draws upon scriptural and other Christian writings in the development of an account of *Dasein*. The questions which then arise are: What exactly is the element of Christian thought which must be 'extruded' from philosophy if we are to arrive at a correct account of our nature? and what are the acceptable theological notions which may help us to effect the necessary extrusion?

Drawing in part on work by John Richardson,[15] Kerr proposes that for Heidegger the essence of our subjective alienation is the result of a movement from practical engagement with the world to (broadly) scientific contemplation of it (*Im anfang war die tat?*). This movement brings with it the notion of an objective view which in turn is associated with the idea of a transcendent status, a possessor of which would be unlimited in cognitive capacity, unconditioned by any historical context and unrestricted in power to realize all possibilities. Such a status is of course that classically ascribed to the Deity. In brief, then, the idea is that like Lucifer we strive to be God. To this, someone might reply that in the myths of the eternal damnation of Satan and the expulsion from Paradise of Adam and Eve the religious tradition provides means enough to deflate delusions of divine grandeur, and to induce gratitude for whatever condition Providence has bestowed. That reply is not considered, but I suppose the thought is that so long as the idea of a transcendent status remains around we are always going to aspire to it, or at least to regard our own condition as, by comparison, defective. In this way, then, the elimination of un-naturalized Christian anthropology becomes the precondition of a true account of 'the being of *Dasein*'.

Heidegger's thought on these issues is somewhat facile and I suspect that Kerr has done more work than his subject in order to fashion the latter's fragmentary remarks into some kind of coherent whole. Even so the conclusions he attributes to him are open to objection. As Kerr remarks: 'The Christian God is already in the world.' Instead of taking issue with the details of Heidegger's story, however, I want to develop a theme touched on by Kerr and consider whether rather than Christian anthropology darkening reflection about our nature it is not a possible source of illumination. I shall argue that if one takes seriously certain central Christian doctrines, even if only as possibilities, and thinks about how they might be accommodated within metaphysics, then interesting prospects for progress in philosophy of mind may come into view.

Theology and philosophical anthropology

Consider the following three ideas.

(i) Traditional Christians believe that, in the person of Jesus Christ, God became a man. The doctrine of the Incarnation finds expression in the words of the Nicene Creed: 'For us men and for our salvation he came down from heaven: by the power of the Holy Spirit, he became incarnate from the Virgin Mary and was made man.' (*Qui propter nos homines et propter nostram salutem descendit de caelis: Et incarnatus est de Spiritu Sancto ex Maria Virgine, et homo factus est.*) It is heretical to hold that Jesus Christ was a union of two persons, one divine the other human (*Nestorianism*), or that Christ had only a divine nature (*Docetism*) or that he had only a human nature (*Arianism*).

(ii) In Genesis 1.26–8, we read the following: 'Then God said, "Let us make man in our image, after our likeness...". So God created man in his own image, in the image of God he created him; male and female he created them.' In his First Letter to the Corinthians 11.7, St Paul is concerned with implications of this doctrine for liturgical practice, advising 'that a man ought not to cover his head, since he is the image and glory of God'. This injunction presupposes a theological anthropology but does not articulate it. That task was begun by the Church Fathers and continued in the Middle Ages by the scholastics. In his *Commentary on the Sentences*, Aquinas repeats the claim that man is made in the image of God (strictly, that he *is* an image of God – *imago Dei*). As was seen, this is the sort of endorsement by a Christian philosophical theologian which, together with the original Genesis text, Heidegger blames for alienating us from our natural environment. Anyone disposed to agree with him, however, would do well to consider what exactly Aquinas means by this phrase as used of human beings. He writes as follows: 'Similarity is considered with regard to the form. Now the form of the human body is the rational soul, which is an image of God (*imago Dei*); for this reason the human body not only enjoys the similarity of a vague general copy (*vestigium*) but also the similarity of a specific likeness (*imago*), inasmuch as it is informed by the soul.'[16] Admittedly, the sense of this is not transparent, but it could hardly be thought that the insistence upon the body's participation in the 'image' encourages a dualist reading.

(iii) Returning to his First Letter to the Corinthians 15.35, we find St Paul teaching that Christ is raised from the dead and that resurrection awaits those whom he chooses to save. Towards the end of his epistle Paul writes as follows:

> But some will ask, 'How are the dead raised? With what kind of body do they come?' You foolish man! What you sow does not come to life unless it dies. And what you sow is not the body which is to be, but a bare kernel, perhaps of wheat or of some other grain. But God gives it a body as he has chosen, and to each kind of seed its own body...
>
> So it is with the resurrection of the dead. What is sown is perishable, what is raised is imperishable. It is sown in dishonour, it is raised in glory. It is sown in weakness, it is raised in power. It is sown a physical body, it is raised a spiritual body. If there is a physical body, there is also a spiritual body (*soma pneumatikon*). Thus it is written, 'The first Adam became a living being; the last Adam became a life-giving spirit.'

In each of these three cases interpretation is called for, but it is worth remarking in advance that dualistic readings are not inescapable and indeed there are philosophical and theological difficulties standing in their way.

The Incarnation

Consider again the doctrine of the Incarnation: the claim that the Son of God – co-eternal with the Father – became a human being. This is often charged with contradiction but I cannot see that these charges have been made out. Suppose, for example, that an objector observes that the doctrine commits one to the claim that in so far as He was God Christ was uncreated but in so far as he was a Man he was a creature. This, it is supposed, yields the contradictory claim that *Christ was and was not a creature.*

One reply to this challenge is to deny the commitment ascribed to the doctrine. Certainly God is uncreated, and Christ being God is thus an uncreated being; but while it may be that most men have been created it is not part of what it is to be a man that one have been created.[17] Creatureliness is not of the essence of humanity. If this is right then there is, so far at least, no contradiction (and perhaps not even the appearance of one) in the claim that Christ had divine and human natures – even if possession of the former rules out the possibility that Christ was a creature.

This first sort of response, however, is inadequate as a *general* reply.[18] The orthodox believer *may* be willing to allow that Christ was an uncreated man but he certainly wishes to assert that he was none the less *born* of humankind (*et incarnatus est...ex Maria Virgine*), and the latter is an attribute which, as it stands, *is* incompatible with being divine – at least as divinity is understood in the Christian tradition. Thus the orthodox Christian seems committed to the following two claims:

(A1)　Christ was born.
(A2)　Christ was not born.

How might this difficulty be resolved? It has long been the practice of some theologians – the more thoughtful ones – to refer the characteristics of Christ to the relevant aspects of His person, i.e. the distinct human and divine *natures*. Thus, instead of (A1) and (A2) one might say the following:

(B1)　Christ *qua* man was born.
(B2)　Christ *qua* God was not born.

This, however, may not seem any advance if one supposes that the correct logical form of this second pair of statements is given by first-order predicate calculus. For according to that they would be represented as follows:

(C1)　Fa & Ga.
(C2)　Ha & ~Ga.

This then yielding

(C3)　(Fa & Ha) & (Ga & ~Ga).

But there is good reason to suppose that (C1) and (C2) do *not* give the correct logical form of the statements about Christ and to think this for quite general reasons to do with the logic of what I shall term *aspect-involving predications*, i.e. ones involving such expressions as 'inasmuch as it is', 'in respect of its being', 'under the description', 'as', etc. (these giving rise to what the scholastics termed reduplication; the relevant Latin expressions being *inquantum* and *secundum quod*).[19]

Consider first the following example. My status as a resident and community-charge payer in St Andrews does not entitle me to use the University Library; however, my position as a member of the University does so entitle me. Thus, it seems that the following are both true:

(D1) J.H. is entitled to use the University Library.
(D2) J.H. is not entitled to use the University Library.

The apparent contradiction is avoided by observing that these predications are in fact aspect-related and hence that the perspicuous form of representation is:

(E1) J.H. *qua* University member is entitled to use the Library.
(E2) J.H. *qua* resident is not entitled to use the Library.

Here the appearance of conflict is dissolved and we are left with perfectly compatible statements. The question is whether this solution will serve for the Christological statements (B1) and (B2) above. One might think that it will not since the cases are not analogous. The predicates 'is entitled to use the Library' and 'is not entitled to use the Library' clearly stand in opposition to one another but the exact form of this opposition is a matter for further specification. The expression 'is not entitled' admits of a weaker and a stronger reading which yield, respectively, a contradictory and a contrary to the predicate 'is entitled'. The universe is dividable into those things which are entitled to use the Library and those which are not. Among the latter complement, however, are those who are merely unentitled (the 'contradictory complement') and those who are disentitled, i.e. prohibited (the 'contrary complement'). Accordingly, the suggestion might be that in the example introduced above – of my being entitled and not entitled – the latter is only a matter of *unentitlement* and not one of *disentitlement*, and hence a reconciliation is possible in this case (by means of (E1) and (E2)) though it would not be were I, as a resident, to be *disentitled* to use the library. In this second case an inescapable contradiction results; and, the thought continues, it is this case which is the proper counterpart of the claim that Christ was born and Christ was not born. Being unentitled in one capacity leaves open the possibility of being entitled in some other. Being disentitled does not. The Christological case is like the latter, both sets of predicates cannot be simultaneously satisfied.

One reason for thinking this to be the case in the library example is that entitlement and disentitlement are concerned with licensing and prohibiting actions and processes and it is clear that these procedures are not compossible. But this is a problem for action (a practical conflict) and it does not obviously follow that there is a strict contradiction. Whatever about that, however, the foregoing line of objection does not demonstrate the derivability of a contradiction from the *qua* analysis of the reduplicative Christological claims. Consider

again the question of the logical form of these statements, taking first a generalized version of the library entitlement/non-entitlement claims:

> (F1) Anyone *qua* member of the University, is entitled to use the Library.
> (F2) Anyone *qua* resident and charge payer, is not entitled to use the
> Library.

Applying the orthodox analysis these will be represented as follows:

> (G1) (x) (Fx → Gx).
> (G2) (x) (Hx → ~Gx).

This implies that nothing can satisfy the predicates F and H, for if it did a contradiction would be directly derivable. But something *does* satisfy F and H (many
things do); hence this cannot be the correct analysis. So, my preferred schema
makes essential use of the *qua* construction to introduce aspect-involving
predication. Recall that non-entitlement admits of two readings yielding mere
unentitlement (the straight contradictory complement) and disentitlement (the
contrary complement). This gives us two sorts of cases:

> (H1) x *qua* F is entitled.
> (H2) x *qua* H is not (i.e. is un)entitled.

and

> (I1) x *qua* F is entitled.
> (I2) x *qua* H is not (i.e. is dis)entitled.

If (H2) does not imply that x is unentitled, *simpliciter* – and it does not – then
neither does (H1) imply that x is entitled, *simpliciter*. Thus, x *qua* F is G does
not entail that x is G, *simpliciter*. If this inference were valid then a contradiction would be derivable but we know from the actual case which (H1) and
(H2) represent that it is not. But since the general schema 'x *qua* F is G → x
is G' is not a valid one it cannot be used in respect of (I1) and (I2) either in
order to derive a contradiction.[20] In neither interpretation of the entitlement/
non-entitlement opposition is it *demonstrated* that there is a strict contradiction.
In the one case the reduplicative analysis reveals why this is so, in the other it
shows it not to be, and I have added to this an explanation of our intuition that
here there is a real (and not merely an apparent) contradiction, i.e. the suggestion that it generates a practical impossibility.

Returning, then, to the doctrine of the Incarnation, I am suggesting that
some of the supposed contradictions are eliminable by means of ascribing to
Christ *qua* man the very same attribute as is possessed by Christ in his divinity,
and that others are treatable by the reduplicative analysis. This is not to suggest

that the latter explains how something can be born *qua* man, and not born *qua* God, but the want of such an explanation is part of what lies behind the orthodox claim that this and other doctrines are *mysteries*.

Let me next advert to another feature of the favoured reduplicative analysis. It is important to see that in the schema 'x *qua* F is G' the proper subject term is 'x' and not 'x *qua* F'.[21] '*Qua* F' is part of what is predicated, and this accounts for my introduction of the phrase 'aspect-involving predicates'. (Indeed, this favours using the form x is G-*qua* F.) One good reason to parse things in this way is that otherwise falsities result. Since it is one and the same *thing* that is and is not entitled to use the library, if the subject of the non-entitlement were 'x *qua* resident and charge-payer' then it would be true that 'x *qua* resident and charge-payer is entitled to use the library', but this is false. More pertinently, in the Christological case it would license the statement 'Christ as God was born' which again is false – and heretical (compare the case of 'Christ as God died on the Cross' – *Theopassianism*). The term 'Christ' is a proper name designating a single individual in all of its occurrences: 'Christ', 'the man Christ', 'Christ as man', 'Christ as God', etc., all refer to one eternal person possessed (at different times) of two natures; 'the humanity of Christ' and 'the divinity of Christ' signifying these natures or aspects themselves. What all of this indicates, then, is that a minimally adequate logical treatment of attributions to Jesus Christ, the Incarnate Word of God – i.e. one which avoids contradiction – implies that there is but *one subject* of divine and human attributes. This is a happy result from the point of view of orthodoxy: Chalcedon and Nicaea are vindicated and Nestorianism is avoided, but it also bears upon the treatment of the *imago Dei* and resurrection doctrines, as well as upon the project of mundane anthropology.

Humanity and existence

So far as concerns the latter there is one point which is important to discuss here. In recent times it has again become fashionable to argue that questions of personal individuation and identity must and can be resolved by reference to an account of human subjects which sees them as instances of a natural kind or species. This brings with it the idea of real or *de re* essences. There is much to be said for this sort of account, not least that it saps the power of the mind/brain-transfer thought experiments so beloved of English-speaking philosophers from Locke onwards. A natural-kind theory which eschews individual essences will hold that there is nothing necessary for the individual save what is essential to the species. If it is necessary for men to have hearts, then it is essential that I have a heart but *not* that I have the heart I do have, or indeed any particular other one. Likewise for brains. No metaphysically special status attaches to any given brain. If someone were to achieve the Brown/Johnson brain-exchange a species-essentialist should stand firm in the face of odd co-donor behaviour, knowing all the while that so far as individual *identity* is concerned the operation was of no greater significance than had it involved an exchange of hearts.

The previous thought yields the advice: keep track of the human beings and you will know who is who – *up to a point, that is*! This qualification may need to be added because of an implication of the theological doctrines listed above – most obviously those associated with the Incarnation. Consider the following sentence:

(J)   It is necessarily true that if J.H. is a man then J.H. is a man.

This admits of two familiar readings:

(J$_1$)   *De dicto*: Necessarily, if J.H. is a man then J.H. is a man.
(J$_2$)   *De re*: If J.H. is a man, then necessarily J.H. is a man.

But a further separation needs to be made. The *de re* claim can be associated with two distinct metaphysical views, as follows:

(1)   If J.H. is a man then necessarily J.H. has certain features, such that J.H. could not cease to instantiate these and still be a man.
(2)   If J.H. is a man then necessarily J.H. has certain features, such that J.H. could not cease to instantiate these and still exist.

De re readings of J are compatible with each of (1) and (2). If, however, one were to take seriously the doctrine of the Incarnation then one would want to accept (1) but deny (2). Christ as God existed from all eternity but one and the same person took on a human nature at a given moment in history. At the point of incarnation and thereafter Christ as man possessed a human essence, but the existence of the subject of that essence – the person Christ – existed before assuming it. So notwithstanding that *Jesus of Nazareth* was a human being and as such could not have failed to possess certain attributes, it was not essential that *Christ* be a man, i.e. *his* existence was not tied constitutively to this nature.

This may suggest to some readers a duality of substances: a divine person inside a human one, analogous to the Cartesian duality of a mind inside an organism. But I have already indicated why the former view is not forced upon the believer and noted that Christian orthodoxy set itself against any such dualism. Suppose then one were to accept the *one person/two natures* theological formula and to review the metaphysics of human personhood in the light of it, what might emerge? Clearly not Cartesianism and possibly not an essentialism which makes J.H.'s existence depend upon his being human. Recall in connection with this the other theological ideas listed earlier: the *imago Dei* doctrine and St Paul's eschatology – to which it would also be appropriate to add, in respect of Jesus, the Transfiguration: '[A]s he was praying the appearance of his countenance was altered ['his face shone like the sun' (Matthew 17.2)] and his raiment became dazzling white' (Luke 9.29), and the mysterious post-resurrection appearances:

[S]he turned round and saw Jesus standing, but she did not know that it was Jesus....[He] said to her, 'Do not hold me, for I have not yet ascended to the Father'...the disciples were again in the house, and Thomas was with them. The doors were shut but Jesus came and stood among them...he said to Thomas, 'Put your finger here, and see my hands; and put out your hand, and place it in my side.'

(John 20.14–28)

It has been common to draw connections between the transfigured Christ of the 'high mountain' and the generally unrecognizable condition of the resurrected Christ. As was noted, a yet more direct link is forged by St Paul between the risen Christ and the condition of those who will be raised in glory; we are to have 'spiritualized bodies'. Some writers have taken the occasion of St Paul's enigmatic phrase to challenge the doctrine with a dilemma: are they *spirits* or are they *bodies*? But this may be viewed as much as a symptom of the commentators' intellectual limitations as it is that of St Paul. The point of the phrase, as of that section of the epistle, is to indicate that a glorifying transformation awaits those whom God will save. My interest here is in whether this can be fitted into any coherent metaphysical scheme.[22]

Incarnational anthropology

When reviewing the currently favoured options in philosophy of mind I remarked that most projectivists and (realist) property dualists are inclined to be monistic with respect to the ground or bearer of psychological attributes. This monism is materialistic in the sense nowadays intended by the term 'physicalism'. When reading the work of philosophers of these sorts, and indeed most other writers in the field, it is difficult to resist the thought that, to some degree or another, they are working under the influence of corrupted versions of two Aristotelian ideas. The first is the *substance/attribute* distinction, the second the *form/matter* one.

It is sometimes said, e.g. in connection with discussions of the doctrine of transubstantiation, that the medieval scholastics thought of properties as being metaphysical skins enveloping the objects which possess them. This is historically quite inaccurate and badly misrepresents the view they actually held and had derived from their reading of Aristotle. From Locke onwards, however, there has been a growing tendency, especially among English-speaking philosophers, to think about substances and properties in something like the object/envelope way.

Given the materialist presumption, one might more aptly liken the relationship to that between an object and skins or coatings which cover its surface. Just as one may add further layers and the character of the surface will change in various ways depending partly on the nature of the previous surface; so, in this way of thinking, properties are laid (by nature) one upon another atop an underlying bearer, and the character of any given layer is determined in part by what lies beneath it. This simple picture best makes sense of much of the contemporary discussion of *supervenience*, especially in connection with the psychological aspects of human beings. It is as if there is a something covered in a chemical coating which contributes to but does not exactly determine the character of the animalistic coat, which in turn affects the psychological layer settled upon it. Put another, but no more satisfactory, way, the psychological 'supervenes' upon the biological which 'supervenes' upon the chemical. (Here the etymology suggests that the term fits exactly the relationship it is now employed to describe, one layer 'coming upon' another.)

I shall not dwell upon what is wrong with this picture nor the current uses of the idea of supervenience; it is worth remarking, however, that had they been able to make sense of them Aristotle and Aquinas would very likely have been amused. Certainly this way of regarding the substance/attribute relation is not at all what they had in mind. For them, to be a substance is to be a kind of thing some of the characteristics of which are (metaphysically) constitutive of it but others of which, including, for example, location and volubility, may be possessed at one time but not at another. Clearly, in the Aristotelian tradition it makes no sense, save in special cases, to think (even metaphorically) of characteristics, whether essential or accidental ones, as lying in layers over the surface of the things which possess them.

A further mark of the difference between a sophisticated neo-Aristotelian such as Aquinas and many contemporary writers is revealed by the ways in which each speaks of *matter*. Possibly both might say that a human being is materially composed but what this would be likely to mean in the mouth of each is importantly different. I said earlier that, as currently employed, the substance/attribute distinction suggests that if one could uncover the underlying bearer of the psychological, biological and chemical layers exhibited by a human being one would be left with a 'something'. The question 'What?' might now be met with the answer 'a lump or other quantity of matter'. This way of speaking reveals that the original *philosophical* concept of matter as co-relative with form or nature, has undergone a change leaving in its place (or, more confusingly, lying alongside it) an *empirical* notion. For Aquinas, by contrast, matter is best thought of (when philosophical questions are at issue) not as a kind of experientially encounterable stuff but as a metaphysical aspect of substances, be they countable things or measurable quantities of certain kinds. The only sense in which it is unarguably true for Aquinas that a human being is materially constituted is that the substance, i.e. the individual J.H., is an actual living nature operating in various ways – as opposed, that is, to a mere possibility of a life which we might envisage if invited to consider human nature as such.

Conceived of in the abstract, matter is the potentiality for the instantiation of form, and form is the actualizing principle, that which makes something to be the kind of thing it is. Neither matter nor form can exist outside the individual substance whose concrete existence they mutually determine. Consider in this connection the following passage from Aquinas's discussion of the metaphysics of the creation:

> As to formation, the argument is clear. For if formless matter preceded in duration, it already existed; for this is implied by duration; since the end of creation is being in act. But act itself is a form. To say, then, that matter preceded, but without form, is to say that being existed actually, yet without act, which is a contradiction in terms. Nor can it be said that it possessed some common form, on which afterwards supervened the different forms that distinguish it....Hence we must assert that primary matter was not created altogether formless, nor under any one common form, but under distinct forms.[23]

In the metaphysical sense matter is the potentiality for the instantiation of form. (This claim is comparable to the idea that space is the condition of the existence of material objects.) Clearly, it does not follow from this alone that every individual substance which realizes this potentiality is material in the modern sense. This being so we might entertain the prospect that empirical matter involves but one mode of potentiality and that the same form of determining principle may be realized in distinct (but related) ways corresponding to different species of possibility. And furthermore that it may be realized in each of these simultaneously.[24]

Needless to say all of this is highly speculative and stands in need of much more investigation; but what it encourages me towards is the thought that an account may be available of how one person, Christ, could have two natures: the divine form actualizing one species of potentiality as the *Logos* and another as *Jesus of Nazareth*. Such an account might also be expected to explain how a created person could at one time be a rational animal incarnate in an empirical medium, and at some later stage possibly be transfigured by translation into a different mode of being. In neither case is there need to be drawn back into a form of dualism. It is one and the same person that is actualized through all eternity in the manner appropriate to the Son of God and is realized also in the empirical mode as a human being, and following the Resurrection in a further manner possibly not imaginable by us but in relation to which St Paul speaks of the *soma pneumatikon*. Likewise, one may entertain the possibility of sharing in that glorified form of life, and perhaps thereby warranting the description *imago Dei*, while not doubting for a moment that one's life as a mortal rational animal *is* one's present mode of existence and more likely than not one's only one.

These final thoughts combine a recognition of present immanence with a prospect of future transcendence. I cannot see that Heidegger's rejection of the latter as an unsettling legacy of Christian theology places him in any better position to explain the former. On the contrary, the only prospect I see for explaining the subjectivity of *Dasein*, and its very existence, involves the sort of incarnational anthropology discussed above.[25]

Notes

1 See Fergus Kerr, 'Getting the Subject Back into the World: Heidegger's Version', in D. Cockburn (ed.), *Human Beings* (Cambridge: Cambridge University Press, 1991), pp. 173–90.

2 The original passage comes in Hume's *Treatise of Human Nature*, Book III, Part I, Section I.

3 See D. Dennett, *The Intentional Stance* (Cambridge, Mass.: MIT Press, 1987).

4 In this connection see C. McGinn, 'An *a priori* Argument for Realism', *Journal of Philosophy* 76.3 (March 1979), where a similar line of thought is pursued in response to one version of global anti-realism.

5 See Hilary Putnam, *Reality and Representation* (Cambridge, Mass.: MIT Press, 1988) and for some discussion of this J. Haldane, 'Putnam on Intentionality', *Philosophy and Phenomenological Research* 52 (1992).

6 See J. Haldane, 'Folk Psychology and the Explanation of Human Behaviour', *Proceedings of the Aristotelian Society, Supplementary Volume* 62 (1988), pp. 223–54.

7 Fergus Kerr, *Theology After Wittgenstein* (Oxford: Blackwell, 1987).

8 Martin Heidegger, *Being and Time*, trans. John Macquarrie and E. Robinson (Oxford: Blackwell, 1978). Subsequent references are to this volume. The page numbers are those of later German editions as indicated in the margins of the Macquarrie and Robinson translation.

9 *Being and Time*, Division I, ch. II, sec. 12, p. 57.

10 *Being and Time*, Division I, ch. VI, sec. 44 (c), pp. 228–9.

11 For a relevant account of these see Kerr, *Theology After Wittgenstein*, Part Two.

12 See especially 'A Coherence Theory of Truth and Knowledge', in E. LePore (ed.), *Truth and Interpretation* (Oxford: Blackwell, 1986) and 'What Is Present to the Mind?', in J. Brandl and W. Gombocz (eds), *The Mind of Donald Davidson* (Amsterdam: Rodolpi, 1989).

13 See *Being and Time*, Division I, ch. VI, sec. 44 (c), p. 272; and Kerr, 'Getting the Subject back into the World', p. 177.

14 See Kerr, 'Getting the Subject Back into the World', p. 180.

15 John Richardson, *Existential Epistemology: A Heideggerian Critique of the Cartesian Project* (Oxford: Clarendon Press, 1986).

16 *Commentary on the Sentences* (of Peter Lombard), III d. 2., q. 1., a 3. The translation is taken from B. Mondin, SX, *St Thomas Aquinas' Philosophy in the Commentary on the Sentences* (The Hague: Nijhoff, 1975).

17 This point is made by Herbert McCabe in published correspondence with Maurice Wiles. See 'The Incarnation: An Exchange', in H. McCabe, *God Matters* (London: Geoffrey Chapman, 1987), p. 70.

18 To judge from the discussion in chapter 9 of his *Understanding Identity Statements* (Aberdeen: Aberdeen University Press, 1984) this is the response favoured by T.V. Morris. However, I have not yet had the opportunity to read his monograph on the Incarnation, viz. *The Logic of God Incarnate* (Ithaca, N.Y.: Cornell University Press, 1986), which may depart from this approach, though I doubt it.

19 In *Providence and Evil* (Cambridge: Cambridge University Press, 1977) Peter Geach offers a brief discussion of reduplicatives in connection with Christological predications. At one point he writes: '[C]learly, this predicate [is as P, Q] entails the simple conjunctive predicate "is both P and Q" but not conversely' (p. 27). I agree that the latter does not entail the former but nor, I believe, does the former imply the latter. If 'A is both P & Q' is equivalent to 'A is P & A is Q' then the contradictions which Geach and I both want to avoid would be one elimination step away. The only statements derivable from 'x *qua* F is G' are (i) 'x is F' and (ii) 'x is G *qua* F'. But the second of these is obviously just a syntactical variant of the original.

20 Needless to say, this claim will be regarded as controversial. The following two
objections may occur to readers (the first was put to me by Graham Priest).

(i) The analysis of 'x as f is not (i.e. is un)entitled' presented above is not that
which an objector to my reduplicative account would give. For he could observe the
ambiguity in claims of the form 'it is not the case that x is f' between *external* and
internal readings of the negation, i.e. involving the sentence or the predicate respectively. So, the claim (H2) above should be represented as ~(x) (Hx → Gx), and
not as (x) (Hx → ~Gx). This then unsettles the proposed identity of logical form.
Recall that my thesis is that the following inferences are valid but since they yield a
contradiction their antecedent conditionals cannot give the correct analysis of the
entitlement/non-entitlement claims:

$$(x) \quad (Fx \rightarrow Gx), Fx \vdash Gx.$$
$$(x) \quad (Hx \rightarrow \sim Gx), Hx \vdash \sim Gx.$$

The counter-proposal is that since the correct logical form of the second conditional is ~(x) (Hx → GX), then ~Gx is not validly derivable, and one is not forced
into a contradiction: Gx *simpliciter* does follow, ~Gx *simpliciter* does not.

My reply is as follows: ~(x) (Hx → Gx) is equivalent to (∃x) (Hx & ~Gx). If we
assume, however, that the predicates F and H are co-extensive, i.e. in the example
discussed above, that all members of the university are also community-charge payers,
then the latter is clearly false since everyone is both a rate-payer and entitled to use
the library. Thus, in the case where F and H are co-extensive the claimed existential
consequence is false while the premise 'Anyone who is a resident is not (i.e. is
un)entitled' remains true. So far as concerns the present issue, therefore, the wide
scope reading of the negation fares no better than did the narrow one.

(ii) A second response argues that one may detach non(i.e. un)entitlement *simpliciter*,
while capturing the sense of the *qua* construction in a standard logical form analysis.
Consider the generalized non-entitlement claim (F2) above:

Anyone *qua* resident and charge-payer is not entitled to use the Library.

This, it is supposed, may be represented as follows:

$$(x) \quad (Hx \& \sim Ix \& \sim Jx \& \sim Kx, etc. \rightarrow \sim Gx).$$

Here I, J, K, etc., stand for various entitling properties; thus we have:

Anyone who is a resident and charge-payer and is not a member of the University and is not a visiting scholar, etc., is not entitled to use the Library.

The problem with this proposal, as I see it, is that the reduplicative 'x *qua* H is not
G' is semantically determinate in the way that the counter proposal is not. One could
grasp the sense and determine the truth value of the first without being able to do the
same for the second – indeed, the 'etc.' barely conceals that as it stands there is no
articulable sense to grasp nor truth to determine. Given this fact the proposal fails as
an analysis.

21 The importance of this point was first impressed upon me by reading 'Nominalism',
in P. Geach, *Logic Matters* (Oxford: Blackwell, 1973).

22 For some related discussion of the Christian idea of a bodily afterlife see J. Haldane,
'A Glimpse of Eternity?', *The Modern Churchman* 30.3 (1988).

23 *Summa Theologiae*, Ia, 1.66, a. 1, ad 1. The translation is that of the Fathers of the
English Dominican Province (London: Washbourne, 1912).

24 The idea of different modes of potentiality, different kinds of 'matter', also has application in connection with the question 'How is thought possible?' For discussion of this see J. Haldane, 'Brentano's Problem', *Grazer Philosophische Studien* 35 (1989); and 'Mind/World Identity Theory and the Anti-Realist Challenge', in J. Haldane and C. Wright (eds), *Realism, Reason and Projection* (Oxford: Oxford University Press, 1992).

25 I am grateful to my colleagues Peter Clark and Anthony Ellis for discussions of issues raised in this essay.

Chapter 7

Examining the Assumption

Immaculatam Deiparam semper Virginem Mariam, expleto terrestris vitae cursu, fuisse corpore et anima ad caelestem gloriam assumptam. (The Immaculate Mother [*sic*] of God, the ever Virgin Mary, having completed the course of her earthly life, was assumed body and soul into heavenly glory.)

Pius XII, *Munificentissimus Deus* (1950)

Introduction

Many Christians, for the most part though not exclusively Roman Catholics, believe that at the end of her life Mary, the mother of Jesus Christ, was assumed bodily 'into heaven' where she remains and is exalted by her divine son. This claim, magisterially entitled the Doctrine of the Assumption of the Blessed Virgin Mary,[1] strikes some people as clear evidence of the extent to which religious believers are prepared to abandon reason in favour of nonsense. Even many who hold to the articles of the Creeds, and are in general traditional Christians, are opposed to, or have serious doubts about, this aspect of Catholic doctrine (as they do of its non-defined equivalent among the Eastern Orthodox marked by the feast of the *koimesis* [dormition] of the *Theotokos* – the one who 'gave birth to' God).

Typically, critics of the doctrine regard it as being at best a sentimental piety, misrepresentative of the truth of Mary's significance, and at worst a neo-pagan accretion entirely lacking in support from any appropriate quarter.[2] Others go further, however; suggesting that the doctrine is not simply without biblical or other evidential warrant but is in some way incoherent, or asserts what is altogether impossible. These are important claims, and in what follows I wish to consider some of the sources of the difficulties that confront any attempt to present and defend the doctrine. There is very little contemporary theological writing on the subject.[3] That may reflect a certain discomfort on the part of Catholic academics with dogmatically substantive Mariology (as contrasted with cultural theory); but a consequence of theological neglect has been a loss of a proper sense of the problems and resources in the field. It has also left the subject of Mary open to sensationalist treatment by others. In a recent book, *Mary: The Unauthorized Biography*, Michael Jordan, writing from what he has described as 'an objective journalistic viewpoint', suggests that Mary may have been initiated in early childhood into the role of temple prostitute, and that Jesus was probably the product of a fertility rite honouring a pagan Mother goddess.[4] Without embarking on a discussion of this, I think it fair to say that Jordan's treatment of the subject lacks theological understanding, and it serves to highlight the need for renewed study of the origins, grounds and meaning of Marian doctrine.

Ancient and medieval homilies and treatises on the subject, variously entitled the 'ending', 'laying down', 'committal', 'falling asleep', 'transition' or 'assumption' of the Virgin, tend to appeal to narratives or reports of the circumstances of Mary's final days. Significantly, however, they also invoke religious reasoning to the effect that, given the Holy Mother's unique status as the bearer of God, the Assumption *must* have happened because it *should* have done. A characteristic example of this is the treatise on the Assumption once attributed to Augustine, but in fact dating from the eight or ninth century and possibly authored by the English Benedictine Alcuin. The writer, whom I shall call 'Anonymous', may be responding to a formally posed question:

> What, then, shall I say of the death of Mary? What of her Assumption seeing that the Scriptures are silent on the subject? Surely here reason must find out what harmonizes with truth, and truth must become our authority, since without truth authority must itself be deprived of all weight.
>
> …Though Mary shares in the sorrows of Eve, she is unlike her in that she [conceived though she remained a virgin and] brought forth her child without pain. Her singular sanctity merited this for her as well as her unique grace which rendered her specially worthy to become the Mother of God. Meetly, therefore, does a well-founded opinion except from certain laws that affect all others her whom a special grace protected, and a unique privilege raised to a most lofty dignity. How much the power of Christ may achieve is shown forth by the whole universe; how much his grace may accomplish is proved by Mary's integrity, an integrity as singular as it exceeds the power of nature.
>
> …Now if Christ wished to preserve untouched the purity of his Mother's virginity, why should he not likewise have willed to guard her from the corruption of the grave.
>
> …With these [and other previously mentioned similar] considerations in mind and guided by right reason, I am of the opinion that we must affirm that Mary is in Christ and with Christ; in Christ because she was gloriously taken up into the joys of eternity who here on earth had been favoured by grace beyond all others….And since it is in his power to prevent even one hair from falling from the head of his saints, it assuredly also belongs to him to preserve integrally her soul and her body.[5]

In terms of speculative theology the best case for the doctrine is indeed an argument along the following lines:

(1) The Assumption of the earthly bearer of the divine incarnation is fitting in the order of grace;
(2) The Assumption is possible by God's ordinance;
(3) God ordains what is fitting in the order of grace;
(4) Therefore, God ordained this;
(5) Whatever God ordains occurs;
(6) Therefore, the Assumption occurred.

This sort of deductive theological reasoning was much practised in the Middle Ages, though it is far less evident in recent times. Indeed its practitioners are now more likely to be found among Christian philosophers rather than among theologians. It is clear enough that (with some further explication of its premises) the argument I have sketched can be shown to be deductively valid. The problems, of course, are with the truth of the premises not with the inference from them. The arguments advanced by Anonymous are of the type *argumenta ex convenientia*, reasoning from agreed premises, and it might even have been reasonable for him to hope for a strict demonstration. The present context, however, is very different and every premise may expect to be challenged. Those concerning what is spiritually fitting and the scope of God's providence are strictly theological, and rest in turn on other claims (such as the precedent of Christ's resurrection). That concerning the possibility of the Assumption, however, reaches far into philosophical territory.

Here deep and problematic issues arise, and I hope it may assist discussion of this important but neglected subject if I isolate certain of these difficulties and then consider briefly how, if at all, they might be resolved. Although I shall not have space to do more than touch upon its implications, an examination of the Assumption doctrine is highly relevant to the important task of making sense of the more widely held Christian belief in the resurrection of the dead and the life of the world to come. It is perhaps of some significance that this is another topic in need of sharply focused examination.[6]

Identifying the challenges

Let me begin by emphasizing a distinction between two sets of problems implicit in the objections I have already noted. First, it may be claimed that there are no serious considerations in favour of belief in Mary's bodily Assumption. Second, and more importantly, it could be argued that what the doctrine asserts is incoherent or impossible. Clearly, if the latter were true then one need not try to respond to the former; just as the presumed impossibility of time-travel renders otiose any efforts designed to demonstrate how it can be achieved. On the other hand, if it can be shown that there is an interpretation of the

Assumption by which it is not impossible that it could have occurred, then it still remains to be established that there are compelling reasons to think the doctrine true, and to this end one would need to begin to counter the first set of historical and religious objections.

The task of arguing the case in favour of the Assumption is clearly substantial, even granting a general disposition to Christian faith. Given its theological content, historical inaccessibility and metaphysical oddity, it is not something one could hope to establish by ordinary means; and, of course, no-one has ever supposed otherwise. The most one could aim to achieve by reason alone, therefore, is a possibility; and in view of the asymmetry between the two sets of objections, it is appropriate that I should concentrate on the issues of meaning, coherence and feasibility.[7]

This said, it is also necessary to offer a response to the common complaint that the doctrine lacks any positive historical support. Polemical critics have occasionally suggested that the idea is in essence a medieval one; but no-one can seriously doubt that the broad tradition to which the definition gives particular expression is much more ancient. The earliest written references to the Assumption come in Eastern apocryphal texts some of which date from the late fourth century. The most significant of these, in respect of narrative and theological sophistication, are the following: Pseudo-John the Theologian, *The Dormition of the Holy Mother of God* (fifth century); Pseudo-Melito of Sardis, *The Passing of the Blessed Mary* (fifth century); Pseudo-Cyril of Jerusalem, *Discourse on Mary the Mother of God* (fifth/sixth century); Pseudo-Evodius of Rome, *Discourse on the Dormition of Mary* (sixth century); Theodosius of Alexandria, *Discourse on the Dormition* (sixth century); and Pseudo-Joseph of Arimathea, *The Passing of the Blessed Virgin Mary* (seventh century). There are further literary references in works attributed to St Andrew of Crete, to St John Damascene, and to St Modestus of Jerusalem; and in the seventh and eighth centuries belief in the Assumption of the Virgin was widespread in the Eastern and Western Churches.[8] Interestingly, unlike the other papally defined Marian dogma, that of the Immaculate Conception of Mary, there is no evidence of significant theological controversy about the Assumption or of medieval opposition to it.[9]

St John Damascene records that at the Council of Chalcedon in 451, Juvenal, bishop of Jerusalem, advised the Emperor Marcian and his wife Pulcheria that their wish to have the bodily remains of the Virgin Mary was impossible, for when her tomb had been opened at the request of the Apostle Thomas, it was found to be empty. The Apostles then collectively concluded that Mary's body had been transported to heaven by the will of her divine son. Mention of the conclusion being a collective one may be intended to suggest that it was inspired by the Holy Spirit, and that it was, perhaps, an early exercise of the collegial magisterium.

It is also reported in the 'Lives of the Popes' (*Liber Pontificalis*) that, at some point in the century following Chalcedon, the Emperor Mauritius (who died in 603) ordered that the feast of the Assumption should be kept on 15 August.

Since it refers to the event as an established solemnity, the instruction was evidently directed at a devotion already widely practised.

These various textual sources testify to a mainstream belief in the sixth century and perhaps in the preceding one. There may, however, be other material evidence indicating acceptance of the Assumption among churches in earlier centuries. It has long been accepted that the Roman Marian liturgies were developments of ones originating in the Gallican church, belief in the Assumption being earlier in Gaul than in Rome. The fact that Aquitanian Gaul abutted what is now Pyrenean Spain is significant in light of the case made by Dom Ernest Graf in the preface to his translation of the treatise on the Assumption from which I quoted earlier. He refers to a sarcophagus in the crypt of the Church of Santa Engracia at Saragossa in Aragón, on one side of which is depicted a scene which has been taken to be a representation of Mary's bodily Assumption. It shows a line of twelve men with a central female figure who is being drawn upwards by a hand stretched down to grasp her. The probable dating of the sarcophagus, which contains bones presumed to be those of local martyrs, and of the crypt itself, is 312/13, i.e. at the end of the Diocletian persecution around the time of the Edict of Milan.

'Saragossa' (Zaragoza) is a corruption of 'Caesar-augusta', the name given to the ancient settlement of Salduba by Octavius Augustus after the Romans captured it in the first century BCE. According to pious tradition, the Apostle James the Greater travelled to Saragossa while evangelizing among the people of Hispania, and there fell into depression about the ineffectiveness of his apostolic mission. Legend has it that while he was at prayer the Virgin Mary appeared to him and gave him a small wooden statue of herself together with a column of jasper, instructing him to erect a church in her honour. If the story were true this would have been the first church dedicated to Mary in the whole of Christendom. Certainly a church of 'Our Lady of the Pillar' (*Nuestra Señora del Pilar*) exists today on the site of earlier ones, and it houses a gothic wooden statue and marble pillar. Pious tradition also has it that after James's return to Jerusalem and his martyrdom there in 44 CE, several of his disciples took his body back to Spain for final burial in the place where several centuries later was built the Cathedral of Santiago de Compostella ('St James of the Starry Field').

Whatever the details of the early Christian presence in Spain, it is clearly very ancient, if not apostolic. And if the interpretation of the Saragossa tomb is sound it yields a date for a sophisticated illustration by Christians in Roman Spain in the early years of the fourth century. This would then imply a prior origin in at least the third century and also bring into view a possible source of the Marian liturgy of the Assumption associated with Gaul and later developed in Rome in place of an already existing Mass of the Blessed Virgin Mary. Indeed, the rites of Spain and of Gaul were so closely linked as to give rise to the expression 'Hispano-Gallican Rite'.

Assessing the evidence

Such considerations go some way towards establishing the antiquity of the conviction that the end of Mary's life was attended by a most remarkable event. It will be objected, however, that while these various observances and devotions may be testimony to the special status accorded to Mary in the early Church, they are in no way *evidence* for her Assumption. In support of such denials it is usually noted that no account of Mary's death is given in scripture, and there is no first- or second-century evidence from Ephesus, Jerusalem or Rome. Had it been widely believed that her death was followed by her Assumption it is most unlikely that such a miracle would not have been recorded, particularly as it might be thought to be further testimony to the divinity of Christ.

This objection can be generalized so as to maintain that Mary's absence from the greater part of the New Testament undermines the claims made on her behalf mostly by Catholic and Orthodox Christians concerning her immaculate conception, perpetual virginity, and suitability for veneration as the Mother of God. Certainly, references to Mary are few and far between. Following the Easter events her only appearance comes at Acts 1.14 (the gathering in the upper room after Christ's ascension leading up to Pentecost). It is far from obvious, however, what conclusions we are entitled to draw from the scriptural evidence, given that the announced purpose of the gospels is to present the life, teachings, death and resurrection of Jesus Christ. Likewise Acts and the epistles concern evangelization on behalf of the risen Messiah. Interestingly, Luther's insistence on *sola scriptura* did not prevent him from endorsing the Marian claims made above, and on the Assumption itself his attitude is agnostic rather than hostile. In his sermon on the feast of the Assumption he observes that 'There can be no doubt that the Virgin Mary is in heaven. How it happened we do not know.'

The absence from scripture of any mention of Mary's death and burial may even be interpreted as of some positive significance, as may the absence from tradition of any affirmation of her bodily corruption, and likewise the lack of any cult of Mary's bodily relics. Moreover, the point is not just that there is no tradition or cult of Mary's remains, but that, as Pius XII observes, drawing on a set of considerations assembled in the fifteenth century by St Bernardine of Siena, 'since the Church has never looked for the bodily relics of the Blessed Virgin, nor proposed them for the veneration of the people, we have a proof in the order of sensible experience' *(Munificentissimus Deus,* 33 [drawing from Bernardine's *In Assumptione B. Mariae Virginis, Sermo* 11]).

However one interprets what is and what is not said about Mary in scripture, it is inescapable that as the mother of Jesus Christ, the Word Incarnate, Mary occupies a unique position in the historical faith of Christians. There is a need to do full justice to this truth, taking into account the evidence of early devotion in both the Western and Eastern Church, as well as developments of the abstract theological argument sketched earlier. It may also be relevant to consider that, as an Anglican commentator observed of one apocryphal text: 'the belief [in the Assumption] was never founded on that story. The story was founded on the belief. The belief, which was universal, required a definite shape, and that shape at length it found.'[10] Likewise, Anonymous writes that 'Certain things have not been recorded at all by the Scripture though we rightly hold them to be true, inasmuch as our very sense of what is seemly leads us to the knowledge of them.'[11]

The various ecclesiological and doctrinal issues are complex and obviously require a better response than I am now able to give them. For the present, therefore, I can do no more than note the antiquity of the tradition in regard to Mary's life, her special role and her death, and observe that in defining the Assumption as a dogma of the Catholic Church, Pius XII was giving formal and magisterial expression to an ancient and widely held belief in an event taken to be a visible acknowledgement of Mary's special place in human history and a demonstration of God's love of her, as well as being a sign of the promise of the life to come. Such considerations are no less powerful now than they were in the period in which the first homilies and treatises on the Assumption were composed, and something of them will reappear later when I consider the meaning of talk of eternal life.

Metaphysical concerns

Having offered these observations in response to the first set of objections, I now turn to the task of considering the suggestion that the very idea of Mary's bodily Assumption is somehow an incoherent one; that it must be confused, since what it asserts could not possibly have happened. Anonymous acknowledges that what he has said of Mary is 'beyond the customary laws of nature'; and if the complaint were merely that such things do not happen, that bodies are not miraculously transported 'into the sky' but are subject to decay and decomposition, then the reply is simple. Absolutely no-one has ever believed that this was a 'natural' event; any more than anyone has supposed that Christ's resurrection, or the raising of Lazarus, or the cases of healing, or the multiplication of the loaves and fishes and so on, were events in the ordinary course of nature. To look for a *natural* explanation in all these cases is to reject their significance as *praeternatural* interventions by a divine agent in the service of a further *supernatural* (i.e. gracious) purpose.

I entirely agree with those who reject the picture of Christ as a spectacular wonder-worker, and who seek instead the moral-cum-spiritual point of his actions within a wider account of his ministry. It is important to insist, however, that the latter approach is not incompatible with the belief that among Christ's actions some were miraculous and involved interruptions in, and reversals of, ordinary causal processes. To insist that such things do not and cannot happen by nature is to refuse to allow any but natural events (so defined) a place in the broadest scheme of things. The concept of a miracle may be problematic, and many hold to a strictly naturalist view; but naturalism is a form of materialism which has no place for religious belief other than as a psychological phenomenon. The appropriate question, therefore, is not whether such a thing can occur in the ordinary course of nature (even if only exceptionally), but whether such a thing could happen at all. In short, is it logically and metaphysically possible that the Assumption could have occurred? With respect to the first question, everything we know about nature suggests not. As regards the second, however, the answers are by no means so clear.

One method of testing if some state of affairs is impossible is to consider whether any contradiction follows from the description of it. Constructing a triangular square is an impossible task because anything that has the property of being a triangle thereby, and necessarily, has the property of not being a square. The one property, by its very nature, excludes the other. Likewise, a philosophically minded objector to the Assumption doctrine might hope to show that under analysis the very description of it can be shown to involve some similar contradiction. We may grant that the state of affairs it envisages would involve the violation of natural causal processes, and since these are liable to be explained in terms of higher-order physical principles, it may be supposed that they too would have to have been transgressed. This supposition presents some difficulties inasmuch as it challenges a familiar nomological conception of the status of the patterns of cause and effect in nature. It is worth noting that this conception may itself be unwarranted,[12] but in any case unless one held the implausible view that such physical laws are logically necessary, it is not contradictory to hold that they might possibly be violated. Indeed, I cannot see that any logical contradiction can be derived from a literal interpretation of the doctrine itself.

To allow this much, however, does not fully answer the complaint that the doctrine is incoherent. An objector may concede the point so far as concerns logical possibility, yet insist that it is nevertheless inconceivable that such a thing could have happened because it is contrary to the metaphysical nature of things, a possibility not revealed by mere *conceptual* analysis.

According to the believer, when Mary had completed the course of her earthly life her 'body and soul' were transported from earth 'into heavenly glory'. What in this case, exactly, is it that the believer holds to have been assumed? Three possible replies suggest themselves:

(a) the *corpse* of Mary;
(b) the *living woman* Mary, who thereby was saved from death; or
(c) the *resurrected woman*, who had suffered death and then, at some point, was restored to life.[13]

There is little to commend the first option, involving as it does the continuing existence of a preserved corpse – even though Mary's soul might be held to be 'alive'.[14] The second and third replies are those offered by the 'immortalists' and 'mortalists', respectively. It might be supposed that in defining the dogma the Church of Rome would have made clear its position in this regard, but interestingly it did not, and the terms of the statement allow either interpretation. This ambiguity is not accidental, for the ancient discussions often disagree or are imprecise on the issue, and the matter was one of some dispute prior to the definition. Tradition, the liturgy and the pious belief of those who follow the devotion to Mary are somewhat ambiguous between the second and third replies. A case for immortalism can be made through connecting the Assumption dogma to that of the Immaculate Conception; arguing that death is an inherited effect of original sin, and since Mary was conceived free of this there was no intrinsic factor or internal cause (*causa ab intrinseco*) that would lead to her death. Interesting as this suggestion undoubtedly is, I am inclined to think that theological considerations, principally those involving the precedent established by Jesus' death and resurrection (the 'first fruits' of those that are to follow) lend further weight to the mortalist view. Nevertheless the issue remains one of contention among Mariologists and I shall not pursue the debate directly here.[15]

Indeed, from the point of view of the objection I am concerned with, all these replies are as one. For each holds that the Assumption involved the transportation of Mary *body and soul*. The complaint then is this: We are told where Mary departed from, viz., earth, but where was she transported to? The definition speaks of 'heavenly glory', and though strictly this is a state and not a place we can take the expression to refer to the glory that is enjoyed by a subject in heaven. But where is that? Or, if this seems too question-begging a formulation, we may ask how heaven is to be understood such that it can be true that two thousand years ago Mary was assumed into it. One recent French writer, Jacques Bur, assessing the significance of the dogma, repeats the claim that 'Mary was received body and soul into heavenly glory', and then continues:

> This sober affirmation does not go into theological explanations about the glorious condition of the human person and the nature of her transfigured body. The dogmatic definition avoids all spatial language.
>
> The Kingdom of God is not situated above, in heaven, in the physical sense, in some planet or star of the firmament. The glorified Virgin and her risen Son do not dwell in one or other of the galaxies. We speak of heavenly life in order to express the superiority of a glorious eternal life to our terrestrial and temporal life...
>
> [I]t must be remembered that the glorified body is not situated in a heaven that can be located, and the glorious resurrection of the body is not a reanimation of a corpse, like the resurrection of Lazarus. It is a supernatural transfiguration of the human body which cannot be the object of natural experience or of any scientific explanation.[16]

It is certainly true that the definition omits theological explanations, and that it avoids spatial descriptions of Mary's circumstance; however, the absence of theoretical speculation from the definition can hardly be an excuse for others to set aside the obvious issues that arise from its claims; and talk of bodies being 'assumed', 'glorified' and 'transfigured' calls for some interpretation, be it literal or metaphorical. Bur's observation that such terms are warranted by the greater glory of eternal life may be part of the story but it cannot be all of it; indeed it simply forces the question: In what mode may we hope to enjoy eternal life?

Traditionally, Christians have adopted two main views of the nature of 'the life of the world to come', according as to whether they subscribed to an Augustinian–Platonic or a Thomist–Aristotelian account of man's essential nature. Thus two ideas of heaven are available. According to the first, it is a non-spatial reality in which the disembodied and incorporeal souls of the departed join with other immaterial beings, most significantly, with God. (Bur's remarks suggest but fail to embrace this possibility.) According to the second, it is a future state of the universe following the bodily resurrection of the dead when men and women will live again as materially individuated human beings. Certainly both accounts face difficulties and scripture is not unambiguous between them. When, for example, in addressing the concerns of the Corinthians (1 Cor. 15), St Paul answers the question of future life by saying it will be that of a 'spiritual body' (*soma pneumatikon*), one is left wondering whether this is a spirit or a body.

What is relevant here is that on the first view heaven is not a location in physical space that a body could occupy. So wherever Mary (assumed *body and soul*) is, she is not there. According to the second tradition heaven is a place but it is, as the final article of the Creed says, 'the world to come', i.e. it is a condition of the spatio-temporal continuum to which we may look forward, but one that does not yet obtain. So once again it seems that Mary could hardly be there. In short, the substance of this objection is that whatever befell Mary she cannot have been assumed into heaven 'body and soul', but since no other possibility seems plausible we should be sceptical about the central claim of the dogma.

How then might a defender reply to this objection? All I wish to do here is sketch various possibilities and invite consideration of them. One option might be to relax the claim that Mary was assumed and exists body and soul, so as to allow that her body was destroyed but that she, the essential person, lives on as a disembodied soul. On this view Mary's present state is no different from that of others who have died in Christ, though it might be supposed that the manner of her body's destruction was extraordinary. Second, it could be argued that the resurrectionist conception of the future life maintained by Paul and endorsed by Aquinas is to be preferred,[17] but that it is enjoyed now by any post-mortem individual who has been resurrected to a new bodily life. Thus Mary's Assumption would have consisted in her being transported to some location where she joined or was subsequently joined by these others.[18] Once again it could be allowed that the mode of her passage to the 'other world' was out of the (extra)ordinary. Doubtless some will find the idea of heaven as a determinate place rather bizarre. Yet the notion is not a novel one, for many have thought of life everlasting as a form of bodily existence, though they have avoided the seeming absurdity of this prospect by projecting far into the future the time when it will obtain.

On the suggestion I am entertaining, however, this state of affairs has been in existence for some time. Hence it invites the question: Where is heaven? Some have proposed that the resurrection world is located in another space, thereby meeting the requirement that it be dimensive, so to allow its occupancy by material beings, while at the same time avoiding the extraordinary and counter-intuitive corollary that one could initiate a search for heaven in the sure know-ledge that it lies in some direction and at some distance from earth.[19] As it stands, however, this proposal is inadequate. Perhaps there could be a plurality of spaces without there being spatial relations between them, but this is not well suited to present purposes. There cannot be two spatio-temporal continua sub-ject to the same physical laws between which a body could pass. That is to say, if the latter conditions were fulfilled then what we would have are two regions of a single spatio-temporal system. Conversely, if the continua were distinct and unrelated then there could be no passage between them.

Even relaxing the condition of sameness of physical laws, there can be a passage of an object between two distinct spaces (such that it is one and the same object that was in the first space and is now in the second) only if they are causally related. Otherwise, we would have to say that the disappearance of an object from the first space and the appearance of a similar object in the second may provide the impression of continuity, and hence of identity, they neither constitute nor guarantee the reality of it. Here it will not do to say that God can do anything, for the issue is not the extent of a power, but rather of what it is that would have to be achieved. If one wishes to claim that Mary was assumed body and soul, from earth into heaven (conceived of as a place), it seems to follow that she is spatially located in some direction and at some distance from here; or at least that she is in a space causally continuous with this one; and hence that in principle physical contact could be achieved. Perhaps in years to come pious (hyper)space travellers might go in search of Mary, as in the Vic-torian period religious enthusiasts went in search of the Ark of the Covenant.

Religious meanings

I am wholly in sympathy with those who will find this last suggestion bizarre, and in some sense profane. Yet it appears to present the only possibility, given a literal interpretation of the dogma. This being so, some may prefer to articu-late their belief in the Assumption in the way I have outlined above: adopting a dualist conception of *post-mortem* existence, and placing Mary as a disembodied soul within it. But others will conclude from my result that it is so much the worse for any form of belief in the Assumption. For while the original objection does not demonstrate a metaphysical impossibility, the conclusions it leads to are quite absurd and serve to reveal the incoherence of the premise.

It may be supposed that anyone who takes the second view and maintains that the doctrine is strictly and literally false, must thereby hold that the beliefs associated with it are of no value and have no significant basis. Yet this latter does not necessarily follow. Consider, for example, the position elaborated in various works by D.Z. Phillips.[20] He has never been concerned with the issue of the Assumption, but he discusses the character of religious language in general, and has considered ways in which Christians are accustomed to speak of death, the soul and immortality in particular. On his account such modes of talking are not literally true but nevertheless they have real and moral importance, being concerned with the character and quality of this life.

Influenced by certain of Wittgenstein's insights into the character of meaning, Phillips wishes to say that expressions of belief in the immortality of the soul, the resurrection of the dead, or the life of the world to come are attempts to recognize a system of value that is independent of loss and fortune as it is assessed by one whose eyes are fixed on the goods the world has to offer. Such talk still has 'life' (in Wittgenstein's term) even though death may be the end, because it still has a use – this latter being to express a realization of, and a commitment to, value. To speak of a man's 'soul' is to observe the quality of his life; and to invoke images of eternity and of a condition removed from this one is to convey to others the belief that there is a way of living that is not solely concerned with the needs of the moment; a way of being *in* the world but not *of* it.

Likewise the religious conception of overcoming death is an expression of the possibility of ceasing to see ourselves as having a special importance. It is to affirm that there is a way of judging and of acting that does not have at its heart concern with self; but which is founded on a vision of the world as indifferent to one's own progress through it. To learn through this discovery what it means to judge fairly, to forgive completely, and to live unselfishly *is* to enjoy God's reality. On this account eternal life is not a state or a place into which one passes (whether or not one chooses to do so) at some point following death when the body ceases to function. Rather it is a way of being alive now, the only route to which is one involving the death of self. In short, the doctrine of the life of the world to come is essentially a metaphor pointing to a way of life in the world that is. Those who relish the paradoxical mode might well render this as the view that what the final article of the Creed asserts is *a false doctrine having a true meaning*.

Without detailing Phillips's thesis further, it should be apparent that whatever insights he has to offer into the value of the eternal perspective, his account of the metaphysics of the person and of immortality involves a rejection of what most Christians believe their faith to proclaim. What motivates his denial of such beliefs is, in part at least, his assessment of the difficulties facing any attempt to elaborate a coherent account of life after death. He is prepared to say that understood as involving an ontological claim it is false, if not meaningless, to hold that men are immortal, or that they will live again following the destruction of their bodies. Here I think his conclusions are unwarranted. Certainly there are significant problems in the way of the traditional interpretations of the hope for the life of the world to come: what are the identity and individuation conditions for incorporeal souls? what constitutes the continuing existence of one and the same soul over time? what makes two souls to be different? and so on. What these suggest, however, is a mystery in need of a solution, not an impossibility that demands abandonment of any form of belief in the life of the world to come.

Setting aside the important matter of whether it is possible to give a coherent and literal content to a future-life doctrine, I am in agreement with Phillips in so far as concerns the rest of his analysis of religious language. I take it to be a feature of such ways of talking that they are *value sensitive*. They express a range of views of how things are that is only available to one who can adopt a certain evaluative-cum-spiritual perspective on the world. To fully occupy such a position involves, for example, ceasing to deliberate solely on the basis of a concern to maximize material well-being or social fulfilment. For one who is able to live a religious life, in this sense, some course of action is not to be followed simply according to whether it may be judged as being in his or her best material interest. The latter mislocates the value of value; for ultimately the good commands us because it is good and not because it is a means to some non-ethical end. This is not at all to deny that a man's flourishing is good because it realizes his need for values; but it is to say that putting flesh on his bones or a spring in his step are at most partial constituents of a good life, the proper integration and completion of which lies in the attainment of spiritual values – ultimately entering the company of God.

By drawing attention to these features of its discourse, Phillips has made an important contribution to our understanding of religious belief; though, as I have implied, such an understanding is compatible with a commitment to the literal truth of various doctrines. Whether or not to accept the believer's claim is in part a matter for historical, theological and philosophical analysis; and here as elsewhere particular considerations have to be judged on their merits. There is no overarching argument by which one may pass with certainty from the character of certain ways of talking to discovery of how things are in reality. Phillips's account salvages meaning from contexts where, in his view, a belief is strictly false, or 'literally' meaningless; but the traditional conception of a doctrine as stating truly what is the case independently of our beliefs and concerns is not excluded simply because the other analysis is possible.

The meaning of Mary

Returning to the issue of the Assumption, the relevance of the foregoing should be clear. We might suppose that talk of Mary's being taken up 'body and soul into heavenly glory' serves to express the believer's devotion to the mother of Christ. Reflection upon her special place in the lattice-like structure of stories, ethical principles and patterns of action that forms his religion yields the thought that it is inconceivable that so central a figure should not be accorded great respect. Indeed, she might be expected to occupy a position of importance that places her below one figure alone – that of Christ himself, from where she could be held to act, again according to Catholic teaching, as a *mediatrix* between her son and the body of believers.

This latter theme echoes her earlier role as the willing vessel in whom Christ was conceived and through whom he entered the world; and it leads naturally to her presentation as a mother to all. The initial exemplification of this may be discerned in Christ's words from the cross: 'Woman, behold, your son' (John 19.26–8). Given this background of special respect, the idea that the end of Mary's life was marked by some extraordinary event seems altogether fitting; and it is hardly surprising, therefore, that from very early times the belief in Mary's Assumption developed through tradition, the liturgy and pious devotions. It expresses a commitment to a way of living that focuses upon the life and death of Christ. Yet Mary's is not merely reflected glory. It is due her in her own right, albeit that what is glorified is her role as Christ's mother. In saying that Mary was assumed, therefore, one may give expression to the belief that the means by which the living paradigm of goodness was given to the world could hardly have been other than good herself; and further, that such a person's value could not merely pass away and be lost to us forever, as is the way of material things, but instead continues to exist and to exert its influence upon us. To see the matter in this way interprets the dogma of the Assumption as stemming from the reification of the value of Mary's life.

I have no doubt that something such as I have outlined is correct and must needs form a part of a full discussion of this belief. Yet while this way of recovering meaning from religious discourse was introduced in connection with the view of one who might take the objections to the Assumption to constitute a refutation of it, I have also argued that this type of interpretation does not exclude the acceptance of the dogma as stating what is strictly and literally true. It is quite compatible with this, as it is with the dualist conception of Mary's glorification. Indeed, any plausible account must include considerations similar to those I have rehearsed concerning the place of Mary if it is to explain the development of the doctrine.

Towards a conclusion

I have tried to isolate and to clarify certain concerns one may have about the warrant for, and the coherence of, the doctrine as it is presented in the Roman definition. It is evident, I hope, that there is need for a clearer understanding of the truth of this important matter. To this end a review of certain theological concerns is called for. In particular, one might look to earlier proofs of the Assumption and to the scriptural basis of their premises, viz., the intimate relation between Mary and Jesus, the divine maternity, and Mary's co-redemption, whereby she (the new Eve) and Christ (the new Adam) are seen to have 'co-operated' in overcoming sin and death. Whether or not reflection on these claims may yield sound arguments in favour of the dogma, it remains a prior task to show the Assumption is possible, and that is a genuinely philosophical problem to which no very obvious or compelling solution has yet been provided.

The traditionally hostile reaction of Reformed theologians to Mariology is no doubt due in part to the suspicion of Catholic and Orthodox inclinations to invest Mary with some kind of semi-divine, or even super-human nature. Happily, recent studies of the positions of each side on other hitherto divisive matters have brought greater clarification and a degree of common understanding. This is testified to by the continuing work of the Anglican–Roman Catholic International Commission (ARCIC) and in French-speaking Europe by Le Groupe des Dombes, both of which have, in recent times, addressed themselves to the place of Mary in the life of the Christian Church. These and other developments (including Roman Catholic–Lutheran and Roman Catholic–Methodist discussions) suggest the prospect of a widening consensus that while any positive account of the issue of Mary's status must never stray from the truth that she was wholly of humankind, it is also a mistake not to acknowledge the uniqueness of her position in history, and this latter feature must be reflected in an understanding of the ancient belief in Mary's Immaculate Conception and Assumption[21] It is significant, therefore, that recent meetings of ARCIC have taken up the question of the meaning of the Marian dogmas, agreeing that 'Mary, the Mother of God incarnate, was prepared by divine grace to be the mother of our redeemer, by whom she was herself redeemed, and received into glory.'[22] Working through a similar agenda of topics, Le Groupe des Dombes has published two volumes on Mary. In these it recommends that while the Catholic Church 'must recognize that since the two dogmas do not belong to the common faith, they cannot oblige other Christians', Protestants should not 'consider them contrary to the Gospel or to faith, but regard them as free and legitimate consequences of Catholic understanding', and should themselves 'again accord to Mary her true place in the mind and faith of the Church'.[23]

Returning to the metaphysical dimension, and acknowledging Aquinas's insistence on the impoverished nature of disembodied human souls, and their ultimate need of resurrected embodiment,[24] I believe it is consistent with Mary's unique role that the mode of her present existence is of a different order to that of other separated subjects. Elevation to a higher realm of spiritual being, with a corresponding increase in powers, is a coherent supposition within the framework of Aquinas's ontology, and is one which might serve to satisfy the essence of the doctrine, viz., that Mary enjoys special proximity to Christ. The latter addresses the issue of Mary's relation to God and to eternity; there remains the other aspect of her special status, namely, her relation to the rest of humankind. Gnostic occultism apart, there has never been any suggestion that Mary was an angelic (i.e. spiritual) being who was accorded a phenomenal 'body'. The whole theology of Christ's incarnation depends on his having a human nature acquired in the process of conception within a human womb. Mary was a bodily being, and according to the dogma she retains some kind of 'bodily' standing.

In partial understanding of this, one might suppose that while her post-earthly mode of existence is spiritual it is nevertheless possible that she enjoys a 'spatial presence' thus far denied to others. Consider the fact that it is customary to interpret the claim that God is 'everywhere' not as holding that he is dimensively omnipresent but in terms of his capacity to act immediately through-out creation *as if* the world were his body – though it is not. Also, a traditional understanding of angelic apparitions has it that these spiritual creatures have powers to effect material appearances – though not their own 'appearings', for *ex hypothesi* they are outside the material order. It would not, I think, be philosophically or theologically problematic to suppose that Mary is specially elevated, and uniquely privileged, in being accorded immediate, though derived and dependent, powers of material agency, i.e. by having the ability to produce effects in the world directly, as if the localities in which that agency is mani-fested involved her bodily presence.

It should be clear, I hope, that while this present suggestion draws back towards the dualistic interpretation introduced above, it differs from it in pro-posing that the character of Mary's present state is unique among those who have died in Christ. Earlier I quoted Jacques Bur's gloss on the language of the dogmatic definition, where he writes that 'we speak of heavenly life in order to express the superiority of a glorious eternal life to our terrestrial and temporal life'. Were it the case that one who entered that state did so without there remaining behind a corrupted earthly body, and that this person was specially empowered to act as if a bodily being, albeit a transformed one, then we might speak of such a person as having entered into heavenly glory 'body and soul'; even though, in fact, this spiritual agent had no intrinsic bodily or spatial properties, or extrinsic ones of the usual, natural, sort.

With regard to this speculation, and more generally, there is much that remains to be discussed and I acknowledge that what has been proposed is not unproblematic. However, there is now the prospect that, in contrast to earlier times, the study of Mary's place and role may serve as the occasion for genuine understanding between believers in different (and in the same) traditions who are divided on what truths their faith proclaims. As has ever been the case since the completion of her earthly life, the study of Mary's special standing offers the prospect of a deeper comprehension of the Christian hope for the life of the world to come. It would be a welcome benefit if this understanding extended to the metaphysical dimensions of the dogma as well as comprehending its spiritual meaning.[25]

Notes

1 Defined as a dogma of the Roman Catholic Church by Pope Pius XII on 1 November 1950: 'We pronounce, declare, and define it to be a divinely revealed dogma: that the Immaculate Mother of God, the ever Virgin Mary, having completed the course of her earthly life, was assumed body and soul into heavenly glory': *Munificentissimus Deus*, in *Acta Apostolicae Sedis* (Rome: The Holy See, 1950), pp. 753–73. The dogma was reaffirmed by the Second Vatican Council in the Dogmatic Constitution *Lumen Gentium*: 'preserved free from all guilt of original sin, the Immaculate Virgin was taken up body and soul into heavenly glory, upon the completion of her earthly sojourn'. *The Documents of Vatican II*, ed. W.M. Abbott, SJ, trans. J. Gallagher (New York: Guild Press, 1966), p. 90.

2 In his *Panarion* ('medicine chest' of antidotes to poisonous heresies) written around 375, Epiphanius of Salamis cites two heresies concerning Mary: that of the 'Anticomarianites' who denied her perpetual virginity; and that of the 'Collyridians' who made sacrificial offerings to her of cakes or rolls (*kollyris* = small loaf). This second sect appears to have regarded Mary as a deity and to have connected her with a pre-Christian goddess/queen figure.

3 This is not to say that there is no interest in Marianism. Three (primarily) English-language periodicals are dedicated to the field. In order of creation they are: *Marian Studies* (founded in 1949 as the journal of the Mariological Society of America); *Marian Library Studies* (established in 1969 by the Marian Library of the University of Dayton, Ohio); and *Maria* (founded in 2000 and edited from the Centre for Marian Studies at the Margaret Beaufort Institute of Theology in Cambridge, UK). For the most part, however, these are concerned with ecclesiastical, liturgical and cultural aspects of Mary. In the area of dogmatic theology Karl Rahner's 'Fundamental Principle of Marian Theology' has only recently been translated into English by Sarah Jane Boss and Philip Endean, *Maria*, 1.1, pp. 86–122. See also Rahner, 'The Interpretation of the Dogma of the Assumption', in *Theological Investigations*, vol. 1 (London: Darton, Longman & Todd, 1961), pp. 215–27.

4 Michael Jordan, *Mary: The Unauthorized Biography* (London: Weidenfeld & Nicolson, 2001).

5 *An Eighth-Century Treatise on the Assumption of Our Lady*, translated from the Latin by Dom Ernest Graf (Buckfast: Buckfast Abbey Publications, 1950).

6 On this see John Haldane, 'The Examined Death and the Hope of the Future', in M. Baur (ed.), *Philosophical Theology: Reason and Theological Doctrine, Proceedings of the American Catholic Philosophical Association* 74, 2000 (New York: ACPA, 2001), pp. 245–57.

7 A full treatment of this important topic might be expected to include at least the following: (a) an account of the history of the doctrine, with particular emphasis on the circumstances of its origin; (b) a hermeneutical study relating the content of the dogma to other Christian claims; and (c) a philosophical analysis of the problems associated with the relevant forms of belief in post-mortem existence. While this is not the occasion to attempt such a major project, there is undoubted need of an extended discussion along the lines I have indicated. For material relevant to (a) and (b), see J.B. Carol (ed.), *Mariology* (Milwaukee: Bruce, 1957); G. Turner, 'Mythology and Marian Dogma', *New Blackfriars* 54 (July 1973), pp. 303–13; and G. Ashe, *The Virgin* (London: Palladin, 1977). It will be clear that the present essay is presented from a Roman Catholic perspective.

8 Extracts from some of these together with other relevant texts are gathered in P. Palmer, SJ, *Mary in the Documents of the Church* (London: Burns & Oates, 1953). See also J.K. Elliott, *The Apocryphal New Testament* (Oxford: Oxford University Press,

1993); and B.J. Daley (ed.), *On the Doctrine of Mary: Early Christian Homilies* (New York: Continuum, 1998). Translations of most of these texts can be found at the New Advent website, www.newadvent.org.

9 Though see Pseudo-Jerome, who expresses some reservation in his *Letter to Paula and Eustochius on the Assumption.* The *Decretum Gelasianum* of the fifth/sixth century condemns one Assumption discourse, but this is most likely to be on grounds of its Gnosticism.

10 J.B. Mozley, *Reminiscences of Oriel College and the Oxford Movement*, vol. 2, p. 368 – cited in Palmer, *Mary in the Documents of the Church*, p. 65.

11 See *An Eighth-Century Treatise on the Assumption of Our Lady*, p. 12.

12 See G.E.M. Anscombe, 'Causality and Determination', in her *Metaphysics and the Philosophy of Mind* (Oxford: Blackwell, 1981), pp. 133–47.

13 See K. Rahner 'The Interpretation of the Dogma of the Assumption', in *Theological Investigations*, vol. 1 (London: Darton, Longman & Todd, 1961), pp. 215–27.

14 It has been argued that fulfilment of the Christian hope for resurrection requires that deceased corpses be preserved (somewhere) to await resuscitation, and that the bodies we see disintegrating are *simulacra* put in their place by God. See P. Van Inwagen, 'The Possibility of Resurrection', *International Journal of the Philosophy of Religion* 9 (1978), pp. 114–21.

15 See L.P. Everett, 'Mary's Death and Bodily Assumption', in Carol, *Mariology*, pp. 461–92. This article seeks to interpret the meaning and scope of the definition of the dogma, and to review the considerations in its favour. It contains references to a great number of relevant writings bearing on this and other issues in Marian theology.

16 See Jacques Bur, *How to Understand the Virgin Mary* (New York: Continuum, 1994; translated by J. Bowden and M. Lydamore from the French *Pour Comprendre la Vierge Marie* (1992), p. 74.

17 I Corinthians 15:12–54, and Aquinas's commentary on this text; also *Summa Contra Gentiles*, 4, 79.

18 See again Van Inwagen, 'The Possibility of Resurrection'.

19 For variants of this idea, see: J. Hick, *Death and Eternal Life* (London: Collins, 1976), p. 279; A. Farrer, *Saving Belief* (London: Hodder, 1964), p. 145. The conceptual issues relating to the idea of plural spaces are helpfully discussed by A. Quinton, 'Spaces and Times', *Philosophy* 37 (1962).

20 Of particular interest here is D.Z. Phillips, *Death and Immortality* (London: Macmillan, 1970), esp. ch. 3, pp. 41–60. Similar points are made by Nicholas Lash in 'Eternal Life: Life After Death?', *Heythrop Journal* 19 (1978), pp. 271–84.

21 For an account of some of these interdenominational dialogues, see David Carter, 'Ecumenical Dialogue on Mary', *Maria* 2.1 (2001), pp. 105–20.

22 From material deriving from the ARCIC meeting held at Mississauga, Ontario, Canada, August–September 2001. For an account of Anglicanism's re-approach to the status of Mary written by a member of the Church of England Doctrine Commission, see Ann Loades, 'The Position of the Anglican Communion regarding the Trinity and Mary', *New Blackfriars* 82 967 (September 2001).

23 See *Marie dans le dessein de Dieu et la communion des saints*, 2 vols: *Dans l'histoire et l'Écriture* (1997); *Controverse et conversion* (1998) (Paris: Bayard Editions/Centurion).

24 Commentary on 1 Corinthians 15. For reinforcement of this view, see the Wittgensteinian considerations adduced by P.T. Geach in 'Immortality'; see *God and the Soul* (London: Routledge & Kegan Paul, 1969), reprinted as 'What Must Be True of Me if I Survive My Death?' in B. Davies (ed.), *Philosophy of Religion: A Guide and Anthology* (Oxford: Oxford University Press, 2000).

25 A version of this article was delivered as the 2001–2 Annual Philosophy–Theology Lecture at Creighton University, Omaha, Nebraska. The event was jointly sponsored by the Center for the Study of Religion and Society and the Departments of Philosophy and Theology. I am grateful to members of the audience for their observations and questions, and especially to Ronald A. Simkins, Director of the CSRS, and Patrick Murray and Jeanne A. Schuler of the Department of Philosophy for generous hospitality and helpful conversation. The present text was completed while holding the Royden Davis Chair of Humanities at Georgetown University, Washington, DC. I am grateful to the University and to the Department of Philosophy for the appointment and the opportunities it provided.

Part III

Ethics and politics

Chapter 8

Medieval and Renaissance ethics

The Human will is subject to three orders. Firstly, to the order of its own reason, secondly to the orders of human government, be it spiritual or temporal, and thirdly, it is subject to the universal order of Divine rule.

St Thomas Aquinas, *Summa Theologiae*, Ia IIae, q8, aı

Introduction

The central timespan covered in this chapter extends from the eleventh to the sixteenth centuries – a period of half a millennium of considerable philosophical activity only matched in its variety and vigour by the modern and contemporary periods. Yet, somewhat surprisingly, between the end of the Renaissance and the middle of the twentieth century the philosophy of those five hundred years was largely forgotten. Indeed, it is only in the last twenty or so years that philosophers in the English-speaking world have begun to appreciate the intrinsic quality of medieval and Renaissance thought, and its relevance for the continuing effort to understand the central issues in philosophy.

Part of the difficulty in evaluating the philosophy of the Middle Ages, and to a lesser extent that of the Renaissance, is that it is couched in a largely unfamiliar theoretical vocabulary. This is connected with the nature of *scholasticism* – the dominant philosophical tradition – which was uncompromisingly technical. A further problem for understanding and assessing the argument and conclusions presented by authors of these periods arises from the very different assumptions about the nature of the universe and the situation of mankind within it that they and we are apt to make.

In order, then, to make sense of the patterns of ethical thought which developed through the medieval and Renaissance periods, it is necessary to begin with an account of the historical and philosophical background to the emergence of scholasticism towards the end of the eleventh century. Following that, I shall discuss some of the ideas and disputes of the one-hundred-year period falling roughly between the middle of the thirteenth and that of the fourteenth century. This was without doubt the high point of medieval thought, a period in which intellectual seeds were sown and entire philosophical gardens grew up, flourished and bloomed. The authors of the great works of this era were members of two religious orders – the *Dominicans* and the *Franciscans* – whose activity determined much of the character of a fruitful age in the history of Western culture.

Following upon this, however, was a period of relative infertility. Significantly, not a single historically important philosopher was born in the fourteenth century. (The best candidate for this status, namely John Wyclif (1320–84), was too much a theologian and churchman to qualify.) Yet by its close, new growth had begun which in due course produced several new species of ideas and transformations of older ones. Discussion of this period will lead on to an examination of the main elements in Renaissance ethics, which can be divided into two traditions: first that of the late scholastics, who elaborated and synthesized the products of the geniuses born in the thirteenth century, and second that of the humanists who looked back to classical antiquity and forward to a secularized political future.

From the Church Fathers to the scholastics

The earliest post-classical origins of medieval philosophy lie in the patristic period of Christianity, in the writings of the Church Fathers. These works were produced between the second and fifth centuries by religious teachers belonging to the Eastern and Western Churches. The aim of these theological authors was to interpret Judaeo-Christian scriptures and traditions with the assistance of ideas derived from Greek and Roman philosophy. Although the Fathers were not themselves speculative thinkers, they introduced into their theistic ethics notions of considerable importance which recur throughout medieval and Renaissance philosophy.

The first of these, which appears in the writings of Clement of Alexandria (150–215) and in subsequent authors, is the idea that, by the exercise of natural reason, some of the philosophers of antiquity had arrived at conclusions concerning the kind of life fitting for human beings which were coincident with parts of Christian moral teaching. This concurrence was later to become a theme in the defence of philosophy, and of the study of pagan writers, that scholastics would offer to the charge that their inquiries endangered faith. The particular discovery of Greek philosophy which interested the Fathers was that of practical reasoning (*ratio practica*) or 'right reason' (*recta ratio* in the Latin, *orthos logos* in the Greek). Both Plato and Aristotle had argued that there is a faculty of rational judgement concerned with choosing the right way of acting. Excellence in the exercise of this power constitutes the intellectual virtue of practical wisdom – *phronesis* (Latin: *prudentia*) – and conduct in accord with its deliverances is moral virtue.

Generally there was little concern with the philosophical arguments supporting these suggestions. The points of interest were rather that some of the conclusions about how to live concurred with religious teachings derived from revelation, and, implicit in this, that an alternative model of moral knowledge might be available. In addition to knowing how to act by having received public instruction, it might be that an individual could think his own way towards moral rectitude. This possibility would relieve the difficulty with the idea of public revelation: that, through no fault of their own, those who have not received it directly, or had it communicated to them, are deprived of the means of salvation. For if the pagans could reason their way to virtue, then perhaps all men have the same innate resource to lead good lives. This indeed became a model of *universal salvific grace*; that is, of the idea that each man is given sufficient means for his salvation – though, of course, he may choose not to follow the route this grace prescribes.

Notice, however, that the idea of an innate power of moral knowledge is open to at least two interpretations. On the first, men are endowed with a capacity for rational thought, and starting from certain premises, knowledge of which is not dependent on revelation, they can arrive at conclusions about right conduct. On the second interpretation, the relevant endowment is one of a faculty of moral sense by which men can simply intuit what it is right or wrong to do. Borrowing from the vocabulary of later theories it may be useful to describe these views as 'rationalist' and 'intuitionist', respectively.

Following the introduction of the term by St Jerome (347–420), writers of the earlier and later Middle Ages referred to the innate power of distinguishing good from evil as *synderesis*. Jerome himself describes this as the 'spark of conscience...by which we discern that we sin', but it later became usual to reserve the term 'conscience' (*conscientia*) for the ability to distinguish good from bad at the level of particular actions. In the thirteenth century, for example, Aquinas (1224–74) argues that the first principle of thought about conduct is that good is to be done and pursued and evil avoided. This '*synderesis* rule' is, he maintains, a self-evident principle, such that anyone who understands it must assent to its truth. What it concerns, however, is not the rightness or wrongness of this or that particular action, but rather the polarity of the axis on which conduct lies and the intrinsic attraction of one pole and repulsion of the other. Even granting the truth of the principle, however, knowledge of it will not suffice to guide one through life without a more specific capacity to distinguish good from bad courses of action, and it is this capacity which Aquinas follows tradition in identifying with *conscientia*. Furthermore, given his distinctly rationalistic account of moral knowledge (which I discuss below) it should come as no surprise to learn that he regards conscience as equivalent to practical or 'right' reason (*recta ratio*). In the pre-scholastic period, however, the tendency was to take an intuitionist view of moral thinking. On this account, versions of which are to be found in the writings of St Jerome and St Augustine (354–430), conscience is an innate faculty which reveals God's moral law as this is inscribed in men's souls. Something of this idea persists today in contemporary Christian discussions which (adapting the sense analogy) speak of conscience as if it were the mind's 'inner ear' by which one may attend to the word of God.

In Augustine's moral theology this account of conscience is connected to a line of thinking which constitutes the second major contribution from earlier tradition to later medieval moral philosophy. This is the idea of moral purification as resulting in a 'flight of the soul' away from the world. The more distant origins of this notion lie in Plato's *Republic* and in equally ancient mystical traditions. It features in the writings of Plotinus (204–69) but was introduced into patristic thought by his Christian fellow student Origen (185–255). Indeed it was a widely held doctrine, advanced in one form or another by St Gregory of Nyssa (335–95), Dionysius the pseudo-Areopagite (fifth century) and John Scotus Eriugena (810–77), and it was taken up again with some enthusiasm in the Renaissance period by Mirandola (1463–94) and other Neoplatonists. According to Augustine, God endows each man with a conscience whereby he may know the moral law. However, this knowledge is not sufficient for virtue, which requires that the will should also be turned towards the good. In order to achieve this benevolent orientation God illuminates the soul by a revelation of his own goodness, and this induces virtue as the soul becomes charged with love for God's perfection and strives to be united with him. This psychology of grace is less prosaically expressed by Augustine in the claim that love draws a soul to God as weight draws a body to the earth; but, of course, since God is 'above' all things, the direction of pull is upwards and so the movement effected by grace becomes a flight of the soul away from the world.

A further issue raised by this theory of moral knowledge concerns the nature of that which conscience reveals. Earlier it was said that conscience discloses the moral law, but this latter notion is in turn open to at least two interpretations, both of which influenced medieval and Renaissance thought. The expression 'law' translates the Latin word *ius*, which may mean either order or ordinance, systematic regularity or prescribed regulation. Hence the claim that conscience is a form of knowledge of the moral law could be read as holding that it is a means of discerning states of affairs and properties which constitute moral facts and values, just as science is a method for discovering those facts which are constitutive of the laws of physics, for instance. Alternatively, the claim could be interpreted as maintaining that conscience is a way of coming to know what God commands, much as consulting a textbook may be a way of discovering the content of a nation's law.

Writers of classical antiquity, of the patristic period and of the early and later Middle Ages often use the expression 'natural law' (*ius naturale*) to refer to whatever principles are taken to govern human conduct, other than those which originate in human legislation or positive law (*ius positivum*). To the modern reader the expression 'natural law' probably suggests the idea of an objective moral order independent of the mind or will or any being. It should be clear, however, that for those living in these earlier periods it might signify a number of distinct ideas. The common element is the contrast with human legislation, but beyond that lie differences. It was held by some that natural law pertains to the ordered structure of the world into which each kind of thing fits and by reference to which a proper pattern of its development may be determined. On this view, the idea that natural law yields *prescriptions* for human conduct is a metaphorical way of referring to preconditions of man's natural development, but it has no implication that their prescriptivity issues from the will of a legislator. They are not in that sense *commands*. According to a second view, however, natural law is precisely the set of rules legislated by God and promulgated to mankind via the presentation of the decalogue to Moses, and via the revelation afforded to individuals through their exercise of conscience.

The first of these views partly originates in the pre-Socratic period of Greek philosophy and was known to authors of the early Middle Ages in the form of the Stoic doctrine that all processes are governed by cosmic reason (*logos*), and that law (*nomos*) is what this universal rational principle dictates concerning the various spheres of activity. This idea was usually combined with two others which, taken together, yielded a more theologically acceptable account of natural law as metaphysical order. The first of these additional notions was the Platonic theory that individual entities and characteristics are instances of ideal forms (*eide*), and are better or worse of their kind to the extent that they approximate to, or deviate from, these perfect paradigms. The second related notion derived from patristic exegeses of Chapter 1 of Genesis, which suggested that in creating the world God gave material instantiation to a plan which preexisted as an eternal idea (*ratio aeterna*) in his mind. (This notion, sometimes referred to as 'divine exemplarism', was undoubtedly influenced by the previously mentioned element of Plato's metaphysics and by the creation myth he presents in the dialogue *Timaeus*, in which the supreme God or Maker (*demiurge*) is attributed with the desire to create a world that embodies the forms.) Put together, these ideas provided an account of natural law as the proper pattern of activity in accord with the rational order of creation.

It is important to appreciate that in the foregoing account the role of God in relation to the moral law is an indirect one. An action is good because fitting, given the nature of things – a nature owing to God's design and manufacture. But according to the second view mentioned above, God's role is wholly direct, for the natural law is nothing other than a body of legislation willed into existence by God for the governance of human affairs. And this law need have no relation to the design of the created world.

In the thirteenth century there was a major dispute between proponents of these two views of the universal moral law. I shall return to this in the next section. For now, however, it is enough to point out that there are further complexities in the structure of pre-scholastic theories which were transmitted to later periods. For example, as was previously noted, it was held by some that the innate capacity to determine the requirements on conduct is the ability to discover the proper nature of things, most centrally of man himself, and to reason to conclusions about how to perfect these natures. For others, while the truths discovered by the exercise of *synderesis* and *conscientia* are indeed those pertaining to self-perfection, their discovery is not a matter of empirical investigation and practical reasoning but simply apprehension of prescriptions pronounced to the soul by God. (In a famous passage in his work *On the Trinity*, Augustine writes that 'men see the moral rules written in the book of light which is called Truth, from which all other laws are copied' (*De Trinitate*, 14, 15, 21).) For others yet, the form of discovery is of this latter style, but what is apprehended is simply the ungrounded will of God expressed in commands to act or to refrain from action, and not guidance offered in accord with a law of nature.

So much for the developing complexity of pre-scholastic thought about the source of morality. There was also a variety of views concerning the objects of moral assesment, i.e. those features which are properly judged to be right or wrong. St Augustine had claimed that merit only attaches to actions which conform to God's moral law if they are performed with the appropriate motive, i.e. a love of God and a wish to perfect oneself so as to draw closer to him. As he puts it: 'To live well is nothing other than to love God with all one's heart, soul and mind' (*De Moribus Ecclesiae Catholicae*, I, 25, 46). This introduces a focus on the state of mind of the agent, rather than on the performance as such, and introduces the possibility that while two people could perform actions of the same type, e.g. nursing the sick, only one would do something creditable, inasmuch as his motive was *love* whereas that of the other was *Pharisaism*, i.e. the self-righteous desire to be thought well of.

Other authors, drawing upon the parable(s) of the talents (Matt. 25) or pounds (Luke 19), tended to regard merit as appropriate to the achievements or consequences of conduct. The most wide-ranging and exacting account of moral assessment, however, held that for an action to be good, everything about it – its type, its motive and its outcome – must be good, and that should just one of these be bad, then the action is bad and the agent culpable. This strict doctrine seems to have originated in a work written in the fourth or fifth century by Dionysius the Areopagite entitled *On the Divine Names* (*De divinis nominibus*). This author's writings, known collectively as the *Corpus Dionysiacum*, were of great influence from the sixth century onwards into the Renaissance. Indeed, he was the main channel through which Platonic and Neoplatonic ideas passed from the Greek into the Christian world. Besides being one of the main sources of the 'flight of the soul' theological psychology and of the strict doctrine of moral assessment mentioned above, he advanced the view (as did Augustine) that evil is nothing other than the privation of good, just as sickness may be thought of not as a distinct independent condition but merely as the absence of health. This idea, and the doctrine about what is required for an action to be good, were endorsed and elaborated by Aquinas in the thirteenth century and have remained as part of the general body of Thomist teaching. The considerable respect accorded the *Corpus Dionysiacum* throughout the Middle Ages and the Renaissance was due in part to its value as a source of Platonic philosophy but also because of a mistaken belief about its authorship. The writer claims to have been a witness to events recorded in the New

Testament and uses the pseudonym 'Dionysius the Presbyter', from which he came to be identified with an Athenian converted by St Paul. However, from internal evidence, it has long been generally agreed that these writings were produced around the year 500.

Before proceeding to consider the central period of scholasticism, it is appropriate to give some rough idea of relevant historical developments within the preceding centuries. This history is in effect that of the fall and re-establishment, as a Christian institution, of the Roman Empire. In the fifth century the Western Roman Empire succumbed to Teutonic invasions from the north, and when the Eastern Roman Empire, based on Byzantium, succeeded in the sixth century in re-establishing a hegemony in the Mediterranean, it was in turn attacked by the Arabs in the east and the south. Among the damage wrought by these invasions was the destruction of the Roman educational system which, through schools located in the main cities, had provided administrators for the Empire. As was the case in Britain in the twentieth century, an education suited to the staffing needs of a civil service also produced men of wide culture with something of a philosophical cast of mind. Following the invasions, however, such centres of education as remained or were created were attached to monasteries situated in isolated rural areas. In the very changed circumstances, the aim of these monastic schools became the more limited one of preserving the culture of the past.

In the year 800, Charlemagne was crowned first Holy Roman Emperor, and for a period following this there was something of a revival of the imperial idea and associated with it a cultural renaissance. Indeed the only original Western philosopher writing between Boethius (475–525) and St Anselm (1033–1109), namely Eriugena, was head of the Palace school founded at Charlemagne's court. A series of wars, political conflicts and disputes beween the Church and the Empire led by stages to the recovery of Christendom and the victory of the Papacy over the Emperor, marked by Pope Gregory VII's reforms of the Church, begun in 1073, and by the Emperor Henry IV doing penance before the Pope at Canossa in 1077.

The golden age of scholasticism

During the patristic and early medieval periods, educated discussion of morality was of an entirely theological sort. It was either concerned with *normative* questions about which virtues to cultivate, what actions to avoid and what goals to aim for, or else it set out the *general structure* of morality, indicating, for example, its relation to natural processes or to revealed doctrine. By and large, however, it was neither systematic nor interested in what are now characterized as *meta-ethical* issues; that is, issues about the content and logical character of moral concepts. In the eleventh and twelfth centuries this began to change, as there evolved the scholastic method of enquiry.

The 'father' of scholasticism was St Anselm, Archbishop of Canterbury and now best known as the originator of the 'ontological proof' of the existence of

God. In the sixth century, Boethius had held that some propositions, including some moral principles, are intuitively self-evident. He also favoured a more rigorous style of reasoning than was then common. In Anselm's writings these two factors come togeher to yield a logically ordered discussion proceeding from 'axioms' to implied conclusions. He applied this method of systematic and discursive reasoning to a range of theological issues, and in citing authority (*auctoritas*), in the form of quotations from scripture or patristic writings, was concerned to use it as a means of proceeding towards additional conclusions. This innovative attitude is expressed in a passage, the concluding words of which compose the motto of scholasticism. He writes: 'It seems to me to show negligence if after we have become established in the Faith we do not strive *to understand what we believe*' (*Cur Deus Homo*, i, 2).

In his moral theory Anselm is influenced by Augustine's psychology, and adopts the view that grace induces in the soul a disposition to move towards the good (*affectio justitiae*) by conforming its actions to the will of God. The importance of the will is also emphasized by Abelard (1079–1142). The August-inian tendency to voluntarism (from the Latin: *voluntas*, meaning 'will') is pursued in relation to both the subject and the criterion of goodness. As regards the latter the standard is, as mentioned, conformity to the divine will. In regard to the former, Abelard insists that in themselves actions are morally neutral. Moreover, he suggests that desires or inclinations are likewise not good or bad as such. The appropriate object of moral assessment is the agent's *intention*. Vice is nothing other than knowledgeable consent to sin, that is to action performed in the knowledge of its disobedience to God's commands. As he writes: 'Defect, then, is whereby we are...inclined to consent to what we ought not to do....What is that consent but to despise God and to violate His laws?' And later in the same work he illustrates how vice lies not in desire but in consent. The example is of a man who in seeing a woman has his 'concupiscence aroused; his mind enticed by fleshly lust and stirred to base desire but who yet bridles this lascivious longing by the power of temperance' (*Scito Teipsum*, ch. 2), and so reaps the reward of obeying God's commandment (presumably the ninth: Thou shalt not covet thy neighbour's wife).

This view, shared by Anselm and Abelard (and later adopted in part or in whole by Henry of Ghent (1217–93), Duns Scotus (1266–1308), William of Ockham (1290–1350) and in the Renaissance by Francisco Suarez (1548–1617) has certain potentially troublesome implications. If virtue consists in rightness of intention, and this in turn is analysed in terms of consent to God's commandments (conceived of under *that* description, i.e. as 'conduct com-manded by God'), then a problem arises if the agent does not know what God commands, or that he commands anything, or indeed that there is even a God to issue commands. Certainly if one lacks this knowledge then one cannot be sinful or vicious (i.e. vice-filled), since in that circumstance one cannot know-ingly intend to breach a divine commandment. By the same token, however, neither can one be virtuous, not knowing to what to give consent. And if virtue is necessary for salvation then the ignorant are in trouble, albeit perhaps a less damnable predicament than that facing those who know God's law and intend to contravene it. As regards the first of these implications, Abelard took it to show that those who (in ignorance) persecuted and crucified Christ committed no sin – an opinion apparently not shared by his contemporaries, for it was condemned at the Council of Sens in 1141. In connection with the second implication, he offers an unconvincing version of the suggestion discussed earlier, that those existing outside the scope of the Christian revelation might yet be virtuous inasmuch as they conform their intentions to the content of the moral law as this is revealed to reason.

The second problem facing the Anselm/Abelard view arises from the location of moral character in the agent's intentions rather than in the type of actions he performs. If one believes that it is publicly determinable what kind of action each of several people has performed but that it is not determinable what intention each has, then, if intention is the locus of moral quality, one is not in a position to say whether they have all acted virtuously even if one somehow knows that one of them has. For Abelard this problem is overcome by the claim that God can 'see' into the hearts of men, though they are unobservable to others. That possibility, however, will be of little comfort to those mortals who may have a responsibility to assess moral character, which in any event we do often take to be manifest in publicly observable events. This latter presumption suggests a different solution: to deny that agents' intentions are necessarily private objects and to allow that they are sometimes open to assessment.

The greatest of medieval and scholastic philosophers, St Thomas Aquinas, was born eighty years after the death of Abelard. Only those who have made the effort to comprehend the philosophy of Aquinas can properly appreciate the extent of his system and the power of his mind. Albertus Magnus (1206–80) – St Albert the Great – his sometime teacher and patron, said of the young St Thomas, who had acquired the nickname 'the dumb ox' on account of his taciturnity and stout figure, that 'he will eventually bellow so loudly in his teaching that it will resound throughout the whole world'. At least by the standard this suggests, viz. renown, there can be no doubt that Aquinas is the greatest of the scholastics and perhaps of all philosophers born between Aristotle and Descartes.

The Thomistic genius lay in the capacity to see how Greek thought and Catholic doctrine might be synthesized into a Christian philosophy. So far as this vision concerned ethics, it took the form of showing that the previously noted parallels between ideas of virtue originating in the philosophy of classical antiquity and those recurrent within Christian thought could be developed so as to give a rational foundation to ethics and thereby demonstrate an account of true virtue which could be compelling to any intelligent human being. The scale of St Thomas's synthesis of ethics and moral theology is vast. It covers both theoretical and normative issues and is spread through many texts. Fifteen volumes of the current Blackfriars edition of the *Summa Theologiae* and many other independent commentaries and treatises are concerned with ethics and value in one form or another. Given the extent of this corpus, therefore, it would be absurd to do other than identify the essence of the theory.

Something of Aquinas's views has already been indicated, including the fact that he held a rationalistic account of moral thinking – regarding the 'natural law' as discoverable by the exercise of 'right reason'. In arguing for this he was greatly assisted by the recent availability in the Christian West of the ethical writings of Aristotle. Drawing on these he was able to develop a form of teleological eudaimonism, according to which right action is conduct that either tends to promote or actually realizes human flourishing. On this view there is a distinctive and essential human nature, and associated with it a set of values constituting excellence in the conduct of life. Hence, virtues are those habits of action which are conducive to the fulfilment of an agent's rational nature.

To speak of the 'natural law' is thus to refer to that part of the general order of things which involves humankind and its progress to perfection. This law is embodied in natural human tendencies, such as the inclinations to preserve one's life, to mate and rear children, to co-operate with others in society, and so on. In addition to this empirical source of moral values and requirements there is the 'law of God' promulgated to mankind via the Mosaic law and other parts of the divine revelation. However, for Aquinas this is not a source of alternative or additional commandments, but rather a supplementary source of those pre-scriptions conformity with which is necessary for achieving well-being. What Christian theology adds to the basically Aristotelian moral theory is first, super-natural assistance, through revelation and grace, and second, a supernatural transformation of the goal of virtue, from the state conceived of by Aristotle as flourishing (*eudaimonia*) to that of blessedness (*beatitudo*) consisting of eternal union with God.

In giving due place to the religious dimension of morality while combining it with a broadly rationalist theory, Aquinas trod a path between two groups of contemporary philosophers: the Latin Averroists and the Franciscan voluntarists. The former, of whom the most important was Siger of Brabant (1240–84), maintained an unqualifiedly naturalistic version of Aristotelian eudaimonism. The latter, by contrast, challenged the idea that divine law is in effect a 'users' guide' to human life, and maintained that it is an independent source of obliga-tion rooted in God's legislative will. This revival of Augustinian thought began in St Thomas's lifetime in works of a mystical inclination by St Bonaventure (1217–74), Ramón Lull (1235–1315) and Meister Eckhardt (1260–1327) which emphasized divine illumination and the turning of the soul's will to God. More philosophically significant, however, were the writings of the two greatest Franciscan thinkers of this period, namely, Duns Scotus and William of Ockham.

Until recently it was common to regard both men (but especially Ockham) as espousing straightforward versions of theistic voluntarism, i.e. the view that an action is good if and only if God commands or approves of it. However, the situation is not so simple. Scotus holds much in common with the 'right reason' theory of Aquinas but he accords two special roles to the will. On the one hand, the object of moral assessment is always an act of will, and on the other, God is able to invest moral prescriptions with the additional status of absolute obligations by willing that they be obeyed (*Opus Oxoniense*, III).

Ockham moves further towards locating the source of morality in the divine will by arguing that since God is omnipotent he can do anything save the logically impossible. The criterion of logical impossibility is contradiction. So, if a statement is not a contradiction, then the situation it describes is at least logically possible and hence is such as can be brought about by God. But a moral statement such as 'theft is permissible' is not contradictory – even if it is false. Accordingly, if God is omnipotent then it must be possible for him to make it the case that theft is permissible without this being achieved by changing any other logically independent fact of the matter. One, and perhaps the only, way in which this could be achieved would be if permissibility, requirement and prohibition are constituted simply by God's attitudes. That is, if the moral character of an action is an immediate logical consequence of God's allowing, commanding or prohibiting it. In fact, Ockham was willing to allow that much of what we hold to be right and wrong is so for reasons presented by natural law theory. But he also saw, like Scotus, that such a theory has some difficulty accounting for the legalistic character of some moral requirements, and he further held that belief in the absolute omnipotence of God must imply that the moral order could be reversed by nothing other than God's willing it to be so (*Reportatio*, IV, q9).

Renaissance pluralism and the decline of scholasticism

Ockham was the last philosopher of the golden age of medieval scholasticism. In the century following his death the intellectual and political worlds were transformed by the rise of science and the decline of the Church of Rome. Once again Western Europe became subject to political and religious warfare, but in regard to the latter the source of attack was not, as before, an alien faith; rather it came from within the Christian Church, from scandalized or disaffected clergy and other members of the religious orders. It is not altogether surprising, therefore, that the leaders of the Reformation and those of the new natural science were both apt to set aside a philosophical tradition which had by then come to be closely associated with the old order.

This said, the movement to develop Aristotle's ethical theory did not come to a halt. Rather, it split into two directions and proceeded onwards for some while longer. The division corresponded to secular and religious interests and was also largely geographical. In Italy a group of writers and natural scientists located in and around Padua looked back to the Latin Averroists of two hundred years before, and beyond them to Aristotle himself, as sources for a wholly naturalistic ethical theory consonant with their wider scientific worldview. The most renowned of this otherwise little-known group was Pietro Pomponazzi (1462–1525), who, given his philosophical materialism, sceptical epistemology and quasi-utilitarian ethical theory, would no doubt find the contemporary philosophical environment rather congenial.

Meanwhile in the Iberian peninsula the Thomist tradition persisted among a group of Catholic neo-scholastics. Much of their work consisted of expounding and commenting upon the writings of Aquinas and Aristotle, but they also contributed something to the tradition by attempting to relate it to the changed circumstances. The Dominican Francisco de Vitoria (1480–1546), for example, considered the legitimacy of using violence in defence of society, and thereby advanced the development of 'just war' doctrine. The same issue also formed part of the normative ethics proposed by the Jesuit Francisco Suarez. He was probably the most distinguished of all the Iberian Thomists, though while he was a major commentator on Aquinas his ambitions went far beyond re-presenting the 'Angelic Doctor's' teachings. His own synthesis of scholasticism also drew from the metaphysical ideas of Ockham, and this led to his espousing a view in which the will of the agent and that of God play a large part in determining the moral value of conduct. Perhaps the main historical significance of Suarez's writings, however, is as the channel through which Thomist moral philosophy was made available throughout Europe to those who had not been educated in the scholastic tradition, including those who, like Hugo Grotius (1583–1645), were deeply hostile to its particular religious associations but who nonetheless, often unknowingly, developed moral views similar of those of the Catholic scholastics. Much closer in theological outlook to Suarez, but living in isolation from Thomist circles, was his English contemporary Richard Hooker (1553–1600) who drew upon the natural law theory presented by Aquinas to develop an account of the relation between natural and revealed law. So great, indeed, was the influence of Thomist ideas upon Hooker in his writing of *The Laws of Ecclesiastical Polity* that he came to be known as the 'Anglican Aquinas'.

Several factors contributed to the post-medieval reaction against scholasticism. Besides the rise of empirical science and the fragmentation of the Universal Church, there was a movement within philosophy against Aristotelianism and in favour of a return to Platonic doctrines. The latter trend was due in part to the rediscovery of the authors of classical antiquity and to the increased availability of their works through translation. This encouraged a somewhat uncritical eclecticism, there being less interest in determining the internal consistency of compilations of ideas than in admiring the aesthetic qualities of both parts and wholes. Early on in this development Nicholas of Cusa (1401–64) had drawn upon Pythagorean and Platonic metaphysics and Christian mysticism to construct an account of reality according to which there is a general movement of all humanity towards God, directed under the guidance of mystical love.

Such ideas were to the fore in the writings of those associated with the Neoplatonic Academy founded in Florence in the fifteenth century under the patronage of Cosimo de' Medici. The two main figures in this circle were

Marsilio Ficino (1433–99) and Giovanni Pico della Mirandola. Like Nicholas of Cusa, Ficino blends pre-Socratic and Augustinian ideas about the causal efficacy of love as a universal principle, but then manages to identify this with a generalized concept of man, thereby giving rise to the idea of humanity (*humanitas*) as the primary moral value.

More important, perhaps, than the intoxication resulting from such rhapsodic associations of ideas were the numerous translations of classical texts produced by members of the Florentine Academy. Besides introducing new notions into Renaissance thinking, these texts encouraged the development of a different form in which to cast moral and social thought, namely, lyrical fables of past or future golden ages. While the Renaissance scholastics sought to extend the philosophical methodology of the *Summa Theologiae* by drawing in yet more material for logical analysis and subsequent systematization, the Renaissance humanists looked back to the *Republic*, finding in it the perfect model for the literary expression of ideas. Thus it was that during the long eve of the modern period Vitoria was writing his *Commentary on the Second Part of the Summa Theologiae*, while Sir Thomas More (1478–1535) penned *Utopia*; and Suarez wrote *De Legibus* as Tommaso Campanella (1568–1639) was composing his *City of the Sun*. (Some small degree of essayist's licence should be allowed in relation to the chronological pairings of these works.) Of interest also is the fact that whereas Vitoria and Suarez preserve the theocentrism of medieval ethical theory, More and Campanella offer homocentric views presented through visions of secularized political futures. Such was the state of moral thought at the end of the Renaissance.

References

Works by individual authors

Abelard: *Peter Abelard's Ethics*, ed. D.E. Luscombe (Oxford: Clarendon Press, 1971).

Anselm: *Basic Writings*, trans. S.N. Deane (La Salle, Ill.: Open Court, 1962).

Aquinas, Thomas: *Summa Theologiae*, ed. T. Gilby et al. (London: Blackfriars and Eyre & Spottiswoode, 1963–75).

Aquinas, *Summa Contra Gentiles*, ed. A.C. Pegis et al. (Notre Dame, Ind.: University of Notre Dame Press, 1975).

Augustine: *The Essential Augustine*, ed. V.J. Bourke (New York: Mentor-Omega, 1964).

Augustine, *The Confessions*, ed. E.B. Pusey (London: Dent, 1962).

Campanella, T.: *Città del Sole*, trans. D.J. Donno, *City of the Sun* (Berkeley, Calif.: University of California Press, 1981).

Dionysius the Areopagite: *On the Divine Names*, trans. C.E. Rolt (London: SPCK, 1950).

Duns Scotus: *God and Creatures: The Quodlibetal Questions*, ed. F. Alluntis and A. Walter (Princeton: Princeton University Press, 1975).

Hooker, R.: *The Laws of Ecclesiastical Policy* (1594), ed. R. Church (Oxford: Clarendon Press, 1876).

More, T.: *Utopia* (1513), ed. G.M. Logan and R.M. Adams (Cambridge: Cambridge University Press, 1989).
Plato: *Timaeus*.
Plato, *The Republic*.
Pomponazzi, P.: *The Philosophy of Pomponazzi*, ed. Douglas et al. (Hildesheim: Olms, 1962).
Suarez, F.: *De Legibus*, trans. (Oxford: Clarendon Press, 1944).
William of Ockham: *Philosophical Writings*, ed. P. Boehner (Indianapolis, Ind.: Bobbs-Merrill, 1977).

Collections

The most easily available sources of original medieval and Renaissance writings are edited collections of extracts such as:

Hyman, A., and Walsh, J. (eds), *Philosophy in the Middle Ages* (Indianapolis, Ind.: Hackett, 1973).
McKeon, R. (ed.), *Selections from Medieval Philosophers*, 2 vols (New York: Scribner's, 1958).
Cambridge University Press is currently preparing a series of collections of texts to accompany the volumes on the history of medieval and Renaissance philosophy listed above. The first relevant one of these is:
McGrade, A.S., Kilcullen, J. and Kempshall, M. (eds), *The Cambridge Translations of Medieval Philosophical Texts*, vol. 2: *Ethics and Political Philosophy* (Cambridge: Cambridge University Press, 2002).

Chapter 9

Natural law and ethical pluralism

General considerations

The one and the many

Plato, Aristotle and other philosophers in the ancient world were much concerned with the general metaphysical problem of the 'one and the many' – that is to say, the question of the relationship between a universal or common nature, such as horseness or triangularity, and its many instances, the multitude of horses or triangles. They would ask, for example, whether each particular horse possessed a part or the whole of horseness or horse nature, and if triangularity was itself a triangle. Such abstruse questions are very much the stuff of philosophers' philosophy, and they continue to occupy metaphysicians today.

Equally ancient, equally philosophical, but of much wider concern, is the particular question of the relationship between human nature and its many instances as these exist at different times and places. In part this issue is indeed metaphysical, but its interest and importance go beyond the general problem of universals. There is, for example, the matter of how far any common nature might extend.

At one extreme it might be supposed that in all significant respects human beings are constituted in exactly the same ways, with the same physiological, psychological and sociological natures, so that we can generalize from the study of cases in one time and place to the nature of those from history and from other cultures. At the other extreme it may be held that apart from broad physical similarities attributable to common ancestry, human beings vary enormously in all sorts of respects. On this account humans may share no more of a common nature than do buildings. Certainly, the latter are very broadly similar with features such as walls, floor and roof (though not all buildings have even these), but the developed variety now existent is far greater than any underlying unity.

A second set of philosophical questions concerns the ethical implications of human nature and of its unity or diversity. Morality and politics are concerned with wide ranges of values, virtues, norms, requirements and prohibitions. Perhaps the central and certainly the most fundamental philosophical issue concerning these is that of their foundation. What is the basis of goodness? Why is justice a virtue and why is virtue to be sought for? What are requirements and prohibitions founded on? And so on. As well as the very many disagreements about moral and political issues that characterize contemporary debate, particularly in advanced, technological, liberal societies, there are deep theoretical disputes about the foundations of ethics and politics.

Natural law

Arguably the oldest accounts of these foundations are those provided by natural law theories. These originated in the ancient world, and basic versions of them can be found in the mythopoetic texts of the Near East that predate philosophy as it is generally understood. In these mythic writings (use of the term 'myth' does not prejudge their basic truth or falsity) such as the narrative of the Epic of Gilgamesh or the early books of the Hebrew Bible, various episodes are related in which good and evil feature significantly. Whether or not their occurrence is attributed to the action of human or supernatural forces, the main point is that certain states of affairs are identified as having positive or negative value, and the question arises as to what the basis for this identification might be. Generally, the answer is that the author or authors are working with a reflective understanding of the situations they describe that has built into it notions of what is harmful or beneficial for human beings as such.

This suggests two ideas that have come to be associated with natural law theory: first, that of moral objectivity, as grounded in rationally discernible facts of nature, facts concerning what is good or evil for rational animals; and, second, that of ethical universality. Right and wrong, on this account, is not a matter of mere opinion or sentiment, nor is it a relative or local matter like custom. On the contrary, social customs and practices may be, and often are, judged by reference to universal moral norms such as those of 'natural justice'.

These ideas can be found in developed forms in various philosophical writings of the ancient Greeks, particularly those of Aristotle, but they also feature in pagan Roman thought and in the writings of medieval Jewish, Islamic and Christian theologians. By way of example consider the following two important statements of natural law thinking. The former is taken from Cicero's *De re publica* (written in the first century BCE); the latter from Aquinas's *Summa Theologiae* (composed in the thirteenth century CE). First Cicero (106–43 BCE):

> True Law is Reason, right and natural, commanding people to fulfil their obligations and prohibiting and deterring them from doing wrong. Its validity is universal; it is unchangeable and eternal. Its commands and prohibitions apply effectively to good men and have no effect on bad men. Any attempt to supersede this law, to repeal any part of it, is sinful; to cancel it entirely is impossible. Neither the Senate nor the Assembly can exempt us from its demands; we need no interpreter or expounder of it but

ourselves. There will not be one law at Rome, one at Athens, or one now and one later, but all nations will be subject all the time to this one changeless and everlasting law.[1]

To the natural law belong those things to which a man is inclined naturally, and among these, it is proper to man to be inclined to act according to reason. Now it belongs to reason to proceed from what is common to what is proper as stated in [Aristotle's] *Physics*. I. Speculative reason, however, is different in this matter from practical reason. For, since speculative reason is concerned chiefly with necessary things, which cannot be otherwise than they are, its proper conclusions, like universal principles are invariably true. Practical reason, on the other hand, is concerned with contingent matters, about which human actions are concerned, and consequently, although there is necessity in the general principles, the more we descend to matters of detail, the more frequently we encounter deviations.... Accordingly, in matters of action, truth or practical rectitude is not the same for all in respect of detail but only as to the general principles, and where there is the same rectitude in matters of detail, it is not equally known to all.[2]

The second passage is especially relevant to the subject of this essay. First, because Aquinas was highly influential in the development of natural law theory, particularly, but by no means exclusively, within the tradition of Roman Catholic Christianity. But second, because Thomas expresses an appreciation of the fact that the options of unqualified universalism or of unrestricted diversity may not be the only ones, and that the truth may lie somewhere between them. Furthermore, he allows that, as one moves from general principle to detailed application, the scope for doubt and error, and hence for one kind of ethical disagreement, increases.[3]

Natural law and religious ethics

These points are important for the task of addressing pluralism and we shall return to them in due course. For now, however, it is worth emphasizing what is often not appreciated, namely that not all advocates of natural law have been theists; that not all natural law theists have been Christian (Moses Maimonides (1135–1204) is an important Jewish example); and that within Christianity natural law is by no means the preserve of Catholicism. These facts may be news to some readers but the third is likely to be the most surprising, for in the twentieth century especially, the term 'natural law' has generally come to be associated with the moral teachings of the Roman Catholic Church.

As mention of Aquinas suggests, that association is long-standing. It became widespread, however, following publication in 1968 of the encyclical *Humanae Vitae* in which Pope Paul VI reaffirmed traditional Catholic opposition to artificial contraception. Whereas conservative Protestant views on sexuality are nowadays primarily (and often exclusively) scripture-based, Catholic teaching invokes styles of argument in which certain kinds of actions are proscribed on grounds of violating a natural norm. This marked difference of approach is, however, a somewhat modern development and is connected with the fragmentation of Protestantism into a multitude of different groupings and with the trend, as theological differences increased in depth and number, to go back to scripture as a basis for doctrine.

In earlier centuries, by contrast, natural law was widely appealed to by non Catholic Christian thinkers. Indeed, some of the greatest writers in the natural law tradition have been non-Catholics. Examples of these are the Anglican Richard Hooker (1554–1600), who wrote *The Laws of Ecclesiastical Polity*, and the Dutch Protestant Hugo Grotius (1583–1645), author of the *Law of War and Peace*. In the eighteenth century, versions of natural law were espoused by the largely Presbyterian Scottish philosophers of 'common sense', most famously Thomas Reid (1710–96), and advocated by the English legal theorist Sir William Blackstone (1723–80) in his *Commentaries of the Laws of England*. From Britain and Continental Europe these passed to North America and the rhetoric, if not always the substance, of natural law features in the Philadelphia Constitutional Convention of 1787.[4]

A common mistake

In the popular mind, however, the association of natural law with Catholicism has been strengthened by the continued reference to it in the widely discussed encyclicals of Pope John Paul II, especially *Veritatis Splendor* (1993) and *Evangelium Vitae* (1995). One common feature of this association, particularly as it dates from *Humanae Vitae*, is the belief that opposition to contraception on the basis of natural law amounts to the claim that it is 'not natural'. Because the context is one where 'artificial' contraception is at issue, this further suggests that Catholic ethics, and natural law ethics more generally, revolve around a contrast between what happens in the ordinary course of events (nature) and what might occur as a result of human interference (artifice).

This ill-informed impression has had some interesting consequences. Initially the view attributed to Catholic moral theology was criticized on the basis that it is absurd, cruel and superstitious to confine actions and policies to ones that do not interfere with natural processes. Medicine, for example, is precisely designed to interfere with a course of events and to reverse or redirect them. If that is acceptable, how can interfering with other processes so as to avoid conception be intrinsically wrong?

This argument rests on a mistake about the way in which appeal to nature features in the anti-contraception argument, but before commenting on that let me say something about a recent trend in public thinking, which, ironically as it turns out, might seem to support what is often taken to be the Catholic view. This is the rise of environmentalism, and more generally of 'nature holism'.

Within a decade of the storm of criticism that surrounded *Humanae Vitae* a movement had begun, the main claim of which was that techno-industrial consumer societies have become polluters and corrupters of nature. On this account environmental degradation, species exploitation and human physical and mental illness have all resulted from an attempt to secure false goods by interfering with long-standing natural processes. Eco-activists, new-age travellers and holistic healers represent one broad strand of this movement, with commercial and state environmental policies falling into line in the general campaign to 'get back to nature'.

As with the critics of Catholic teaching mentioned earlier, opponents of environmentalism and nature holism are quick to point out that human activity is unavoidably interventionist and that many of the processes and products that 'naturalists' favour themselves are or result from interference in the course of events. Organic farming, homoeopathy and species conservation are all forms of intervention and in that respect are contrary to nature.

At more or less the same time, therefore, we find progressive sentiment criticizing traditional Catholic teaching for restricting liberty and inflicting misery on the grounds that it is wrong to interfere with nature, and the same sentiment criticizing techno-industrial society for treating nature as something that can be overridden in order to secure material goods and affluent lifestyles. In short, and somewhat paradoxically: Catholic ethics is bad for insisting on respect for the natural order, and capitalism is bad for failing to respect it. This combination echoes something of the sound heard in recent years of traditional sexual morality voiced in unison with feminist criticism of pornography. And just as there is now an alliance between conservative and radical critics of the commercial exploitation of sex, so too there are signs of an alliance between old and new advocates of nature's ways.

However interesting and suggestive this may be, it is also deeply confused. The appeal in Catholic moral theology to the idea of acting 'in accord with nature' is not a recommendation of general non-interference, or of letting what will happen happen. For apart from running into contradiction (implementing non-interference will itself constitute interference), such a policy stands in need of some account of 'what happens anyway'. Setting aside the bare idea of an unchosen causal process, the notion of 'the naturally occurring' or of 'what happens normally' remains ambiguous between what is in keeping with a statistical pattern, and what is in accord with a value-protecting or value-promoting norm. And, of course, the idea of natural law concerns the latter. That is to say, it concerns the natural as *that which ought to be*, not merely that which happens to be. In the traditional view, then, therapeutic medical interventions are warranted because they are aimed at protecting or restoring normal functioning; while contraceptive intervention is improper because it is intended to inhibit or destroy proper functioning.

Recognition of this point should bring with it the realization that there is nothing essentially religious about natural law thinking. Apart from the consideration that the very possibility of there being natural norms depends upon purposeful creation, one could advance a natural law theory without invoking the law of God.[5] Indeed one might hold that religious ethical teachings that appeal to a natural law foundation actually go further than can be supported on that basis. This, indeed, is exactly what some Catholic moral theologians of broadly natural law persuasion do maintain with regard to their church's teachings on contraception and divorce. According to such critics, natural law reasoning may establish the good of marriage and procreation, but it does not show them to be absolute in the sense associated with traditional teaching.

Reducibility and plurality

Without engaging in the debate about artificial contraception, it may be useful to illustrate something of the general character of natural law by considering its bearing on the issue of sexuality in general. This will also be relevant to the theme of the final section.

In a recently published book *Ethics and Sex*[6] the Israeli moral philosopher Igor Primoratz contends that there is no distinctive sexual morality, that is, no values or norms specific to this sphere of human life. That is now a very common view, and it is often matched by similar rejections of the idea that the major departments of life are governed by specific values or virtues. Setting aside general moral scepticism, which involves the rejection of the cogency of *any* moral reasoning, even those who think that something rational can be made out of morality usually contend that particular moral claims derive from a non-specific, general ethical rule.

The two leading candidates for the ultimate principle from which particular claims derive are (in some or other version) the principle of utility and the principle of pure practical reason. An action or policy is permitted, required or prohibited in relation either to the maximization of preference-satisfaction, or to conformity with universal prescriptivity. For example, an action will be permissible according to the former principle if performing it creates no less (total) happiness than other available options, and according to the second if it is of a type that one can consistently prescribe both for oneself and for others.

Given these accounts and their current dominance one can see why contemporary moral philosophy can find no place for department-specific values, virtues or norms. If there is anything wrong with telling a lie, or having casual sex, or taking goods from a shop without paying for them, or killing someone, it will have to consist in an intentional violation of the basic principle. Accordingly, that will be the only morally relevant description of it. More strictly, it will be the only non-reducible moral description, for, as a matter of convenience, one might mark out in other terms actions liable to violate the principle, say for purposes of training children.

In rejecting the idea of irreducibly distinct values, each proper to different areas of life, these moral philosophies disallow the possibility of at least one kind of ethical pluralism. Rather than it being something to think twice about, however, to advocates of these views this is likely to seem inevitable and quite proper. For it has often been supposed that ethical pluralism is equivalent to ethical relativism, which in turn is taken to be the thesis that reason cannot show some action or policy to be right or wrong as such. That then leaves us with either moral scepticism (in the strict sense, i.e. things may be intrinsically right or wrong but that fact cannot be known) or moral subjectivism (there are no moral facts). In short, moral rationalism excludes moral pluralism inasmuch as the former asserts and the latter denies that universal reason can determine unqualifiedly true moral claims.

There are those, however, who reject the assumed equivalence of pluralism and relativism. One such group includes figures in the British moral intuitionist tradition, especially Moore, Ross and Pritchard.[7] Another related group comprises philosophers from the Austrian value-phenomenological school.[8] Common to both groupings is the idea of moral reflection leading to conclusions about what is good or bad. From this perspective there is no a priori reason to suppose that all moral phenomena will turn out to be instances of the one value, any more than it is rationally determined that the proper sensibles – colour, flavour, odour, sound and texture – be reducible to some foundational 'perceptible quality'. On this account, then, there is scope for the idea that right conduct in the area of sex is not reducible to conformity with a single general ethical principle, but consists in respect for particular sexual values and virtues such as those of modesty, chastity and fecundity.

Recognition of the possibility of real plurality is, I believe, commendable. However, what is called for philosophically is a legitimation of experience, and an explanation of how what is diverse can be so and of how variety might yet be unified. At one extreme stand the rational monists for whom all moral value must be one; and at the other the phenomenologists for whom things float free in their evaluative diversity. Traditional natural law walks a via media between these positions. It recognizes that life has departments, and thus that there are activity-specific values and virtues. On the other hand it sees that departments can only be viewed as such when seen as parts of a greater whole. That greater whole is human life. Mere material aggregates have no principle of dynamic unity; non-living compounds are sustained through a balance of attractive and repulsive forces; but life involves the integrated operation of vital functions. Not every human good must be an expression of *the* human good, but every such good must be intelligible as part of human life. By rooting value in animate nature, and by recognizing that a species-nature involves a plurality of functions, this most ancient variety of ethical theory combines plurality of values with unity of foundation.

Just as one and the same plant has roots, stem, branches, leaves and flowers and functions associated with each, all subserving the well-being of the whole, so human nature has many parts and functions, each subject to particular norms, yet each integrated within a whole. In this sense there is a dimension of the ethical corresponding to each distinct voluntary activity. And so there are sexual norms as well as communicative ones. It should be clear that such a doctrine of moral pluralism has nothing to do with relativism as that is nowadays understood.

Nature and right action

Before turning to questions of application, it will be as well to clarify further the claim of natural law and to note important points of difference and disagreement between its present-day advocates. Among contemporary theorists, particularly in North America, there is an important debate between two prominent parties: first, those who maintain that what qualifies a position to be a natural law one is simply the claim that right and wrong are objective, universal and naturally knowable; and, second, those who go further by insisting that it is part of the theory that what makes something right or wrong is its relation to natural human good (or the good of other animals). More precisely, the latter view is that the moral character of actions derives from their contribution as means toward, or as constituents of, well-being. In philosophical circles in which there is little if any historical knowledge of natural law traditions, this second view is better known as 'objectivist naturalism', or more commonly as 'naturalism'. The first position, by contrast, has no commonly used title but for purposes of contrast we might term it 'naturalist objectivism'.

Both views regard moral knowledge as naturally available – that is, as not depending on divine revelation or on some mystical power of ethical intuition. The difference between them concerns the role of nature in providing the *content* of morality. Besides disputing which is the best position philosophically speaking, advocates of these two views argue about the correct attribution of them to historical figures such as Aristotle and, most especially, Aquinas. Given the latter fact it will perhaps come as no surprise to say that this debate is largely confined to Catholic moral philosophers.[9]

This is not the place to enter into these disputes, let alone to try and resolve them. But it is appropriate that I should indicate where my own view lies. To some extent, in fact, I think that the opposition is overstated, but to the extent that it exists my sympathies lie with the objectivist naturalists.[10] Such a view, I believe, provides a powerful way of thinking about the objectivity of value and practical reasoning. In the twentieth century moral objectivism has often been challenged with the claim that what we now know of reality leaves no scope for the existence of non-natural values, let alone of 'free-floating' requirements and prohibitions. On this account objectivism faces the task of showing how there could be such 'objects' as moral facts and values. This has proved to be a *real* difficulty. At the same time, however, the subjectivist reduction of value to preference and sentiment has seemed contrary to experience and liable to undermine commitment to right action.

A better response is to reject the idea that moral objectivism requires moral 'objects'. The approach of objectivist naturalism draws from the writings of

Aristotle and Aquinas (at least on its interpretation of them) the idea that right action is best understood in terms of the exercise of dispositions – virtues – the having and practice of which serve to advance natural human well-being. Virtues such as prudence, temperance, justice and courage are as necessary as health and sanity in order to achieve and maintain a good life. Its goodness is not to be understood in terms of the presence in or around it of 'values' in the sense of metaphysical objects. Rather it consists in the integrated and balanced operation of various natural functions, including physiological, psychological and social ones. Goodness in human life on this view is metaphysically neither more nor less mysterious than goodness in the life of plants.

MacIntyre and the challenge of relativism

One might now ask whether this account of value is too good to be true. Ironically grounds for doubt arise from within the family of ethical naturalists. Forty years ago, in an essay whose importance for modern English-language moral theory could hardly be exaggerated, the British philosopher Elizabeth Anscombe advanced several bold and very interesting theses.[11] Among these is the claim that the basic moral vocabulary of requirement and of prohibition – 'ought', 'ought not', 'must', 'must not' and so on – is a cultural remnant of an earlier religious way of thinking in which morality consists of a series of divine commands. Because people in general no longer subscribe to such a view (indeed, it is uncommon even among moral theologians), Anscombe proposed that it be abandoned in favour of the language, and the philosophy, of human virtue and flourishing.

Twenty years later a second British philosopher, Alasdair MacIntyre, took up both this historico-conceptual analysis and the option for virtue. In *After Virtue* he argued that modern ethical language is an incoherent assemblage of disordered fragments left over from earlier moral systems.[12] However, whereas Anscombe focused exclusively on the remains of divine law and proposed the re-adoption of a traditional Aristotelian approach, MacIntyre argued that as things stand, contemporary secular, liberal consciousness is no better placed to make sense of virtue talk than it is of the strongly prescriptive vocabulary of the Judaeo-Christian moral law. In both cases what we lack are the historical and cultural contexts that give meaning to these ways of evaluating and commending character and conduct.

A further point of important difference between Anscombe and MacIntyre is that whereas she seemed to believe that we could reconstruct the philosophical anthropology by which Aristotle was able to prescribe a natural end for humankind, MacIntyre regarded this sort of quasi-philosophical anthropology as committed to a form of ahistorical, acultural 'metaphysical biology', which he then believed was no longer tenable. In keeping with the general character of Aristotelian moral psychology, however, he still argued that the value, and indeed the moral meaning, of actions flows from habits whose standing as virtues derives from their orientation toward ends constitutive of good human lives. Like Anscombe and other neo-Aristotelians, therefore, MacIntyre hoped to restore coherence to morality by relating it to an account of life as teleologically ordered. In part for the reasons mentioned, and in part because of conclusions drawn and retained from his earlier studies in Marxism and sociology, however, he viewed that order in terms of social practices rather than of culturally invariant natural functions. In asking the question, What ought I to do? one is, in effect, asking a question about the kind of person one should be. The unit of moral assessment is not, strictly, individual actions but the form of life from which they issue and the agent's overall character. Furthermore, this character is formed and developed in a social context, out of participation in practices whose meaning is given by their traditional goals.

In summary, to understand the moral identity and value of individual actions one has to relate them to the agent's life, and through this to the practices and social forms of his or her culture. The very obvious problem presented by modernity, therefore, is that there is no single unifying culture and hence no shared set of values and virtues by reference to which actions may be interpreted: 'The rhetoric of shared values is of great ideological importance, but it disguises the truth about how action is guided and directed. For what we genuinely share in the way of moral maxims, precepts and principles is insufficiently determinate to guide action and what is sufficiently determinate to guide action is not shared.'[13]

The considerable interest of MacIntyre's explorations of these issues is testified to by the attention his work has attracted. Yet his thoughts also raise a problematic question about the claim to objectivity. If the standards of moral assessment are not given by extra-moral and uncontested values, or by ahistorical principles of practical reason, but are entirely immanent within the particular social traditions and practices in which agents are situated, then how is relativism to be avoided? If what is right is determined by virtues whose form and content is specific to a tradition, how can it even make sense to raise questions about the morality of conduct from a perspective outside that tradition? Because the diagnosis of modernity, and a fortiori of 'post-modernity', is that there is no single moral order, the threat of relativism is not merely speculative, it is real.

Back to nature

MacIntyre's concern with the question of competing moral traditions is reflected in the title of the book that followed *After Virtue*, namely, *Whose Justice? Which Rationality?*[14] In this, and in the sequel *Three Rival Versions of Moral Enquiry*,[15] he developed a dialectical account of how one tradition of reflection can establish its rational superiority over another. In broad outline it maintains that a tradition may run into philosophical difficulties and recognize this fact without having the resources to solve the problems. It might yet, however, be able to appreciate that another, rival tradition does possess the means to diagnose and to resolve these difficulties. Acknowledgement of these facts therefore amounts to recognition of the superiority of the rival. Thus, while styles and principles of inquiry may be tradition-specific, the ultimate goal of moral inquiry, namely goodness, is tradition-transcendent.

But if virtue and moral reasoning are necessarily formed in interpersonal contexts, can this really be squared with claims to transcendent objectivity? MacIntyre believed himself to have provided the basis for a positive answer but his critics have maintained the charge that his position is a version of relativism – be it a very sophisticated one. While MacIntyre has always denied this, in recent writings he retracts his earlier rejection of Aristotelian appeals to nature.

Certainly he still maintains that we must recognize the diversity of times and circumstances and acknowledge culturally situated histories but he no longer takes the acceptance of these requirements to be incompatible with a naturalistic philosophical anthropology. In the past he has emphasized 'deep conflicts' in our cultural history over what human well-being (and hence human nature) consists in. Now he points to the fact that an understanding of value has to be placed within an account of human animality and of what befits its flourishing. He writes:

> In *After Virtue* I had attempted to give an account of the place of the virtues, understood as Aristotle had understood them, within social practices, the lives of individuals and the lives of communities, while making that account independent of what I called Aristotle's 'metaphysical biology.' Although there is indeed good reason to repudiate important elements in Aristotle's biology, I now judge that I was in error in supposing an ethics independent of biology to be possible...no account of the goods, rules and virtues that are definitive of our moral life can be adequate that does not explain – or at least point us towards an explanation – how that form of life is possible for beings who are biologically constituted as we are, by providing us with an account of our development towards and into that form of life.[16]

If, as MacIntyre now accepts, the rejection of universal human anthropology was unwarranted, he is surely right to emphasize the importance of second nature: what time, place and community add to what God or evolution has established. Our movement toward self-realization is in no small part as beings nurtured and formed by the communities of our birth, adoption, education or career. What this suggests, though, is not that Aristotelian anthropology is redundant but only that it must needs be attendant to historical and cultural diversification. As MacIntyre himself has come to emphasize, there need be no opposition between *historicism* understood as the claim that reason has a variety of cultural and historical starting-points, and *realism* conceived as the view that truth is something objective and transcendent of these perspectives.[17]

Applications

Problems of pluralism

While this reconciliation may be theoretically satisfactory, it would be facile to suppose that it can easily be invoked to resolve deep moral disagreements. Recall again the words of Aquinas:

> [S]ince speculative reason is concerned chiefly with necessary things...its proper conclusions, like universal principles are invariably true. Practical reason, on the other hand, is concerned with contingent matters, about which human actions are concerned, and consequently, although there is necessity in the general principles, the more we descend to matters of detail, the more frequently we encounter deviations.... Accordingly, in matters of action, truth or practical rectitude is not the same for all in respect of detail but only as to the general principles.

The conclusion of the previous section was that according to natural law, most clearly in the interpretation that associates it with objectivist naturalism, the plurality of human values is located within the broad unity provided by a common human nature. If the various points and arguments are found cogent, it will be agreed that moral questions admit of objective answers, though not necessarily of exclusive ones.

But several issues now arise. First, to what extent do the relevant facts prescribe particular policies? Consideration of what pertains to human nature may be insufficient to determine a unique course of action, just as the knowledge that it would be good to apply colour to a wall leaves open the question of precisely what colour to apply. Second, even where it is determined what would be good, the context of action may be such that the effort required to realize this, and the collateral damage of doing so, would be too great to warrant it. For example, it would be good if all parents treated their children with loving care and refrained from any psychological or physical abuse of them. Given this fact, a community might seek to encourage norms of good parenting and intervene in cases where these norms are violated. However, the effort required to eliminate parental abuse would be enormous, and the social and familial effects of surveillance and intervention might be immensely destructive and themselves violate rights of privacy. Where prevention or cure may be more harmful than the disease, prudence may need to temper idealism. This is not to say that nothing should be done but only that social regulation has to take account of a range of values and be mindful of the costs of coercion and restraint. Third, it is one thing to defend the coherence and even the plausibility of natural law theory and to suggest what its stance on various ethical questions might be; it is yet a further task to show how it might deal with a situation in which not everyone shares that perspective; in which, indeed, some reject both it and the particular judgements it gives rise to. The second and third of these considerations are particularly relevant to the business of managing ethical pluralism.

Citizenship and social regulation

In and of itself the mere idea of natural law does not prescribe any particular form of social life or political organization. How it may be appropriate for human beings collectively to live, and what constraining and enabling structures it may be just to impose, depend in no small part upon one's understanding of the extent and modes of human sociability. Here is one point at which the relation of natural law to philosophical anthropology becomes important. If, for example, one's account of human nature conceives of persons as constituted independently of any social relations into which they may enter, then the argument for an individualist politics looks strong. If on the other hand one views human beings as essentially social, as did Aristotle and Aquinas, then one will look to the political order to realize the goods of community. For the most part contemporary theorists who are drawn to natural law have taken inspiration from the Aristotelian–Thomistic tradition and have favoured communitarian accounts of political society. There are, though, distinguished exceptions who combine an appreciation of Aristotle with forms of liberal individualism.[18]

Given the 'social animal' anthropology now most commonly associated with natural law theory, the good of citizenship (or, more generally, of membership in a community) is both instrumental and constitutive. Collaboration makes possible the achievement of projects and benefits not otherwise attainable; and social life provides the necessary context for the realization of certain aspects of human nature. It is not merely, as any individualist might be willing to grant, that collective action is an effective means to the achievement of ends that, as a matter of fact, no individual could attain by themselves. Rather, collective endeavour is a form of group activity through which bonds of community are strengthened and by which goods may be secured for members of society that *logically* could not be available to them as individuals. These latter benefits are what, strictly speaking, constitute 'common goods'.

To clarify this point it may be useful to distinguish and then illustrate several ways in which values can be possessed or enjoyed:

1. As *individual goods*: attaching to individuals independently of the states of well-being of others, for example, physical comfort.
2. As *collective goods*: as sets of individual goods, for example, aggregate wealth.
3. As *common goods*: as ones attaching to collectivities and thus only available to individuals as members of groups – for example, the happy mood at a social gathering.
4. As *private goods*: the possession of which by one party prevents their possession by another, for example, food.

5.   As *public goods*: the possession or enjoyment of which by one party does not preclude similar benefit to others, for example, fresh air.

The state of happiness felt by those at a social gathering may be and typically is something other than the addition of the separable states of happiness of each. It is something emergent that comes into being through social interaction and is enjoyed by each participant derivatively through membership of the group and not directly as an individual. By way of chemical analogy, the resultant of interaction is not a 'linear combination' or additive sum of antecedent quantities. Common goods are neither individual goods nor mere collections of such goods; they are irreducibly communal. Notice, however, that the distinction between private and public goods is tangential to this, inasmuch as not every public good is possessed commonly and not every individual good is a private one.

Part of the considerable importance of Aquinas in the development of natural law is his insistence on the social nature of human beings; his explicit identification of the existence of common goods (or as he says 'the common good' (*bonum commune*)); and his claim that in order for this to be realized and protected it is necessary that a community should have leadership with the authority to regulate the activity of its members. All three points are present in the following short passage from his treatise on *The Governance of Rulers* (*De regimine principum*):

> When we consider all that is necessary to human life it is clear that man is naturally a social and political animal, destined more than all the other animals to live in community.... The fellowship of society being thus natural and necessary to man, it follows with equal necessity that there must be some principle of government within the society. For if a greater number of people were to live, each intent only upon his own interests [individual goods], such a community would surely disintegrate unless there were one of its number to have a care for the common good: just as the body of a man or of any other animal would disintegrate were there not a single controlling force sustaining the general vitality in all the members...the particular interest and the common good are not identical.[19]

Citizenship in this account serves to complete human social nature and is a common good. It is clear, then, that Aquinas and anyone following him is committed to some form of communitarianism as against individualism. Popular political opposition between these views is sometimes drawn in terms of alternative values and ideals of social life. Only among theorists, however, is the opposition cast in terms of conflicting metaphysical accounts of persons. Yet, as the passage from Aquinas suggests, the two contrasts are not unrelated: for the priorities of political governance have to take account of the essential nature of the governed. Unsurprisingly, therefore, philosophical individualists who believe that social relationships belong to persons *per accidens* and not *per se*, are willing to see the state act so as to limit interference with the lives and liberties of individuals and are resistant to the idea of coercion for the sake of common goods or of society as a whole. By the same token, philosophical communitarians are often suspicious that an emphasis on individual liberty has behind it an antisocial disposition, and they favour the idea of collective action as an end in itself or as a practice part of whose benefit is intrinsic to it.

Rationality features twice over in determining the content of natural law theory. It is *by* the use of reason that we determine our good and the routes to it; and it is *because* we are rational animals that our good has the form it does, embracing intellectual, moral and spiritual aspects as well as material ones. These are universal features of human nature and hence the goods of citizenship should be open to all. Any attempt to restrict them on the basis of race or gender is liable to be unjust, and members of civil society have a responsibility to ensure that the goods of community are not denied to those who have a human right to them. Within pluralist societies there are groups whose historic culture does discriminate on such grounds. For the sake of civil order, and mindful of the value of autonomy, a society might tolerate minor injustices but at the level of fundamental natural rights, entitlements flowing from one's human nature, there can be little if any room for compromise within a society. Happily, natural law's commitment to the rationality of human beings gives grounds for optimism that a change of view can be effected by argument. Typically, this will take the form of showing that the basis on which one individual or group claims for himself, herself or itself the status and privileges of citizenship is also possessed by those to whom they would deny this benefit. This argument to consistency is one of the oldest and most commonly used methods in political debate and has had notable (if less than complete) successes, such as the end of slavery and the emancipation of women.

While the communitarian account imposes constraints on policy, it nevertheless allows considerable scope for the variety of arrangements that might realize social goods. In considering conflicts, for example, what have to be balanced are, first, the demonstrable need of an individual or group to pursue projects that are recognizably variants of the general human good; second, the impact of this on the similar need of others; and, third, the resulting effect of the combination of arrangements on the common good. Natural law on this account sees social regulation not as an undesirable necessity but as an expression of communal existence, which is itself a basic good. However, it must also recognize that the circumstances of social life, particularly in contemporary developed societies, involve immense diversities of lifestyle, considerable ranges of values and no little amount of conflict. To some extent it can treat pluralism as a desirable consequence of the fact that basic values, such as those of intellectual or physical activity, can be realized in different but equally good ways. However, not every difference is benign. Where there is conflict, the advocate of natural law must deploy moral reasoning and prudence in order to determine whether the harms or evils resultant from conflict, or from the pursuit of goals that are, on its account, disvaluable, are so great that they must be ruled against, or whether they are such that the effort and measures required to act against them would themselves cause more harm than good. These issues are best pursued by considering examples, and not merely speculative ones but those which represent some of the deepest and most conflicted divisions within our societies, namely, matters of life, death and sex.

Life-and-death decisions

Because all human values are instrumental toward, or constitutive of, the actualization of human nature in individual persons, these lives are the primary loci of value and hence must be respected. Unlike certain other traditions that separate morality and politics, natural law sees these as necessarily related, political values being a subset of moral ones. Accordingly, for natural law no policy that provides resources for, let alone promotes, the intentional and direct destruction of human life will be morally acceptable. One only has to write or read such a claim, however, to recognize that for all its initial plausibility it faces a number of challenges.

First, there is the fact that communities are vulnerable to attack both from within and without and consequently have need of protection. Where the attacks are life-threatening the means of defence against them may themselves pose mortal threats. Government rules society using the apparatus of the state, itself the organized institution through which the community is regulated and protected. For this reason it has been characteristic (and in some accounts definitional) of the state to claim for itself a monopoly of the legitimate use of coercive power. Combining this prerogative with the need to protect their citizens, states have established and maintained police and military forces with the means and the entitlement to use lethal force. This is qualified in various ways but the fact remains that the killing of human beings is provided for within common justifications of the state. For the natural law theorist this derives from the right of self-defence.

Typically, however, natural lawyers have gone on to say that what this right provides for is not the intentional and direct destruction of human life, but only the use of force, which it is conceived may result in death, *though that end is not intended*. Although this distinction (of 'double effect') is open to abuse it is a coherent and morally significant one, as is brought out by the following 'counterfactual test'. Suppose an agent acts in his own defence, or in the defence of those he is charged to protect, in such a way as results in the death of an aggressor. Now consider whether, had his action been equally successful but not lethal, he would have regarded this as a failure or as a success. If the former, then his intentions were murderous; if the latter, they were not.

Capital punishment is a more difficult issue, for this certainly does involve the intentional and direct destruction of human life (as the counterfactual test shows: if the condemned survives the executioner's actions, that is regarded as a failure of the process). It may nevertheless be argued that such killing is justified by the fact that society has a right to protect itself and to exact due penalty for the most serious crimes. This claim is highly controversial and cannot be explored here beyond noting the following. Most philosophers and political leaders in societies in which natural law theory has had an influence are against capital punishment, and yet most ordinary people tend to favour it. At least they do so when asked for their opinion, and that is usually at times when some brutal murder has been in the news. However, when at other, less emotional, times the point is made that not all who have been executed have been guilty, and they are then asked whether they would prefer a situation in which someone whom they think might deserve to die escapes that fate, or one in which mistakes having been made the innocent are put to death, they tend to favour the former option. Interestingly, given its association with natural law, the Catholic Church in the form of its Catechism and the pronouncements of John Paul II has moved toward the conclusion that in stable and civilized societies capital punishment cannot be justified.

If liberal intellectual opinion and Catholic moral teaching find themselves in agreement on this life-and-death issue, they are deeply opposed on those of abortion and euthanasia. More than proponents of any other ethical theory, advocates of natural law tend to be opposed to abortion. Their argument is straightforward, combining the general prohibition on the taking of innocent human life with the claim that a foetus in the womb is an innocent human being. Equally and for parallel reasons they tend strongly to oppose non-voluntary and involuntary euthanasia – that is, those cases in which a patient is constitutionally incapable of giving, or has not given, consent to having themselves killed. The matter of voluntary euthanasia and assisted suicide is more complex but again the preponderance of natural law opinion is probably against it.

Unlike certain increasingly prominent versions of political liberalism that hold that it is not the business of the state to advance or protect any conception of the morally good life but only to provide a safe and procedurally just sphere for individual activity, natural law holds the laws of the state *should* reflect moral values and requirements. Accordingly it can hardly take a neutralist stance on questions of killing where it believes this killing to be unjustified. Consider in this connection the following passage drawn from a recent statement on abortion issued by the Vatican Congregation for the Doctrine of the Faith:

> The inalienable rights of the person must be recognised and respected by civil society and the political authority. These human rights depend neither on single individuals nor on parents; nor do they represent a concession made by society and the state.... Among such fundamental rights one should mention in this regard every human being's right to life and physical integrity from the moment of conception...a consequence of the respect and protection which must be ensured for the unborn child from the

moment of conception, the law must provide appropriate legal sanctions for every deliberate violation of the child's rights.[20]

There is scope for argument even in natural law terms about the blanket opposition to abortion and euthanasia. For example, the claim that the foetus is an innocent human being carries greater weight than does the claim that the *immediate* product of conception is such. Additionally it may be recognized that respecting the rights of autonomy, which natural law regards as integral to human self-realization, gives scope for tolerating error and wrongdoing at certain levels and to certain extents. However, anyone who believes that the laws of the state should embody fundamental moral principles and who also believes that certainly abortion and probably euthanasia are gross violations of such principles has little option but to resist legislative changes in the direction of liberalizing these practices, and to strive to repeal such legislation once it has been enacted. At the same time, concern for the overall good of society and acceptance of the fact that many seriously and sincerely hold a different view on such issues must limit the forms of opposition. In this and in other matters the following balanced compromise may be reasonable: while one may certainly not give support to legislation that provides for or permits what one holds to be evils, one may yet accept the constitutional right of the state to enact such legislation and thus confine one's opposition to legally permissible forms. Necessarily this formulation is qualified by the phrase 'may yet accept'; for the evils might be so great that one then has no moral option but to break the law and, at the limit, to regard lawful government as having ceased to exist. If this seems extreme it is worth recalling that precisely this situation has faced the citizens of more than one state during the course of the twentieth century. Put another way, there is a limit to how much ethical difference a society can withstand.

Human sexuality

Along with abortion, sexuality has become one of the main issues of contention between traditional natural law morality and politics, and the moral and social philosophy of 'liberal pluralism'. Although a range of matters are in contention, the most prominent is the issue of homosexual practice (by which I include lesbianism) and its legitimation by the state. It is only relatively recently that homosexual relations have been decriminalized in many societies, and in some they are still illegal. Yet in many of the states where homosexual activity was once prohibited there are now moves to bestow legal rights on homosexual partners and even to extend the institution of marriage to them.

For those liberals who uphold the moral neutrality of the state this latter prospect can be perplexing. For on the one hand while they do not believe that it is for the state to proscribe sexual practice on moral grounds, nor do they believe that it should endorse, let alone prescribe, forms of sexual union as expressions of moral values. Yet this latter is precisely the basis on which some gay activists seek the extension of marriage to homosexual partners. In this respect at least they share with the traditional defenders of heterosexual marriage a common belief in the value of publicly recognized partnerships.

Once again what the natural law theorist has to say will depend on what he or she believes about human nature and the goods that perfect it. What is generally, and unsurprisingly the case, however, is that most proponents of natural law take a 'conservative' position. According to traditional natural law ethics, judgements as to the moral acceptability of sexual practices must be keyed to an understanding of the proper role of sex in human life. Sexual organs are defined by function and their (primary) function is that of reproduction. What follows is that the definitive use of sexual organs is intersexual, that is, between male and female, and for the sake of procreation. This is not to say that the only function of sex or of the sexual organs is to reproduce. Sex obviously gives pleasure and serves to express and deepen emotional bonds; but these features are located within the boundaries of its primary, reproductive function.

Suppose, then, that the natural law theorist believes homosexual practice to be contrary to nature, and thus at odds with right reason. What should follow so far as policy is concerned given the fact that this opinion is now widely contested? Here it may be useful to relate a real case in which moral and political views on just these issues have been in heated conflict. In 1988 under the Conservative administration of Margaret Thatcher a piece of legislation was enacted in the United Kingdom regulating local government. This contained within it the following clause, known universally as Section 28: 'A local authority shall not (a) intentionally promote homosexuality or publish material with the intention of promoting homosexuality; or (b) promote the teaching of homosexuality as a pretended family relationship.'[21]

This clause was introduced in legislation designed to curb what were viewed as doctrinaire policies then being advanced, and sometimes implemented, by far-left activists particularly in London. The general legislation was contested by the parliamentary opposition, and the clause was viewed with some disquiet by others, but it was presented as part of a general block to policies for which the public certainly had no sympathy. Then, as now, the dominant feeling was probably one of wishing not to know what people do in private so long as it is not contrary to the well being or interests of others.

Since the removal from power of the Conservatives in 1997 and the election of New Labour, moves have been made to repeal Section 28, and that has now happened in Scotland and seems likely to happen elsewhere in the UK. However, such proposals have met with considerable opposition from various quarters including many leaders of Christian, Jewish and Islamic faiths – all traditions in which natural law has had an influence. On the other side the proponents of repeal divide into three broad groups: first, liberals of the sort who do not believe that it is the business of law either to promote or to prohibit behaviour on moral grounds; second, advocates of alternative sexualities who insist that the state has a responsibility to encourage attitudes and actions favourable to these sexualities, not in the sense of teaching people to adopt them but of teaching them to affirm or even to celebrate them; and, third, moral conservatives who, while not favouring the neutral state, are unhappy about the way in which matters of sexual morality are now dealt with.

There is certainly ground for complaint that the clause is discriminatory in singling out one particular sexual group. So far as public opinion is concerned, it is hard to suppose that those who maintain the moral superiority of heterosexual over homosexual activity would be happy to have local authorities promote sadomasochism or fetishism. And if that is not the case, then the charge of homophobia commonly levelled against opponents of repeal does indeed begin to look justified.

What is in fact the case is that most people do not want local authorities or schools to promote, recommend or celebrate any particular form of sexual activity though they would, I suspect, be happy and indeed wish to see heterosexual marriage, or at least stable, domestic heterosexual family life, presented as a desirable norm. Clearly, though, this would be unacceptable to sexual radicals. Moreover, they will regard mere social toleration of homosexuality (or of other alternatives) as insufficient, noting (correctly) that toleration is compatible with moral disapproval. But approval cannot be coerced, and it is evident that the majority do not regard all forms of sexual activity as 'equally valid'. If pressed as to why, they will usually speak in terms of what is 'normal' or 'natural'.

Such replies are now regularly countered by the suggestion that, while homosexuality or fetishism may be statistically abnormal, it occurs in nature and hence cannot be objected to as unnatural. Whether by accident or design, however, such rejoinders confuse the two senses of the terms identified earlier. 'Normal' may mean usual (i.e. according to a pattern), or it may mean conforming to an appropriate standard. Likewise 'natural' may mean not artificial or according to design or proper function. In each case it is the latter meaning that is intended by the critic of alternative sexualities, and his or her position is untouched by pointing out that these occur 'in nature'. So too do inclinations to obsession and addiction, but that is hardly a basis for maintaining equivalence between these and the human norm.

Of course, such natural law reasoning is unlikely to persuade those who maintain the moral equivalence of all forms of sexual lifestyle. And against this background of fundamental moral disagreement the liberal idea of state neutrality may have some appeal. But it is neither practical nor consistent with the natural law view of the state. In such a view morality does and should constrain the public sphere insofar as policies bear upon basic rights and interests. The state exists in part to promote the common good and, more fundamentally, to protect its members' interests from harm or injury arising from the actions of others. On this at least moral conservatives and radicals are likely to agree.

How then to proceed? On the one hand, discrimination in law on the basis of private sexual practice cannot be justified. On the other hand, society has a right to expect its commonly shared interests to be protected, and these include the norm of heterosexual marriage, particularly as that bears upon the needs and formation of children. With that in mind one might see some wisdom in the search for a middle way between repeal and retention. When the matter was debated in the Westminster Upper Chamber – the House of Lords – Lord Brightman drafted the following replacement clause:

> Subject to the general principle that the institution of [heterosexual] marriage is to be supported, a local authority shall not encourage or publish material intended to encourage the adoption of any particular sexual life-style. This section does not prohibit the provision for young persons of sex education or counselling services on sexual behaviour and associated health risksy.[22]

In the event this was not put to the vote and the issue remains to be brought back to Parliament, but the proposal has merit. Reasoning about what policy it is rational for an individual or a government to pursue has to be related to the question of what burdens and harms arise from the effort to encourage or to enforce any given option. Here it may be useful to recall the distinction between value-promoting and value-protecting policies. Natural-law-based legislation will seek to protect the good of heterosexual union open to procreation and it will not promote forms of union other than this. Equally, however, where there is strong demand for alternatives, it will consider the cost of opposing this, and where that seems too great in its impact upon civil order and the common good, it may elect to tolerate what it cannot endorse.

Conclusions

Having quoted severally from Aquinas, the principal medieval author of natural law ethics and politics, I end with a quotation from one of the leading twentieth-century contributors in the same tradition, Jacques Maritain. In his classic work *The Person and the Common Good*, Maritain writes as follows:

> [T]he common good of political society is not only the collection of public commodities. . . . It includes the sum or sociological integration of all the civic conscience, political virtues, and sense of right and liberty, of all the activity, material prosperity and spiritual riches, of unconsciously operative hereditary wisdom, of moral rectitude, justice, friendship, happiness, virtue and heroism in the individual lives of its members. For these things are, in a certain measure, communicable and so revert to each member, helping him to perfect his life of liberty and person.[23]

This is an inspiring conception of the life of a civil and political community and it should serve to win friends if not converts to the view it represents. But anyone reviewing the degree of ideological and moral diversity and conflict

exhibited today, half a century after Maritain wrote these words, must wonder
how feasible in countries such as the United States is the project of a civil
society and political culture based on natural law. Lying behind the foregoing
applications of natural law theory has been the question of the social preconditions of the possibility of protecting or promoting certain fundamental values.
This raises the interesting though somewhat unsettling thought that an advocate of natural law, who for that reason is likely to be a moral and social
conservative (a non-libertarian communitarian), may find himself or herself in a
situation in which the diversity of opinions and the plurality of positions within
society is so great that there is no possibility of ordering the institutions and
policies of the state according to natural law reasoning. In that circumstance the
conservative may be persuaded that the best option is to urge the dismantling of
the state. If a polity cannot be well ordered, then better, *perhaps*, that it be
abandoned. It is for this reason that natural law ethics and practical politics
(conceived as the art of the possible) may not always go hand in hand.

Notes

1 Cicero, *De re publica*, I, 43 as translated by Michael Grant in *Roman Readings*
(Harmonsdworth: Penguin, 1958). The complete text – Latin and English facing –
can be found in Cicero, *De re publica* and *De legibus*, trans. C.W. Keyes, Loeb
Classical Library (London: Loeb, 1977).

2 Aquinas, *Summa Theologiae*, 1-2, q. 94, a. 4 *responsio*. The translation is based on
that of the Fathers of the English Dominican Province (London: R. & T. Washbourne,
1915). The relevant sections of the *Summa* (1-2, 22, 90–7) are given in Latin and in
English translation together with commentary in R.J. Henle, *Saint Thomas Aquinas:
The Treatise on Law* (Notre Dame, Ind.: University of Notre Dame Press, 1993).

3 Two interesting accounts and discussions of Aquinas's thought in relation to natural
law and the ethical foundations of politics are provided by Anthony J. Lisska, *Aquinas's
Theory of Natural Law* (Oxford: Oxford University Press, 1996), and John Finnis,
Aquinas: Moral, Political and Legal Theory (Oxford: Oxford University Press, 1998).

4 For an excellent account of political thought from antiquity to the Renaissance,
which situates natural law throughout this period, see Janet Coleman, *A History of
Political Thought*, vol. 1: *From Ancient Greece to Early Christianity*, vol. 2: *From the
Middle Ages to the Renaissance* (Oxford: Blackwell, 2000). For an introduction to and
selections from the writings of moral and social philosophers of the modern and
Enlightenment periods, see J. Schneewind (ed.), *Moral Philosophy from Montaigne to
Kant*, 2 vols (Cambridge: Cambridge University Press, 1990). For a general history
of moral philosophy, see Alasdair MacIntyre, *A Short History of Ethics*, 2nd edn
(London: Routledge, 1998).

5 Such, in a sense, is the case with Cicero, as quoted earlier. For while he writes of
attempts to supersede the law as being 'sinful' and refers to 'God' as its author, these
references are regularly set aside as rhetorical and non-theistic. On the other hand,
however, in his dialogue *On the Nature of the Gods*, composed around 4 BCE but set
some thirty years earlier, Cicero has one of the interlocutors, the Stoic philosopher
Lucillus, speak as follows: 'The point seems scarcely to need affirming. What can be
so obvious and clear, as we gaze up at the sky and observe the heavenly bodies, as
that there is some divine power of surpassing intelligence by which they are ordered?'
On the Nature of the Gods, trans. P.G. Walsh (Oxford: Clarendon Press, 1991), p. 48.

The parallel between this and the following from Saint Paul's Letter to the Romans is striking: 'What can be known about God is plain to men for God has shown it to them. Ever since the creation of the world his invisible nature, namely his eternal power and deity, has been clearly perceived in the things that have been made' (Romans 1.19–20).

6 Igor Primoratz, *Ethics and Sex* (London: Routledge, 1999).

7 For a brief account of the ideas of these figures, see Jonathan Dancy, 'Intuitionism', in Peter Singer (ed.), *A Companion to Ethics* (Oxford: Blackwell, 1991), pp. 411–20.

8 This is now an unduly neglected group. For an introduction to the main figures and their ideas, see J.N. Findlay, *Axiological Ethics* (London: Macmillan, 1970).

9 For representations of these positions, see (1) on the side of naturalist objectivism: John Finnis, *Natural Law and Natural Rights* (Oxford: Oxford University Press, 1980); Robert George, 'Natural Law and Human Nature', in Robert George (ed.), *Natural Law Theory: Contemporary Essays* (Oxford: Clarendon Press, 1992), reprinted in Robert George, *In Defence of Natural Law* (Oxford: Clarendon Press, 1999); and Patrick Lee, 'Is Thomas's Natural Law Theory Naturalist?' *American Catholic Philosophical Quarterly* 71 (1997), pp. 567–87; and (2) on the side of objectivist naturalism: Russell Hittinger, *A Critique of the New Natural Law Theory* (Notre Dame, Ind.: University of Notre Dame Press, 1987); Lloyd Weinreb, *Natural Law and Justice* (Cambridge, Mass.: Harvard University Press, 1987); and Mark Murphy, 'Self-Evidence, Human Nature, and Natural Law', *American Catholic Philosophical Quarterly* 69 (1995), pp. 471–84.

10 For further discussion, see John Haldane, 'Thomistic Ethics in America', *Logos* 3 (2000), pp. 150–68, and for some historical background, John Haldane, 'Medieval and Renaissance Ethics', Chapter 8, above.

11 G.E.M. Anscombe, 'Modern Moral Philosophy', *Philosophy* 33 (1958), p. 1–19, reprinted in Anscombe, *Ethics, Religion and Politics: Collected Papers*, vol. 3 (Oxford: Blackwell, 1981), pp. 26–42.

12 Alasdair MacIntyre, *After Virtue* (London: Duckworth, 1981).

13 Alasdair MacIntyre, 'The Privatisation of Good', in C.F. Delaney (ed.), *The Liberalism–Communitarianism Debate* (Lanham, Md.: Rowman & Littlefield, 1994), p. 6.

14 Alasdair MacIntyre, *Whose Justice? Which Rationality?* (London: Duckworth, 1988).

15 Alasdair MacIntyre, *Three Rival Versions of Moral Enquiry* (London: Duckwroth, 1990).

16 Alasdair MacIntyre, *Dependent Rational Animals: Why Human Beings Need the Virtues* (Notre Dame, Ind.: University of Notre Dame Press, 1999), p. x.

17 I discuss the character and coherence of MacIntyre's account of the structure of rational inquiry in John Haldane, 'MacIntyre's Thomist Revival: What's Next?' Chapter 2, above. For MacIntyre's reply see the original volume, J. Horton and S. Mendiss (eds), *After MacIntyre* (Cambridge: Polity Press, 1994), pp. 294–6.

18 See Fred D. Miller, Jr, *Nature, Justice and Rights in Aristotle's Politics* (Oxford: Oxford University Press, 1995); also, Michael Novak, *Free Persons and the Common Good* (Madison, Wis.: Madison House, 1989).

19 Translated as 'On Princely Government' by J.G. Dawson, in A.P. D'Entreves (ed.), *Aquinas: Selected Political Writings* (Oxford: Blackwell, 1959), p. 3.

20 From *Donum Vitae* (1987) as quoted in the *Catechism of the Catholic Church* (London: Geoffrey Chapman, 1994), part 3, section 2, paragraph 2273.

21 *Local Government Act* (London: HMSO, 1988), section 28.

22 Lords Hansard for 7 February 2000 (London: HMSO, 2000).

23 Jacques Maritain, *The Person and the Common Good*, trans. John Fitzgerald (New York: Scribner, 1947), pp. 52–3.

Chapter 10

From law to virtue
and back again
On *Veritatis Splendor* think about that

> *The dialogue of Jesus with the rich young man*, related in the nineteenth chapter of Saint Matthew's Gospel, can serve as a useful guide *for listening once more* in a lively and direct way to his moral teaching: 'then someone came to him and said "Teacher, what good must I do to have eternal life?" And he said to him, "Why do you ask me about what is good? There is only one who is good. If you wish to enter into life, keep the commandments." He said to him, "Which ones?" And Jesus said, "You shall not murder; You shall not commit adultery; You shall not steal; You shall not bear false witness; Honour your father and your mother; also, You shall love your neighbour as yourself." The young man said to him, "I have kept all these; what do I still lack?" Jesus said to him, "If you wish to be perfect, go, sell your possessions and give the money to the poor, and you will have treasure in heaven; then come, follow me"' (Matt. 19.16–21).
>
> *Veritatis Splendor*, §6

Introduction

The invitation to reflect upon the use of the Bible in ethics is a welcome challenge. For a philosopher working within the analytical tradition, who thinks of ethics principally as moral philosophy, it is rather like being asked to consider the role of woodcarving in the decoration of supermarkets – generally speaking it is not to be found there. But, as in that case also, one cannot help wondering whether the omission is not to be regretted.

Certainly some philosophical authors make reference to the idea of divine commands and occasionally even go so far as to specify one; but that is usually in the context of setting up the Euthyphro dilemma in order to show the purported irrelevance of religion to morality.[1] The dilemma (deriving from one posed by Socrates in the dialogue from which it takes its name) involves the question of whether God commands what is good because it is good, or whether what is good is so because God commands it. The apparent problem for the believer in divine commands is that the first option accords antecedent (prelegislated) standing to values and so seems to render God's prescriptions irrelevant or, at best, instrumentally useful after the manner of advice; while the second preserves the ontological priority of God's commands but at the price of rendering them ungrounded or arbitrary, with God being like a whimsical sovereign simply willing that this or that be done.

This is an old problem, but discussions of it rarely engage with the form and content of Judaeo-Christian scripture. An interesting and little-known exception to this neglect, however, is the debate between Christian philosopher–theologians of the medieval and Reformation periods. These divided on 'realist' and 'voluntarist' lines – taking the first and second horns respectively – and often cited scripture in challenge and defence. The two most often quoted and debated episodes are the command to Abraham to sacrifice Isaac (Gen. 22) and the order to the Israelites to despoil the Egyptians (Exod. 11). Much theological and philosophical ingenuity went into the reading of these cases. Aquinas, for example, introduces the idea of *mutatio materiae* (change of matter) to argue that God was able to prescribe the taking of goods from the Egyptians without revoking or violating the prohibition against theft because he had changed the underlying material facts by transferring property – which in truth is his – from the Egyptians to the Israelites. In short, the Jews were taking what, by virtue of divine reassignment, was already rightly theirs.[2]

This sort of serious and respectful attention to the content of a biblical text is hard to find in present-day philosophical writings. Occasionally, however, a philosopher will cite an episode recounted in scripture in order to make some general point about the nature of evil, or about a form of moral thought. Peter Winch's fine essay 'Who Is My Neighbour?' is an interesting instance of the latter. He begins as follows: 'Philosophical discussion needs well-formulated examples; and I want to introduce my subject with a very well known example from the New Testament: the parable of the Good Samaritan.'[3] There then follow some sensitive reflections on the meaning of Christ's words, but by the end of the essay it is clear that the aim has been to argue for certain ideas about the character of moral psychology which could as easily have been developed (as in others of Winch's essays) by considering a passage from some work of modern literature. Winch concludes: 'My central point is that in questions concerning our understanding of each other our moral sensibility is indeed an aspect of our sensibility, of the way we see things, of what we make of the world we are living in.'[4]

So the use of scripture as a foil, or as a source of examples, is not unknown in analytical writings. What is very much rarer – indeed probably rarer than wood-carving in supermarkets – is any consideration of the general relationship between Judaeo-Christian sacred writings and the form and content of philosophical ethics. This, however, is my theme; and to explore it, if only very briefly (and certainly inadequately), I have chosen the method of case study. I shall be discussing a specific use of scripture: Pope John Paul II's reflections on Matthew 19.16–21, in the encyclical letter *Veritatis Splendor* addressed to the Catholic bishops 'regarding certain fundamental questions of the Church's moral teaching'.[5] While I am concerned with a single case, what I hope to show is that this instance of an appeal to scripture is of entirely general significance; for in one sense what is at issue in the encyclical is the whole of ethics – biblical and philosophical.

Veritatis Splendor is divided into three chapters concerning 'Christ and the answer to the question about morality', 'The Church and the discernment of certain tendencies in present-day moral theology' and 'Moral good for the life of the Church and of the world' respectively. For present purposes the first and the second chapters are of most relevance. I shall not say anything about their detail as my interest is in certain framework issues, but I will give an idea of what they contain. In the following sections, then, I begin with preliminary scene-setting before sketching some of the contents of the encyclical. Following that I take up a series of general questions about the relations between the old law of Moses and the new law of Christ; and between rule and virtue, nature and function; and between scripture and philosophy.

A trend in moral theology

Among the conciliar documents of Vatican II is the 'Decree on Priestly Formation' (*Optatam Totius*). This sets out a series of directives and counsels including several concerning the revision of ecclesiastical studies. There we read that 'the first object in view must be a better integration of philosophy and theology' and later, in the sections on theology, that 'special attention needs to be given to the development of moral theology. Its scientific [systematic and theoretical] exposition should be more thoroughly nourished by scriptural reading.'[6]

Vatican II induced something of a renaissance in Catholic scriptural studies; and certainly it became increasingly common in catechetics and homiletics to focus on the life and teachings of Christ and then on the activities of the apostles in forming the first Christian communities. This attention to what is given in scripture contrasts with earlier approaches which emphasized the doctrines and laws of the Catholic Church, presenting them with a determination and confidence borne of Counter-Reformation thought and subsequent affirmations of the magisterium. So far as concerns moral theology, the tradition of the inter-council years was of the systematic elaboration of prohibitions, requirements, permissions and exceptions deriving from the Decalogue; the Ten Commandments being conceived of as a set of absolute (non-relative and exceptionless) prescriptions.

This somewhat abstract and formal approach then gave way to styles of ethical reflection in which contexts and particularities were emphasized in the service of the idea that few if any general 'for always and everywhere' judgements are possible. In place of the idea that certain types of action are forbidden or morally impossible, there developed notions of 'contextuality' or 'situationality' and of a 'fundamental option' (or, in Karl Rahner's terminology, 'the human person's disposition of his self as a whole') in terms of which it was argued that right action is that which issues from a personality imbued with Christ-like charity and is sensitive to the special circumstances of each occasion. Instead of asking what God has commanded, it became common to wonder what Christ would do, and in answering the latter question to suppose that he would seek to bring about the best outcome for those involved. Thus was effected the transition from a legalistic ethic of strict and largely negative duty to one of positive virtue, with beneficence being the principal disposition in the latter orientation.

Targets of criticism

Pope John Paul II is noted for his theological orthodoxy and for his willingness to censure Catholic theologians whom he judges to have moved outside the sphere of legitimate interpretation. It is unsurprising, therefore, that he should have chosen to address an encyclical to the issue of the moral teaching of the Catholic Church.[7] It was also to be expected that in doing so he would take issue with certain views developed within recent moral theology.[8] Equally predictable were the responses that followed it. Since the publication of *Veritatis Splendor* in August 1993 at least three sets of commentaries and many journal articles have appeared. For the most part the authors of these have been critical of John Paul's theological and philosophical conservatism, and defensive of the revisionist tendencies which he challenges[9] – though there are some distinguished exceptions, including Alasdair MacIntyre. MacIntyre examines the ways in which the encyclical manages to be both a teaching document and a philosophical text and relates its critical moments to a synthesis of these two functions. He writes:

> *Veritatis Splendor* is and will remain a striking Christian intervention in moral debate, at once authoritative teaching and a voice in that continuing philosophical conversation between Christianity and modernity to which Pascal and Kierkegaard, Newman and Barth and von Balthasar, have all been contributors. *Veritatis Splendor* continues the same evangelical and philosophical conversation with secular modernity, and the appropriate initial response of each of us to it should concern our own past and present defects and errors rather than those of others. There is much work to be done.[10]

The nominal targets of the Pope's criticisms are moral philosophical-cum-theological positions (e.g. 'consequentialism' and 'proportionalism') and not the individuals who occupy them. However, it is easy enough to identify some of those who might be in the line of fire: Charles Curran, Bernhard Häring, Joseph Fuchs and Richard McCormick. (It is also interesting to speculate, on stylistic grounds, on the identity of the Pope's philosophical and theological consultants – Fr Andrzej Szostek of Lublin and John Finnis of Oxford[11] have been mentioned in this connection, especially with regard to ch. 2.) What the Pope objects to as much as anything else in the 'new' moral theologies is the suggestion that reflection on the words and deeds of Christ, as given in scripture, permits or requires a departure from familiar moral teaching, including most especially its exceptionless prohibitions. His aim, therefore, is to uphold that teaching by the ancient method developed by Anselm, Aquinas and others, of showing it to be warranted by Holy Scripture, Church tradition and philosophical argument.[12]

Although the last of these is broadly in line with scholastic Aristotelianism as represented by Aquinas, the Pope adds a distinctive note by adopting a 'personalist' perspective. In the form associated with the University of Lublin (where he had previously taught philosophy and theology), personalism is a blend of Thomist metaphysics and anthropology, with phenomenological epistemology and ethics. That is to say it assumes that persons are unified substances possessed of rational powers and that we come to understand (and change) ourselves by reflection upon the meaning of our agency as this is implicit within deliberative consciousness.

One of the central elements of Thomist personalism is the denial of Cartesian and Kantian dualisms according to which the true subject of deliberation – and thus the true moral agent – is an entity (a *res cogitans* or *noumenal self*, respectively) distinct from and transcendent of its contingent embodiment in nature. Arguing on anti-dualist lines that human beings are rational animals whose bodies are already in the domain of meaning, an interesting connection between personalist philosophy of mind and sexual ethics is suggested in ch. 2:

> [O]ne has to consider carefully the correct relationship between freedom and human nature, and in particular *the place of the human body in questions of natural law.*
>
> A freedom which claims to be absolute ends up treating the human body as a raw datum, devoid of any meaning and moral values until freedom has shaped it in accordance with its design. Consequently, human nature and the body appear as presuppositions or preambles, materially necessary for freedom to make its choice, yet extrinsic to the person, the subject and the human act...
>
> This moral theory does not correspond to the truth about man and his freedom. It contradicts the *Church's teachings on the unity of the human person,* whose rational soul is per se *et essentialiter* the form of his body...
>
> *A doctrine which dissociates the moral act from the bodily dimensions of its exercise is contrary to the teaching of Scripture and Tradition.*
>
> (*Veritatis Splendor*, pp. 75–7)

Virtue and reason

Veritatis Splendor was an ambitious attempt to reaffirm orthodoxy on the eve of the third millennium, and in the face of challenges to the effect that what it teaches is no longer tenable. If I am broadly right in my interpretation and in the argument of the following section, then this reaffirmation can be seen to be an interesting and, to some extent, effective deployment of the same range of resources that dissenters have sought to use on behalf of their own reformed moral theology. This may be in part an *ad hominem* response but it is much more an application of methods long-established within Catholic thought – a pre-modern challenge to modernist and postmodernist errors.

Chapter 1 is an extended reflection on the meaning of the exchange between the wealthy questioner and Christ. In asking 'what good must I do?' the young man represents the general human search for a source of meaning; and in replying '…come, follow me', Christ shows that the question is in essence a religious one to which God himself is the answer. Later, John Paul links this idea with natural and revealed law by arguing that both the exercise of reason and the commandments 'show man the path of life' (p. 20). What the encounter with Christ adds is a model of perfected virtue: 'Jesus' way of acting and his words, his deeds and his precepts constitute the moral rule of Christian life' (p. 34).

In chapter 2, the tone is less inspirational, more systematically philosophical and in parts unmistakably critical. The main concern throughout is to show that a proper understanding of human agency implies that certain kinds of actions are intrinsically bad (*intrinsece malum*) and not such as can be justified by a pre-established fundamental option, good motives (*causis bonis*) or by a specific intention to produce beneficial outcomes. As before, appeals to scripture and reason are interwoven:

what does this mean?

> Reason attests that there are objects of the human act which are by their nature 'incapable of being ordered' to God, because they radically contradict the good of the person made in his image…
>
> In teaching the existence of intrinsically evil acts, the Church accepts the teaching of Sacred Scripture [cf. 1 Cor. 6.9–10]…
>
> Consequently, circumstances or intentions can never transform an act intrinsically evil by virtue of its object into an act 'subjectively' good or defensible as a choice.
>
> (*Veritatis Splendor*, p. 125)

The concluding chapter then addresses various implications for the Church's prophetic function of Christ's call to perfection and the rational defence of moral absolutes – in one guise the dictates of right reason attuned to the proper goal of human life, and in another the revealed will of God. Against the background of rampant secularism and moral relativism, the task of instruction is taken to be urgent and the duty to bear witness inescapable.

The philosophical-theological framework

John Finnis has written that the theme of *Veritatis Splendor* is faith not sex.[13] There is in fact very little said about specific kinds of behaviour, though contraception is mentioned along with other offences against chastity and justice.[14] Unsurprisingly, though, it was sexual issues that caught the interest of the press and other media. Here I am not concerned to challenge or defend papal teaching on these or any other any specifics;[15] for my interest is in the way in which the encyclical brings together scripture and reason, and law and virtue. If some interpretation of this constructive enterprise provides a correct and adequate *form* of moral-cum-religious thinking, then one may adopt it in advance of agreeing to particular norms and requirements. Let me offer, then, an outline of what I believe to be such an interpretation.

It is often claimed that there is an ethical contrast between Hebrew and Christian scriptures inasmuch as the former emphasize the regal dominion of God over his people and the promulgation of his commandments, while the latter advance the idea of divine concern and the restoration of a fallen order of nature through the perfection of Christ. Allied to this contrast is a somewhat less familiar distinction between deontological and virtue-ethics; that is to say, between an account of right action that ties it to the observance of various categorical duties, and a view which sees it as the expression of a certain kind of valuable character. It is natural, then, to see Christ as the perfect embodiment of virtue and to read into the encounter with the rich man the superiority of good character over obedience to law. After all, we read that the rich man observed the latter but was not on that account morally perfect.

With these sorts of contrasts in mind, and recalling what was said earlier about the styles of moral theology pre- and post-Vatican II, it is perhaps tempting to regard John Paul's emphasis on moral absolutes as an effort to return to a narrowly deontological and decalogical interpretation of morality and to downplay the role of character and circumstance in the determination of right action. However, this is difficult to square with the choice of Matthew's text; and it neglects the Pope's Thomistic-cum-phenomenological philosophy. Of course, one might take the view of some of its critics that *Veritatis Splendor* is a mishmash of disparate elements; but I think a more plausible reading of it as a fairly systematically ordered and largely unified thesis is available. There are irregularities in its style, and its general character is somewhat scholastic. These are, however, recurrent features of Vatican documents and should be set aside when considering the overall form of its argument.

The basic philosophical-cum-theological framework is that provided by St Thomas in the *Summa Theologiae*. We are part of a created and beneficial order, an interlocking system of substances possessed of defining powers and characteristics. What it is to be a such and such – an oak tree, a cat, or a human being – is to be so much matter organized to function in various ways so as to attain certain (species-specific and species-transcendent) ends. Matter is taken up by the form of the tree and is maintained in a dynamic organization involving nutrition, growth and replication. Likewise a human being is an organized substance in which various vital processes are subordinated to the service of rational action. All being well, the end-related functions and activities contribute to the movement of life towards some enduring state of well-being (for Aristotle *eudaimonia*, for Aquinas *beatitudo*). But Judaeo-Christian scripture tells us that all is now not well, that creation is 'fallen', not irredeemably impaired but liable to go dangerously wrong; and as cancer is to healthy tissue so wrongdoing is to the moral self – that is, progressively destructive.

It may be useful to think of this in terms of an object, a sphere say, that is perfectly fashioned and provided with a principle of self-directed movement. Imagine further that the terrain across which it moves is likewise well-formed and free of threats and dangers. Under these conditions it makes its way easily, rolling onwards towards its destination. Suppose, however, that something happens to damage the sphere and its environment. Its surface becomes deformed, its guidance system is rendered less reliable, and the terrain is now strewn with obstacles and pitted with craters. In these changed circumstances the object is unlikely to reach its destination unless some external influence is applied, say by the introduction of a system of barriers and tracks and by the periodic application of pressure in the direction of its goal.

This serves as an image of the human condition before and after the Fall and makes sense of the Decalogue as a device for trying to keep us away from deathly dangers, and of the prophets as (themselves flawed) pilots attempting to reorient us towards our eternal destiny. It also suggests the form of a better solution: the restoration of the pre-lapsarian order starting with the reformation of human beings. This is the condition and role of Christ in whom human nature is made perfect. The specialness of Jesus in this regard is not the example offered by his divine nature – after all, what do we, or most, if not all, of those who encountered him know of that? – it is the example presented by his humanity.[16] To adapt Paul, 'as in Adam humankind fell, so in Christ it is raised up again'. Whereas before a series of instructions was required to try and help to reach our destination, now an example of proper functioning is available, as is the promise that if it is followed we will ourselves become perfect.

On this account the transition from an ethics of law to one of virtue is not a matter of changing direction, but that of acquiring an adequate principle of movement from within (*ab intrinseco*, as the scholastics had it) whereby one is better able to reach the same destination as one was previously directed towards. Grace perfects and does not repeal nature; and Christ comes to fulfil and not to annul the law. So the difference between the Hebrew and Christian Testaments and between duty and virtue lies not in what each prescribes but in how they achieve one and the same end. What is sought under the species of the virtuous and aimed at under the guise of the obligated are one and the same thing, that is, realization of one's nature in union with God. The rich man asked, 'What must I do to have eternal life?' and Christ replied 'If you wish to enter into life, keep the commandments.' The young man said, 'I have kept these, what do I still lack?' Christ's second answer does not revoke the commandments; indeed, it does not obviously add to them, for giving to the poor might reasonably be thought to be an instance of loving your neighbour as

virtue ethics

yourself. The significance lies in what follows the instruction to act charitably, in the words 'then come, follow me'.

Notice that in effecting this reconciliation between moral law and moral virtue it was necessary to draw upon certain metaphysical resources – the Thomistic account of nature as a system of teleologically ordered substances. This philosophical understanding gives rise to a further sense in which morality pertains to law, for it has long been the practice in Catholic moral theology to speak of human goods and of patterns of action directed towards them in terms of 'natural law'. Again, this is not something to be contrasted with scriptural ethics, whether in decalogical or Christological forms; rather it is the same reality towards which both direct us but it is now regarded from the point of view of reason rather than of revelation.[17] And just as the requirements and prohibitions of the Decalogue are not rescinded or relaxed by Christ's injunction to charity, so the conclusions of practical reasoning about how to attain the end of human life must include absolute prohibitions, inasmuch as a course of action that is at odds with this goal is thereby excluded, both as an end and as a means. The evil of torture does not lie solely nor for the most part in its effects, as if these might in some cases be outweighed by beneficial consequences. In the first instance torture is evil and thus morally prohibited because of what it *is* and not simply because of what it produces. To act in that way is to attack a basic human good; and it is a teaching both of Aristotelian ethics and of Christian scripture that some actions are such that they may never be performed and that those who violate these prohibitions thereby show themselves to be of vic[e]ious character. First Aristotle and then St Paul:

> Some [actions and passions] have names that already imply badness, e.g. spite, shamelessness, envy, and in the case of actions adultery, theft, murder....It is not possible then ever to be right with regard to them; one must always be wrong. Nor does goodness or badness with regard to such things depend on committing adultery with the right woman, at the right time, and in the right way, but simply to do any of them is to go wrong.[18]

> Do you not know that the unrighteous will not inherit the kingdom of God? Do not be deceived: neither the immoral, nor idolaters, nor adulterers, nor sexual perverts, nor thieves, nor the greedy, nor drunkards, nor revilers, nor robbers will inherit the Kingdom of God.[19]

Conclusion

Here I have been concerned to argue that the use made of the opening gospel passage in *Veritatis Splendor* is not at odds with the appeal to revealed and natural law, and that it is not incompatible with the teleological virtue-theory elaborated in chapter 2, or with the moral absolutism upon which the Pope insists at every turn. On the contrary, the elements of philosophy and scripture are effectively integrated and pose a significant challenge to those contemporary moral theologians who favour weaker and often relativistic interpretations of Christ's invitation to be perfect.

Let me end by indicating why in these matters scripture, and in particular the New Testament, is not merely an interesting route to a conclusion which can be reached by other means. Thomistic Aristotelianism provides a compelling account of the *form* of morality as a set of rational dispositions to act and to refrain from acting – dispositions that are in part instruments to our flourishing and in part constituents of it. But, thus far, this is only a formal characterization without any specification of the human *telos* or of the virtues that lead to and form part of it. Experience and reason can help inform us of how we should live; but given the wounded condition of human nature their deliverances are at best partial and underdetermine the content of morality. Thus the encounter with Christ, the Son of Man and the perfect human being, offers a unique possibility of answering fully the principal questions of ethics: *What should we be?* and *What should we do in order to be it?* That is why, I believe, Pope John Paul begins with and returns to the young man's encounter, and also why he uses a good deal of philosophy and theology to integrate the general meaning of this resonant episode within a rational and affective moral psychology. Rather than being a reactionary and retrograde tract, as the revisionists assume, *Veritatis Splendor* presents a challenge and offers a model for a new phase of religious ethics; one in which scripture, reason and tradition are worked together to produce an authoritative theology of the right and the good.[20]

"the sense of the faithful"

Notes

1 See, for example, Jonathan Berg, 'How Could Ethics Depend on Religion?' in P. Singer (ed.), *A Companion to Ethics* (Oxford: Blackwell, 1990), pp. 525–33.
2 For further discussion see J. Haldane, 'Voluntarism and Realism in Medieval Ethics', *Journal of Medical Ethics* 15 (1989), pp. 39–44.
3 Peter Winch, 'Who Is My Neighbour?', in idem (ed.), *Trying to Make Sense* (Oxford: Blackwell, 1987), p. 154.
4 Winch, 'Who is My Neighbour', p. 166.
5 *Veritatis Splendor* (London: Catholic Truth Society, 1993).
6 'Decree on Priestly Formation', in W.M. Abbot, SJ, and J. Gallagher (eds), *The Documents of Vatican II* (New York: Guild Press, 1966), pp. 450, 452.
7 More recently he has returned to the theme of moral absolutes in discussing the ethics of life and death – see *Evangelium Vitae* (London: Catholic Truth Society, 1995).
8 He writes: 'The specific purpose of the present Encyclical is this: to set forth, with regard to the problems being discussed, the principles of a moral teaching based upon Sacred Scripture and the living Apostolic Tradition, and at the same time to shed light on the presuppositions and consequences of the dissent with which that teaching has met'. *Veritatis Splendor*, p. 11.
9 See the various contributions in J. Wilkins (ed.), *Understanding Veritatis Splendor* (London: SPCK, 1994); these were originally published in the *Tablet*. Another cluster of responses is to be found in *Studies in Christian Ethics* 7 (1994); and a third

The appeal of virtue ethics is that it unites the whole human person, rather than separating out ends and means.

in J.A. Selling and J. Jans (eds), *The Splendor of Accuracy* (Grand Rapids, Mich.: Eerdmans, 1994). See also the following: J. Berkman, 'Truth and Martyrdom: The Structure of Discipleship in *Veritatis Splendor*', *New Blackfriars* 75 (1994), pp. 533–41; F. Kerr, 'The Quarrel over Morals in the Catholic Church', *New Blackfriars* 75 (1994), pp. 500–11; R. McCormick, 'Some Early Reactions to *Veritatis Splendor*', *Theological Studies* 55 (1994), pp. 481–506; and S. Pinckaers, OP, 'The Use of Scripture and the Renewal of Moral Theology: The *Catechism* and *Veritatis Splendor*', *The Thomist* 59 (1995), pp. 1–19.

10 A. MacIntyre, 'How Can We Learn What *Veritatis Splendor* Has To Teach?', *The Thomist* 58 (1994), pp. 171–95 (195).

11 Compare ch. 2 of the encyclical with J. Finnis, *Moral Absolutes: Tradition, Revision, and Truth* (Washington, DC: Catholic University of America Press, 1991).

12 It is interesting in this connection to note what M. Daniel Carroll R. writes when discussing the work of the Dominican Bartolomé de Las Casas (1474–1564). Carroll observes that 'His use of the Bible is best exemplified in H.R. Parish (ed.), *The Only Way to Draw All People to a Living Faith* [trans. F.S. Sullivan; New York: Paulist Press, 1992]. In this work Las Casas presents arguments based on papal pronouncements, tomes of ancient philosophers, and Church tradition for evangelising in a peaceable manner so as to win the willing consent of the indigenous to the Catholic Faith. *The Only Way* is also heavily sprinkled with biblical references [including Matt. 19].' See 'The Bible and the Religious Identity of the Maya of Guatemala at the Conquest and Today: Considerations and Challenges for the Nonindigenous', in J.W. Rogerson, M. Davies and M.D. Carroll (eds), *The Bible in Ethics* (Sheffield: Sheffield Academic Press, 1995), p. 196.

13 John Finnis, 'Beyond the Encyclical', in Wilkins, *Understanding Veritatis Splendor*.

14 See *Veritatis Splendor*, §§49, 80 and 81 (pp. 77–8 and 122–5).

15 Given the interest in the issue, perhaps I might note in passing that even educated commentators seem to misunderstand the logic of the teaching on contraception. In his introduction to *Understanding Veritatis Splendor*, John Wilkins recognizes the unambiguous nature of the condemnation of 'contraceptive practices' as *intrinsece malum*, but observes that many Catholics do not regard contraception as intrinsically wrong. He then adds: 'They observe, for example, that in Paul VI's encyclical *Humanae Vitae* it is stated that contraception is admissible for therapeutic purposes. So intention counts' (p. xiii). No-one could seriously suppose that John Paul II denies that intention counts; the point is that it is not sufficient to determine the morality of an act: 'Activity is morally good when it attests to and expresses the voluntary ordering of the person to his ultimate end and the conformity of a concrete action with the human good as it is acknowledged in its truth by reason' (*Veritatis Splendor*, p. 110). As regards permissible uses of contraceptives, the point is that while it is always forbidden intentionally to render a sexual act infertile (to *practise* contraceptive sex) it is not necessarily forbidden to provide or receive a therapy the foreseen but unintended consequence of which is infertility. The distinction is between using something which is contraceptive in effect, and intentionally acting contraceptively. The conditional permissibility of the former is an instance of a principle of double effect.

16 In other words, I am claiming that Christ-*qua*-human (not *qua* Second Person of the Trinity) was a perfect human agent. For some discussion of a proposed logic of Christological predications, see Chapter 6, above.

17 For a short account of the history of this tradition in Christian ethics see Chapter 8, above.

18 Aristotle, *Nicomachean Ethics*, in *The Basic Works of Aristotle*, trans. W.D. Ross, ed. R. McKeon (New York: Random House, 1941), 1107a9–18.

19 1 Cor. 6.9–10, as quoted in *Veritatis Splendor*, p. 124.

20 A further aspect of the interest of *Veritatis Splendor* is its potential to expose inadequacies, or at least controversial elements, in secular accounts of moral and social thought. One implicit thesis of *Veritatis Splendor* is the indivisibility of practical reasoning. So put this may sound like a characteristically scholastic doctrine, but it has important implications for political philosophy. Contemporary deontological liberalism of the sort advocated by John Rawls and others distinguishes between the right and the good and then argues that different principles of each are appropriate for conduct within the ethical and the political spheres. On this basis it is argued by Rawls that any view that excludes or greatly restricts a woman's right to abortion in the first trimester is thereby 'unreasonable' (*Political Liberalism* (New York: Columbia University Press, 1993), p. 243). This argument derives from assumptions – about what may legitimately count as a political consideration – which are challenged by the unified notions of right and wrong articulated in *Veritatis Splendor* and in its sequel *Evangelium Vitae*. For further discussion, see J. Haldane, 'The Individual, the State and the Common Good', *Social Philosophy and Policy* 13 (1996), pp. 59–79.

Chapter 11

Can a Catholic be a liberal?
Catholic social teaching and communitarianism[1]

> As in the Church, God has established different grades of orders with diversity of function so that all should not be 'Apostles, nor all Doctors, nor all Prophets', so also He has established in Civil Society many orders of varying dignity, right and power. And this to the end that the State, like the Church, should form one body comprising many members, some excelling others in rank and importance but all alike necessary to one another and solicitous for the common good.
>
> *Quod Apostolici Muneris*

Introduction

The question posed in my title is meant to be thought-provoking, but it and the topics announced in the subtitle are broad and not altogether easy to discuss. Moreover the difficulty is not simply one of the scale of the subject matter. For it is by no means clear that there is any single political view that may claim the title 'Liberalism', or that there is a definite set of historically articulated principles that can be set out as giving the content of something called 'Catholic Social Teaching', or that there is one thing that deserves the label 'Communitarianism'. Fortunately, however, there is more that can be said, since there are elements and continuities which these various terms properly suggest and which it may be of philosophical and practical interest to discuss.

My strategy, then, will be to say something first about the recent history of Roman Catholic social teachings and their relation to older sources and then to outline certain ideas in contemporary political philosophy associated with the phrase 'the liberalism vs. communitarianism debate'. By that point certain connections between the topics will have become clear and I shall conclude by considering some implications of these. Perhaps I should add that political philosophy is currently in a state of considerable confusion over issues very close to some of those I shall be discussing and this fact may give a certain edge and relevance to what might otherwise seem, at least to some, to be a rather parochial interest. Finally I should add that my perspective on the title question is one which assumes the truth of Catholicism. That may seem to limit the interest of the discussion for those who do not share this belief, but whether the dominant version of Christianity is incompatible with the leading political ideology of the Western world is an issue that should be of general concern, and in any case part of what I have to say in criticism of liberalism is independent of any distinctly Catholic or even Christian doctrine.

Catholic social teaching

1991 saw the celebration, and not just in Roman Catholic circles, of the centenary of Pope Leo XIII's encyclical *Rerum Novarum*. In that document the Pope focused his attention, that is to say in non-punning terms, focused the mind of the Church, on the question of the contemporary condition of the working classes and produced a line of thought that wove its way between two opposing attitudes to private property: that of communism which denied that private ownership was or could be legitimate; and that of economic liberalism which rejected the idea that the state could be justified in constraining the operations of the market for the sake of the common good. Leo's *via media* allows that the acquisition of property is a legitimate aspiration for individuals but insists that ownership is responsible to wider moral and social interests and is thus answerable to the requirements of social justice. In this he was building on a philosophical tradition associated with natural law as that was interpreted and developed by the scholastics of the Middle Ages. This ancestry is important and I shall return to it later but for now I want to consider other aspects of papal teaching in the nineteenth and twentieth centuries.

In 1864, under the Papacy of Pius IX, there was published the *Syllabus of Errors*, a compilation of ideas held to be dangerously false. Among these were such theses as that there should be a separation of church and state (55); that morality is autonomous of divine sanction natural law (56); and that universal religious toleration does not imply indifference or lead to corruption (77). A proper appreciation of the contrary claims upheld by the Church would need to take account of the historical setting of the *Syllabus*, including the fear of revolution and of atheistic humanism, and this would yield interpretations less narrow in respect, for example, of church/state separation than an uninformed reading might suggest. All the same it is clear and undeniable that there is a strong anti-liberal current in this and other nineteenth-century documents. In 1888, for example, Leo XIII, the author of *Rerum Novarum*, offered a further rejection of a central theme of liberal thinking about the relationship between religion and politics when he wrote:

There are [those] who affirm that in public affairs the morality of God may be passed over and entirely disregarded in the framing of laws. Hence follows the fatal theory of the need of separation of Church and State.

(*On Human Liberty*)

Similarly, and as uncomfortable for many modern Catholics, church teaching has exhibited a repeated hostility to radical socialism. In his encyclical *Quadragesimo Anno* (1931) celebrating, as the title indicates, the fortieth anniversary of *Rerum Novarum*, Pope Pius XI wrote that 'Religious Socialism, Christian Socialism are expressions implying a contradiction in terms. No one can be at the same time a sincere Catholic and a sincere Socialist.' As before, a proper appreciation of these words would require an understanding of their context,[2] and in particular of what was meant by socialism. But it is important to see that there is an ineliminable opposition and to understand its basis. Pius writes:

> It follows from the twofold character of ownership, which we have termed individual and social, that men must take into account in this matter not only their own advantage but also that of the Common Good. To define in detail these duties [where that is not already done by the Natural Law] is the function of Government.

A central element of Catholic social teaching which can be extracted from these various documents is the idea that the basic laws governing the relations between citizens should take account of the requirements of an objective moral order which, in respect of social justice, involves the protection and promotion of the common good. Before saying something about the philosophical justification of this, and going on to consider its relation to the contemporary 'liberalism vs. communitarianism' debate, it is worth noting how the same idea as can be found in the encyclicals of Pius IX, Leo XIII and Pius XI informs the social doctrine of a more recent Pope, namely John XXIII. This bears upon the continuity of the teaching and ought to be noted particularly because it is commonly supposed that Pope John reversed the Church's attitude to liberalism. As will emerge, this is certainly not so.

One reason for thinking otherwise is that in his 1963 encyclical *Pacem in Terris*, the Pope adopted the, by then dominant, liberal rhetoric of rights:

> Every human being has the right to respect for his person; to his good reputation, the right to freedom in searching for truth and in expressing and communicating his opinions...
>
> Every human being has the right to honour God according to the dictates of an upright conscience and therefore the right to worship God privately and publicly...
>
> Human beings have the right to choose freely the state of life which they prefer and therefore the right to establish a family with equal rights and duties for man and woman and also the right to follow a vocation to the priesthood or religious life.

Superficially this can look to be entirely at odds with earlier teaching, such as the rejection of universal religious toleration contained in the *Syllabus of Errors*.

Certainly there is, as I remarked, a difference in the political vocabulary, and of course John XXIII made efforts not to speak with the authoritarian tones of his predecessors; but on closer inspection it becomes clear that while the teaching may have developed it has retained its original and essential orientation, *and its (presumed) authority*. Compare, for example, what I have quoted from *Pacem in Terris* with what the *Syllabus* implies about religious toleration:

> civil liberty for any religious sect whatever and the granting to all of full right to express any kind of opinion and thought whatever, openly and publicly, conduces to the easier corruption of the morals and minds of peoples and the spread of the disease of indifferentism.

Note first that what is condemned is 'liberty for any religious sect whatever' and 'full right to express any kind of opinion and thought whatever', and then look again at John XXIII's declaration of rights. What he speaks of is 'freedom in searching for truth', 'the right to honour God according to the dictates of an upright conscience', 'the right to establish a family...and also the right to follow a [religious] vocation'. In short, John, no less than Pius, regards the legitimacy of the free pursuit of human activities as related to an objective moral and theological order. The difference is not one of substance but of application and presentation.

What lies behind this tradition of social teaching is a moral and political philosophy that originates in the weaving together, through the patristic and medieval periods, of Greek theories of value and Judaeo-Christian moral codes. The history of this construction is too lengthy and complex even to summarize here,[3] but its product is a general theory of natural law which holds that men and women should act in accord with certain values related to their nature as rational creatures. Just as a plant has a range of functions the operation of which conduces to, and in part constitutes, its flourishing as an entity of a certain sort, so human beings are equipped with various powers the proper operation of which promotes and realizes their well-being as rational animals. Unlike plants, however, man is both rational and spiritual. That is to say, his well-being is not constituted organically, though bodily health is not unimportant, but in terms of a transcendent destiny: the attainment of union with his Maker, whose company he may hope to enjoy through an eternal and inexhaustible beatific vision. An important element in the Catholic version of this theory is the claim that, in respect both of the earlier mundane phase of their existence and of the later heavenly one, human beings are essentially social creatures. As Aquinas has it:

> It is natural for man to be a social and political animal, living in community; and this is more true of him than of any other animal, as is revealed by his natural necessities.

> (*De Regimine Principum*)

The fact that man is a social creature not by voluntary choice but through his created nature has an implication for the politics of society. The civic community, or the state, is not a product of individuals' chosen associations with one another; rather it is an 'organic' unity, the continuing existence and well-being of which depends upon morally guided government. And the primary duties of human governments are to protect and promote the common good. As the opening quotation from *Quod Apostolici Muneris* has it:

> the State, like the Church, should form one body comprising many members, some excelling others in rank and importance but all alike necessary to one another and solicitous for the common good.

Liberty and justice

Political philosophy in the English-speaking world has undergone a renaissance during the last twenty years. Arising from that rebirth is the current domination of the subject by one issue more than any other, that being what I shall call *'the question of liberalism'*. The dominance of this question has different aspects. One is simply *statistical*: in some guise or another it is the question most often addressed by writers in the field. A related but more fundamental aspect of its domination, however, is *philosophical*. The question of liberalism exerts a gravitational pull attracting other issues to its surface and often drawing them deep into its core. The author who above all others has been the midwife of political philosophy's renaissance and has also been largely responsible for the current centrality of the question of liberalism is John Rawls. Just over twenty years ago Rawls published *A Theory of Justice*[4] in which he sought to articulate a conception of interpersonal justice adequate to found principles which might govern the political institutions of society. Rawls's theory is developed within certain self-imposed limits. These include restrictions on its *scope* and on its *structure*. As regards the first, it eschews any ambition to arrive at a general theory of morality, an overall account of how one ought to live; and as regards the second, it accords priority to the right over the good. I shall discuss both points. The first restriction arises from a view of the task and circumstances of contemporary Western political philosophy. This aims to provide legitimate forms of social organization in a situation in which the members of society may hold quite different moral views about how best to live. Accordingly, no political philosophy should or could supplant morality as a guide to individual conduct. I shall return to this issue shortly. The second restriction has, in part, a similar origin in a view of what society is actually like, but it is also philosophically motivated by a consideration of other accounts of justice.

The idea of the priority of the *right* over the *good* is that principles which direct conduct, i.e. which indicate what it would be right to do or to avoid, may override considerations of what it would be good to be or to have. If one kind of reason has the power to 'trump' another it must have an independent grounding. By way of a parallel, considerations of taste may outweigh those of cost when a company is redecorating its boardroom; but if so it cannot be that taste is measured by expense, it must have a separate foundation. Likewise, if considerations of what is right, i.e. of what is required or prohibited, may outweigh those of what is desirable then it cannot be that the desirable is the measure of the right.

Here, however, one may ask why should the right have priority over the good, why can it not just be a function of it, in the way that price is a function of demand and supply? Rawls's argument on this point is direct and telling. Justice is, as he puts it, the first virtue of civil society. It is the norm or principle which governs the operation of the fundamental political institutions. It is, for example, what legitimizes law-making and warrants the enforcement of law through the courts. In civil society the state takes to itself the exclusive right of coercive power. Law-makers set patterns for the distribution of goods and the regulation of behaviour and law-enforcers push those who depart from these patterns back into position. What legitimizes these regulative and coercive activities is the claim that justice permits or requires them.

This suggestion has attracted quite general support but it leaves unspecified the nature of justice, and as soon as one begins to specify it certain difficulties arise. Consider, for example, a utilitarian theory of justice. The utilitarian regards an action, policy or practice as warranted to the extent that it maximizes overall welfare. On this basis, then, it seems possible to justify individual political rights, according to each person a protected zone of activity within which he or she may do as they please, compatible with non-infringement of the protected zones of others. Thereby, we can imagine, each maximizes his or her personal utility without interference (or the threat of it) from others and in that way overall welfare is also maximized.

One only has to understand the structure of utilitarian theory, however, to realize that it is incapable of generating inviolable rights. It is committed to maximizing welfare, and given this fact we can easily imagine how any pattern of distributed rights could, under changed circumstances, become an obstacle to welfare rather than a means to it. Then, of course, the rights lapse, the zone of personal activity is entered for the benefit of others. But that is just to say it never was an inviolable zone as such, only a contingently protected one. In addition, and as Rawls was among the first of recent philosophers to observe, utilitarianism fails to respect the *distinctness of persons* – treating the interests and aims of each as if they were items in the desire-stock of a single agent to be weighed without consideration of their different ownership.

Rights, then, seem to need a different kind of foundation to well-being if they are to resist its claims to be promoted. Rights are part of what justice accords the citizen and hence the principles of justice, if they are to generate trumping but untrumpable entitlements, must involve the priority of the right over the good. As I said, this is a direct and telling argument, but we shall soon see that in the context of liberal assumptions it runs into difficulties.

Before coming to these, however, let me return to the question of the scope of justice, for this too is interesting but ultimately problematic. Rawls has given greater emphasis in recent writings to what he calls 'the circumstances of justice', that is the social conditions in which principles of justice must operate. These conditions induce the existence of different and incompatible systems of belief and value. At some level it was always so, but whereas in the Middle Ages, western Europe formed a broadly Christian culture, and more specifically a Catholic one, religious homogeneity then gave way to Christian disunity which in turn became part of a greater diversity of belief and disbelief. Likewise, the broadly Judaeo-Christian-cum-Hellenic–Roman natural law morality came to be questioned and often rejected in favour of other ethical theories and of moral nihilism. So, by stages, the West moved from a condition of ideological unity to one of pluralism.

That transition was neither continuous nor smooth. Rearguard actions on behalf of ruling orthodoxies are a familiar and recurrent feature of its history. In the nineteenth and twentieth centuries, the focus of dispute has been of a sort which invites the description 'belief against unbelief' – theists defending religion against atheism, objectivists fighting on behalf of moral realism against the onslaught of subjectivism. In previous centuries, however, the battles were between religious believers and between advocates of different forms of moral objectivism. Doubtless moral theorists have come to blows, but the metaphor of ideological battles has most often had a literal counterpart in the area of religion.

This fact is often adverted to by Rawls in his criticisms of those who look for a more wide-ranging political and social philosophy. He sees the modern political consciousness, upon which his own theory builds and to which it makes appeal, as deeply (if now indirectly) influenced by the religious wars of Europe. Whatever view one takes of the truth of rival Catholic and Protestant doctrines, and of the Christian Creed more generally, we are not now disposed to take arms on behalf of any party to theological debates. This disengagement from religious warfare has not been the result simply of seeing people die, or of loss of all conviction in the truth of claims in this area; rather it represents an advance in our thinking about the relationship between religious and moral doctrines on the one hand, and collective public life on the other. Recognition of the reality of irreconcilable differences in belief has produced a separation of aspects of life into different spheres. The general scheme of division into *public* and *private* realms arises from, and gives principled expression to, the division between the political order and the moral and religious ones.

Thus, the *scope* restriction on a liberal theory of justice is the claim that, given the condition of pluralism, political philosophy must eschew comprehensive doctrines of value and conduct and concern itself with principles which can govern the public interaction of persons holding radically different basic beliefs. As it is now often put, more under the influence of Dworkin[5] than of Rawls, liberalism aims to regulate political life without reference to any particular conception of the good for human beings as such. More strongly, it has to proceed on a neutral basis if it is to gain the allegiance of persons committed to different philosophies of life. In this connection Rawls speaks of the '*principle of tolera-tion*' and extends the range of its application. Not only must a theory of justice adequate for the modern world remain free of deep moral commitments of a comprehensive sort, it must also be independent of controversial philosophical assumptions and, one may add, styles of argument. For, as before, the theory has to be acknowledged as yielding authoritative principles of political life by all participants in the political order whatever their philosophical viewpoints. If a disagreement between individuals over a matter of property, say, should reach the point of requiring legal settlement, then one of the parties to the dispute would have grounds for complaint if it should transpire that the principles of public justice rest upon controversial philosophical ideas subscribed to by his opponent. It is out of this way of thinking that there emerged a phrase and almost a slogan which Rawls uses to characterize his theory: Justice as Fairness: *political not metaphysical.* As he writes:

> [The] public conception of justice should be, so far as possible, independ-ent of controversial philosophical and religious doctrines. Thus, to formulate [it], we apply the principle of toleration to philosophy itself: the public conception of justice is to be political not metaphysical...
>
> No political view that depends on [such] deep and unresolved matters [as questions of philosophical psychology or a metaphysical doctrine of the self] can serve as a public conception of justice in a constitutional democratic state.[6]

Thus the restrictions on *structure* and *scope* now come together in the idea that a liberal theory of politics is, and can only be, concerned with such prin-ciples and procedures for regulating social life as give priority to the right over the good and do not invoke any comprehensive theory of value or controversial philosophical doctrines.

Two questions now suggest themselves. Given these restrictions, can liber-alism deliver a satisfactory political system? and if it cannot, is there a viable alternative? As one might expect, there are lines of criticism proceeding from two opposing directions: from the side of those who think that liberalism offers too little in the way of guidance for social life, and from the wing of those who regard it as enlarging the area of public interest beyond what is legitimate. Here I shall not be concerned with this latter 'libertarian' critique. I know of no philosophical anarchist who argues that the domain of human life is exhausted by the private sphere, i.e. who holds that there is no public realm over which governance by political principles is required. That being so, the anarchist can be seen for what increasingly he takes himself to be, viz., a radical (or, as it has become fashionable to say, a 'classical') liberal.

It is for this reason among others that the most significant challenges to Rawlsian liberalism have come from those who think it is too weak a structure to hold political society together. This thought is linked with a more general claim to the effect that Rawls, Dworkin and others make a series of assumptions

about the nature of persons and the constitution of value which are misconceived and which, if acted upon, can only result in persons becoming alienated
from the kinds of things that give human life its meaning. Here philosophical
and empirical considerations are taken to converge. If one looks at contemporary Western society the alienation from common values and traditions is presumed to be evident and evidently damaging to both public and private interests.
And if one reviews the theoretical presuppositions of liberal politics, then
an incoherent individualism is taken to be apparent. Obviously these anti-
individualists' criticisms address the first question – that of whether liberalism
can deliver an adequate politics; but the 'communitarian critique', so-called,
is intended simultaneously to indicate an alternative and better theoretical
foundation for thinking about the conduct of social life. Before considering
this, however, let me offer a few remarks about the negative criticisms of philosophical liberalism.

These criticisms, delivered by authors such as Alasdair MacIntyre, Michael
Sandel and Charles Taylor,[7] have two targets: a theory of *persons* and a theory of
value. The occasion does not permit of more than an outline sketch of the
arguments but this should be sufficient.[8] Liberalism, requires that the various
participants in social life agree to be bound by principles of a strictly impartial
sort in which no reference is made to the identity-constituting facts of particular
individuals and communities. Justice, as we say, is blind. Accordingly, its principles must be such as would be affirmed by someone who knew nothing of
the contingent circumstances of their own life-history. In that sense justice as
fairness is the virtue affirmed by the anonymous chooser who knows only that
he or she will have some or other values and projects which they will want to
pursue. But the identity and specific nature of these goals may not inform the
principles of social life; and nor may the fact, if it is one, that any values and
projects may be shared and pursued with others. Similarly, the particular values
which one may come to affirm must be held in abeyance when questions of
public policy arise, for then only the transcendent requirements of justice can be
recognized to have universal authority.

The communitarian objections are easy to anticipate given these descriptions.
Liberalism requires that we think of ourselves as characterless, atom-like agents
constituted as subjects of one or another political community without reference
to the distinctive circumstances and histories which have influenced us. However, this ignores the empirical dependency of self-consciousness upon social
environment. Moreover, philosophical reflection reveals that social influence is
not a contingent fact about our actual identities, additional to a necessary truth
about the essences individuals possess as persons. Rather, the original social
context of a human life shapes it – in the sense in which we might speak of
sphericality shaping a ball – it makes it to be the kind of thing it is. The very
idea that we can conceive of ourselves as agents entering into a scheme of
political association independently of knowing ourselves to have a particular
socially constituted nature is incoherent. As incoherent, indeed, as supposing

that one could think of oneself as entering into a commercial transaction as a banker independently of locating oneself within a pre-existing order of financial exchange. The very acts of lending money – of being a *financier* – and of borrowing it – of being a *debtor* – presuppose a complex system of social relationships in terms of which these particular roles, as of that of *money* itself, can be defined. The charge, then, is that liberalism is committed to a philosophical theory of social agents as constituted independently of societies – as pre-social individuals – and that this theory is incoherent.

Just as there are several variations on the basic themes of liberalism so there are a variety of communitarian theories. Abstracting from the differences, however, the 'communitarian challenges' all attack the individualism of liberalism and give an alternative account of persons as being to some degree socially constituted and of political virtues as depending upon wider shared moral values. Thus it is generally argued that Rawls's way of thinking about justice as protective of rights rather than as productive of well-being, and Dworkin's insistence that the state may not promote any distinctive idea of the good life for human beings but must be neutral as between rival moralities, both rest upon a view of citizens as autonomous and atomic moral agents. Rather than seeing society as an organic entity into which human beings are born and within which they find their identities, the liberal views it as a voluntary association, rather like a club. This, it is claimed, is both descriptively false and morally and politically harmful inasmuch as it denies people a true understanding of themselves and of the means of their fulfilment. Where there could, and should, be a morally informed social existence what liberalism has produced is moral anarchy and political disaffection.

Liberalism assessed

By now it should be very clear how the elements within Catholic social teaching which I identified in Section II connect with the central issue of contemporary political philosophy as outlined in Section III. The tradition, deriving from the synthesis of Catholic Christian thought and Greek philosophy, which has informed the encyclicals of the last two centuries is a version of communitarianism. When, in the thirteenth century, Aquinas wrote on *Princely Government* and produced his great *Summa* his opponents were heathen or ungodly tyrants and Augustinian pessimists, liberalism not then having been invented. But the individualism that was a factor in the Reformation found its political expression in a tradition conceived by Locke, nurtured by Kant and Mill and developed by Rawls and Dworkin. It is, I believe, a tribute to the prescience of the Popes whose encyclicals I have quoted that from the middle of the nineteenth century they saw liberal individualism, even more than socialism, as one of the major ideas standing in opposition to Catholic social teaching. That opposition is faced on two fronts: concerning the place of morality in politics, and the status of the community and the common good.

It would take far more space than is available here to pursue the arguments in favour of Catholic social teaching and to advance to any satisfactory conclusion the general debate between liberalism and communitarianism. Rather than embark upon that now it may be more useful to anticipate some worries of an objector arguing from the side of secular liberalism. Two concerns are likely to be to the fore. First, that the Catholic view as set out above implies an extensive role for the Church in the determination of government policy; and second and related, that allowing moral considerations into the shaping of legislation is certain to prove intrusive in areas where individuals should be free to act as they please. In short, the Catholic view is illiberal and oppressive.

As regards the first point, it should by now be clear from my comments on the encyclical texts that what the Popes were arguing is that a truly just political order will, by that very fact, be in accord with the natural law which is the law of God promulgated to mankind through reason. From the point of view of religious concerns and theological understanding one should certainly recognize that the moral law is an aspect of divine law, but from the perspective of social philosophy it is not necessary that moral considerations be invoked as divine commands. The claim on behalf of the Church as a moral authority, therefore, is not for quasi-theocratic rule but only for a right to be heard and for the moral opinions voiced to be attended to in the shaping of policy. A recent and still topical example of this claim is that made by the British archbishops in their statement on abortion:

> We live in a society where many differing moral and political opinions are conscientiously held and pursued in practice. We make no attempt to override the consciences of our fellow citizens. We do not seek to have all Catholic moral teaching imposed by law, or even adopted as public policy. But we too have the right, as members of this pluralistic society, to appeal to the consciences not only of our fellow Catholics, but also of our fellow citizens and our political leaders and representatives.[9]

The charge of illiberal intrusion into the sphere of private choice invites two responses. First, the critic may simply be begging the question against the Catholic view. In everyday parlance 'illiberal' is a pejorative term implying bigotedness or narrow-mindedness. But the only sense in which what I have been arguing shows Catholic social teaching to be 'illiberal' is the technical one, meaning contrary to liberal doctrines. What the critic has to show is that this is a bad thing, and it will not do to insist that an illiberal (in the technical sense) social philosophy is, *ipso facto*, erroneous. Some independent argument has to be given.

A familiar candidate for such an argument appeals to the disagreeableness of external constraint, such as in the case of censorship. According to liberalism each should be free to pursue his or her own chosen interests so long as thereby harm is not caused to others. The implication of Catholic social teaching, however, would seem to be that in formulating law government should attend to moral requirements, including those relating to the conduct of personal life; but this will lead to illegitimate intrusion into the private sphere. Once again there is a drift towards *petitio principii*, for the question as to whether legislation on censorship is 'illegitimate' is precisely what is at issue. A more subtle 'begging of the question' lurks in the use of the expression 'private sphere', as if it were an uncontroversial matter what does and does not fall within it. Each of these matters deserves attention, but for now I want to end by directing attention towards some features of the liberal social order.

In the last twenty to thirty years, that is to say during the period in which advanced Western societies have legislated themselves into a liberal political order, there has been a considerable development in the supply of pornography, in the scale of abortions and in the dissolution of marriages. I choose these examples because the facts are undisputed and the cases are ones of deep concern to Catholics and, more widely, traditional Christians. To their credit, I doubt that those who reformed the laws in respect of censorship, abortion and marriage had any idea of how far practice would have moved in so short a time. But the fact is that in the United Kingdom deviant and fetishist pornography is now available in high street shops in every major city, millions of foetuses are killed and one in three marriages ends in divorce.

Of course, grossly obscene material has always been produced, abortions performed and marriages ended. That is not the issue; nor indeed is it the increased scale of these phenomena as such, though what is to the point is related to this increase. The issue is that things which in the reflective view of most people are social evils are regarded by liberal theory as not being the business of government to remedy. There is certainly the recourse to the avoidance of harm, and it is to be hoped that policymakers will become more attentive to harms caused by the factors I have mentioned. But the liberal's grounds for social action are both too narrow and too shallow. Injury is not the only evil, there is offence to the common decencies of civilized life; and there are harms that are not injuries, in the sense of independent consequences of exposure to evils, but moral evils in themselves. The liberal makes much of the idea of social tolerance but risks overlooking the possibility that an attitude of toleration may itself be an expression of corruption. Furthermore, in fixing one's attention on the liberties of individuals one may fail to see what is happening to society. The claim of Catholic social teaching is that government has a duty to protect and promote the common good, and to legislate in accord with the fundamental precepts of the moral law. That outlook is not antagonistic to individual interests, but unlike liberalism it sees them as partly constituted by the political order and conditioned by its moral character. Writing in 1991 in celebration of the centenary of *Rerum Novarum* Pope John Paul II puts the point as follows:

> there is a growing inability to situate particular interests within the framework of a coherent vision of the common good. The latter is not simply the sum of particular interests; rather it involves an assessment and integration

of those interests on the basis of a balanced hierarchy of values; ultimately, it demands a correct understanding of the dignity and rights of the person.
(*Centesimus Annus*)

Finally, then, my answer to the question posed in the title is that someone who follows the social teaching of the Catholic Church, as this has been developed out of the dominant 'Thomistic' trend in scholastic natural law theory and promulgated through the relevant papal encyclicals of the nineteenth and twentieth centuries, cannot accept the central doctrines of philosophical liberalism as these have been characterized above. Viewed more positively, the Catholic has reason to reflect upon the course of recent political theory and history – including the collapse of totalitarian socialism – and take satisfaction from the fact that the world seems to be learning what the Church has long been teaching. We need a truly social philosophy, in which the goods of communal life are combined with the legitimate liberties of private interests.

Notes

1 This essay originated in a lecture of the same title delivered in the Mediterranean Institute in Valletta during the period of a Visiting Lectureship at the University of Malta in the spring of 1992. I am grateful to my hosts, in particular to the Rector, Professor Fr. Peter Serracino-Inglott and to Professor Joseph Friggieri of the Department of Philosophy, for their kind hospitality. The present text was written during the period of a Visiting Scholarship at the Social Philosophy and Policy Centre, Bowling Green, Ohio, later in the same year. I am indebted to the Director and the staff of the Centre for their generous support. A shorter version was presented to a meeting on 'Religious Identity and Political Community' held in Queen's University, Belfast, in November 1992.
2 It is worth quoting the preceding text which runs as follows: 'If, like all errors, socialism contains a certain element of truth (and this the Sovereign Pontiffs have never denied) it is nevertheless founded upon a doctrine of human society peculiarly its own which is opposed to true Christianity.'
3 For a short account of it see Chapter 8, above, 'Medieval and Renaissance Ethics', from P. Singer (ed.), *A Companion to Ethics* (Oxford: Blackwell, 1991).
4 *A Theory of Justice* (Oxford: Oxford University Press, 1971).
5 See R. Dworkin, 'Liberalism', in S. Hampshire (ed.), *Public and Private Morality* Cambridge: Cambridge University Press, 1978), reprinted in Dworkin, *A Matter of Principle* (Oxford: Oxford University Press, 1985).
6 See J. Rawls, 'The Idea of an Overlapping Consensus', *Oxford Journal of Legal Studies* 7 (1987).
7 See especially A. MacIntyre, *After Virtue* (London: Duckworth, 1981); C. Taylor, 'The Diversity of Goods', in A. Sen and B. Williams (eds), *Utilitarianism and Beyond* (Cambridge: Cambridge University Press, 1982); and M. Sandel, *Liberalism and the Limits of Justice* (Cambridge; Cambridge University Press, 1982). A useful source of readings is M. Sandel (ed.), *Liberalism and its Critics* (Oxford: Blackwell, 1984).
8 For further discussions see J. Haldane, 'Individuals and the Theory of Justice', *Ratio* (1985); and 'Political Theory and the Nature of Persons', *Philosophical Papers* (1991). A clear account of the main issues can be found in G. Graham, *An Introduction to Contemporary Social Philosophy* (Oxford: Blackwell, 1989).
9 *Abortion and the Right to Life* (London: CTS, 1980).

Chapter 12

Religious toleration

Religion is not a theological virtue like faith, hope and charity....It is a moral virtue linked with justice, measured not by emotion but by the fairness of the actions offered to God.

St Thomas Aquinas, *Summa Theologiae*, 2a 2ae, q. 81, a. 5, ad. 3

Introduction

As in antiquity each city was dedicated to a deity, so today each year is dedicated to a good cause. Long in advance (no doubt taking account of the interests of relevant organisations) 1995 was designated 'The Year of Tolerance'. But annual dedication tends to devalue the practice, and the mere fact of this designation is unlikely to focus the minds, let alone change the hearts, of those most needing to acquire tolerant dispositions. In any case it will not be obvious to all that tolerance is a good thing. What are called for are inducements or arguments. Here I am interested in preparing the ground for an argument in favour of mutual tolerance on the part of religious believers.

Questions of religious toleration arise in a number of different contexts. First, it might be asked to what extent religious authorities should be concerned with maintaining orthodoxy among those appointed to teach the faith. Consider in this connection the charges of intolerance brought against Vatican authorities on occasions when they have withdrawn licences from academics whose teaching they judged to be at odds with Catholic doctrines. Second, there is the question of how a secular state may act with regard to the religious claims and practices of its citizens where those are at odds with general social policies. The most common forms of this question in Europe and North America concern the compatibility of liberal values with religious fundamentalism. A third context in which issues of toleration arise is where proponents of different religious traditions meet and come into conflict. It is with questions arising from this last circumstance that I shall be concerned in this brief discussion.

True believers, non-believers and false believers

Suppose one believes that outside one's own religious tradition there is no, or perilously little, prospect of salvation – *extra ecclesiam nulla salus*. A question then arises as to what one's attitude as a true believer ought to be to those who are not of the faith. The latter are likely to fall into two categories: *non-believers* and *false believers*; that is to say there will be those who lack the relevant religious beliefs but who do not hold contrary ones, and those whose beliefs are judged to be at odds with one's own.[1] One might then regard both non-believers and false believers with indifference, with pity or with contempt; or one might take different views of the two groups depending perhaps on how one saw their failure to be possessed of the one true faith. Of course, for many people the appropriate attitude will be held to be that of respectful tolerance, but here I want to consider the position of someone who argues that true believers ought not to tolerate false believers. What not tolerating them amounts to will vary from mild discrimination in the distribution of social goods, including respect, to a policy of what might be termed 'credocide' – the systematic elimination of a faith and, perhaps, of its followers.

What can be said about the advocate of religious intolerance? More important what can be said *to* him? Well, he clearly is not likely to be a proponent of philosophical liberalism in either its perfectionist or neutralist variants. That is to say, he is unlikely to hold, or to be amenable to, the view that the business of the state is to promote autonomy and respect in accord with secular notions of reason and value; and nor is he likely to be open to the thought that the institutions of civil society should remain neutral between competing conceptions of the good. He might, however, be persuaded of the merits of that from which increasingly John Rawls has been concerned to distance himself, viz. the idea that the state should be organized on the basis of a *modus vivendi*.[2] One might argue, then, that while there are circumstances in which it might be in his interest to press intolerant policies these either do not obtain or are unstable, and that given that false believers may move into power, or non-believers may follow his example of intolerance to the extent of seeking to suppress *all* believers, it is in his interest to accept a policy of live and let live.

Unlike Rawls I think that a *modus vivendi* is a credible and creditable response to a pluralism of what he calls 'general comprehensive doctrines'. It need not be unstable because the conditions that make rational its original introduction need not remain the only, or the main, grounds for its justification. The stability it achieves may become a cherished political value in its own right. Indeed it is plausible to suppose that this is precisely what happened in Western societies in the centuries following the religious wars of Europe. However, the fact that a *modus vivendi* can achieve this kind of success is likely to ground an objection from the true believer. For he may see it as peace purchased at the price of indifference. To the extent that believers are willing to value stability over a policy of relentlessly prosecuting their religious mission they can be thought to be corrupt.

There is something (but perhaps not much) in this view. Consider, for example, the attitudes to permissive abortion legislation of certain Catholic politicians in recent US Presidential and Congressional election campaigns. A common refrain runs 'Personally I am pro-life and anti-abortion, but in a free society in which I can maintain that commitment it is necessary that women also have the legal right to choose whether to have an abortion.' Notice, here, the difference between the position of one who tolerates permissive abortion laws, having lost the policy debate, and that of one whose contribution to the debate is the proposal that there should be permissive legislation. Advocacy of the latter on the part of those who claim to be anti-abortion suggests confusion or indifference.[3] The lesson so far as the true believer is concerned is that tolerating the intolerable is here a consequence of tolerating the non- or false believer.

Toleration and religious reason

So, can toleration be separated from indifference? Consider the philosophical position of the true believer. Let us suppose, minimally, that he or she believes (1) that God exists – *the doctrine of theism*; and (2) that God commands intolerance towards the false (and perhaps the non-) believer – *the doctrine of intolerance*. Why does the true believer affirm these and why should we believe them? I mean what reasons might be given in support of these doctrines? Consider some possibilities: (1) the true believer has a sound deductive proof of them derived from premises generally known to be true; (2) he has an inductive argument based on empirical evidence and involving inference to the best explanation; (3) he asserts that they are so and does not countenance the idea that rational assessment is in order.

The doctrines of theism and intolerance are obviously significant ones for theory and practice (or for 'faith and works'). The true believer can hardly deny this, and nor will he want to. Given their importance the question arises of why their (purported) truth is not generally acknowledged. One possibility is 'cognitive failure', another is 'revelatory deprivation'. According to the first, the deficiency is just in our knowledge. If we attend to the premises and carefully follow the reasoning we will come to share the conclusions. According to the second, God has not revealed the truth to us but only communicated it to the Gracious Chosen. In either event, there now looms the problem of the 'Hiddenness of God'. For if large parts of the world's human population not otherwise remarkable for their ignorance and inferential incompetence cannot see or infer what the true believer can see or infer, then it may as well be that God has favoured some and not others.

This is a general problem for any theist (one structurally parallel to, or perhaps even an instance of, the problem of evil), and I am not interested in making a special difficulty of it for the true believer. However, a further problem is suggested by it. If the doctrines of theism and especially of intolerance are true, then significant consequences ought to be wrought upon large parts of the divine creation which cannot, or do not know of their requirements. That being so we face the claim that advancing the cause of the good involves a policy of suppressing those who are ignorant of the goodness of the policy. I do not say that this is incoherent, but I do suggest that at the relevant level of generality it is not something that we, even if we are religious believers, have reason to accept.

Recalling the Euthyphro dilemma, let us ask whether something is good because God commands it or whether God commands it because it is good; and following an established usage let us call the position that favours the first possibility 'voluntarism' and that which favours the second 'realism'.[4] Voluntarism has a long-standing appeal for a certain kind of religious believer but it faces considerable problems of which I will mention just two. First by allowing the possibility that everything else could be the same though the moral facts were different – depending upon God's attitudes – it implies that God's view of how things should be is unconstrained by how they actually are, which in turn suggests that his commands are arbitrary. Second, it denies the possibility which realism offers of testing proclaimed revelations by reference to the independently assessable moral adequacy of their contents. Neither consequence can be attractive to the true believer. That leaves him realism and the conclusion that God commands intolerance because it is good. Perhaps that is the case. I do not believe that there is any direct disproof of this possibility. But if the ground of its merit is independent of its being willed, and if the true believer hopes to support his belief by appealing to the virtue of its content, then he has to demonstrate this merit. How can he do that? Only by argument or by appeal to further revelation. The latter option now threatens to be regressive; the former invites demonstration by shared standards of reasoning.

Conclusion

So what may be said about, and to, the intolerant true believer is that he has to meet the challenge of demonstrating the virtue of intolerance to those he would intolerantly suppress. I doubt that he can provide an adequate argument, but I am more than willing to consider any he may offer. Not least, of course, because if he can produce telling arguments to this conclusion then the policy of intolerance is hardly likely to be necessary. By proving the independent merit of an initially implausible doctrine, but one advanced by the faith, he will have advanced the cause of his religion; and the more extensively that is done the more likely it is that false (and non-) believers will become true believers. What though if he will not accept the challenge and seeks to prosecute a policy of intolerance? Then, I suggest, we press the merits of mutual non-interference as a *modus vivendi*.[5] And if that is ineffective and the threat persists? Then we pray and/or build defences. Having cast doubts upon its religious credentials we have added a theoretical reason to the obvious prudential case for not tolerating intolerance.

Notes

1 In fact, of course, this distinction is not always so easy to make or to apply.
2 See 'The Idea of an Overlapping Consensus', *Oxford Journal of Legal Studies* 7 (1987); and more recently, *Political Liberalism* (New York: Columbia University Press, 1993), lecture IV.
3 For a discussion of this issue see Terrence McConnell, 'Permissive Abortion Laws, Religion and Moral Compromise', *Public Affairs Quarterly* 1 (1987).
4 For a historical discussion see John Haldane, 'Voluntarism and Realism in Medieval Ethics', *Journal of Medical Ethics* 15 (1989).
5 For an interesting defence of a *modus vivendi* model of a liberal order see Patrick Neal, 'Vulgar Liberalism', *Political Theory* 21 (1993).

Part IV

Education and spirituality

Chapter 13

Chesterton's philosophy of education

> Every education teaches a philosophy; if not by dogma then by suggestion, by implication, by atmosphere. Every part of that education has a connection with every other part. If it does not all combine to convey some general view of life it is not education at all.
>
> Chesterton[1]

Introduction

In an essay written for the thirtieth volume of the *British Journal of Educational Studies*, R.F. Dearden surveyed philosophy of education during the period 1952–82.[2] As might be imagined he was largely concerned with the emergence in and development through these years of analytical philosophy of education, as the influence of linguistic or conceptual analysis spread beyond the somewhat ill-defined boundaries of core philosophy and was taken up by those interested in the theoretical presuppositions of educational practice. After charting the course of this development, and having reached the point at which certain worries arose about the limits of conceptual analysis as a method, Dearden turned to consider what if any alternatives might be available. The first possibility which he mentions in expectation of its having received explicit articulation is Catholic philosophy of education. However, as he notes, nothing meeting this description was developed during the period in question – in effect, since the war. The one book which he mentions, viz. Jacques Maritain's *Education at the Crossroads*,[3] is barely known of in professional philosophy of education and in style and content is quite out of the mainstream.

The question as to why there should be virtually no recent work in what historically was a major tradition in the development of Western education would probably require a many-part answer. Dearden notes, as if to emphasize the mystery of its absence, that while no distinctive Catholic school of philosophy of education has developed, none the less many philosophers working in the field of education are themselves Catholics who, however, 'follow the mainstream in their choice of topics and methods'.[4] But in this, I think, may lie some part of the explanation. The most distinctive pattern of philosophical thought present in Catholic approaches to this and other departments of life is that associated with the tradition of Thomism and this tradition is a branch of Aristotelianism. As some commentators on post-war Oxford philosophy have rightly observed, the concerns and methods of this contemporary school are also closely related to those of Aristotle, save, of course, that thanks to the preference for semantic ascent and to the more general arguments in favour of examining speech rather than thought, the '*analytical* Aristotelians' explored the *linguistic* counterpart of what in earlier works, including those of St Thomas and later scholastic Aristotelians, were presented as *ontological* categories. One possible reason, then, why some Catholic philosophers were content to follow the mainstream rather than to branch out on their own was that this stream continued the direction of flow of their own intellectual tradition. The explanation in the case of many others is likely to be much simpler, viz. that they were educated in mainstream analytical philosophy.

This said, however, Dearden is right to note as surprising the absence of any well-known and respected statement of the Catholic tradition in post-war philosophy of education. Turning, then, from the historical question as to why there is this absence it may be more useful to consider what might be the content of a Catholic philosophy of education. One way of approaching this would be by investigating the general character of Catholic philosophy and then proceeding to its implications for educational theory and practice. This strategy, however, is neither unproblematic nor especially efficient. Anyone familiar with the history of philosophy within the Catholic tradition will be aware of the disputes between Augustinians, Thomists, Scotists, Ockhamists, etc., and also within these schools: for example, within Thomism between Cartesians, transcendentalists, existentialists and so on. Hence there is no single uncontroversial answer to the question: what is the nature of Catholic philosophy? Likewise for the derivation of views about education. One might, therefore, favour the more direct, if narrower, approach of investigating an obvious instance or instances of Catholic thinking in connection with education and this I propose to do by considering something of the educational philosophies of Thomas Aquinas and G.K. Chesterton – the first by way of elaborating the second.

Chesterton assessed

Save for the ignorant or the disputatious I cannot imagine anyone doubting that Aquinas was a major philosopher. It is not unreasonable, however, to wonder whether Chesterton even qualifies as a practitioner of the same discipline. Most who know of him at all are familiar only with his fiction, in particular the 'Father Brown' stories. And of the decreasing number who are aware that most of his writing consisted in non-fictional work very few would venture to call him a philosopher in the sense associated with the style of thought of major historical figures, still less with that of contemporary academic philosophy. None the less, I believe Chesterton achieves genuine insights in his writings and discloses fallacies in those of others, both of which capacities reveal a philosophical mind.

It is appropriate to add here that this assessment is not wholly eccentric as might be supposed. Indeed, since I first began to think of Chesterton in these terms and then looked around to see whether other philosophers regarded him as one of their kind I was surprised not so much by the absence of reference to him – for professional philosophy is an academic discipline and somewhat exclusive of amateurs – but by the variety of those, admittedly relatively few, sources of informed opinion on Chesterton as a philosophical thinker and of the level of their estimation of his abilities.[5]

By way of illustration of this esteem let me cite from philosophers of quite different types: the Hungarian phenomenologist *Aurel Kolnai*; the German Marxist *Ernst Bloch*; the French Thomist *Etienne Gilson* and the Scots/Australian empiricist *John Anderson*. In a brief *curriculum vitae* prepared three years before his death in 1973, Kolnai set down the main elements of his life and career and in the penultimate section of this document writes as follows:

> *Conversion to Catholicism* resulted from various influences, mainly that of G.K. Chesterton and the writings of the German Phenomenological School of Philosophy from 1923. I was baptised in 1926.[6]

From the dates given and from other writings, including most importantly his *magnum opus*, *The War Against the West*, it seems that the aspects of Chesterton's writings which Kolnai most valued were his social theories and his broadly rationalist and objectivist outlook – features of Chesterton's thought to which I shall return later. Bloch, who by commitment and cast of mind could hardly be expected to be sympathetic to Chesterton's view or to his intellectual style, writes of him as being 'among the most intelligent men who have ever lived'.[7] Somewhat similar language was used by Etienne Gilson in commenting on Chesterton's short study of Aquinas.[8] In an appreciation written after Chesterton's death Gilson, who is widely held to be the leading Thomist scholar of the twentieth century, wrote the following:

> I consider it as being without possible comparison the best book ever written on St Thomas. Nothing short of genius can account for such an achievement.... Chesterton was one of the deepest thinkers who ever existed; he was deep because he was right; and he could not help being right; but he could not either help being modest and charitable, so he left it to those who could understand him to know that he was right, and deep; to the others, he apologized for being right, and he made up for being deep by being witty. That is all they can see of him.[9]

This and Bloch's assessment of Chesterton's philosophical abilities both greatly exaggerate his talent. Yet they show how deeply his thinking can impress itself upon minds given to complex and abstract thought. A more measured and indirect tribute to Chesterton's capacity to expose and undermine the philosophical presuppositions of both theory and practice is contained in John Anderson's essay on 'Socrates as an Educator', where he credits Chesterton with recognizing the Sophistical character of those modern educational social-policymakers who 'try to discover what job a man is fit for, instead of asking what way of life is fitting for man…[they] do not ask what is right'.[10]

So much, then, for philosophers on Chesterton. Before proceeding to consider the content of his thoughts about the nature and value of education (an important element in his general metaphysical anthropology) it is worth considering the question: What was Chesterton's view of philosophy? There is no shortage of relevant sources for the answer. Of his many books, *Orthodoxy*[11] (1908), *The Everlasting Man*[12] (1925) and *St Thomas Aquinas*[13] (1933) are the most self-consciously philosophical, and to these may be added a handful of short essays including 'The Revival of Philosophy – Why?'[14] To the question posed by this latter title Chesterton answers as follows:

> The best reason for a revival of philosophy is that unless a man has a philosophy horrible things will happen to him…struck down by blow after blow of blind stupidity and random fate, he will stagger on to a miserable death with no comfort but a series of catchwords…[which] are simply substitutes for thoughts.…Some people fear that philosophy will bore or bewilder them; because they think it is not only a string of long words, but a tangle of complicated notions. These people miss the whole point of the modern situation. These are exactly the evils that exist already; mostly for want of a philosophy.…Political and social relations…are far more complicated than any page of medieval metaphysics; the only difference is that the medievalist could trace out the tangle and follow the complications and the modern cannot.…Philosophy is merely thought that has been thought out. It is often a great bore. But man has no alternative, except between being influenced by thought that has been thought out and being influenced by thought that has not been thought out. The latter is what we commonly call culture and enlightenment today.[15]

My earlier question about Chesterton's view of philosophy might also be interpreted as asking about his assessment of what he took to be the moral and metaphysical thinking of his own period. So understood it must receive a rather different answer from that concerning the value of philosophy *per se*. In Chesterton's view the two dominant ideas of the modern age were opposed to one another but united in their oppressive effect on common thought and action. The first was a form of *Irrationalism* which denied that the world is intrinsically intelligible, that there are objective values, that man has a moral nature which determines an appropriate teleology of action and that free thought rather than blind causation is the moving force in human life. This view had several sources and forms of expression. In antiquity and in the Middle Ages it emerged from speculative metaphysics and voluntaristic theology – from pre-Socratic cosmology and Manichaean religion – and in more recent times it had been developed by the evolutionary theory of human origins, the Freudian theory of motivation and the Romanticist emphasis upon emotion and free expression. In connection with these last two examples Chesterton writes of the effect of Freud's occult doctrines as having been to advance the 'breakdown at once of the idea of reason and of the idea of authority'.[16] And elsewhere he castigates D.H. Lawrence for having urged the abandonment of reason in favour of instinct.[17]

Set against these anti-intellectualist philosophies of unreasoning power Chesterton identifies a form of *Rationalism* no less destructive in its effects. The main contemporary expression of this he took to be *Scientism* – the view that the methods and conclusions of science exhaust the possibilities of knowledge. It is clear from his writings that he regarded this as presenting the greater threat to both philosophical understanding and practical affairs:

> Imagination does not breed insanity. Exactly what does breed insanity is reason.... To accept everything is an exercise, to understand everything a strain.... The poet only asks to get his head into the heavens. It is the logician who seeks to get the heavens into his head.[18]

As it stands, of course, this is easily dismissable as shallow word play, but as one reads on, the target under attack becomes clearer as does the accuracy of Chesterton's aim. The scientistic rationalist is like the consistent maniac in combining 'an expansive reason with a contracted common sense':

> They are universal only in the sense that they take one thin explanation and carry it very far. But a pattern can stretch for ever and still be a small pattern.[19]

In common sense, by contrast, reason is exercised in association with experience and insight and no presumption operates requiring simple unity either in the phenomena or in their explanation. Thus common sense is open to possibility where pure rationalism of the sort with which he was concerned admits only universal necessity. Chesterton elaborated the point with characteristic style:

> The ordinary man has always left himself free to doubt his gods; but... free also to believe in them. He has always cared more for truth than for consistency. If he saw two truths that seemed to contradict each other, he would take the two truths and the contradiction along with them. His spiritual sight is stereoscopic, like his physical sight: he sees two different pictures at once and yet sees all the better for that. Thus he has always believed that there was such a thing as fate, but such a thing as free will also.... He admired youth because it was young and age because it was not.[20]

Chesterton's general point, put prosaically, is that logical reasoning is necessary but not sufficient for understanding. In the realms of both theory and practice *insight* (or intelligent observation and judgement) is required: 'You can only find truth with logic if you have already found truth without it.'[21] This need of true premises for sound arguments raises the epistemological question of how we may first come to know the truth. For Chesterton, as for Aquinas whom he recognizes to be an ally in this cause, the beginnings of all knowledge lie in perception. But what Chesterton adds to the Thomist idea of abstractive inter-pretation, whereby the objects of experience are brought under general con-cepts, is a method for questioning or enriching accepted classifications. This is the famous Chestertonian use of paradox. At times, especially in later works, the method seems to feature for its own sake and yields diminishing returns. Yet, as Chesterton puts it, the point of paradox is 'to awaken the mind'[22] – and here one is almost tempted to add 'from its dogmatic slumber'.

Chesterton on education

The expression 'awakening the mind' is one which has often been used to characterize education. But, of course, this view of what education is about may not be philosophically uncontroversial, since it presupposes that in some sense the mind is already 'there' prior to the start of the educative process. And assuming the notion of education is understood in a broad sense so as to be applicable prior to formal schooling, this presupposition seems to point towards some kind of innatism. The nearest Chesterton gets to any explicit discussion of this idea is in his book *What's Wrong with the World*,[23] part IV of which is titled 'Education; Or, the Mistake about the Child'. Having argued against the claim that the pattern of human development of mind and character is determined before birth by genetic inheritance, he then considers the contrary thesis that character formation is due entirely to environment. Chesterton identifies an ambiguity in this latter claim and a fallacy on the part of some 'environment-alists' who pass without warrant from one meaning to the other. As he puts it: 'The idea that surroundings will mould a man is always mixed up with the totally different idea that they will mould him in one particular way.'[24] Shortly after this he turns to the nature of education itself and first analyses the idea of it so as to show that it belongs not to the category of *thing* but to that of *process*. The question then arises: What is the nature of this particular process? It is at this point that Chesterton considers the suggestion that education is not, as he himself believes, a method of informing a child's mind by authoritative guidance but rather a procedure 'coming, not from outside, from the teacher, but entirely from inside the boy':

> Education, they say, is the Latin for leading out or drawing out the dor-mant faculties of each person.[25]

Later he goes on to argue that even were the child's mind a pre-existing store of ideas the question would still remain as to which of these to cultivate and which to neglect or even to suppress, and hence the need of guidance and authority in education would remain. However, he is also concerned to reject the strong innatist element in the anti-instructionist view while yet finding a place for the idea that education would not be possible without pre-existing material upon which the process of (in)formation can get to work. He writes:

> There is, indeed, in each living creature a collection of forces and functions; but education means producing these in particular shapes and training them to particular purposes, or it means nothing at all. Speaking is the most practical instance of the whole situation. You may indeed 'draw out' squeals from the child by simply poking him and pulling him about....But you will wait and watch very patiently indeed before you draw the English language out of him. That you have got to put into him; and there is an end of the matter.[26]

As ever Chesterton's style favours brevity and directness rather than detailed argument but it is possible to reformulate his view in more familiar philosophical fashion and to do so in terms drawn from Aquinas with whom in this, as in other matters, he was in general agreement. Here, then, it will be useful to set out in brief something of Thomist epistemology and metaphysics.[27]

Aquinas on the nature of knowledge

Aquinas draws a close parallel between the basic structure of the world and that of the mind. With regard to the former he rejects the Platonic notion that the natural order is not intrinsically intelligible and is only barely describable to the extent that it is a (grossly) imperfect reflection of the structure of the realm of Forms. He also rejects the opposing extreme which likewise denies the intelligibility of the world as a collection of natural kinds and instead regards it simply as varying quantities of matter. In place of these extremes Aquinas follows Aristotle in characterizing nature as consisting of a multitude of particulars, exhibiting common essences and accidents, in the constitution of which Form and Matter are fused together. This implies two levels of composition and, corresponding to these, two stages of individuation. For if one asks, 'What in general is the difference between cats and dogs or apples and pears?' the answer can be given by reference to the different kinds of forms involved. But if one then asks 'And what in particular is the difference between this dog (or cat or apple or pear) and some other individual which is identical in form?' the answer will have to make reference to spatio-temporal location, or what is in effect the same thing, viz. distinct quantities of matter – what Aquinas calls *materia signata quantitate*.[28]

This ontology holds that all things existing independently of the mind are individuals – either particulars, such as cats, dogs, apples, pears, houses, books, etc., or property-instances, such as the blackness of this or that cat, the flavour of some particular piece of fruit, and so on. In sense-experience various causal processes are initiated which give rise to states in subjects which stand in one-to-one relationships with individual elements of the environment. In Aquinas's terminology these processes involve the generation in sense organs of 'sensible species' – corresponding only roughly to what in more recent times have been called sense-impressions. This is the beginning of perception and also of intellectual cognition. But for those activities to take place it is necessary that the subject impose order on the contents of sense-experience by introducing schemes of classification. Perceptions, as contrasted with sensory impressions, involve concepts in partial determination of their contents. Put linguistically, if someone claims to have perceived something then there must be some true description of his or her experience under which it is characterized as being *an experience of a C*, where C in this schema stands for some or other classificatory concept.

The question to which this account now gives rise is that of the origin of these concepts. If Aquinas were an innatist he might say that they are already present in the mind and only require the stimulation provided by the impact of the environment in sense-experience to 'awaken' them. That, in effect, is the view common to Plato and to those 'anti-instructionist' educational writers whom Chesterton criticizes. However, Aquinas rejects concept innatism and offers instead the theory of the *intellectus agens* or active intellect. This may suggest (and in the writings of some scholastics is taken to imply) a kind of quasi-homuncularism of the kind widely favoured among contemporary cognitive psychologists. But such an interpretation involves a mistaken reification of what is in fact a power of whole human beings and not a mechanism located in a part of them. Aquinas recognizes that the difference between sense-experience and perception is one of kind and not one of degree. No mere addition of sense-impressions can yield a perception for the latter involves a classification of the former. In order to explain the transformation, therefore, he posits a natural power of concept-formation activated by sense-experience.

Thus, for Aquinas, something presupposed by knowledge is innate. Not ideas themselves, however, but rather the capacity to fashion them out of the content of sense-experience. This is the process of abstraction whereby the active intellect constructs general notions from the material provided by the senses. Given a series of encounters with numerically distinct instances of circularity, say, the subject becomes active in the construction of the concept *Circle*, or again, though with more sophisticated exercises of the interpretative powers which constitute the active intellect, the subject may form concepts of living substances such as *Cat*, *Dog* or *Man*.

The use of the term 'abstraction' in connection with this account of the origins of ideas may suggest that the Thomist view belongs to a class of theories of concept-formation which were effectively refuted by the anti-empiricist arguments of philosophers such as Sellars[29] and Geach.[30] The general structure of this refutation is that it is incoherent to suppose that a concept is acquired through selective attention to instances of it, since such selective attention is itself an exercise of the concept in question. The capacity to discriminate some feature *f* from other features *g*, *h*, *i*, etc. is (part of) what possession of the concept *F* consists in. Hence it cannot be invoked in explanation of how one comes by the concept. Without getting too involved in the issues raised by this argument I simply want to observe that it is not destructive of all forms of abstractionism. The reasoning involves the claim that discriminating instances of *F*ness from cases of *G*ness presupposes possession of the concept *F*. But this can be conceded while yet maintaining that the concept is acquired in attending to instances of it. The sense in which an exercise of a concept uncontroversially 'presupposes' its possession is *logical* and not *temporal*. An experience of some feature may, therefore, be both the occasion of forming a concept of it and also the first exercise of that concept. By way of (close) analogy consider the example of riding a bicycle. One cannot correctly be said to be riding a bike unless one has the capacity to do so, for the riding is an exercise of that capacity. By the same token, however, one may coherently suppose that the acquisition of this ability dates from the episode which was also its first exercise. In short, coming to possess a capacity and exercising it may be simultaneous events notwithstanding that exercise presupposes possession.

Interestingly, the idea of concepts as involving capacities which is favoured by Geach, Sellars, Hamlyn[31] and other anti-empiricists is also a distinctive feature of Aquinas's own account. In consequence of exposure to the world through experience, subjects come to acquire cognitive dispositions exercisable in judgements. In Aquinas's terminology this disposition is described as a *habitus* (corresponding to Aristotle's notion of *hexis*).[32] A further feature of the Thomistic view is that the theory of acquired habits in terms of which conceptual understanding is characterized should also be invoked in connection with emotion and will. Quite generally habits are directed phenomena, tendencies to do or to refrain from doing something. In cognition a *conceptual* disposition manifests itself most clearly in identifying judgements. In deliberation, *affective* and *volitional* tendencies are likewise exercised as the would-be agent is attracted to or repelled by possible outcomes. At this point in the account an element is present which provides a connection with the Thomist theory of value. For according to Aquinas every tendency has its natural object, and virtue, whether in respect of intellectual, affective or volitional powers, consists in a correct ordering of each faculty with regard to its proper object. Thus intellectual virtue is a habit or disposition of judgement tending towards truth and away from falsity. Likewise, affective and volitional virtues are habits of feeling and choice directed towards goodness and away from whatever is bad. In this way, then, Aquinas integrates cognitive and moral psychology in a single theory of the structure and powers of the human soul.

Mention of the soul in this context should be understood as referring to the biological and rational nature of human beings and not to some immaterial substance located within them. Aquinas rejects Platonic dualism in favour of an incarnational anthropology. Human persons are necessarily embodied, the soul being the form of the living organism. It is for this reason that Aquinas opposes the idea of the Christian afterlife as consisting in permanent disembodiment and argues instead for a resurrectionist eschatology inspired by Paul's first letter to the Corinthians.[33]

In the Thomist theory of human nature, ontology, epistemology and axiology are tightly bound together by the notions of *form, potentiality* (i.e. the possibility of the instantiation or 'reception' of form) and *cause*. The natural world and the human mind are similarly describable as articulated structures the common elements of which are formal principles. These may occur either as properties in nature or as concepts in thought – what Aquinas describes as *esse naturale* and *esse intentionale*, respectively. Movement between world and mind can proceed in either direction. In cognition forms are received into the intellect by way of its abstractive power. In the creation of artefacts, forms first conceived in the mind are then transferred into the world. In a sense, then, both making and knowing involve the coming to be in one fashion or another of new properties as the material world and minds acquire forms through causal interaction between them.

Aquinas on education

Returning now to the issue of education, several implications of the Thomist scheme are directly relevant. First, for Aquinas the acquisition of knowledge is literally a matter of growth – not in size but in respect of properties: receiving information is *ipso facto* acquiring forms (*qua* concepts). Second, it is not mere accretion but growth towards a proper end as the natural tendency to apprehend the two is repeatedly exercised and truth is thereby attained. Third, the primary agent of learning is 'within' the subject, i.e. the abstractive or interpretative power of the active intellect. Fourth, personal development also involves the acquisition of affective and volitional dispositions which again have a proper teleology.

Aquinas does not himself integrate these elements with an explicit philosophy of education. Indeed, he has precious little to say on education in the sense of instruction or schooling though he writes a good deal on the issues of cognitive and moral psychology. He does, however, offer some discussion of the nature of learning which endorses some of the implications derived above, is of interest in its own right, and is salient from the perspective of seeking to understand Chesterton's views. In his *Commentary on the Sentences* (Book IV) and in the *Debated Questions on Truth* (Question 11) Aquinas considers the nature of education (*educatio*) and in the first of these defines it as 'the progression of the child to the condition of properly human excellence, i.e. to the state of virtue'. This description characterizes a very general process in terms of its achievement but elsewhere Aquinas considers how that process is realized in two different forms of learning. The first, *disciplina*, corresponds to the idea of learning through instruction, while the second, *inventio*, is a matter of discovery or learning by oneself. It is the latter of these forms which is most important, but not for the sort of reason one would expect to find given in post-Enlightenment writings, i.e. having to do with individuality and authenticity. Rather the importance of *inventio* is that it constitutes the essential core of all learning. Aquinas puts the same point by saying that 'a teacher should not be thought of as pouring his knowledge into the learner as though particles of knowledge could pass from one subject to another'.[34] The function of an instructor is and can only be to direct the attention of his students towards some phenomenon of which he himself has a proper conception and hope that their own interpretative powers can get to work in abstracting the same concept. Thus a teacher is never the primary agent of learning but only an instrumental cause who is most effective when he organizes his directions (*disciplina*) in accord with the natural order of discovery (*inventio*). Aquinas presents these ideas as follows:

> There is a two-fold way of acquiring knowledge: first, when natural reason itself arrives at knowledge of a truth...second, when another person provides help, this is called instruction. In processes where artifice and nature are mingled artifice operates in the same way and through the same means as does nature....This procedure is followed in the acquisition of knowledge...a teacher follows the same method that a man would adopt in discovering things for himself...a teacher is said to cause knowledge in another through the activity of the student's natural reason.[35]

Conclusion

In his emphasis on the secondary role of the teacher and in his account of concept-acquisition as due to the innate abstractive power of the subject Aquinas tends towards epistemological individualism of a kind which following the writings of Wittgenstein and of more recent philosophers one has reason to query. At the same time, however, he also emphasizes the fact that man is a social animal and that his rational goals must include the company and well-being of others. However, somewhat disappointingly this latter support for social communitarianism is nowhere related to, let alone integrated with, the view that the progression towards self-realization is dependent upon growth in knowledge, and this omission is a weakness in Aquinas's system which for the most part is otherwise highly systematic.

In Chesterton, by contrast, the social context of education is given emphasis and features in a forthright defence of authority in teaching. In observing this, however, it also needs to be noted that he is a fierce defender of the individual against the collective. This combination of attitudes makes Chesterton a thinker worth studying – in part to understand better how his vigorously commonsensical views connect with those deep philosophical ideas of Aquinas with which he judged himself to be in agreement; and in part also because the tension between

the attractions of autonomy and those of community is a distinctive and important feature of much contemporary social philosophy.

The extent to which Chesterton's thoughts about the nature and value of
education independently converge with, or directly draw upon, Aquinas's philosophical anthropology and metaphysics is more than sufficient to warrant the
description of those ideas as constituting a Thomistic philosophy of education.
This assessment is one with which, fear of pretentiousness apart, Chesterton
would not want to disagree. At several points in his study of Aquinas he quotes
with approval St Thomas's incarnational theory of man and his account of
knowledge as growth toward self realization. But in doing so he also manages
with characteristic style to make what are abstract theoretical ideas sound like
nothing so much as solid common sense. Perhaps, then, it is appropriate to
draw to a close with Chesterton making a somewhat similar claim on behalf of
Thomism itself. He writes:

> Since the modern world began in the sixteenth century, nobody's system of
> philosophy has really corresponded to everybody's sense of reality; to what,
> if left to themselves, common men would call common sense...[my] only
> object...is to show that the Thomist philosophy is nearer than most
> philosophies to the mind of the man in the street.[36]

The prospect this offers of a philosophy adequate both to the treatment of
problems of practice arising in social life – such as those bearing upon the
legitimacy of authority in education – and adequate also to the abstract difficulties
which appear at the level of theoretical reflection – such as those concerning the
nature of education – should be sufficient to encourage more people to read
both Chesterton and Aquinas.[37] In doing so they might also consider to what
extent the common views of these authors depend upon a shared theology. For
if it were the case, as some philosophers have come to think, that the reality of
values, the incarnate existence of persons, the objectivity and reliability of knowledge and the existence and structure of the world as a mind-dependent but
intelligible, teleologically ordered system, are intrinsically related and jointly
dependent upon the continuing activity of a caring personal God, then one
might see how Chesterton's Thomistic philosophy of education could be Catholic
in more than a historical-cum-sociological sense.[38]

Notes

1 'A New Case for Catholic Schools', in *The Common Man* (London: Sheed & Ward,
   1950), p. 167.
2 'Philosophy of Education, 1952–1982', *British Journal of Educational Studies* 30.1
   (1982).
3 *Education at the Crossroads* (New Haven: Yale University Press, 1963). See also
   J. Maritain, 'Thomist Views on Education', in Nelson B. Henry (ed.), *Modern Philosophies of Education* (Chicago, Ill.: Chicago University Press, 1955).

4 'Philosophy of Education', pp. 63–4.

5 For a discussion of the extent to which Chesterton's fictional writing was a vehicle for his social philosophy see Ian Boyd, 'Philosophy in Fiction', in J. Sullivan (ed.), *G.K. Chesterton: A Centenary Appraisal* (London: Elek, 1974), pp. 40–57. Something of the philosophical background to Chesterton's view of literature is explored in Lynette Hunter, *G.K. Chesterton: Explorations in Allegory* (New York: St. Martin's Press, 1979), see especially ch. 10.

6 See *Ethics, Value and Reality: Selected Papers of Aurel Kolnai*, ed. F. Dunlop and B. Klug (London: Athlone Press, 1977), p. xiii.

7 *Subject–Objekt* (Frankfurt am Main: Suhrkamp, 1962).

8 *St Thomas Aquinas* (London: Hodder & Stoughton, 1933).

9 See Cyril Clemens, *Chesterton as Seen by His Contemporaries* (London, 1939), pp. 150–1. Gilson's admiration for Chesterton's study of Aquinas seems not to have waned. At the time of its appearance he is quoted as having said: 'Chesterton makes one despair. I have been studying St Thomas all my life and I could never have written such a book.' See Maisie Ward, *Gilbert Keith Chesterton* (London: Sheed & Ward, 1944), p. 524. (Anyone suspicious that this might be an ambiguous tribute should read the remainder of Gilson's appreciation quoted above.) Some thirty years after making this remark he wrote in a letter to the Revd Mr Scanell, dated 7 January 1966, '[in that book Chesterton was] nearer the real Thomas than I am after reading the Angelic Doctor for sixty years' – as quoted in Hunter, *G.K. Chesterton*, p. 173.

10 See D.Z. Phillips (ed.), *Education and Inquiry* (Oxford: Blackwell, 1980), pp. 72, 73.

11 *Orthodoxy* (London: Collins, 1961).

12 *The Everlasting Man* (London: Hodder & Stoughton, 1925).

13 See note 8.

14 See *The Common Man*, pp. 173–80.

15 Ibid., pp. 173–6.

16 'On Twilight Sleep', in *Come to Think of It* (London: Methuen, 1930), p. 161.

17 See 'The End of the Moderns', in *The Common Man*, pp. 196–205. In connection with evolutionary theory Chesterton offers the interesting observation that in addition to undermining the distinction between reasons and causes, it puts at risk the very possibility of knowledge by abandoning the idea of stable and enduring essences. In this thought he parallels Plato's reflection upon the sceptical implications of Heraclitean cosmology. Chesterton observes that '[evolution] means that there is no such thing as an age to change, and no such thing as a man to change him into. It means there is no such thing as a thing. At best, there is only one thing, and that is a flux of everything and anything. This is an attack … upon the mind; you cannot think if there are no things to think about' (*Orthodoxy*, pp. 34–5).

18 *Orthodoxy*, p. 17.

19 Ibid., p. 22.

20 Ibid., pp. 27, 28.

21 *Daily News*, 21 December 1906.

22 *St Thomas Aquinas*, p. 144. In her biography Maisie Ward writes of Chesterton's use of paradox that: 'nearly all his paradoxes were either the startling expression of an entirely neglected truth, or the startling re-emphasis of the neglected side of a truth' (*Chesterton*, p. 155).

23 *What's Wrong with the World* (London: Cassell, 1910).

24 Ibid., p. 191.

25 Ibid., p. 200.

26 Ibid., p. 201.

27 For more detailed discussions of these aspects of Aquinas's philosophy which also relate them to persistent problems in epistemology and metaphysics see J. Haldane, 'Brentano's Problem', *Grazer Philosophische Studien* 35 (1989); and J. Haldane, 'Mind–

World Identity and the Anti-Realist Challenge', in J. Haldane and C. Wright (eds), *Reality, Representation and Projection* (Oxford: Oxford University Press, 1993), pp. 15–37.

28 See *On Being and Essence (De Ente et Essentia)* trans. A. Maurer (Toronto: PIMS, 1968), ch. II, sec. 4, 36–7.

29 See W. Sellars, *Science, Perception and Reality* (London: Routledge & Kegan Paul, 1963), essay 5.

30 See P. Geach, *Mental Acts* (London: Routledge & Kegan Paul, 1957), sec. 6 and Appendix.

31 In addition to the works by Sellars and Geach mentioned above see D. Hamlyn, *Experience and the Growth of Understanding* (London: Routledge & Kegan Paul, 1978), ch. 6.

32 See, for example, his Commentary on *De Anima*, 417a22–b17, which appears as Lectio Eleven in *Aristotle's De Anima in the Version of William of Moerbeke and the Commentary of St Thomas Aquinas* (London: Routledge & Kegan Paul, 1954), pp. 240–1. For some discussion of the Thomist view of concepts as intellectual dispositions see Bernard Lonergan, *Verbum* (London: Darton, Longman & Todd, 1968), ch. 5, and Haldane, 'Brentano's Problem'.

33 *Super Epistolas Pauli Apostoli*; also *Summa Theologiae*, Ia, q 89.

34 *De Veritate*, I, ad 6.

35 Ibid., I, q 11, aa 1 and 2; also *Summa Theologiae*, Ia, q 117 (the translation of the passage from *De Veritate* is from Thomas Gilby, *St Thomas Aquinas: Philosophical Texts* (Oxford: Oxford University Press, 1951).

36 *St Thomas Aquinas*, pp. 172–3.

37 For further discussion of Aquinas in connection with the idea of a normative anthropology adequate to ground judgements of value and requirement, see J. Haldane, 'Metaphysics in the Philosophy of Education', *Journal of Philosophy of Education* 23.2 (1989).

38 Earlier versions of this essay were read to the Scottish branch of the Philosophy of Education Society of Great Britain at a conference held in the University of Edinburgh in November 1988 and to a meeting of the same society held in Cambridge in May 1989.

Chapter 14

Religion in education

In defence of a tradition

> When a man is asked to write down what he really thinks on education a certain gravity grips and stiffens his soul, which might be mistaken by the superficial for disgust.
>
> Chesterton 1910, p. 194

Introduction

Whether Chesterton's observation is regarded as ironical or grave it is certainly true that the topic of education tends to elicit strong reactions whenever it is subjected to public debate. That the place of religion in general education should currently be thought to be a controversial and problematic issue also serves as a reminder of how quickly perceptions of social affairs can undergo radical change. For until about 1970 it was simply taken for granted by most people that religion was one of the things children would learn about at school, and, more positively, that teaching something of the distinctive religious tradition of the country was part of what general education ought to provide.

Move back another score or so of years and one reaches the period in which, assuming not only that religion ought to be taught but that its importance was such that its place in the curriculum should be secured by statute, R.A. Butler and Archbishop Temple devised a series of clauses for inclusion within what was to become the 1944 Education Act, requiring instruction in religious education and daily acts of collective worship. Indeed, these elements of the post-war settlement have been preserved in subsequent acts, and that of course is part of the problem. For now, it seems, law and educated opinion (at any rate some part of the latter) are at odds; as, more importantly, are law and practice.[1]

That this problem should nowadays be regarded as one suitable for philosophical treatment again reminds us of how quickly orthodoxies may come to seem anachronisms. However, if one still operates with a 30-year period of comparison the change is not so much in the prevailing attitude to the possibility of philosophizing about practical topics as in the assumptions about what one would be doing, and could reasonably hope to achieve, through such a discussion. For an author writing towards the beginning of this period the goal would have been conceptual clarification and the method linguistic analysis (see, for example, Hudson 1973). Nowadays, however, philosophy has expanded in a direction that has brought it to a position that does not so much resemble that occupied by Kant's Queen of the sciences as Plato's policy guide to government. And the resultant expectation is that it will offer answers to the question: What should we do?

This change of role has been effected from within the subject largely by a transformed self-image which now includes among its features a responsibility precisely and economically expressed in the first of the stated 'Specific Objectives' of the Social Values Research Centre, University of Hull, (one of a number of philosophy, policy and practice centres), to wit:

> To consider fundamental questions of ethics and values, particularly in relation to practical decision making.[2]

Such a broadening of concerns is now generally accepted. But notwithstanding a strong trend towards consideration of questions of conduct, the dominant view of the aims and methods of the new practical philosophy largely remains that of earlier conceptual dissection. Indeed, the prevailing idea of the relationship between philosophy and practice is indicated by the much favoured expression 'applied philosophy', which strongly suggests a two-stage process beginning with abstract speculation and, once general conclusions have been reached, proceeding to introduce them to particular issues.

I present these observations partly to indicate an ambition to answer certain questions about religion in education rather than simply to discuss the meaning of the questions themselves, and partly to suggest that current discussion of such issues may suffer from operating at too high a level of abstraction. The worlds to which religion and philosophical speculation aspire may be realms of timeless essences but the world their (known) practitioners inhabit is one of contingency, particularity and flux. The place to begin, therefore, is where we currently stand, and if we are serious about seeking answers to practical questions the succeeding movement of thought should be from local historical particularities to similarly conditioned conclusions. The philosophy which follows is, therefore, not so much applied theory as *practical thinking*.

Challenges to religion in schools

Two established practices, the first prescribed and the second protected by law, are currently under attack. They are: the support of religious denominational schools by government grant; and the provision of religious education and collective worship within maintained non-church schools. Opposition to both practices comes from different sources and is backed by different arguments. At one extreme there are those who would legislate for state atheism and prohibit even independent denominational schools on the grounds that they are no more to be tolerated in an enlightened age than the keeping of slaves or the advertising and sale of curses. The polar opposite, in background assumptions though not in practical consequences, is the view of those who regard religion – I mean some particular creed – as too precious to risk corruption by contact with anything other than the sanctified hands of a priesthood moved only by religious will and supported solely by the alms of the faithful.

Both the 'Albanian' and 'Iranian' positions, as one might term these extremes, thus stand strongly opposed to current British practices. But given the grounds and scope of their opposition they need not, I think, detain us. Regarding the first, one might question the claims to enlightenment of those who cannot distinguish between what is demonstrably immoral and that about which well-intentioned and informed parties may reasonably disagree. Meanwhile the untrusting puritanism of the second position faces familiar self-generated theological objections. But independently of such doubts about their assumptions we are entitled to set aside these challenges on the grounds that their practical implications involve the denial of freedoms and benefits of which we are clearly entitled to avail ourselves: the freedoms to congregate, to impart beliefs and to instruct in practices so long as these activities are not directed against others or present serious risk of injury to them, and the benefits of study and instruction in some area without total and unqualified commitment to it.

So much, then, for the extremes and their easy dismissal. The more frequently encountered challenges to church schools and religious education have their source in different and more plausible ideas. Here I shall mostly be concerned with arguments which appeal to the changing character of British society and conclude that whatever may have been appropriate in the past the new cultural complexity and general philosophy of the nation make previous practices unacceptable. (Elsewhere I consider other challenges to the place of religion in education; see Haldane 1986.)

The changes cited are, familiarly, the transition from general ethnic and social identity to multi-racial, multi-cultural variety, and the evolution of a secular conception of life in place of a religious one. Such ideas are powerful tools of analysis and those who wield them are right in supposing that questions of public policy must be settled by reference to social realities. However, these facts should encourage care and sensitivity in the use of sociological arguments. For the size and complexity of the phenomena in question – nothing less than the patterns of national life, and the liability of theorists to advance to large and general conclusions on the basis of little evidence, give reason to be sceptical about claims that the social world has radically changed from one distinctive pattern to another in the short space of a couple of generations, and that in consequence we need to make substantial changes to the education system.

The notions of *cultural pluralism* and *secularism*, and of *religion* and *education*, as these feature in challenges to existing arrangements are often so far abstracted from the multifarious complexities of daily life as to preserve little in the way of significant content. This is a matter which I shall elaborate as I proceed, but by way of example of what is being questioned consider the familiar pattern of reasoning which holds that Britain is now culturally pluralistic and secular to an extent that requires that national institutions (government, the media, school, college and university systems, etc.) no longer give special place to the values historically associated with the country.

This argument, by the way, is not the general and *a priori* liberal one to the effect that social institutions should not base themselves upon any distinctive conception of human life if they are to serve and gain the allegiance of men and women who may, but need not, live by different and conflicting values. Rather the previous argument depends essentially on its *actually* being the case that society is diverse and secularized. But now consider whether this claim is true. Of course, one cannot do that without determining its meaning and as one tries to do so several possibilities come into view. Does 'culturally diverse' just mean 'contains different cultures'? If so are not the long-standing differences between the West Country, Tyne and Wear, and Strathclyde evidence that Britain has always been culturally pluralistic? Perhaps instead cultures are to be individuated by native tongue. But again, by that criterion Britain has long been diverse. At this point the suggestion will be made that what the country is now, but has not been previously, is host to large numbers of people from abroad. Certainly the facts of recent immigration are clear but their relation to the claim about radical cultural diversity remains troublesome. In the past there have been major periods of immigration into the country: Catholic Irish from the west, Protestants from the low countries, Jews from eastern Europe and so on. But all of this belongs to the period before which, on the analysis under examination, Britain became multi-cultural. Here I am not denying that there are new and different ethnic groups, or that they have a right to preserve aspects of their foreign traditions. Indeed, as will become clear shortly, I am in favour of this right extending to the maintenance, with state support, of non-Christian religious schools. What I am suspicious of, however, is the representation of local differences as something new and major in our national history which is the suggestion of the claim that Britain has recently become a multi-cultural society.

Likewise, the contention that in the twentieth century, but especially since the last war, the country has ceased to be religious and become secularized. A country is of course not a thing like a book or a rock formation. In the sense intended here it is a place and an evolving population standing in a certain complex set of yet more complex relations. What meaning can then be given to the claim that a country is or is not secular? Opposing secular to theocratic it is clear enough that Britain is not, while Iran is, a religious state. But in this sense Britain was secularized many centuries ago if indeed it ever was theocratic. It is true, however, that the country has been deeply influenced by Christianity and that the religion gave birth to a number of institutions to which it remains constitutionally attached. Beyond this, certain values and practices originated in and continue to be nourished by Christian thought even though they may be logically independent of it. If such features are sufficient to constitute being a religious state then certainly Britain has long been of this sort. But of course in this interpretation it remains non-secular today and shows no sign of changing its status. Again a reply suggests itself to the effect that these readings miss the point. Certainly Britain may be a non-theocratic yet religious *state*, but it has nonetheless undergone a radical transformation in having become a non-religious *society*. On this account the secularism of contemporary Britain is a feature not of its political and cultural institutions but of the attitude of its people. In short, we have ceased to be a believing nation and thus, to resume the revisionary argument, there is no place within public education for privileged treatment of the Christian religion.

As before, the analysis only appears plausible when considered in isolation from the empirical facts from which it abstracts. Of course, only a minority of the population are churchgoers but when was it ever generally otherwise? Moreover, support for an institution is not only, nor perhaps even best, measured by reference to participation in its activities. All the latter indicates is, truistically, active membership. A better measure is afforded by considering reactions to efforts to dismantle it, or to attacks upon it; or again by looking at the ways it is invoked as a source of authority and is regarded as an object of pride and affection. By these measures it is very far from clear that people's attitudes to Christianity are other than favourable. And certainly there is no good reason to think that there has been a marked shift in attitudes generally over recent decades.

Where there very probably have been changes in social composition and philosophical outlook is among those who spend their time and energies considering such issues, that is among people such as ourselves. But recognizing this it is important also to identify certain possibilities and attendant risks. First, without hint of self-congratulation, academics should acknowledge that they are untypical in being equipped for and disposed to abstract speculation and scepticism. Second, as Hume observed, 'mind has a propensity to spread itself upon the world' and thus to project the distinctive features of its thinking upon the phenomena it takes itself to be investigating. And third, there is a natural, indeed almost irresistible, tendency to invest one's own position with special significance. Thus, an acquired disposition to treat metaphysical and religious claims with scepticism may easily express itself in judgements about what people in general must surely think. (Consider here the fatuous if quaint remark attributed to a well-known bishop: 'Miraculous claims put ordinary sensible people off Christianity. They say, "Tell that to the Marines" and so miss a great opportunity for good.'[3]) Likewise, the ascent to high abstraction in pursuit of an elevation from which to describe and evaluate the trends of human history often yields the flattering Hegelian illusion that one's self-understanding is greater than that of one's predecessors and that what it reveals is the special historical significance of the present. One must be alert, therefore, to the possibility of exaggeration when it is claimed that in the present era society is undergoing major cultural and philosophical transformations. In short, since there are reasons to doubt our capacities for accurate representation and interpretation at this level it will not do to put great weight on sociological analyses in arguing for significant changes in national policy. In any event the burden of proof lies with those who urge reforms to existing arrangements.

Religions and cultures

One feature of contemporary Britain which has been much referred to is the existence of large Asian communities in several cities, who in recent times have been seeking state support for the maintenance of Islamic schools. Apparently some people regard this development as calling into question the whole basis of existing law and refer to it in arguments for the elimination of the voluntary aided sector and repeal of the general requirement to provide religious education. Someone unfamiliar with the details of the debate might well find the first part of this response somewhat bizarre and the second part simply irrelevant; rather as if requests by one individual to join an ongoing system in which goods are distributed, and to be treated in the same way as existing participants, were met with the reply that fairness demands that the system be abandoned. That would, of course, establish parity of treatment but not in a way that would be to the satisfaction of either the newcomer or the former beneficiaries of the scheme. Such a response might be justified if resources were scarce but in the case in question, i.e. the maintenance of community schools, the expenditure is pretty much the same whether it supports denominational or non-church establishments.[4]

However, this way of depicting the issues is not entirely faithful to the details of recent arguments against providing voluntary aid for Islamic schools and for reforming or abandoning the teaching of RE. Moreover, it misses out an important element by failing to mention their stated purpose which is that of promoting social cohesion. Here, then, is such reasoning as drawn from a National Union of Teachers document (NUT 1984):

> The Union, whilst respecting the religious beliefs and practices of the Muslim faith, would not wish to encourage the setting-up of separate Muslim schools, principally because of the likely divisive effect of this step which would separate Muslim young people from their contemporaries. Further, most of the students at present in schools or entering them in the future will probably stay in Britain to live and work, so it will be necessary for them to achieve some accommodation with the society around them and its different values.
>
> (p. 1)

Such aversion to encouraging the foundation of Muslim schools obviously invites the charge of unfairness so long as other religious groups – historically, Catholics, Anglicans and Jews – are granted this privilege. Surprisingly the discussion paper does not address this issue explicitly but it does go on to suggest that Muslim parents might be content to continue sending their children to state schools if the latter were to change in certain respects. Citing with apparent agreement the view of teachers who find the 1944 Act, in its religious clauses, 'inimical to the spirit of multi-cultural education' it continues:

> Some minority groups might feel more comfortable about schools' attitudes to their own religious beliefs, if religious education was not compulsory as it is at present, but instead took its place as an accepted part of the curriculum which reflected Britain's current cultural diversity. Thus, not only would more extreme pressure groups who saw the teaching of Christianity exclusively in schools as a threat to their own religious beliefs be satisfied that this was not the case, but also it would enable more status to be given within schools to other world religions.
>
> (p. 3)

Elsewhere I have remarked upon the peculiarity of the idea that Muslims wishing for their own schools might instead be satisfied by being required to send their children to secular institutions, and also commented upon the reasonableness of the further thought that a society that would respond to their expression of deep attachment to tradition by casting off its own inheritance might not be wholly sincere in its commitment to respect the integrity of Muslim and other essentially religious immigrant cultures (see Haldane 1986, pp. 163–5).

Besides these points several other criticisms of the NUT argument suggest themselves. First, in the passage just quoted the case for repealing the requirement for RE rests upon a caricature of the form and content of both law and practice. For the time being at least, religion certainly differs from other parts of the curriculum in being compulsory – but this feature relates to its *provision* and not to its *reception*.[5] For, again uniquely among school subjects, law explicitly entitles parents to withdraw their children from religious classes. Incidentally, while this renders the subject anomalous it involves no internal inconsistency of the sort suggested by critics, including the Swann Committee. There is no incoherence in thinking that the importance of religion in and for the lives of individuals and communities justifies requiring provision of instruction, while yet allowing that the same consideration supports permitting withdrawal on grounds of conscience. It is only verbally paradoxical to say that something may be important enough to offer and to decline. Relatedly, it is wrong to suggest that law requires the exclusive teaching of the Christian religion. Certainly Christianity has been favoured (whether this should continue is a matter to which I shall return). But the terms of the Act do not prescribe Christian education[6] and, as the NUT paper itself goes on to note, several local authorities have designed syllabuses of panoramic scope.

A second criticism concerns the way in which the argument assumes a division between religion and culture. This is not an easy matter in general, but in the case of Asian immigrants it is especially difficult. The sorts of areas in which problems may occur are familiar enough, e.g. treatment of the sexes, clothing and dietary customs. In each case it seems impossible to separate an essential religious commitment from a contingent cultural expression, and so the idea that one might discourage religious divisions while encouraging the uninhibited expression of different ethnic traditions is in doubt. If cultures are to be taken seriously, non-aggressive commitments are to be respected and freedoms are to be acknowledged then there is no option but to extend the system of voluntary aided schools to the Muslim community.

Nor should this be a grudging concession. For so long as certain educational and social values are respected society stands to benefit in the future just as it has in the past from according educational autonomy to different communities. It remains, however, to note that the avowed purpose of the NUT proposals was the avoidance of social division and this may invite the thought that whatever the worth of autonomy that of social unity is greater. There are two replies to this. First, the use of schools largely as devices of political design offends against educational and moral values in just the ways in which the opponents of denominational schools charge them with being offensive. Second, it is simply fallacious to infer discord from difference. The existence of distinct religious-cum-cultural communities need not give cause of difficulty so long as they share in common and with the wider society a set of civic values including respect for law, and toleration of difference.

It is, indeed, our historical attachment to such values that is engaged by the appeal for voluntary aid for Muslim schools. And in recognizing this a further idea should dawn upon us. For the attachment and the appeal imply a basis for social unity that transcends communal differences. Membership of British society brings entitlements and duties. So far I have been concerned largely with the former but it should be clear that in meeting demands for support the government is entitled to set conditions for it such as that schooling should satisfy general educational criteria and, besides transmitting a distinctive religious perspective, inculcate a common set of democratic values. Among these is religious tolerance. And that is more likely to be acquired by members of religious communities if they are themselves beneficiaries of it. That is to say if instead of being required to attend secular schools they are given support to maintain their own institutions.

Conclusion

In conclusion I turn from the issue of denominational schools to that of religious education in the state sector, and in doing so I want to draw together the themes developed in previous sections to suggest a case for retaining the present arrangement at least in its general outline. One concern expressed in the NUT document was that Muslim children educated in separate schools would not have the opportunity to achieve some accommodation with the surrounding society. This is a familiar claim formerly presented in opposition to church schools of other faiths, but it clearly has greater plausibility when advanced in connection with religious communities that are also culturally very different. On reflection I think it possible to discern two contingently related thoughts enmeshed in this concern. One is a *moral* or *political* idea about how people in a society ought to behave, e.g. that they should be tolerant, respectful of others, value democracy, and so on – and the fear that separate schools will not inculcate these social virtues. The other is the *empirical* hypothesis that pupils of such schools will remain apart from the society and as a result lose out on certain opportunities available to others.

As regards the latter consequence I think we have no way of determining whether it is or is not likely, but its antecedent is either trivially true and insignificant since 'remaining apart' is tautologically derived from 'attending separate schools', or else it is a substantial thesis, in which case, save for those who attend boarding schools located in the countryside and are not exposed to external influences through radio and television, etc., it is almost certainly false. Society is like the air; it surrounds us and we take it in daily without conscious effort. Indeed, it is barely possible to resist it. There is, therefore, no well-founded reason to suppose that Muslim children any more than Jewish or Catholic ones will not be drawn into the general flow of British life, notwithstanding that they may also retain many of their ethnic traditions. Let me consider next the normative question about how any member of society should behave *qua* citizen that has already been attended to in the earlier discussion of the appropriate conditions accompanying government grants. Muslim schools like others may not on ultimate pain of closure inculcate vicious dispositions and should as a condition of continuing support give evidence of imparting basic civic virtues appropriate to the society in which they are located.

The connection between these issues and that of general RE is that the state's duties extend beyond the provision of the means of instruction to aspects of its content. Speaking now of non-church schools this suggests the propriety of some form of value education. Quite independently there are sound academic reasons for teaching children about the formative influences on their society. No-one could doubt that Christianity is one of the most significant of these. Indeed, it would be reasonable to suggest that it, more than any other single force, has formed the social and moral character of Britain. Thus, we have a set of social virtues and values and a history of their development – as of that of many other important institutions. Add to this the universal significance of religion as a field of experience and activity and an educational case emerges for conjoining the general transmission of certain persistent values with the provision of specific instruction identifying and explaining their Christian sources and using the example of Christianity to introduce religious ideas.

This is not of course an argument for catechetics, the only justification of which could be a theological one. Nor does it support the exclusion of reference to other traditions. On the contrary, since part of what it envisages is teaching children about religion conceived of at a level more general than that of particular faiths, it should draw its examples from more than one source. And in going beyond Christianity it will be appropriate to direct attention to the other main religions – as indeed, at some point, to the possibility of life without any faith. Nonetheless, the case remains that an education provided by the state for those of its population who have not sought denominational instruction should include the teaching of the Christian religion as part of the country's cultural and moral heritage.

Here I have not directly addressed the liberal argument referred to in section II (p. 202) and nor have I considered the question of whether statutory regulation is an appropriate device for shaping the curriculum. Since there is soon to be a radical change in the way law is involved in controlling the content of general education, now is perhaps the best and worst of times in which to discuss the issue. To do so, however, would require far more space than is available here. Likewise, the exposition and assessment of the powerful and recently revived arguments for liberal individualism is a task beyond the limits of this occasion. (For some discussion, see Haldane 1986, pp. 163–5.) However, it may be apparent what form an argument against neutralism in education as in other social matters might take, for it is implicit in the discussion presented above. In short, conformity with some inherited values and familarity with others acquired through teaching should not be regarded as an unreasonable constraint on the individual but rather as a precondition of his or her personal development in the circumstances of social life.

A Chestertonian example

I began with Chesterton contemplating the possibility of thoughts of education inducing gravity, let me then conclude by quoting a passage from another of his writings in which he considers the educational presuppositions of delight. The scene is night time in the courtyard of University College, London. Two figures stand beneath the portico of Wilkin's elegant testimony to humanist ideals. They look down from there into the blackness in which the only visible thing is a gardener's fire. From time to time glowing sparks fly out and upwards towards the figures. 'Aren't those sparks splendid?' asks one. 'Yes', replies the other. The dialogue then continues:

> That is all I ask you to admit.... Give me those few red specks and I will deduce Christian morality. Once I thought like you, that one's pleasure in a flying spark was a thing that could come and go with that spark. Once I thought that the delight was as free as the fire. Once I thought that red star we see was alone in space. But now I know that the red star is only on the apex of an invisible pyramid of virtues. That red fire is only the flower on a stalk of living habits, which you cannot see. Only because your mother made you say 'Thank you' for a bun are you now able to thank Nature or

chaos for those red stars of an instant or for the white stars of all time. Only because you were humble before fireworks on the fifth of November do you now enjoy any fireworks that you chance to see. You only like them being red because you were told about the blood of the martyrs; you only like them being bright because brightness is a glory. The flame flowered out of virtues, and it will fade with virtues.

(Chesterton 1939, pp. 137–8)

This is, I think, an inspiring model of how religious education might contribute to the development of our self-understanding. Sad, then, that its author is nowadays so rarely referred to.

Notes

1 See, for example, the evidence of wide-scale failure to meet the morning assembly requirement of the 1944 Education Act presented in *The Times Educational Supplement*, No. 3625, 20 December 1985.

2 The present essay is the text of a paper given to the *Education Now* conference held on 24 October 1987 to mark the establishment of the *Social Values Research Centre* at the University of Hull. I am grateful to Brenda Almond, the then Director of the Centre, for the invitation to contribute to this meeting.

3 The quotation comes from an interview between John Mortimer and Bishop Jenkins of Durham published in *The Sunday Times*, 12 May 1985. Given the link I have discussed between opposition to the present status of religion in education based on sociological assumptions and the liability of theorists and commentators to project their own opinions into society at large, it is interesting to note that in the year following this interview Bishop Jenkins gave an address to an education conference in York in which he is quoted as saying: 'We must face up to our pluralistic society and dissolve [voluntary aided church schools]' *Daily Telegraph*, 26 July 1986.

4 The financial aspect of the voluntary schools issue is complicated by the fact that for demographic reasons they may be more expensive to maintain than 'state' schools. Against this, however, is set the fact that unlike the latter the former receive only 85 per cent of their capital cost from government.

5 At the time of writing, the Conservative government had published a consultation document titled *The National Curriculum 5–16* (Department of Education and Science, July 1987) which introduces among other proposals a plan to amend the Section 8 duty (in the 1944 Act) on local education authorities so as to oblige them to offer instruction to all pupils 'as required by the national curriculum'. If enacted this would bring other subjects within the scope of statute; but without further amendment RE would remain anomalous by the national curriculum and while being compulsory in its provision would, unlike subjects in the core curriculum, be voluntary in its acceptance.

The whole question of the use of law to control the curriculum is fraught with political and philosophical difficulties which cannot be discussed on this occasion. Elsewhere (Haldane 1986) I have suggested that proponents of competing views might consider the position in Scottish law whereby education authorities do not have imposed upon them a requirement to provide RE but are obliged to continue existing provision unless they are able to secure support for its abandonment from a majority of those entitled to cast a vote in local area elections. In the present essay my concern is principally with the case for and against religious schools and religious education, and the issue of how best these traditions may be preserved is partly independent of this.

Thus, I do not take myself to be committed to the present legal arrangement, only to what that is intended to effect.

6 See section 26: 'Special Provisions as to Religious Education in County Schools' which begins as follows:

> Subject as hereinafter provided, the collective worship (a) required by subsection (1) of the last foregoing section shall not (b), in any county school be distinctive of any particular religious denomination, and the religious instruction given to any pupils... shall be given in accordance with an agreed syllabus adopted for the school or for those pupils and shall not include any catechism or formulary which is distinctive of any particular religious denomination...

References

Chesterton, G.K. (1910) *What's Wrong with the World* (London: Cassell).

Chesterton, G.K. (1939) 'The Diabolist', in *Essays by G.K. Chesterton*, ed. J. Guest (London: Collins).

Haldane, J. (1986) 'Religious Education in a Pluralist Society: A Philosophical Examination', *British Journal of Educational Studies* 34, pp. 161–81.

Hudson, W.D. (1973) 'Is Religious Education Possible?' in G. Langford and D.J. O'Connor (eds), *New Essays in the Philosophy of Education* (London: Routledge & Kegan Paul).

National Union of Teachers (1984) *Religious Education in a Multi-Faith Society: A Discussion Paper by the National Union of Teachers* (London: NUT).

Chapter 15

Catholic education and Catholic identity

Introduction

Let me begin with two short passages from writings by G.K. Chesterton. The effect of bringing them together is to suggest the need for a philosophy of education.

> Philosophy is merely thought that has been thought out. It is often a great bore. But man has no alternative, except between being influenced by thought that has been thought out and being influenced by thought that has not been thought out. The latter is what we commonly call culture and enlightenment today.
>
> (Chesterton 1950, p. 176)

> Every education teaches a philosophy; if not by dogma then by suggestion, by implication, by atmosphere. Every part of that education has a connection with every other part. If it does not all combine to convey some general view of life it is not education at all.
>
> (Ibid., p. 167)

Whenever I read Chesterton I am left wondering why his non-fiction writings are not more widely discussed. Certainly there are circles of loyal devotees, but the Chestertonic is most effective when not consumed so liberally as to induce intoxication and nostalgic melancholy. One gains most, I think, from taking small portions of his work, such as an individual essay or book chapter, and letting them refresh one's mind. Chesterton is not best read for reassurance but for stimulation; and the stimulation he provides enables one to start thinking again about matters which previously seemed closed or intractable.

A few years ago, inspired by a chapter of his 1908 book *What's Wrong with the World*, I wrote an essay on Chesterton as a philosopher of education in which I linked aspects of his thought to elements in the writings of Thomas Aquinas (Haldane 1990, Chapter 13 of this volume). It seemed to me then that there was need for a contemporary study of Catholic educational philosophy, and in the meantime I have become convinced that any such work ought to include an account of how concerns with education connect with more general issues in social and political philosophy and with the question of Catholic identity (on this see Carr et al. 1995). Elsewhere I have explored the former issues, arguing that a Roman Catholic cannot accept certain liberal doctrines such as the moral neutrality of the state (Haldane 1992, Chapter 11 of this volume), and on an earlier occasion I defended the traditional idea that general orthodoxy is non-optional for the Catholic (Haldane 1989, Chapter 4 of this volume). Here I want to reflect briefly on such matters as they relate to the question: What is the proper function of Catholic schools? I shall be making five points as follows:

- It is important to distinguish issues of experience from those of identity.
- The question of Catholic identity is inescapable.
- There is a distinctive Catholic identity.
- Catholic identity is partly constituted by authority and dogma.
- The primary function of Catholic schools is to transmit Catholic truths and values.

Questions of experience and of identity

What does it mean to be a Roman Catholic? The question is ambiguous. Understood in one way it enquires about personal and social attitudes and is the sort of thing that an interviewer might ask expecting a personal biography or cultural description. When interpreted in this way let us call it 'the question of Catholic experience'. This contrasts with a second interpretation according to which what is being sought for is some sort of objective essence, or at least a broad definition identifying central features of Roman Catholicism. When taken in this latter sense let us call it 'the question of Catholic identity'.

My first point then is this: When thinking about Roman Catholicism many of those raised in that tradition now tend to confuse the two questions and assimilate the issue of identity to that of experience. At a conference on 'The Contemporary Catholic school and the Common Good' at St Edmund's College, Cambridge, Thomas Groome addressed the issue: What makes a school Catholic? and asked those present to consider what they took to be distinctive of Catholicism. (See McLaughlin et al. 1996, ch. 7.) I found myself immediately thinking about such ideas as the duality of Holy Scripture and Holy Church, the special mediating functions of the priesthood, the Mass, transubstantiation, the extraordinary magisterium, the Papacy, the communion of saints, the Marian dogmas, prayers of intercession and so on. When the time came to report our thoughts, however, I was struck by the fact that those who spoke all recalled personal memories of childhood and youth, memories of priests and nuns, of authority and discipline, of particular rituals and pieties, and the such like. Many, in fact most, spoke in terms that suggested that they thought the old ways had gone and that things in the Church were now better for this. At least two things are significant in these responses: first, the preference for the present over the past;

and second, the fact that no-one else seemed to have taken the speaker to be posing the question of *identity* rather than that of *experience*.

The programme included a couple of 'retrospectives', for one of which I had been detailed to reflect on some of the main issues discussed throughout the conference. These fell under several heads including the different legal and institutional circumstances of schools in the US and in the UK, questions of social justice, the role of Catholic schools and the issue of Catholic identity. Commenting on the latter, I began by noting that my own perspective was partly determined by the fact that I live and work in St Andrews, a town and university strongly associated with the Scottish Reformation. The legacy of the sixteenth century in Scotland continues to give greater prominence to questions of religious identity than they generally have in England, and Roman Catholicism has only recently begun to enjoy 'non-alien status'. Additionally, something of the reformed heritage was in my own Scottish childhood, since although my mother was a cradle Catholic and I spent ten years at a Jesuit school, my father had a Presbyterian upbringing and only converted to Catholicism in middle-life.

Such circumstances, together with the fact that as a philosopher I am concerned with trying to understand the 'essences' of things, contribute to my interest in the question of identity. However, and this is my second point, this issue is anyhow inescapable if one begins to think seriously about the nature and purpose of Catholic schools. In recognition of this necessity and in the hope of getting clearer about differences in attitudes to the distinguishing features of Catholicism, I produced the following diagram and considered various possible differentiae:

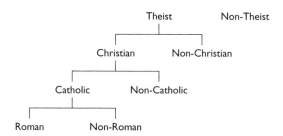

My third point arises from this exercise. However difficult it may be to produce a definition of the essence of Roman Catholicism there are relevant and important differences between theists and non-theists, Christians and non-Christians, Catholics and non-Catholics, and Romans and non-Romans. This may seem too obvious for comment. However, I have been struck by the fact that as well as conflating questions of personal experience and of ecclesial identity, many people in Catholic circles are concerned to deny that there are differences of genuine significance between Catholics and certain other religious groupings – at least at any level that really matters. One illustration of this point would be to say that the issues between Anglicans and Romans over the matter of authority are not theologically deep but reduce to variety in the cultural realization of certain ideas. Or again it is sometimes said that the religious practices of non-Christians are equally significant and deserving of religious respect to those of Catholicism – as when, for example, members of a Catholic Commission suggested that Rastafarianism is a 'valid religious experience' and that its followers should be allowed the use of Catholic premises for worship. Similar claims are made by many Anglicans and other Christians.

One way of bringing out disagreements over such matters of purported identity and difference – and I believe it is important for Catholics to recognize and explore these disagreements – is by considering the diagram and asking oneself the following questions: Where am I located? Why should I be there? Do I want to bring others there also? For those in the Victorian and Edwardian periods confronted with challenges to religion from science and politics, as for those in the inter-war years struggling with the competing claims of Catholicism and Communism, or like George Orwell trying to find a humanist philosophy different from each, the resolution of issues of theological and philosophical doctrine and the implementation of their practical corollaries were not viewed as unwelcome intrusions in the effort to live well, or to establish respectful relations with others, but as preconditions of the possibility of doing so (Norman 1985, chs 4 and 5; Haldane 1989, Chapter 4 of this volume). What has changed? One possible answer is 'the Roman Catholic Church'.

Authoritative and dogmatic: vices or virtues?

There is a widely held view that sometime during or after the Second Vatican Council the Church underwent a radical and irreversible change in its self-conception. To the extent that such distinctions are drawn, proponents of this view, whom I shall call the 'revisionists', would say that the transformation in question is not just, or even primarily, a sociological one but is theological and cognitive. In other words the Church has not merely undergone certain stylistic changes. Rather, the initiatives of the Council and the resulting post-conciliar reorientation mark a progression towards a truth previously unseen, lost sight of, or even deliberately obscured. For instead of regarding itself as an autocratic structure primarily concerned with preserving Tridentine orthodoxy through authoritative teaching and priest-administered sacraments, the Church now knows itself to be a community of equals moving uncertainly as a pilgrim body towards a more just social order.

Of course this way of speaking raises the question: Who or what is the Church? And one problem in maintaining the revisionist view is that it seems to be at odds with that presented by Pope John Paul II and by Cardinal Ratzinger, the Prefect of the Sacred Congregation for the Doctrine of the Faith, both of whom have been concerned to combat what they regard as serious lapses from authentic Catholic teaching. Given some perspectives, to find oneself in disagreement with the occupants of these offices is to have reason to presume that one is in error. But of course from the revisionist perspective the authority of these papal and congregational offices is precisely a matter on which traditionalist occupants are likely to be mistaken. In other words assertions of, and demands for, orthodoxy are regarded as question-begging, reactionary measures against revisionist advances.

Clearly there is no quick or single way to resolve this dispute. But it is worth considering the plausibility of the competing interpretations of Catholic teaching during what both parties can agree has been a period of social change and religious questioning. Consider, for example, the important area of social issues as these have been addressed in papal documents during the last century. According to the traditionalist the Church is committed to a core of unchanging norms and values which it has long propagated and which it continues to affirm with authority. On this account the passage from Leo XIII's *Rerum Novarum* (1891), via Pius XI's *Quadragesimo Anno* (1931) and John XXIII's *Pacem in Terris* (1963), to John Paul II's *Veritatis Splendor* (1993) is one of unbroken commitment to the same essential doctrines. In the revisionist view, however, Vatican II marked an important shift in the Church's understanding of morality and politics as it belatedly came to terms with liberalism and contextualism. Thus while it will be conceded that the present Pope's thinking is similar to that of pre-conciliar Pontiffs, that very fact is taken to show that he is a reactionary, drawing back from enlightenment and retreating into the darkness of anti-modernism.

This latter impression is widely shared, but it is doubtful whether it stands up to much scrutiny. Consider for example the claim that in his social teaching John XXIII inaugurated a new liberalism in Catholic thought. In *Pacem in Terris* he writes:

> Every human being has the right to respect for his person; to his good reputation, the right to freedom in searching for truth and in expressing and communicating his opinions within the limits laid down by the moral order and the common good.
>
> Every human being has the right to honour God according to the dictates of an upright conscience and therefore the right to worship God privately and publicly...
>
> Human beings have the right to choose freely the state of life which they prefer and therefore the right to establish a family with equal rights and duties for man and woman and also the right to follow a vocation to the priesthood or religious life.
>
> (John XXIII, *Pacem in Terris*, 16, 25)

Initially this may seem to be at odds with the anti-liberal claims of previous Popes and the purported 'illiberalism' of the present incumbent, but while it is certainly true that John XXIII sought to avoid the authoritarian tones of his predecessors and recognized the fact that many societies had become pluralist democracies, the teaching retains its original and essential orientation towards an objective moral order and preserves its papal authority. Notice, for example, the way in which the liberties are qualified by reference to permissible or required ends. The right to intellectual freedom is specified in terms of the pursuit of truth and is constrained by the demands of morality; religious liberty is described as the right to worship God; the right to choose freely one's state of life does not extend to pre- or extra-marital affairs or homosexual relationships. In other words the heralded freedoms are tied to prescribed ends.

In addition to the *matter* of papal and conciliar teaching there is the critical question of its *form*, more precisely that of its authority. Traditionally the Church claims to be the repository of divine revelation and to possess an apostolic magisterium, in respect of the essentials of the faith. Within this it defines an extraordinary magisterium, the agents of which may be Councils or the Pontiff pronouncing *ex cathedra*. This 'magisterial' aspect of Catholicism has been the subject of much revisionist criticism. It is sometimes said to be a relatively late accretion at odds with the understanding of the early Church. At other times it is rejected as triumphalist and offensive to non-Catholic and non-Christian believers. Furthermore it is held to be philosophically untenable in a post-Cartesian age.

Once again I can do little more than suggest considerations to the contrary. First, the idea that the Church is possessed of a special teaching authority is as old as systematic reflection upon the nature of Christ's mission and of that of the Apostles. Famously in Matthew we have the commissioning of Peter (Matthew 16.17–19), and prominent in John's Gospel are Christ's repeated promises of the coming of an Advocate, the Holy Spirit, who will be with the Church forever as a source of truth (John 14–16, *passim*). Writing in the fourth quarter of the second century and building upon such scriptural foundations Irenaeus advises:

> It is not necessary still to seek amongst others for the truth which it is easy to receive from the Church. Since the Apostles most fully committed unto the Church as into a rich repository all things pertaining to the truth, that whosoever wills may draw out of it the drink of life.
>
> (St Irenaeus 1868 edn, p. 264)

And elsewhere he writes:

> This, beloved, is the preaching of the truth, and this is the manner of our salvation, and this is the way of life, announced by the prophets and ratified by Christ and handed over to the Apostles and handed down by the Church in the whole world [i.e. the ecumenical or 'Catholic' Church] to her children. This must be kept in all security, with good will and by being well-pleasing to God through good works and sound moral character.
>
> (St Irenaeus 1952 edn, p. 108)

Of course such claims can be rejected, but that is not to the point. I have no ambition here to argue the truth of Catholic teaching, only to maintain that it has a distinctive content of the sort I have indicated and to urge that reference to this is central in answering any question about Catholic identity.

As regards the notion of doctrinal authority as such, and of its correlative, viz. *dogma*, it is a long-standing claim of the Church of Rome that it shows its truth in part precisely through its making authoritative pronouncements. This idea needs to be properly understood. The assumption is not the obvious absurdity that claiming an inerrant teaching authority is *sufficient* for possessing it; but rather that a *necessary* condition of having such authority is that one presumes oneself to be in possession of it. As a matter of philosophy, but independent of Cartesian or any other theory of epistemological warrant, no person or institution that does not claim to teach with authority, either explicitly or by implication, can coherently be regarded as authoritative. While this fact does not guarantee the truth of doctrine it undermines the claim of revisionists to be advancing legitimate developments of Catholic teaching. My fourth point, therefore, is that whatever the nature of a Church that has only the most limited, if any, defined doctrines, that claims no special authority and regards itself as on a par with other faiths in respect of its grasp of truth, it is *not* that of Roman Catholicism.

The Catholic Church has a distinctive nature, part of which unites its members with other non-Christian theists and with the faithful of other Christian denominations, and parts of which distinguish them as separate. At the level of essences this is a matter of theology not of sociology or of psychology. While Catholic identity, therefore, is not a question of experience, nevertheless membership of the Catholic Church or extended encounters with its members should make a difference to one's experience. Sadly of course the difference is not always found to be beneficial, as was testified to by some of the reminiscences prompted by Thomas Groome. While that must be a matter for regret, the Catholic can only regard it as providing reason for improving the quality of lived Catholicism and not as grounds for shifting to some other religious foundation.

Catholic education and Catholic schools

At this point, then, let me return to the question of Catholic education and again quote from Chesterton.

> The fashionable fallacy is that by education we can give people something that we have not got.... These pages have, of course, no other general purpose than to point out that we cannot create anything good until we have conceived it.... Education is only truth in a state of transmission; and how can we pass on truth if it has never come into our hand?
>
> (Chesterton 1910, pp. 198–200)

In the context of schooling, education is a deliberate process whereby the cognitive, affective and practical potentialities of the pupil are realized and given determinate content (Haldane 1995). The primary function of Catholic schools, therefore, is to provide forms of education through which the essential doctrines and devotions of Catholicism are transmitted. In the present day that is not an easy task either to plan or to implement; but nor was it unproblematic throughout most of Christian history, and I believe it follows from what has been said that the task is a non-negotiable one. It is a duty.

Against this, however, may be brought such objections as that the vocation of the Church is primarily to promote social justice, and that in multi culture, multi-faith societies the religious function I describe is 'exclusivist' and as such both undesirable and impractical. In their book *Catholic Schools and the Common Good*, Anthony Bryk, Valerie Lee and Peter Holland attribute part of the success of Catholic secondary schools in the USA to what they describe as 'an inspirational ideology that directs institutional action toward social justice in an ecumenical and multicultural world' (Bryk et al. 1993, p. 11). However, since others who do not share Catholic, Christian or any religious beliefs are also moved by considerations of social morality the question arises: What is this 'inspirational ideology' and how is it related to other aspects of Catholic faith?

In tracing the origins of this ideology the authors refer to the neo-scholastic revival initiated by Leo XIII's encouragement to Catholic scholars to study the work of Aquinas, and they go on to describe something of Maritain's Christian philosophy of education, one of the foundations of which is a social ethic involving the idea of the common good. In brief, this builds upon the natural law tradition giving special emphasis to the Thomistic–Aristotelian claim that human beings are social creatures constituted as persons through their relationships with others (Maritain 1943). This is all to the good; however, it hardly seems to point to an 'inspirational ideology' that is necessarily religious, never mind distinctively Catholic. Indeed, in what they say subsequently, Bryk and his co-authors appear to widen the gap between the social philosophy of the common good and traditional Catholic theology.

> Although selected Neoscholastic scholars such as Maritain...offered Catholics a way to engage with modernity, the more conventional and doctrinaire interpreters of Thomas wreaked much havoc. Their scholarship reinforced a hierarchical conception of the institutional Church, in which the magisterium would think and the flock would follow...
>
> Further, Neoscholasticism's very strengths were also its weaknesses. Its aggressive resort to intellectualising faith diminished the common appeal of the Christian message....Neoscholasticism distracted many Catholics from the more concrete imperatives of the gospel message to advance human goodness through hope in the vision of the 'final Kingdom'.
>
> (Bryk et al. 1993, pp. 40–1)

What follows this is an account of the adaptation of Catholicism to the facts of 'modernity' and 'postmodernity', the upshot of which is said to have been the shattering of 'the monolith of Neoscholastic thought as the authoritative synthesis of the "Catholic position"', leading to the employment of 'multiple rationales to ground social action'. However, something of the earlier neoscholastic tradition is said to remain and to constitute the Catholic contribution to social thought:

> Postmodern thinkers increasingly speak of the need to rekindle a sense of social responsibility and public participation in a diverse and pluralistic American life. In the search for a grounding for this renewed social commitment, these two residuals of Neoscholasticism – the capacity of reason to arrive at truth and the need for moral norms and principles in social life – represent an active, vital, coherent Catholic voice in this extended dialogue.
>
> (Ibid.)

Admiring as I am of the authors' sociological study, I think that this assessment bears the marks of the revisionist tendency with which I was concerned earlier. It is undeniable that as a matter of historical fact moral theologians have drawn back from the claims of their predecessors. More to the point I am happy to admit that some of the assertions and arguments of the scholastic manuals do not bear close (or even middle-distance) scrutiny. The critical issue, however, is approached when one asks the question: Is Catholic social teaching coincident with an objectivist ethic of the common good? There is scope for much philosophy here. Certainly it asserts the objectivity of values and claims that certain goods attach to society as a whole. But the interesting and troublesome issues arise when it is asked if such a view is tenable on other than theological grounds, and whether a theological foundation supports, and even necessitates, more extensive claims.

In place of lengthy argumentation permit me to conclude by merely sketching a line of thought. Just as in Catholic metaphysical theology grace perfects nature, so in its moral and social teaching a theological ethic transforms what would otherwise be a mundane natural law structure. From this perspective no account of values can begin to be adequate unless it has at its heart the recognition that mankind has an eternal destiny. The primary purpose for which we were created is certainly *not* that of loving ourselves, as the ethical egoist might have it; but nor is it that of loving one another. Rather it is that of loving *God*. Of course this last is not incompatible with an ethic of brotherly concern – we are not to love God *as opposed to* loving one another – but such brotherly concern is made sense of, as more than a romantic metaphor, by the claim that we are fellow creatures brought into existence by the one and only divine creator.

A Catholic philosophy of education cannot limit itself to the claim that there are objective social goods. It must build an extensive structure around the simple yet unlimited claim that we exist for the sake of God's glory. It has to be acknowledged that this is nowadays an extraordinary and divisive claim. It is certainly 'exclusivist' in the sense of being incompatible with certain other secular and religious philosophies. But it is surely not open to the Catholic to believe that the design and implementation of an educational philosophy based on this assumption is 'undesirable' and 'impractical'. On the contrary, it is the thought that in pursuing it we are doing God's will that assures us that it can, and ought to, be achieved. My fifth and final point, then, is that the primary function of Catholic schools is to transmit Catholic truths and Catholic values. Everything else, no matter how important, is secondary to this

References

Bryk, A.S., Lee, V.E. and Holland, P.B. (1993) *Catholic Schools and the Common Good* (Cambridge, Mass.: Harvard University Press).
Carr, D., Haldane, J., McLaughlin, T. and Pring, R. (1995) 'Return to the Crossroads: Maritain Fifty Years On', *British Journal of Educational Studies* 43, pp. 162–78.
Chesterton, G.K. (1910) *What's Wrong with the World* (London: Cassell).
Chesterton, G.K. (1950) 'The Revival of Philosophy: Why?', in *The Common Man* (London: Sheed & Ward).
Haldane, J. (1989) 'Critical Orthodoxy', *Louvain Studies* 14. (Chapter 4, this volume.)
Haldane, J. (1990) 'Chesterton's Philosophy of Education', *Philosophy* 65. (Chapter 13, this volume.)
Haldane, J. (1992) 'Can a Catholic Be a Liberal?: Catholic Social Teaching and Communitarianism', *Melita Theologica* 43, pp. 44–57. (Chapter 11, this volume.)
Haldane, J. (1995) 'Education: Conserving Tradition', in B. Almond (ed.), *Introduction to Applied Ethics* (Oxford: Basil Blackwell).
Johnstone, R. (1982) *The Will to Believe* (Oxford: Oxford University Press).
McLaughlin, T., O'Keefe, J. and O'Keefe, B. (eds) (1996) *The Contemporary Catholic School* (London: Falmer Press).
Maritain, J. (1943) *Education at the Crossroads* (New Haven, Conn.: Yale University Press).
Norman, E. (1985) *Roman Catholicism in England: From the Elizabethan Settlement to the Second Vatican Council* (Oxford: Oxford University Press).
St Irenaeus (1968 edn) *Adversus Haereses*, III, 4, 1, in *Anti-Nicene Christian Library*, ed. Roberts and Rambant (Edinburgh: T. & T. Clark), 1.
St Irenaeus (1952 edn) *Proof of the Apostolic Preaching*, ed. and trans. J.P. Smith (London: Longmans, Green & Co.).

Chapter 16

The need of spirituality in Catholic education

Introduction

By the time someone reaches college or university he or she will already have a definite moral character. This may change, but for the most part subsequent development will be in directions already determined at earlier stages – the child is almost always 'father to the man'. Even so, higher education should not neglect the personal formation of students. In the past, particularly in small institutions, there was a concern for the moral well-being of what were perceived to be young people in transition to full adulthood. One form – perhaps I should say one 'forum' – in which this concern could be expressed was the individual tutorial. Tutors thought of themselves as charged with the responsibility of helping students form themselves, or as it might have been said in the nineteenth century, 'cultivate virtue'. Now, however, reference to this way of thinking would almost certainly be derided as paternalistic, patronizing and unduly 'directional', an infringement of student autonomy.

It is harder, though, to deny that school teachers have responsibilities to provide moral guidance for their pupils. Sometimes it can happen that what is taught in schools, and the general ethos that is created therein, undermine the attempts of parents to inculcate one or other set of values. In recent years this has been a problem in some larger cities where teachers have pursued ill-considered philosophies against the grain of society and of folk wisdom. Here, though, I hope I can set this danger aside by assuming that where Catholic schools are concerned, parents and teachers are agreed on the importance of cultivating Catholic habits of thought, feeling and action. This may sound fine and comforting but it begs a major question, namely, what the relevant virtues are and what the end is that they help promote. The main issue to be considered, therefore, is the proper content of Catholic education.

Complainers and converts

In 1993 I was invited to contribute to a US/UK conference on Catholic schools which resulted in a publication about the contemporary Catholic school

(McLaughlin et al. 1996). Much of the discussion at the conference revolved around notions of Catholic identity. Most of this took the form of reminiscences about childhood or complaints about the inadequacy of the Church. Let me say at this point that it is striking how much Catholics complain. My conjecture is that this is often an expression of immaturity born of an unreasonable dependence on the all-too-human aspects of the Church, and on a failure to distinguish between offices and their occupants. Over-clericalized and, historically, often tribal, Catholics tend to suffer from an inability to form an objective perception of themselves; and instead of getting on with things, they stay at home in their backyards and grumble about not getting out into the wider world. It really is an excuse to go on saying that Catholics are discriminated against in the professions, the arts and in academic and public life.

For all the recent excitement about a return to Catholicism akin to that experienced between and after the two world wars – a 'Second Spring' or 'Catholic Moment' – it remains the case that in the twentieth century (and the nineteenth) English-speaking cradle Catholics have contributed little to higher thought and culture. The great and oft-cited figures such as G.K. Chesterton, Compton Mackenzie, Eric Gill, David Jones, Arnold Lunn, Christopher Dawson, Ronald Knox, Evelyn Waugh, Graham Greene, Walker Percy and Thomas Merton, were *all* converts – as in my own field (philosophy) have been the leading Catholic thinkers: Jacques Maritain, Gabriel Marcel, Frederick Copleston, Elizabeth Anscombe, Peter Geach, Michael Dummett and Alasdair MacIntyre. So it continues: in journalism, John Wilkins formerly of the *Tablet*, Clifford Longley formerly of *The Times*, Charles Moore formerly of the *Daily Telegraph*; in literature, Muriel Spark and Alice Ellis Thomas, and so on – all are converts! Whatever it is that attracts these people to Catholicism, we must ask whether Catholic schools and colleges succeed in transmitting it to their own pupils and students. I fear they do not. In fact, I see evidence of their continuing to abandon those features of Catholic faith and culture that have attracted – and continue to attract – good and thoughtful converts.

At any rate there was much grumbling at the aforementioned conference. Indeed an auction developed, reminiscent of the Monty Python 'Self-Made Yorkshiremen' sketch, with successive speakers outbidding one another in their accounts of the privation and cruelty of their upbringings. In the Python scene the recounted deprivations were material, but at the conference the miseries were those of having a Catholic identity. As well as suggesting an amusing parallel, this appears odd in two ways. First, it is somewhat difficult to believe that the reports were accurate and not the familiar exaggerations of group-therapy sessions. Second, this construal of the idea of Catholic identity is self-obsessively sociobiographical. Religious identities are more properly to be thought of in terms of founding scriptures, declared doctrines, authoritative teachings, established liturgies and spiritual traditions. Yet of these the conference participants had literally nothing to say. This omission may be construed as a real sign of a failed Catholic education (for further discussion, see previous chapter).

It is worth comparing such views with that presented by another convert, this time a figure of the old (socialist) left. In 1979 Brian Wicker wrote a piece entitled 'Adult Education' for *The Tablet*. In this he describes his feelings at being admitted to the Church nearly thirty years previously, in 1950:

> One was joining something which put a strange gulf between oneself and the world as one knew it. . . . I discovered there were people about me who lived by vows (of poverty, chastity and obedience) so strange and extraordinary that in meeting them I felt I was moving into another world. Until then I had thought only remote people of moral genius, like Tolstoy and Ghandi, lived by renunciations as total as that in the modern world. Now I found they existed in absurd places like Birmingham or Peckham Rye. One could actually meet them. What is more, the ordinary Catholic in the street lived a hidden life by which he shared, in his own way, that amazing world. For example, by being solemnly committed to attending mass every Sunday without fail, whatever other so called 'commitments' he might have . . .
>
> (Wicker 1979, p. 18)

I shall return to the difference between Wicker's appreciation and the attitudes of the conference participants in due course. But first let me say something very general about what ought to be the fundamentals of any Catholic philosophy of education.

Starting at the end

Briefly stated, the main point of a Catholic education should be to lay down the foundations of a good life and of a good death. The pagan Romans could say '*Mors ianua vitae*' (death is the gateway to life); yet these days many Catholics seem more disposed to say 'life the gateway to personal self-fulfilment'. The four last things, death, judgement, heaven and hell, are in danger of being seen as unhelpful and perhaps removable intrusions from the Dark Ages. But life in the natural order is conditioned by death, and human activity should be measured against this end. It is not morbid to think often of mortality when the point of doing so is to reflect back on one's present condition and actions. It might be said that those best love life who know its meaning, and since for the Christian a key to its meaning is the inescapable fact of death, no-one can love life who seeks to deny its finitude.

It is within this context that a Catholic philosophy of education should be developed. Education is an activity or process. As such it is defined by its goal, what it aims to achieve. Chesterton had this in mind when he wrote that 'Education is only truth in a state of transmission' and immediately raised the rhetorical question 'how can we pass on truth if it has never come into our hand?' (Chesterton 1910).[1] For Aristotle and Aquinas the theory of education belongs to the domain of practical reason, and both philosophers had a definite view of how such reason should proceed. First, define as best you can your ultimate aim; revision and refinement will come later. Next, ask what has to be the case for this to be realized: let us call this the 'ultimate realization conditions'. Now consider what needs to be done in order to bring these about. Next, think of what is required in order to effect these intermediary circumstances – this last reflection introduces the 'penultimate realization conditions'. On goes the reasoning, working backwards until arriving at the present situation.

When conducted with respect to any complex or distant goal, what this sort of exercise in reverse syllogistic usually reveals is that the various enabling conditions are themselves many and complex, and the processes required to realize them may be many-staged and multi-dimensional. Once one appreciates this, and turns to consider the purpose of human life, namely communion with God, and the role of the Apostles and their successors in bringing people to this goal, it begins to become clear why the Catholic Church is a complex and multi-faceted institution. The destination may be mono-verbally described, viz. heaven; but the journey and the modes of transport reflect the complexity of the human condition – a condition, it is important to recall, of inherited fallenness; that is, of sin.

The point of these reflections is to suggest that the traditional patterns of Catholic life and formation which those in their forties and older will recall had their rationale in a definite and well-developed moral theology. Recalling religious texts from the 1950s and before, it is easy to form impressions of dull and doctrinal scholasticism, or of petty rigorism. Of course both may have featured. However, if one actually takes the trouble to look at this material there is much to be found that is both impressive and instructive. Moreover, it is dangerous hubris on our part to suppose that the fruits of two thousand years of doctrinal development and spiritual reflection can be discarded as outmoded impediments to religious well-being. Brian Wicker is no *Daily Telegraph* Tory, or even a 'New Labour' Tory; indeed he and others of the old 'new left' were frequently unwelcome critics of the political conservatism of the hierarchy. However, as the passage quoted earlier makes clear, he saw something sublime in the pre-conciliar Catholic traditions of spiritual discipline and liturgical devotion. Yet it is precisely this order that the conference participants were keen to distance themselves from. Converts have generally had to overcome ignorance, indifference or hostility to the Church. Thus it is unsurprising that they are often better judges of what is good or bad than are cradle Catholics; nor is it surprising that they are frequently the best apologists for the faith.

Three into one must go

Before moving on to look at some aspects of traditional spirituality there is a need to sort out some confusions about the nature of religion. As I have pointed out elsewhere (Smart and Haldane 1996, 2003, sect. 4) there is a marked tendency to distinguish and separate three broad approaches to religious belief: the spiritual, the historical and the philosophical. Those who follow the first emphasize experience, emotion and contemplative reflection; followers of the second concentrate on sacred scripture and Church tradition; and those partial to the third favour abstract and general argument.

Part of what is implied in distinguishing between these approaches is that there is some kind of tension or opposition between them – or at least that they are in marked contrast to one another. This frequently emerges in people's characterization of their religious attitudes. Currently, for example, there is a fashion for the spiritual approach, often under the description of personal renewal or integrative healing. Those who are drawn to this will often say that they are not tied to any Church or scriptural revelation but have a more personal or experiential understanding of religion. Such people are also inclined to regard philosophical theology as dry and overly rationalistic. The latter complaint is also voiced by the advocates of scripture and ecclesial practice, but they take issue with the rootlessness and self-absorbed individualism of New-Age spirituality. Finally, the philosophically disposed tend to be suspicious of the uncritical reliance upon emotion and similarly regard scripture and Church as going far beyond what reason warrants. Readers may recognize themselves in one or other of these portraits.

Doubtless these tendencies reflect differences of personality types, and it is true that each approach appeals to genuine aspects of the religious. However, the division of religion into these three approaches is neither necessary nor desirable. Indeed, I believe that its effect is generally malign and that there is therefore a pressing need to reintegrate the spiritual, the historical and the philosophical.

As a general principle one should not presume that because one approach or form of understanding is available others are thereby excluded. Not only may they be compatible but one may have to draw upon several or all of them in order to construct an adequate account and practice. Praying for the dead is a characteristic religious activity around which rituals and liturgies have been developed. This does not make philosophical questions about the possibility and nature of an afterlife irrelevant. On the contrary, the meaning of such prayer is given in part by the metaphysical idea that natural death is not the end of personal existence. So if there are philosophical objections to the ideas of disembodiment, reincarnation or resurrection then the point and value of the religious practice is threatened. As St Paul noted in writing to the Corinthians, 'if there is no resurrection of the dead then Christ has not been raised...and your faith is in vain' (1 Cor. 15.13–14).

Similarly, although the 'god of the philosophers' is characterized in abstract terms, as a self-existent, eternal, immutable, omnipotent, omniscient, omnibenevolent, immaterial creator and sustainer of the universe, it is a serious mistake to sever the links between spiritual reflection, revelation and philosophy. Each has a part to play in the task of coming to know, to love and to serve God. In this connection consider St John's Prologue:

> In the beginning was the Word, and the Word was with God, and the
> Word was God...all things were made through him. And the Word was
> made flesh and dwelt among us, full of grace and truth.... And from his
> fullness we have all received grace upon grace.

In the space of a few lines, John informs the Greeks and the Greek-speaking
Jews of Alexandria that what the philosophers had long sought after – the
Logos, or the ultimate account of things – has been with God from all eternity
and is that through which all things were made; and that this very same Logos
was incarnate in Jesus of Nazareth, 'the Way, the Truth and the Life'. Thus are
philosophy, history and spirituality united. To separate them would diminish
each, for what John teaches is at once metaphysical, revelatory and a theme
for meditation. A further example, this time from liturgy, supports the same
conclusion. Gerard Manley Hopkins (another convert) gives a fine English
rendering of the eucharistic hymn traditionally ascribed to Aquinas. The first
two verses run as follows:

> Godhead here in hiding whom I do adore,
> Masked by these bare shadows, shape and nothing more;
> See, Lord, at thy service low lies here a heart,
> Lost all lost in wonder at the God thou art.
>
> Seeing, touching, tasting are in thee deceived;
> How says trusty hearing? That shall be believed;
> What God's Son has told me, take for truth I do;
> Truth himself speaks truly, or there's nothing true.
>
> (Hopkins 1970, p. 211)

What is believed of the consecrated host rests upon the words of scripture.
The text itself is a testimony of personal and ecclesial belief couched in poetic terms
and adverting to the philosophico-theological doctrine of the real presence.

Some religious believers take pride and comfort in the idea that their faith
owes nothing to reason, historical testimony or doctrinal authority. Perhaps
they believe that by treating their belief as a personal relationship with God they
incur fewer troublesome burdens. However, such an attitude is quite alien to
the central traditions of Western and Eastern Christianity (as it is to those of
Judaism and Islam). The three monotheistic faiths are all religions 'of the book';
but neither value nor sense can be attached to the idea of discerning and
trusting the word of scripture unless it is possible to specify which writings and
interpretations are to be accepted and which rejected. Every faith of 'the book'
presupposes some sort of canon of authentic and authoritative scripture, and
one need only ask the question of how such a canon came to be determined,
ratified and transmitted and how it would be defended against rivals, to realize
the ineliminable role of reason and general understanding.

G.K. Chesterton said of philosophy that it is 'merely thought that has been thought out' and added that 'man has no alternative, except between being influenced by thought that has been thought out and being influenced by thought that has not been thought out' (Chesterton 1950).[2] Holy scripture together with the creeds and biblical spirituality which it inspired are religious experience that has been thought out. Nothing less would be worth transmitting across the centuries, and nor should the religiously disposed settle for anything else. The spiritual, the historical and the philosophical are no more separable in reality than are the three sides of a triangle or, dare I say it, the three Persons of the Trinity.

Religious knowledge and religious education

Accordingly, however Catholic education (at any level) proceeds, it needs to attend to the integration of these three aspects of faith. The ultimate concern on this occasion is with the spiritual, but the others are equally important and my sense is that we are failing in our educational task with regard to them. It used to be the case that Catholics knew that the Church placed great emphasis on reason and that theology was closely identified with philosophy. They were aware of the great figures of the Middle Ages, such as Aquinas and Bonaventure, and they knew in very broad terms the two main styles of argument for the existence of God: from the contingency of the world and from the order within it. They had some sense of the Catholic argument against the Protestant doctrines of the exclusivity of scripture, and of salvation by faith alone.

Of course their knowledge in these matters was from testimony, and they deferred to the expertise of others. But that is no disqualification. In general, think of how little of what we know we are in a position to confirm by our own efforts. In any society there is division of labour by competence, and this is true also with regard to matters religious. Just as my scientific knowledge rests on the say of others whom I take to be (sufficiently) expert, so my knowledge of dogma is based on the word of those who have it from those who know. Certainly this assumes that someone somewhere does know or that the knowledge is set down and may be recovered, but it ill behoves a Catholic, as it would not a sceptic, to deny this. The following counsel of prudence may be recommended to all Catholics: 'Cultivate the habit of thinking that if the Church teaches it as a matter of faith and morals then somewhere there is a good case for it drawn from revelation, tradition or natural reason.' This may seem utterly obvious, but there are many who would regard what I have said as intellectually naive and as encouraging an attitude of docility. Well, the more I pursue questions of doctrine the more I am impressed by the richness of the Church's resources, and so far as docility is concerned, it is a virtue whose corresponding vice is ineducability. Better to be teachable than not!

Similar points of contrast may be drawn in relation to historic practice. It once was the case that Catholic children had developed in them a reverence for the sacraments and the liturgy. This effect was produced through a variety of means: by pious devotions, modes of dress and behaviour, stories of heroic devotion and so on. One benefit of these efforts was to prepare them for the idea that amidst the ordinariness of life there were channels of transcendence. It is much easier for a child to believe that God is present on the altar if the setting is physically special, if the demeanour of older children and adults is reverential, and if the priest later takes evident care to clean the vessels and consume the residue of the body and blood of Christ.

Talk of the Mass as a family meal encourages quite different ways of thinking. It is unsurprising when later in life those raised in the 'get-together-with-Jesus' style wonder why the Church should make so much fuss about restricting the Eucharist to Christians in communion with Catholicism. Again, they are liable to regard caution against participation in the religious services of other denominations as mean and prejudiced. It is as if having been taken regularly to McDonald's one were to be told that one's friends who eat at Burger King are not free to share one's meal, and moreover that one should not eat there oneself. This is liable to seem 'Burgophobic'. Yet the well-educated Catholic knows better. The Mass is not a religious service, nor is it a family meal, nor a community feast. It is an event in which heaven and earth come together, as mundane time and sacred time are united. In it the sacrifice of Jesus Christ, a divine Person, is made really present – not re-enacted or remembered, but made actually present as a means of sacrifice by which our sins and those of humankind generally are atoned. He is the Messiah for whom the Jews longed and for whom many still wait, whose voluntary death opened the gates of heaven and who is presented to us as the priest speaks the words of consecration. Children cannot be taught this sacred doctrine all at once, but they should be taught it rather than the deflationary, desacralizing account of the Mass as a devotional service akin to that of other religions.

It may be suggested that these recommendations would make Catholicism seem esoteric, supernaturalist and exclusive, whereas we should be celebrating the complexity and beauty of the natural order and opening children's eyes to the universally shared features of all religions. Certainly creation is wonderful, but in order to appreciate the extent of its glory one has to understand how limited are scientific and naturalistic accounts of it. The most compelling evidence for God's existence comes precisely as one realizes that the natural order is not self-explanatory and that preternatural causes are effective in it. The 'supernatural', as Catholics should know, is not a scientific, quasi-scientific or metaphysical category; rather it is a theological one pertaining to the order of divine grace. This, not spooky magic, is what is made available through the sacraments. Furthermore, it is exclusive in as much as it is not generally available in all religions – unlike French fries in fast-food outlets – and in so far as it is freely and electively bestowed by God and is not an entitlement to all who feel benignly disposed towards the universe or to the ground of its being. If these matters have been confused or lost sight of it may be because too much attention has been afforded comparative religious education and too little given to Catholic religious knowledge.

The sacrament of the present moment

So on to spirituality; or rather a return to it, since it has been implicit in things said already, and the point of the section on the three approaches to religion was to argue that the spiritual, the historical and the philosophical-cum-theological are aspects of the same reality. Now, however, there is a need to discuss the character of spiritual development and question how it may be communicated to children and others. Earlier it was pointed out that activities and processes are identified by reference to the goals towards which they are aimed – not any old 'as it happens' goals, but their proper objects. The goal, in this sense, of spiritual development is union with God. Such union is in part a mystery, but to the extent that it can be understood it is well described by the great teachers and mystics of the Church. Those more familiar with modern ideas of spirituality might have expected a characterization of the spiritual goal in terms of becoming a certain kind of person (a fully integrated one, perhaps), or of deepening one's understanding of reality. However, unless these are just elliptical ways of talking about union with the divine Persons, then they are at best misleading and at worst plain wrong. Certainly, as the journey proceeds the traveller is changed and his or her understanding becomes more profound, but these are effects and not causes or constituent features of increasing proximity to God.

In the past when there was still a lively sense of the strangeness and dangers of unknown terrain, travellers sought out experienced and prudent guides, and where these were not available in person they studied any maps and topographical writings they may have left behind. Thinking, then, of human life as a journey towards God, it is unsurprising that the Church Fathers and those who succeeded them often used the metaphor of the guide to describe one competent and willing to lead others along the way. In earlier days the names of the great Catholic spiritual writers and the titles of their works would have been fairly well known, even if most people had not read them: Augustine, *On True Religion* and the *Confessions*; Benedict, *Rule of the Master*; Gregory the Great, *Dialogues*; Catherine of Sienna, *Dialogues*; Catherine of Genoa, *Purgation and Purgatory*; Thomas à Kempis, *Imitation of Christ*; Ignatius Loyola, *Spiritual Exercises*; Teresa of Avila, *The Interior Castle*; John of the Cross, *The Dark Night*; Francis de Sales, *Introduction to the Devout Life*; and Jean-Pierre de Caussade, *Self-Abandonment to Divine Providence*. At this point in the list it might have been added 'and one could go on'; but there are reasons to hesitate, one being the familiar feature of any list of 'greats' that it is a product of the judgement of time, and the nearer the past the less determinate the judgement. So let this list be left as it stands.

The title of this section is 'The sacrament of the present moment'. That phrase is taken from De Caussade and I will draw my conclusions about the role of spirituality by referring to his work (my knowledge of which I owe to the writings of Fr Benedict Groeschel, CFR; see, for example, Groeschel 1984 and 1988). Jean-Pierre de Caussade was born in 1675 near Toulouse. At the age of eighteen he entered the Jesuit novitiate there and eleven years later was ordained a priest of the Society. In 1720 he was transferred to preaching missions, and in 1728 was sent to Nancy, where he began work as spiritual director to a convent of Visitation Sisters. He left Nancy twice, in 1731 and again in 1739, and after tours of duty in various Jesuit houses he returned to Toulouse as spiritual director, dying there in 1751. Exactly a decade before his death he published *Dialogues on the Various States of Prayer* (De Caussade 1931), but the works that contain his greatest teachings are the posthumously published letters to the Visitation Sisters, and the treatise known as *Self-Abandonment to Divine Providence*.[3] I will quote from the latter to give the flavour of de Caussade's general guidance:

> God still speaks to us today as he spoke to our fathers, when there were no spiritual directors or set methods. Then, spirituality consisted in fidelity to the designs of God....Then it was enough for those who led a spiritual life to see that each moment brought with it a duty to be faithfully fulfilled. If the work of our sanctification presents us with difficulties it is because we do not look at it in the right way. In reality holiness consists in one thing alone, namely, fidelity to God's plan. And this fidelity is equally within everyone's capacity in both its active and passive practice.
>
> The active practice consists in accomplishing the duties imposed upon us by the general laws of God and the Church, and by the particular state of life which we have embraced. Passive fidelity consists in the loving acceptance of all that God sends us at every moment. Which of these two requirements of holiness is beyond our strength?....Not active fidelity, since the duties imposed by it cease to be such when they are really beyond our powers.... What excuse can we plead? Yet this is all that God demands of the soul in the work of its sanctification. He demands it from the high and the low, from the strong and the weak; in a word, from all, always and everywhere.
>
> The passive part of holiness is even more easy, for it consists merely in accepting what most frequently cannot be avoided, and in suffering with love, that is to say with resignation and sweetness what is too often endured with weariness and discontent.
>
> Perfection does not consist in understanding God's designs but in submitting to them....They are God working in the soul to make it like himself....The whole essence of the spiritual life consists in recognising the designs of God for us at the present moment.
>
> Souls who walk in the light sing the hymns of light, those who walk in darkness, the hymns of darkness. They must both be left to sing to the end the part and the motet which God allots to each.
>
> The more we seem to lose with God, the more we gain; the more he deprives us of the natural, the more he gives of the supernatural.
>
> (De Caussade 1959, pp. 3–9)

The meaning of the expression 'the sacrament of the present moment' will be clear. For de Caussade the search for God begins (and in a sense ends) exactly where one is at any given moment. No occult incantations, no esoteric diagrams, no strange exercises, no theatrical props, just a call to sanctity through willing service and acceptance. There is a striking contrast between this and many contemporary calls to spirituality. In, for example, an advertisement from a community of a well-established religious order which appeared in an issue of a prominent Catholic periodical: the advertisement featured a circular logo showing three joined figures stretching upwards towards a smaller circle in which a winding road or river heads towards the sun-rayed horizon, and the accompanying text read as follows:

SABBATICAL CHALLENGE FOR WOMEN RELIGIOUS

'Out beyond ideas of wrongdoing and rightdoing there's a field.
I'll meet you there.' – Rumi

- Experiential program; process-oriented
- Call to inner growth; self-empowerment, inner wisdom
- Supportive, loving community; safe environment to grow wholistically [*sic*]
- Surrounded and supported by a variety of resources
- Powerful, deep healing; loving integration leading to inner freedom

Jalal ad-Din ar Rumi was a thirteenth-century Sufi poet whose disciples formed the fraternity of Mawlawiyah, better known as 'Whirling Dervishes'. While not very familiar with the writings of Rumi (the quote is taken from a work entitled *Open Secret*), I suspect that those women religious who respond to the challenge will receive rather different guidance from that offered by Father de Caussade to the Visitation Sisters – but I may be wrong!

Recall Chesterton's remark about education being truth in a state of transmission. Then ask what truths we know about the spiritual state and about how to advance it. Young people at school and college live in times where spirituality is often equated with pantheistic psycho-babble. This generally involves vague injunctions to be 'at one with oneself' and 'develop holistically', in accord with the unity of nature. Like the command to 'do something' these offer little direction and it is hard to think what they could exclude. De Caussade, by contrast, tells us exactly what to do: first, obey God's will as communicated through Holy Scripture and Holy Church; and second, within the structure this creates, accept what comes each moment as part of gracious providence.

The theology of acceptance is at odds with a culture that has extended the idea of consumer rights to the conditions of life itself. A few years ago commentators and politicians wrote of a 'dependency culture' in which people expected resources to come to them from the state. Now we are taught to be self-confident claimants to various moral entitlements. We have rights to be upheld: rights of ownership, of association, of free expression, of respect; in general, rights to fulfilment on terms chosen by ourselves. Ironically, since it wears the mantle of virtue, this ideology of entitlement undermines the notion of an objective moral order, for it treats subjective preferences as the determinants of value. Crudely, what is good (for me) is what I want. Any appeal by others to independent standards of right and wrong then appears as a threat to frustrate my efforts at self-fulfilment. It is, in other words, a violation of my rights.

This twisted logic of entitlement can be seen operating daily in discussions of abortion, adoption, care of the elderly, euthanasia, genetic therapy, human reproduction, sexual orientation and practice, and so on through the familiar list. We are left with the impression that young Catholics are often no better equipped to deal with such issues than are others of their age and general level of education. Given the riches of Church teaching and magisterial moral theology this must be construed as an indictment of educational practice. But I am not blaming the schools as such, for the explanation lies at an earlier stage in the failure to substitute sufficient lay expertise at the level of higher education in place of seminary clerics. In consequence, the current state of religious knowledge among teachers is often frighteningly limited.

There is little point, though, in continuing to condemn the failures of the past. The question is how to make our way forward to something better. One might try to begin with doctrine, or by retelling the story of the Church. Both are important, but before anyone will attend to these they must first be brought to the point of recognizing that doctrine and Church form part of a single divine answer to a deep human need – the need to be united in love with an unfailing companion. This is the role of spirituality in education.

The guide identifies the destination and the starting-point, and traces the route between them. De Caussade makes the point that we need travel for no longer than the present moment, and for no further than the spot on which we stand. Slow the pace of discussion to this, lower the volume of talk, and teach children to discern what the moment calls for – sometimes action to change the world, sometimes patience to accept it. With these habits acquired, it will quite naturally occur to them to ask what we know about God and of God's will for us. From that point on, education will construct itself in accord with the Aristotelian–Thomistic pattern of practical reasoning, working backwards from ends to means. I have faith that this will bring true happiness and contentment as well as other less important forms of success. Any education that could achieve this would be a great gift to future generations.

Notes

1 Here it is especially helpful to see Conroy 1999, Part IV, 'Education or the Mistake About the Child'. For a further discussion see J. Haldane, 'Chesterton's Philosophy of Education', *Philosophy* (1990), reproduced as Chapter 13, this volume.

2 The section on 'The Revival of Philosophy' is interesting here.
3 I am grateful to Roger Pouivet of the University of Nancy for bringing to my attention the most recent French edition of *The Abandonment to Divine Providence* in which the editor argues that the work is in fact not by Jean-Pierre de Caussade but was written in the eighteenth century by a 'Lady of Lorraine' to whom he served as spiritual director: see *L'Abandon à La Providence*, ed. Jacques Gagey (Grenoble: Editions Jérôme Millon, 2001). The case is not at all conclusive, and most will judge that the matter of authorship neither adds to nor detracts from the content of the work.

References

Chesterton, G.K., *What's Wrong with the World* (London: Cassell, 1910).
——, 'The Revival of Philosophy' in *The Common Man* (London: Sheed & Ward, 1950).
Conroy, J.C. (ed.), *Catholic Education: Inside-Out; Outside-In* (Dublin: Veritas, 1999).
De Caussade, J.-P., SJ, *On Prayer: Spiritual Instructions on the Various States of Prayer According to the Doctrine of Bossuet, Bishop of Meaux*, trans. A. Thorold (London: Burns, Oates & Washbourne, 1931).
——, *Self-Abandonment to Divine Providence*, translated by A. Thorold, edited by J. Joyce, S.J. (London: Burns & Oates, 1959).
Gardner, W.H. and MacKenzie, N.H., *The Poems of Gerard Manley Hopkins* (Oxford: Oxford University Press, 1970).
Groeschel, Benedict J., *Spiritual Passages: The Psychology of Spiritual Development* (New York: Herder & Herder, 1984).
—— *Stumbling Blocks on Stepping Stones: Spiritual Answers to Psychological Questions* (Mahwah, NJ: Paulist Press, 1988).
Haldane, J. 'Chesterton's Philosophy of Education', *Philosophy* 65 (1990), pp. 65–80.
——, 'Catholic Education and Catholic Identity', in T. McLaughlin, J. O'Keefe SJ and B. O'Keefe (eds) *The Contemporary Catholic School: Context, Identity and Diversity* (London: Falmer Press, 1996).
McLaughlin, T., O'Keefe, J., SJ and O'Keefe, B. (eds), *The Contemporary Catholic School: Context, Identity and Diversity* (London: Falmer Press, 1996).
Smart, J.J.C. and Haldane, J.J., *Atheism and Theism* (Oxford: Blackwell, 1996); Second Edition (2003).
Wicker, Brian, 'Adult Education', *The Tablet*, 24 February 1979.

Part V

Beauty and contemplation

Chapter 17

Medieval and Renaissance aesthetics

There is no single correct answer to the question of when medieval philosophy began and ended, and the Renaissance period is similarly indeterminate in its chronological boundaries. For present purposes, however, it will be useful to regard the medieval era of art and thought as beginning between the birth of Anselm of Canterbury (1033–1109) and of Abbot Suger of St Denis (1081–1151), and to view the end of the Renaissance period as falling early within the lifetimes of Shakespeare (1564–1616) and Hobbes (1588–1679).

These vague boundaries contain over five hundred years of magnificent architecture, painting, sculpture, literature, philosophy and theology; and along with the centuries of classical antiquity they constitute the greatest eras of Western humanism. Thus no effort to understand the history of that tradition can succeed without taking something of the measure of the medieval and Renaissance contributions. In attempting to do so, one soon notices a striking structural feature of the cultural activities of these centuries. If one places on a timechart of the period 1100–1600 the names of the greatest figures in the various branches of art and learning, it becomes clear that there is a difference in the development of those branches. The era of greatest philosophical and theological achievement lies between 1200 and 1350, while the period of greatest artistic progress and accomplishment is 1400–1550.

Aesthetics and changing philosophical contexts

In briefest outline, one might characterize medieval aesthetics as an aspect of a tradition of theologically informed metaphysics and epistemology. In similarly broad terms one may represent Renaissance aesthetics, where it does not simply repeat medieval thinking (in largely secularized versions), as an emergent theory of the nature of artistic activities and of the value of their exercise.

The task of working these outlines into a comprehensive and comprehensible history faces two problems. First, the scale of the subject-matter; and second, the conceptual incongruity involved in using the contemporary idea of the *aesthetic* to capture the concerns of these earlier periods. As regards the problem of scale, the obvious difficulties are compounded by the fact that the histories of philosophy and art have not yet reached a point of interconnection that allows the easy passage of information between them; in particular we remain, in general, fairly ignorant about the relationship between art and philosophy in the Renaissance period (though see Summers 1987).

The problem of incongruity arises because thinking about art and beauty shifted importantly in the late modern period – that is, during the eighteenth century. Up to that point, the focus of philosophical attention was principally upon the unifying *objects* of certain kinds of experience – namely, *beauty*, and what it manifests or betokens, which is to say, reality. Thereafter, however, attention passed to the nature of the experience itself, and writers came to discuss what features and attitudes mark out an experience as *aesthetic*. This shift was itself a consequence of a movement in speculative inquiry away from the structure of the world, conceived of as something independent of the human mind, towards the structure of human psychology.

One reason for this movement was a change of view of how thought stands with respect to its objects. In antiquity, in the Middle Ages, and even in the time of Descartes (1596–1650) and Locke (1632–1704), philosophers were apt to regard *ideas*, the building blocks of thought, as being in one or another way identical with the structuring principles of reality itself. Whether these principles were taken to be received into the mind through experience (*abstractionism*) or to be placed there pre-natally (*innatism*), their presence in the intellect guaranteed that all thought is either directly about reality or traceable back to it. With Hume (1711–76) and Kant (1724–1804), however, a quite new picture was developed, within which concepts originate in the mind itself. Accordingly, the objects of thought and experience came to be regarded as in some sense mental constructions. Given this imagery, it becomes intelligible that Kantian and post-Kantian aesthetics should focus on the nature of aesthetic experience rather than on its objects. For if we think that what we encounter is what we have placed before ourselves, then speculative interest will attach to the modes of placement and the conditions of repossession. It is no accident, then, that Kant's three great *Critiques* replace the tradition of metaphysical descriptions of reality with interconnected logical analyses of the three different modes of thinking: the theoretic (*Pure Reason*), the practical (*Practical Reason*) and the imaginative (*Judgement*). Of course, it is possible to find anticipations of philosophical aesthetic psychology in writings earlier than the eighteenth century; but this does not tell against the general point that in the medieval and Renaissance periods the primary focus of interest was on those aspects of an independent reality which induced experiences of beauty.

Medieval aesthetics

The royal portal at Chartres was built around 1150, and is one of the earliest surviving parts of the cathedral. On it are carved various figures. Some are recognizably religious: Christ, the Virgin Mother and various prophets and saints. Others are of regal bearing – Old Testament kings and queens – but not easily identifiable; and there are figures of yet other sorts. In the moulded framing above the left-hand door are representations of the signs of the zodiac, while the right-hand portal includes personifications of the seven liberal arts (the medieval *trivium* and *quadrivium*): Grammar, Dialectic and Rhetoric, Arithmetic, Music, Geometry and Astronomy. Along with these allegorical representations are depictions of ancient practitioners of each of the arts, and among them are set the figures of Euclid and Pythagoras, the former with geometer's compasses, the latter, oblivious to place and time, hunched over a musical instrument.

In the twelfth century, Chartres and the abbey of St-Denis were the sites of a number of architectural innovations associated with the emergence of what was first known as the 'French style' and later, in the Renaissance, as the 'Gothic'. These included the development of pointed arches, rose-windows, ribbed vaulting and representational (often narrative) decoration. At St-Denis, Abbot Suger had an inscription placed on the original brilliant gilded doors of the west front: 'Bright is the noble work; but being nobly bright, the work should brighten the minds so that they may travel, through the true lights, to the True Light where Christ is the true door. . . . The dull mind rises to truth, through that which is material and in seeing this light, is resurrected from its former submersion.'

This text reveals the influence of two ideas. According to the first, which has its philosophical origins in Plato and which was associated with Neoplatonism, sensible forms and images are symbols of an invisible transcendent reality and channels of communication with it. The Judaeo-Christian counterpart of this notion is found in scripture: 'From the greatness and beauty of created things comes a corresponding perception of their Creator' (Wisdom 13.5); and 'Ever since the creation of the world his invisible nature . . . has been clearly perceived in the things that have been made' (Romans 1.20). These scriptural passages also provide a source for the second idea, which is that, in creating forms embodying a transcendent meaning, the artist is showing one way in which he is himself an image of God (*imago Dei*).

The design of St-Denis and the narrative scheme of the Chartres royal portal embody important aspects of the medieval worldview at a critical stage of its development; thus they are apt and useful focal points for studying its ideas about art and beauty. Chartres was also the site of an influential cathedral school. This integrated the theology of the Church with the philosophy of antiquity and the earlier medieval period. The latter was Neoplatonic, but in the twelfth century Chartres was one of the significant points of reception of the more naturalistic philosophy of Aristotle. (The influence of Greek ideas is evident in the representations of Pythagoras as a practitioner of music.) In the scheme of liberal arts, music featured as a branch of mathematics – being concerned with the proportions and relations between fixed elements, the notes. The choice of Pythagoras derives from his association with the mathematical study of music, but more important is his authorship of the idea that all reality is ultimately mathematical in nature and that beauty is the manifestation of this perfect order. Here, then, the notion that the sensible symbolizes the transcendent becomes the thought that in making things according to due proportion, as in the work of the arts, one creates beauty and, *ipso facto*, establishes a link with the divine.

The rise of naturalism

These ways of thinking were pervasive throughout the medieval period, and find poetic expression in *The Divine Comedy* of Dante (1265–1321). By that point in the early fourteenth century, however, the reception of Aristotelian ideas encouraged by Albert the Great (1206–80) and their extensive development by Aquinas (1225–74), together with the elaboration of Gothic artistic innovations, had produced a more naturalistic view. In Byzantine religious art the human figure was treated abstractly, without reference to its solidity or occupancy of a natural environment. Images of Christ and of the saints were mere icons located within the timeless, depthless plane of heaven, where natural light was replaced by celestial illumination – the point being to affirm the spiritual nature of reality. At Chartres, however, one can see stylized forms giving way to naturalistic representations. The volume of the human body, the disposition of its limbs, and even the facially expressed character of its emotions begin to be depicted; likewise, the shapes and details of flora and fauna.

So, by stages, Platonic dualism came to be replaced by a view of spirit as incarnate and of order as immanent within nature. This trend continued through the medieval period, and with William of Ockham (1290–1350) and the rise of nominalism (which, in insisting that every real thing is an individual entity, went even further from the Platonic belief in transcendent forms) led to a type of humanistic naturalism that ushered in the Renaissance. Indeed, so strong was the naturalizing trend, even within religious art, that it became common to affirm the humanity of Christ by emphasizing his sexual identity through depicting the naked infant or the loin-cloth-clad figure of the crucifixion.

Renaissance aesthetics

The Vatican fresco now known as *The School of Athens* was painted by Raphael (1483–1520) in the years 1509–11, and is one of the very finest works of the High Renaissance. Like the Chartres portal, it includes a representation of Pythagoras, this time engaged in mathematical calculation involving the measure of musical intervals. Notwithstanding the quasi-ecclesiastical location of the fresco (the Vatican Palace), however, the realistically depicted setting is quite different from that of Chartres. It shows, as if seen through an aperture, various figures from antiquity gathered within a classical temple, and behind them a series of archways open to the sky. The central magisterial characters are Plato (modelled on the features of Leonardo da Vinci) and Aristotle; but around and below them are gathered several groups of metaphysicians, mathematicians and scientists, including Socrates, Heraclitus (modelled on Michelangelo), Empedocles, Euclid and Ptolemy (Raphael offers a self-portrait in the depiction of one of the figures standing with these last two). The architectural interior of the temple is itself dominated by two sculpted figures representing Apollo, god of the sun and divine patron of the arts, and Athena, goddess of wisdom and patroness of Athens.

That such a work should grace a papal study room is a striking measure of how the new humanism, inspired by the rediscovery of the art, literature and science of antiquity, had taken hold of educated minds. Fifty years before its completion Marsilio Ficino (1433–99) had founded the Neoplatonic Academy in Florence under the patronage of Cosimo de' Medici (1389–1464). There the identification of beauty with mathematical proportion, and of each with a transcendent reality, was formulated in neo-classical-cum-mystical vocabulary. In connection with this idealizing of compositional order, painting and sculpture began to be separated from practical crafts and treated as branches of higher learning.

It was in Florence, also, that Raphael came under the influence of the ideas, methods and sensibilities of the two senior figures of the High Renaissance trinity – namely Leonardo and Michelangelo – both of whom were native Florentines. While the subject-matter of Renaissance art owes much to the revival of classical mythology and mystical philosophy, the *manner* of depicting scenes was transformed, from what had been common in the medieval period, by technical advances in painting and design. In his *On Painting* of 1435, Alberti (1404–72) describes a system of linear perspective based on a single vanishing point; and the possibility of depicting spatial depth and solidity through geometrical composition and other devices (as effectively realized in *The School of Athens*) was a major preoccupation of the period. Similarly, Alberti and Leonardo urged upon their contemporaries the importance of studying the details of natural forms in order to be able to produce worthy images. According to Alberti: 'The function of the painter is to draw with lines and paint in colours on a surface, any given bodies in such a way that at a fixed distance and with a certain position what you see represented appears to be in relief and just like those bodies' (*On Painting*, vol. 3, p. 52).

Likewise, in his writings on art (later collected in what is known as the *Treatise on Painting*), Leonardo presses the case for precise empirical observation – 'The mirror, above all, should be your master' – and connects this with a belief in the mathematical order of reality. He also argues for the superiority of painting over other arts on the grounds that, through its wide range of representational resources, it is best able to reflect the forms of nature. The idea of painting as a reflective medium, and of other arts (including music) as similarly representational of an ordered world, suggests that art itself is an activity governed by rational and codifiable principles of operation. Leonardo voices this thought in the *Treatise*, and it became a dominant theme of later writings about the nature and status of painting. Interestingly, there is in this development a parallel with the sort of thinking about thinking which led in due course to Descartes's *Rules for the Direction of the Mind* (1628).

To some extent, my earlier claim that 1400–1550 was a period of greater artistic progress and achievement than 1200–1350, which saw more in the way of philosophical genius, disguises the fact that it was the innovations made at Chartres, St-Denis and elsewhere which made possible the profound representational realism achieved in the Renaissance. But to this it must be added that the later period was more concerned with developing the techniques of art than it was with questioning the nature of the reality it sought to represent. There would not be another period of innovative thought on these matters until the rise of rationalism in the seventeenth century, and it was over a hundred years after that that philosophical aesthetics, as we understand it, came into being.

References

Alberti, L.B., *De pictura* (1435), edited by M. Kemp, translated by C. Grayson, *On Painting* (London: Penguin, 1991).

Baxandall, M., *Painting and Experience in Fifteenth Century Italy* (Oxford: Oxford University Press, 1984).

Beardsley, M., *Aesthetics from Classical Greece to the Present: A Short History* (Tuscaloosa, Ala.: Alabama University Press, 1975).

Blunt, A., *Artistic Theory in Italy: 1450–1600* (Oxford: Oxford University Press, 1973).

Da Vinci, Leonardo, *Leonardo on Painting: An Anthology of Writings by Leonardo da Vinci*, edited by M. Kemp, translated by M. Kemp and M. Walker (London: Yale University Press, 1989).

Eco, U., *Art and Beauty in the Middle Ages*, translated by H. Bredin (London: Yale University Press, 1986).

Fubini, E., *The History of Music Aesthetics*, translated by M. Hatwell (London: Macmillan, 1991).

Martindale, A., *The Rise of the Artist in the Middle Ages and Early Renaissance* (London: Thames & Hudson, 1972).

Panofsky, E., *Gothic Architecture and Scholasticism* (New York: Meridian, 1976).

Suger, Abbot, *Abbot Suger on the Abbey Church of St Denis and its Art Treasures*, edited and translated by E. Panofsky (Princeton, N.J.: Princeton University Press, 1979).

Summers, D., *The Judgment of Sense: Renaissance Naturalism and the Rise of Aesthetics* (Cambridge: Cambridge University Press, 1987).

Tatarkiewicz, W., *History of Aesthetics*, 3 vols (The Hague: Mouton, 1970), vols 2 and 3.

Chapter 18

Form, meaning and value

A history of the philosophy of architecture

Introduction[1]

The question of whether there are enduring principles of architecture is naturally interpreted as asking whether there are rules of design or construction which are universally valid, or at least which hold for the most part. This is an important issue for architects and an interesting one for architectural historians; though for the latter it may be secondary to the question of whether over the centuries certain principles have actually been adhered to. For a philosopher, more abstract questions arise as to the possible status of any such principles, and how they could be anything other than cultural commitments. Yet more generally, the issue becomes that of subjectivity and objectivity with regard to architectural descriptions, interpretations and evaluations.

In philosophical aesthetics it has been common for writers to draw a distinction between art and craft. The limitations of this distinction soon become apparent, however, when one considers architecture, for the attempt to locate an understanding of this within the art/craft dichotomy results in such absurdities as that buildings should be thought of as inhabitable sculptures, or else viewed as decorated habitation machines. In fact, architecture provides a particularly powerful refutation of the idea that aesthetic value is one thing and practical function another.[2]

Happily some contemporary writers acknowledge the significance of the built environment as a unified field of value and meaning,[3] but there is still insufficient appreciation of the history of speculative thinking about architecture, and because of this certain older ideas have come to be overlooked. Here, therefore, my principal aim is to offer a short history of the philosophy of architecture, and secondarily to draw from it one or two ideas about how this branch of aesthetics might now be developed. In particular I shall suggest that in escaping the alienating abstractions of modernism we need not adopt the fanciful ironies of postmodernism, for there remains the pre-modern understanding of architecture as a domain of embodied meanings and values.

Durability, convenience and beauty

Two works have influenced Western architectural theory throughout most of its history: Vitruvius's *De architectura libri X* (*Ten Books of Architecture*),[4] and Alberti's *De re aedificatoria* (*On Architecture*).[5] The first bears a dedication to Augustus Caesar and the second, which derives from it, is a product of the Italian Renaissance. Ironically, although they were written fifteen hundred years apart they were first published in printed form within a year of one another – Alberti in 1485 and Vitruvius in 1486 – and they have stood side by side as foundational texts ever since.

Like most writers of treatises on architecture, Vitruvius and Alberti are largely concerned with practical questions of design and construction, but they also address aesthetic aspects of the subject. Commenting on the 'departments of architecture' Vitruvius writes:

> all of these must be built with due reference to durability (*firmitas*), convenience (*utilitas*) and beauty (*venustas*)...[and beauty will be assured] when the appearance of the work is pleasing and in good taste, and when its members are in due proportion according to correct principles of symmetry.[6]

Earlier he explains that symmetry consists in 'a proper agreement between the members of the work itself, and relation between the different parts and the whole general scheme, in accordance with a certain part selected as standard'.[7]

The classical idea that architectural beauty rests upon compositional unity is taken up by Alberti and developed in a direction that raises a further philosophical issue, viz., that of the proper object of aesthetic assessment. At the outset of *De re aedificatoria* he writes:

> It is the property and business of the design to appoint to the edifice and all its parts their proper places, determinate number, just proportion and beautiful order; so that the whole form of the structure be proportionable. Nor has this design anything that makes it in its nature inseparable from matter...which being granted, we shall call the design a firm and graceful pre-ordering of the lines and angles conceived in the mind, and contrived by an ingenious artist.[8]

Subsequent authors have returned to these ideas of the nature and of the true bearer of architectural beauty; mostly to endorse them, but also to develop or reject them. In the seventeenth century, for example, the English theorist Sir Henry Wotton coined a much-quoted formula that derives (via Palladio and Alberti) from Vitruvius, when he wrote that architecture must aim to provide 'commodity, firmness and delight', while in the following century the French architect and theorist Etienne-Louis Boullée echoed Alberti's claim that architecture should be identified with abstract design rather than with material construction:

What is architecture? Shall I join Vitruvius in defining it as the art of building? Indeed, no, for there is a flagrant error in this definition. Vitruvius mistakes the effect for the cause. In order to execute it is first necessary to conceive...it is this product of the mind, this process of creation, that constitutes architecture.[9]

Although none of these writers was a philosopher, the issues they raise are instances of two central topics in aesthetic theory, viz., the basis of value and the objects of appreciation. Reflection on architecture gives rise to further questions concerning its status in respect of the fine arts, the character of our experience of designs and buildings, and the relation of the built environment to other aspects of human existence, for example, religion, morality and politics.

Conceived as the systematic exploration of these and similar issues, the philosophy of architecture is a modern subject, for although the roots of architectural theorizing run deep into the foundations of Western culture the writings so far cited contain, at best, incidental reflections on normative and ontological issues. It is only with the development of aesthetics as a distinct branch of academic philosophy, a process begun in the eighteenth century, that conceptual resources were fashioned for constructing comprehensive philosophical accounts of architecture. Indeed, it might even be argued that the existence of the subject as a sub-section of academic philosophy of art dates from the publication of Roger Scruton's *The Aesthetics of Architecture* in 1979, for until then philosophical discussions were partial and generally ill-informed.[10] What Scruton offers, by contrast, is a sustained investigation of the aesthetic experience of architecture which draws upon several parts of analytical philosophy, most prominently the philosophy of mind and action, and the theory of meaning.

One way of reading Scruton's work is as addressing the question of how there can be a critical experience of architecture – a formulation that corresponds to the Kantian conception of the general form of a philosophical question, viz., 'How is such and such possible?' Scruton is indeed an avowed admirer of Kant and particularly values his account of aesthetic experience as set out in *The Critique of Judgement*, even though Scruton's own view departs significantly from that. It is unsurprising, therefore, that the perspective developed in *The Aesthetics of Architecture* is broadly Kantian in nature. Before coming to this, however, and in order better to appreciate it and its point of departure from a pure Kantian aesthetic, it is necessary to return to antiquity and to examine some of the central ideas that informed pre-Kantian thought.

Proportion and the metaphysics of regularity

In Book IX of *De architectura* Vitruvius discusses the wisdom of the ancients, illustrating this with accounts of the geometrical discoveries of Plato and Pythagoras. In connection with the latter he cites the famous triangle theorem and adds, 'When Pythagoras discovered this fact, he had no doubt that the Muses had guided him…and it is said that he very gratefully offered sacrifice'. Although Vitruvius is concerned with its practical applications, mention of Pythagoras and the occult nature of his discovery expressed the common view that perceptible forms are underwritten by an abstract, numerically expressible, transcendental order.

Thus when Vitruvius, Alberti, Palladio, Wotton and others write of the importance of *proportion* they are drawing upon a metaphysical theory of regularity. On this account beauty is obtained by designing compositions in which symmetry (*symmetria*) and due proportion (*eurythmia*) are realized, these being determined by relevant units or modules and various operations ('modulations') performed on them. The central Pythagorean idea refashioned by Plato and subsequent Neoplatonists is that empirical order results from the imposition or expression of abstract principles upon or through a medium, in this case matter. In some accounts the units and modes of combination are few and underlie all compositions; in others the modules differ according to the nature of the thing in question. Thus, one might hold that human anatomy expresses the same basic order as the relative positions and movements of the planets, or that each system is based upon its own units and modulations. Such differences, however, are less important than the extent and duration of the consensus that beauty attends correct composition which is a matter of cosmically legitimated proportion.

Although Vitruvius was not printed until the fifteenth century many manuscript versions survive from the medieval period, and it is clear from this and other evidence that the ancient Graeco-Roman metaphysics of architecture informed the theory and practice of design throughout antiquity and the Middle Ages. This raises the question of what, if any, philosophical difference underlay the development from Greek to Romanesque to 'Gothic' in European architecture. Here it is important to emphasize that at the *philosophical* level the difference was one of addition and interpretation rather than of replacement. For the medievals, Platonism was maintained in a Christianized version which included the ideas of divinely ordained symmetry and proportion. Additionally these notions came to be associated with elements from scripture, and architecture was seen as offering an enduring medium for the symbolic representation of a transcendent reality. As before, the application of geometry to part and whole dominated the practice of design but a growing interest in natural forms and their variety led to an enrichment of architectural forms.

In his *Gothic Architecture and Scholasticism*, Erwin Panofsky proposes an interesting, though contestable, general parallelism between High Gothic cathedrals and High Scholastic philosophical and theological treatises (such as Aquinas's *Summa Theologiae*), arguing that each aspires to *totality, articulation* and *coherence*.[11] So far as concerns architecture this involves an integration of theology, morality, nature and history in the plan, elevation and furnishings of the great cathedral churches. In consequence their interpretation and appreciation calls for more than *but not less than* an ability to discern and enjoy geometrical proportion.

Given their shared assumptions about the proper sources of architectural form it is unsurprising that the ancients and the medievals thought of its beauty as objective, and of aesthetic experience as an encounter with properties whose nature is independent of our perception of them. Like most philosopher–theologians of the medieval period, Thomas Aquinas (undisputedly the greatest of them) has no treatise on the nature of beauty or of art-making. Yet contained within his writings are suggestions of lasting interest.

The two most important sources of these are remarks in the *Summa Theologiae*, and in his *Commentary on the Divine Names*. In the second of these he reflects on themes developed in a text (*De Divinis Nominibus*) at that point still credited to 'Dionysius the Areopagite', the Athenian converted to Christianity by St Paul on his visit to Athens. In fact the work is by a much later figure referred to subsequently as 'Pseudo-Dionysius', probably a Christian monk writing at the end of the fifth century. The author seeks to express Christian doctrine through the medium of Neoplatonic philosophy, and it is interesting therefore to see Aquinas try to accommodate himself to a synthesis of faith and reason significantly different from his own.

In the *Commentary* he observes that something is not beautiful because we like it, but that our liking it is due to its being beautiful (c. IV, *lectio* 10). Earlier he remarks that anyone who depicts a thing does so for the sake of making something beautiful, and that each thing is beautiful to the extent that it manifests its proper form (c. IV, *lectio* 5). In the *Summa* this notion of manifest form occurs implicitly within the famous Thomist analysis of beauty:

> Three things are required for beauty. First, integrity or perfection (*integritas sive perfectio*), for what is defective is thereby ugly; second, proper proportion or consonance (*proportio sive consonantia*); and third, clarity (*claritas*).[12]

Later in the same work he writes: 'Beauty is the compatibility of the parts in accordance with the nature of the thing.'[13]

Before commenting on these ideas it is relevant to refer to another of Aquinas's interesting theses. This is the suggestion that beauty is a transcendental quality, identical in an entity to that thing's being, its unity, its goodness, and its truth. Moreover, according to Aquinas it is part of what it is to be a transcendental quality that everything possesses it. Thus he writes:

> There is nothing which does not share in goodness and beauty, for according to its form each thing is both good and beautiful.[14]

The key to understanding what appear, as they stand, to be rather obscure claims, is the Thomist notion of form – more exactly, that of the substantial form of a thing (*forma rei*). This is what makes a particular object to be the kind of thing it is, constituting its principle of organization, and in the case of something animate its life. Carbon, cats and cars all have organizing forms: chemical, biological and mechanical structures, respectively. The form of a thing gives it existence, and inasmuch as its existence is an object of value for it or for others it has goodness. Equally, when that existence is affirmed in the mind of a thinker the thing has truth. Finally, when viewed as an object of contemplation it takes on the character of beauty. In speaking of goodness and beauty (as of being and truth), therefore, one is not speaking of intrinsically different properties but of one and the same quality considered in relation to different concerns.

In short, beauty is only ascribable in the context of actual or potential contemplation of the form of a thing. This introduces an element of subjectivity but relates it directly to an objective ground, viz., the nature of the object being contemplated. The earlier analysis of beauty now emerges as an account of the necessary conditions under which the meeting of an object and a subject gives rise to aesthetic experience. The thing in question must be possessed of the elements apt to something having the relevant form or nature (*integritas*), these elements must be properly related to one another (*proportio*) and these states must be evident when the entity is perceived or contemplated (*claritas*).

Aquinas's definition of beauty is a significant post-Platonist statement of the ancient view that aesthetic experience involves an encounter with properties whose existence and nature are independent of our perception of them; but as we have seen, it also introduces an element of relativity inasmuch as being 'clearly manifest' is a relational property requiring a potential, suitably primed, knower.

Once introduced, this relational element was bound to give rise to a question of the degree to which the nature of the knower serves to condition the experience of beauty – and indeed of the extent to which the grounds of beauty are themselves relative. In the seventeenth century a famous dispute concerning just these matters broke out between two French classical architects: Claude Perrault and François Blondel.[15] Beginning with his edition of Vitruvius (published in 1673) Perrault contested the standard view that the object of aesthetic experience is harmonious unity established by true order and proportion. Instead he distinguished 'convincing' (*convaincantes*) and 'arbitrary' (*arbitraires*) types of beauty, the first being universally pleasing, the second depending on subjective factors such as convention, familiarity and contingent associations. On this basis he reasoned that proportion and its beauty are arbitrary, i.e. not fixed by an independent reality but determined by intersubjective agreement. In reply, Blondel argued for the importance of architecture as a bridging art between painting and sculpture, and upheld the objectivity of the harmonious unity of proportionate orders. In this latter he was subsequently and emphatically supported by Boullée, who insisted upon the certainty that proportion derives from natural symmetry: 'the basic rule and the one that governs the principles of architecture, originates in regularity' (*Essai*).

To some extent the debate was misconceived since, like Aquinas, Blondel acknowledged human relational elements in the analysis of beauty (as did Boullée) and Perrault conceded the objectivity of certain kinds of aesthetic properties. Nonetheless, it marked the beginning of a period in which philosophers and others turned towards non-objectivist aesthetic theories. Edmund Burke, for example, gave various psychological explanations of architectural features and of our approval of them, including the claim that Stonehenge is judged 'grand' because of the idea it induces of the difficulty of its creation.[16]

Free and dependent beauty

Like all such generalizations the claim that philosophical aesthetics began with Kant is open to contention. It is undisputed, however, that his *Critique of Judgement* like his other major works represents one of the points of definition of modern philosophy In aesthetics, as in respect of theoretical and moral thought, Kant's principal innovation is to convert the relationship between subject and object, and to argue that sceptical doubts are answered by the consideration that since the structure of the human mind conditions the realm of its experience and understanding, there is no general possibility that facts should elude the powers of the mind to grasp them. The metaphysical conditions of something being the case include its being a possible object of experience.

In the realm of aesthetics Kant's aim was to show how judgements of beauty could be subjective and yet assessable as correct or incorrect. When I say 'This arched doorway is beautiful' I am not simply saying I like it, but rather that my liking of it arises from my judgement of its quality. For Kant the explanation of this involves the free play of the imagination engaged by something possessed of form. Since form in this sense is a function of the mind's organizing tendency, and this and the imagination are powers common to all rational subjects, if I regard the gateway as a formal object and view it apart from any practical or scientific interest, then the experience I have and the pleasure this involves will be similar for anyone else in an equivalent condition. In other words aesthetic judgement admits of the possibility of intersubjective validity.

From the perspective of the older metaphysical rationalism of Vitruvius, intersubjectivity is still subjectivity and thus falls short of what on that account a recognition of architectural beauty implies; but whether the Kantian view is incompatible with the kind of formal objectivism advanced by Aquinas and Blondel is another and more subtle question to which I shall return. Where, however, even a sympathizer with Kant's general perspective may wish to take issue so far as concerns aesthetic experience in general and that of architecture in particular, is in relation to Kant's distinction between 'free' and 'dependent' beauty.

The experience of sensible forms such as a rainbow or a curling plume of rising smoke, attended to for their own sake and without any concern for their scientific nature or practical function, is the occasion of pure judgements of free beauty. Contrasted with, and very much secondary to, these are applied judgements of dependent beauty. In the case of the latter the experience and judgement is conditional upon a conception of the nature of the thing in question. Thus if in judging that a chapel is beautiful I take account of its religious function and relate its aesthetic qualities to this, judging it to be *a beautiful chapel*, then the beauty is dependent and the judgement is applied.

It is clear, however, that a theory of aesthetic experiences of architecture must accommodate the fact that buildings are functional objects. Someone whose judgements always abstracted from the fact that what he or she was looking at was an occupiable structure designed as such – a house, a church, an airport, or whatever – would rightly be held to be missing the whole point of these things. Architecture is not abstract sculpture and any theory of its nature and of our experience of it that seeks to assimilate it to this status is on the wrong track.

Scruton's appropriation of Kant takes the form of accepting much of his general theoretical and practical philosophy, and adopting the structure of his aesthetic theory with the major qualification that what in the *Critique of Judgement* was secondary and derivative, in the *Aesthetics of Architecture* becomes paradigmatic. The experience of architecture is typically a felt judgement of something recognized to be a building and found to be pleasing as such. With this foundation in place Scruton is able to build a theory that incorporates other elements from idealist and other anti-empiricist sources. From Hegel and Wittgenstein, for example, he takes the idea that the conditions of individual subjectivity, and hence of creative imagination, include the pre-existence of a community within which relevant forms of practice are operative. The ability to design and to appreciate design, and the experience of occupying built designs, are constituents of given forms of life.

While Scruton's book and subsequent articles comprise the most systematic and extensive conceptual study of the subject, the most active sources of writings now catalogued as philosophy of architecture lie within what is generally described as 'Continental' philosophy, i.e. those branches of speculative and political thought that derive from existential phenomenology and structuralism, and which include post- and neo-structuralism, deconstruction and postmodernism. Following the example of essays such as Heidegger's 'Building, Dwelling, Thinking'[17] some writers have tried to construct a reflective phenomenology of the experience of place and of physical containment. Even when these are effective, however, they stand in need of some more general framework such as Scruton provides, and it may be useful therefore to think of the two approaches as complementary, rather than as opposed to one another.

Architectural historicism

The question of whether, and if so how, buildings convey meaning is a recurrent theme of both analytical and Continental writings[18] as is the issue of the connection between architecture and aspects of the wider culture. Writers of the left such as Habermas, and those of the right, principally Scruton and Watkin, both find reasons to follow Ruskin in relating aspects of architectural theory and practice to political ideas.[19] A common target of much recent criticism is the utopian character of the Modern movement as it found expression in the writings and work of its leading figures such as Gropius and Le Corbusier. To some extent the latter's theories of the nature of architecture and the basis of its aesthetic values recall the earlier, pre-modern, Neoplatonic traditions; but they also embody a notion of the architect as a messiah bringing to a heedless world the salvific truths of a revolutionary social message – a creed the time of whose coming has been determined by the logic of history. As Le Corbusier expressed it:

> A great epoch has begun. There exists a new spirit.... If we challenge the past, we shall learn that 'styles' no longer exist for us, that a style belonging to our own period has come about; and that there has been a revolution.[20]

Any plausibility such views might once have had was long ago undermined by the conspicuous failures of modernist architecture; but the philosophical attack upon them has been directed against their historicist and totalitarian assumptions.[21] The collapse of Marxism–Leninism and the rise of radical relativism among thinkers of the left have produced less ambitious, more provisional and contextual ideas about the role of architecture as an element in social policy.[22]

This last trend also contributes to one important and much-cited strand of postmodernist thought. The term 'postmodernism', though since deployed very widely, had some of its earliest uses in architectural criticism;[23] and it was within this context that a distinction came to be drawn between two reactions to modernism. First there is that associated with the post-rationalism of the likes of Derrida and Rorty, the defining characteristic of which has been the claim that rational legitimation is impossible. On this account metaphysical theism and the foundationalist projects of Cartesian and Kantian rationalism have all failed and no other 'metanarrative' is available. Thus we should recognize that appeals to reason are usually veiled exercises of power, and appreciate that all that remains is the ironic affirmation of ideas and images that are without any means of validation.

The second, less celebrated, 'postmodern reaction' is that characterized by Kenneth Frampton as 'Critical Regionalism'.[24] Like its radical counterpart it too rejects universal doctrines and policies, but not as part of a general attack on reason as such. Instead it favours local customs and practices and looks to vernacular solutions to contextually defined problems. Interestingly this way of thinking about architecture in terms of narrative orders, traditions and established modes has certain parallels with the style of moral and social philosophy argued for by Alasdair MacIntyre in a series of works beginning with *After Virtue*.[25]

Synthesis

The historical movement from the Neoplatonism of Vitruvius to the anti-rationalism of contemporary architectural theorists such as Peter Eisenman[26] serves as a reminder of the power of architecture to summon deep thoughts about its nature, and as an indicator of how far and wide such thoughts can range. The question then arises of where on this spectrum a true position lies. Earlier, in connection with the debate between Perrault and Blondel, and the aesthetic theory of Kant, I raised the possibility that certain disputes about the subjectivity or objectivity of architectural values might be misconceived. Another way of putting the point would be to say that the truth of the matter transcends simple formulations of the subjective/objective distinction.

It would be vain to attempt to refute postmodern anti-rationalism in a sentence or two; but besides observing its liability to pragmatic self-refutation (of the 'there are no truths' sort), it is worth adding that its proclamation of the 'end of reason' generally attributes to earlier realist traditions a core of epistemological and metaphysical commitments which they have not all shared.[27] Neo-Aristotelians in particular have little to fear from attacks directed against Cartesian and Kantian projects of 'modernity and enlightenment rationality'. Indeed, they have their own criticisms to contribute. More positively, however, they can give account of objectivity, and acknowledge its varieties and degrees, without always having to posit transcendental objects. In the theory of value, for example, it is often asked whether something is good because we desire it or whether we desire it because it is good. A non-trivial possibility is that *both* are the case. That is to say, we can only make sense of considered aesthetic valuations, with their attendant marks of rationality (groundedness, corrigibility, critical expertise and so on), by conceiving of them as responses to objective features; yet at the same time part of what constitutes value is that such features elicit, in appropriately equipped human beings, a certain kind of appreciative response. This Janus-like structure might be analysed in terms of objective and subjective conditions of value, each set being individually necessary and only jointly sufficient for value itself.

This idea suggests the interpretation of Aquinas's analysis of beauty which I discussed earlier. In the *Summa*, prior to defining beauty he writes:

> [T]he beautiful is the same as the good...they differ in aspect only. For since good is what all seek, the notion of good is that which calms the desire; while the notion of the beautiful is that which calms the desire by being seen or known....Thus it is evident that beauty adds to goodness a relation to the cognitive faculty: so that good means that which simply pleases the appetite; while the beautiful is pleasant to apprehend.[28]

What is 'pleasant to apprehend' depends in part on the sensibility of the subject. Focusing on this responsive aspect can, however, encourage forms of radical subjectivism. One way to resist that trend is to think, as does Hume in his essay 'Of the Standard of Taste'[29] of regularizing the notion of sensibility. Thus we might arrive at some such formula as that

> X is beautiful if and only if it would be judged to be so by a normal observer under normal conditions.

The problems for such analyses are familiar. For present purposes all that need be noted is that 'normal' is ambiguous between statistical and normative readings. For a radical empiricist such as Hume, ultimately the only available interpretation is the first one; but if we follow Aquinas we can make sense of a normative reading. We can suppose that certain subjective conditions have to be satisfied (and here the Kantian tradition is relevant); but also see them as preparing the subject to respond appropriately to certain objective features – such as formal composition, expressive character and representational significance – that have been designed and embodied in the structure of a building and which are conceived of as *meriting* critical responses. On this account the way to understand architectural values is as the joint upshot of intelligent design and aesthetic sensibility. Without the former (objective) features we would have nothing other than ungrounded (as opposed to uncaused) preferences; and without the latter (subjective) ones we would only have inert geometry.

Any attempt to understand why architecture matters must attend to the fact that we are creatures for whom the perceptible and intelligible forms of things can be pleasing. Empiricists have emphasized the role of pleasure in aesthetic experience but neglected its intentionality; or when they have recognized that aesthetic pleasure has an object they have tended to restrict this to phenomenal features such as colours, textures and shapes. The truth is that the *experience* of architecture may encompass sensuous quality, geometrical form, human purpose, symbolic significance and historical context; and that such experiences are generally conditioned by multifaceted conceptions of their objects.

In addition, serious thinking about the nature of the built environment cannot long proceed without taking account of the natural one. It is again a philosophical question what the distinction between nature and artifice is, but it can hardly be denied that however this is defined there are differences of kind or of degree between what has been built and the landscape within which it is set. As Continental, analytical and historical traditions come into further contact and moral philosophers and aestheticians from each learn about one another's concerns it seems very likely that interest in the philosophy of architecture will grow and that it will become part of a larger philosophy of environment; at which point the metaphysics of embodied form can be expected to make a reappearance.[30]

Notes and references

1 This article is the text of the opening keynote address given to the 1998 History in Schools of Architecture Conference sponsored by the University of Westminster and South Bank University and held in the latter on 26 and 27 June. The theme of the conference was 'Are there Enduring Principles in Architecture?' The historical material is drawn from J. Haldane, 'Aesthetics of Architecture', in E. Craig (ed.), *Routledge Encyclopedia of Philosophy* (London: Routledge, 1998).

2 For further discussion of these issues see J. Haldane, 'Aesthetic Naturalism and the Decline of Architecture (Part 1)', *International Journal of Moral and Social Studies* 2.3 (1987).

3 See, for example, A. Berleant, *The Aesthetics of Environment* (Philadelphia, Pa.: Temple University Press, 1992), and *Living in the Landscape: Toward an Aesthetics of Environment* (Philadelphia, Pa.: Temple University Press, 1997).

4 Vitruvius, *De architectura libri X*, trans. M. Morgan (Cambridge, Mass.: Harvard University Press, 1914).

5 L.B. Alberti, *De re aedificatoria*, ed. J. Rykwert; trans. J. Leoni, *Ten Books on Architecture* (London: Tiranti, 1955).

6 *De architectura libri*, bk I, ch. III, 2.

7 *Ibid.*, bk I, ch. II, 4.

8 *De re aedificatoria*, bk I, ch. I.

9 E.-L. Boullée, 'Architecture, Essai sur l'art', trans. S. de Vallée, in H. Rosenau (ed.), *Boullée und Visionary Architecture* (London: Academy Editions, 1976).

10 R. Scruton, *The Aesthetics of Architecture* (London: Methuen, 1979),

11 E. Panofsky, *Gothic Architecture and Scholasticism* (London: Thames & Hudson, 1957). For further reflection on the relationship of medieval architecture to the contemporary intellectual culture see C.M. Radding and W.W. Clark, *Medieval Architecture, Medieval Learning* (London: Yale University Press, 1992).

12 *Summa Theologiae*, Ia, q. 39, a. 8.

13 *Ibid.*, IaIIae, q. 54, a. 1.

14 *De Divinis Nominibus*, c. IV, *Iectio* 5.

15 See C. Perrault, *Abrégé des dix livres d'architecture de Vitruve*, and F. Blondel, *Cours d'architecture*; selections from both authors appear in W. Tatarkiewicz, *History of Aesthetics*, ed. D. Petsch, vol. 3: *Modern Aesthetics* (The Hague: Mouton, 1974).

16 E. Burke, *A Philosophical Enquiry into the Origin of Our Ideas of the Sublime and the Beautiful*, ed. A. Phillips (Oxford: Oxford University Press, 1990), pt. II, sect. XII.

17 To be found in M. Heidegger, *Poetry, Language, Thought*, trans. and ed. A. Hofstader (New York: Harper & Row, 1975).

18 See, for example, Nelson Goodman, 'How Buildings Mean', *Critical Inquiry* 11 (1985).

19 J. Habermas, 'Modern and Postmodern Architecture', in *The New Conservatism*, trans. and ed. S.W. Nicholson (Oxford: Polity Press, 1989); and D. Watkin, *Morality and Architecture* (Chicago, Ill.: University of Chicago Press, 1975).

20 Le Corbusier, *Towards a New Architecture*, trans. F. Etchells (London: Architectural Press, 1927).

21 J. Haldane, 'Aesthetic Naturalism and the Decline of Architecture (Part 2)', *International Journal of Moral and Social Studies* 3 (1988); and A. O'Hear, 'Historicism and Architectural Knowledge', *Philosophy* 68 (1993).

22 For further aspects of the politics of architecture see J. Haldane, 'Architecture, Philosophy and the Public World', *British Journal of Aesthetics* 30 (1990).

23 It occurs in the title of Charles Jencks's *The Language of Post-Modern Architecture* (London: Academy Editions, 1977). For this and other cultural-theory uses see Jencks, *Post-Modernism: The New Classicism in Art and Architecture* (London: Academy Editions, 1987).

24 K. Frampton, 'Towards a Critical Regionalism: Six Points for an Architecture of Resistance', in H. Foster (ed.), *Postmodern Culture* (London: Pluto Press, 1985).

25 A. MacIntyre, *After Virtue* (London: Duckworth, 1981); *Whose Justice? Which Rationality?* (London: Duckworth, 1988); and *Three Rival Versions of Moral Inquiry* (London: Duckworth, 1990).

26 See P. Eisenman et al., *Re:working Eisenman* (London: Academy Editions, 1993). Writing in reply to Derrida, Eisenman notes, 'In the end my architecture cannot be what it should be, but only what it can be', p. 71.

27 For some discussion of these issues see J. Haldane, 'Cultural Theory, Philosophy and the Study of Human Affairs', in J. Doherty et al. (eds), *Postmodernism and the Social Sciences* (London: Macmillan, 1991).
28 *Summa Theologiae*, IaIIae, q. 17, a. 1, ad. 3.
29 D. Hume, *Of the Standard of Taste and Other Essays*, ed. J.W. Lenz (Indianapolis, Ind.: Bobbs Merrill, 1965).
30 See J. Haldane, 'Admiring the High Mountains: The Aesthetics of Environment', in T.D.J. Chappell (ed.), *The Philosophy of the Environment* (Edinburgh: Edinburgh University Press, 1997). (Reproduced as Chapter 19, this volume.)

Chapter 19

Admiring the high mountains
The aesthetics of environment

Experiences of landscape and environmental aesthetics

My main title is drawn from a passage in St Augustine's *Confessions* (x. 8. 15) as quoted by Petrarch in a famous letter addressed to Francesco Dionigi da Borgo San Sepolcro, an Augustinian professor of theology. Dated 26 April 1336, it recounts an ascent of Mont Ventoux (the 'Windy Peak') made that same day by Petrarch, his brother and two servants. After describing his preparations for the climb and its early stages he turns to religious matters, drawing parallels between the difficulties of the physical ascent and the process of spiritual formation. Having reached the highest summit he reflects on his recent past and then, as the sun begins to set, he looks around again in all directions:

> I admired every detail, now relishing earthly enjoyment, now lifting up my mind to higher spheres after the example of my body, and I thought it fit to look Into the volume of Augustine's *Confessions*. . . . Where I fixed my eyes first it was written: 'And men go to admire the high mountains, the vast floods of the sea, the huge streams of the rivers, the circumference of the ocean, and the revolutions of the stars – and desert themselves.' I was stunned, I confess. I bade my brother, who wanted to hear more, not to molest me, and close the book, angry with myself that I still admired earthly things. Long since I ought to have learned, even from pagan philosophers, that 'nothing is admirable besides the mind; compared to its greatness nothing is great' [Seneca, *Epistle* 8. 5]. I was completely satisfied with what I had seen of the mountain and turned my inner eye toward myself. From this hour nobody heard me say a word until we arrived at the bottom.[1]

This is an interesting passage, and for more than one reason. It belongs within a corpus that bears the marks of the emerging Renaissance humanism, and the letter itself has often been referred to as anticipating later European mountaineering interests; but what I think we should be struck by is the unironic willingness with which Petrarch sets aside his aesthetic delight as unworthy of the human mind. We have become accustomed to praising natural beauty and to thinking of its appreciation precisely as a mark of a refined sensibility and as something to be approved of and cultivated. Thus the implicit opposition of aesthetic and spiritual concerns is hard for us to accommodate. Consider how unexceptional (and congenial to modern environmentalism) seem the ideas, if not the form, of Hopkins's sonnet 'God's Grandeur':[2]

> The world is charged with the Grandeur of God.
>   It will flame out, like shining from shook foil;
>   It gathers to a greatness, like the ooze of oil
> Crushed. Why do men then not now reck his rod?
> Generations have trod, have trod, have trod;
>   And all is seared with trade; bleared, smeared with toil;
>   And wears man's smudge and shares man's smell: the soil
> Is bare now, nor can foot feel, being shod.
>
> And for all this, nature is never spent;
>   There lives the dearest freshness deep down things;
> And though the last lights off the black West went
>   Oh morning, at the brown brink eastward, springs –
> Because the Holy Ghost over the bent
>   World broods with warm breast and with ah! bright wings.

Of course Petrarch was writing over six hundred and fifty years ago, long before romantic quasi-panentheism, and addressing a theologian with whom he shared an admiration for Augustine. This large historical and intellectual gap helps to explain the otherwise puzzling deprecation of the aesthetic appreciation of nature. Yet even in more recent times sensitive and thoughtful authors have dismissed what are now canonized landscapes in terms which are at least striking and which some will regard as blasphemous. Consider, for example, the following description from the pen of Dr Johnson writing of Scottish scenery:

> [The hills] exhibit very little variety; being almost wholly covered with dark heath, and even that seems to be checked in its growth. What is not heath is nakedness, a little diversified by now and then a stream rushing down the steep. An eye accustomed to flowery pastures and waving harvests is astonished and repelled by this wide extent of hopeless sterility. The appearance is that of matter incapable of form or usefulness, dismissed by nature from her care and disinherited of her favours, left in its original elemental state, or quickened only with one sullen power of useless vegetation.
>   It will very readily occur, that this uniformity of barrenness can afford little amusement to the traveller; that it is easy to sit at home and conceive rocks and heath, and waterfalls; and that these journeys are useless labours, which neither impregnate the imagination, nor enlarge the understanding.[3]

This text and Petrarch's letter should serve as reminders that there is nothing perennially obvious about the present-day reverence for nature and the elevation of its appreciation to the higher categories of human consciousness. The 'aesthetics of the environment' is like the 'politics of the home' a term of art invented to label a set of concerns and an associated field of academic study each developed over time and out of particular cultural histories. In what follows I first sketch something of the relevant philosophical background and then discuss an account of the aesthetics of beauty suggested by remarks of Aquinas.

Recent years have seen the rapid rise to prominence of a range of studies, policy directives and initiatives concerned with the environment. These are sometimes unphilosophical, pragmatic responses to perceived threats arising from, for example, heavy industrialization and increasing levels of human activity. Very often, however, they are presented through patterns of judgement and justification that are avowedly moral, not to say moralistic. Those involved in such presentations are then liable to speak in terms of 'environmental *ethics*', or more likely of 'an environmental *ethic*'. Although there are reasons for doubting whether values can be thought of in compartmentalized isolation I want for present purposes, and so far as is possible, to place ethical concerns on one side and to focus on *aesthetic* considerations.[4] More precisely my interest is in whether, and if so how, philosophical aesthetics might be brought into contemporary thinking about the natural environment.

In advance one might suppose that the effect of introducing any kind of objective aesthetic element into the discussion of environmental values (what might be termed 'environmental axiology') would be to strengthen the case for 'deep' ecology. It is, after all, a common plea made by those concerned with protecting the natural environment from the effects of industry, say, that these deface the landscape, transforming what is naturally beautiful into something ugly. How then could an interest in the aesthetic qualities of nature be other than an instance of respect for the environment considered as something valuable in and of itself? In order to answer that question I need to say something about the general character of aesthetic theory.

Some elements of aesthetic experience

From antiquity, through the Middle Ages, the Renaissance and the Enlightenment, to the present day, there has been a movement in philosophical discussions of beauty and other aesthetic values (such as the sublime – and in later periods the picturesque) from attention to the *objects* of aesthetic experience to the character of the *experience* itself, and of the modes of attention or *attitudes* it involves. Although there is no agreed inventory of the elements or aspects of aesthetic experience, and certainly there is no agreement on their interrelationships, Figure 1 sets out something of the broad range of favoured possibilities.

Again considered historically, the focus of interest has moved from left to right. Thus in *pre-modern aesthetics* (to the extent that one can reasonably speak

Aesthetic Object		Aesthetic Value		Aesthetic Response	Aesthetic Attitude
Anything at all	Specific things reality; emotion; form; etc.	Intrinsic values content; form; sensuous qualities; etc.	Extrinsic values satisfaction; release; understanding; etc.	Pleasure; interest; universal validity; satisfaction; understanding; etc.	Detachment; disinterest; contemplation; isolation; psychical distance; interpretation; etc.

Figure 1 The elements of aesthetic experience.

in these terms of a subject that is often thought to have originated only in the eighteenth century[5]) aesthetic objects and values are generally taken to be prior, with aesthetic responses and attitudes being held to be posterior to and explicable in terms of these. So, for example, it might be argued that the 'objects' of aesthetic experience are the forms of natural entities, and that aesthetic value consists in the harmonious organization of parts realized in such forms. An aesthetic experience will then be any experience in which these forms and values are attended to and appreciated, and an aesthetic attitude will be an (or perhaps *the*) attitude induced by such experiences.

Clearly any view of this sort, if it is to avoid explanatory circularity, must postulate certain objective features that are the basis for our experiences of beauty. The task of doing so is a challenging one, and though there are still efforts to complete it many have come to think it is impossible. Such scepticism together with other factors led, in the *Modern* and *Enlightenment* periods, to the development of broadly subjectivist accounts of aesthetics. By 'subjectivist', here, I do not mean arbitrary or idiosyncratic. Rather, the unifying feature of such accounts is that the direction of explanation runs from the attitude or experience to the value or object. One might, for example, identify the aesthetic attitude as one of detachment from theoretical and practical concerns or of disinterested contemplation, thereby specifying the character of aesthetic experience as being that of expressing or being conditioned by such an attitude. Following this one might then say that an aesthetic object is any object attended to in that kind of experience, and an aesthetic value is any feature singled out in such an experience as rewarding of attention, or, and more likely, any feature of the experience itself which is found to be pleasant or beneficial. Once again explanatory circularity will only be avoided so long as one does not at this point appeal to aesthetic objects in order to specify the relevant class of attitudes and experiences.

Even if that can be done, however, it is tempting to suppose that a consequence of a subjectivist approach is that there can then be no question of correct or incorrect aesthetic judgements, or relatedly of better and worse judges; for without autonomous aesthetic objects surely there can be no aesthetic objectivity. One familiar reaction to this thought is to welcome it, arguing that one of the main reasons for favouring subject-based approaches is precisely that aesthetic judgements lack criteria by which to be assessed. However, a subtler response recognizes that in giving explanatory priority to the aesthetic attitude and aesthetic experience one is not wholly precluded from having external criteria of greater or lesser, coarser and more refined aesthetic sensibility; for one may hold that there are *intersubjective* standards.[6]

Consider the case of table manners. At the level of serious reflection we should not be tempted to suppose that there are objectively offensive modes of eating. Rather we should say that manners are a function of culturally shared interests. A mode of eating is offensive for a given community if in normal circumstances it would be judged offensive by a competent member of that community. Competence here being explained not in terms of an ability to discern objectively offensive eating practices but by reference to mastery of certain social conventions governing public eating. Although these norms are *subjective*, in the sense of being rooted in the dispositions of *subjects*, none the less their existence allows for the idea that some member of that community can go wrong in his style of eating, and thereby correctly be described as ill-mannered.

It should be clear then that the resources of certain 'subjectivist' aesthetic theories are more considerable than might initially be supposed. Moreover, as Figure 1 indicates, there are many different elements and combinations that might be included in an aesthetic theory of either objectivist or subjectivist orientations. Rather than pursue these possibilities in detail, however, I want to consider next how the aesthetics of the environment is likely to fare when considered from these perspectives. An objectivist approach will look for certain features of environments which will serve as the basis for aesthetic experience and evaluation. Immediately, however, various difficulties suggest themselves. To the extent that we think of artworks as the paradigm class of objects involved in aesthetic experience we will see a problem in seeking for beauty in nature. If, like Hopkins, one were a creationist, holding that the universe is an artefact fashioned by God, then of course one could treat it formally in just the same way. But traditional theists are likely to be cautious of aestheticizing divine creation; and others will find the theistic assumption at least unwarranted and perhaps incoherent.

However, while denying that the natural world is the product of deliberate design one might nevertheless regard it *as if* designed, and maybe even speak of 'Nature' itself as the source of aesthetic order. This move, however, generates problems of its own. Consider the question of how many pictures there are in a given art gallery, or performances in a particular concert hall. Notwithstanding elements of the avant garde, this would, in principle, be a relatively easy matter to settle by reference to the form, content, matter and source of the works. However, if one eschews any claim of literal creation it seems in principle impossible to say where one work of nature begins and another ends. The category of the scenic view, for example, is all too obviously one of our own fashioning. If there is any element of art-making in nature it is surely present through the selective attention of spectators to aspects of a continuous realm. Furthermore, in deciding where to locate the boundaries of one scene, our designs are influenced by the experience of actual artworks. In short, the effort to identify aesthetic objects in nature tends quickly to return one in the direction of the subject of experience and of his or her interests, cultural presuppositions and classifications.

Whether for these or other reasons, an objectivist might not choose to employ the artwork model but try instead the sort of approach I described as being characteristic of pre-modern thinking. That is to say, he or she might hold that the objects of environmental aesthetic experience are natural forms, by which I mean, primarily, the forms of organisms and derivatively those of non-organic entities. Something of this view is suggested by the fragmentary but very interesting remarks made by Aquinas in his discussions of beauty. He explicitly denies the claim that something is beautiful simply because we like it, insisting by contrast that our appreciation is directed towards the beauty of things, and that a thing is beautiful to the extent that it manifests its proper form or natural structure. He writes:

> Three things are required for beauty. First integrity or perfection (*integritas sive perfectio*), for what is defective is thereby ugly; second, proper proportion or consonance (*proportio sive consonantia*); and third clarity (*claritas*).[7]

The background assumption is that each substance or individual is possessed of a nature which, in the case of living things, is at once a principle of organic structure and a determinant of its characteristic activities. Integrity and proper proportion are directly related to this nature or form (*forma rei*) and the issue of clarity arises from them. *Integrity* consists in the possession of all that is required by the nature of the thing, such and such limbs and organs, active capacities and so on; while *proportion* includes both the compatibility of these elements and their being well-ordered. These two factors are then presupposed in the idea of *clarity*, for that concerns the way in which the form of a thing is manifest or unambiguously presented.

This neo-Aristotelian account has certain merits from the point of view of those interested in developing an objectivist environmental aesthetic. Forms are real, mind-independent entities, there to be discovered and contemplated. Thus the question of whether one member of a natural kind better realizes the species' common nature is one that it makes sense to ask and one which informed attention can hope to answer. Also values and policies seem to be implicit or rootable in such facts. A 'good' specimen is *ontologically* better than a 'poor' one; and it is clear enough how industrial practices can be detrimental to these natural values by causing harm to individual organisms and injuring the species. Thus, unlikely as it might have been supposed given the tone of Petrarch's fourteenth-century reflections, it may seem that in the thirteenth-century writings of Aquinas there is a promising source for a deep ecological aesthetic, i.e. one in which the relevant values owe nothing to man's interests – save of course where the forms in question are human ones.

However, this conclusion would be a mistake and it is important to see why that is so. First, although Aquinas is insistent that beauty is not simply a function of subjective preference his account of its conditions indicates that there is a subtle form of subjectivity, in the sense of relativity-to-a-subject, in its very constitution. Recall that beauty requires perfection, proportion and clarity. The last of these I glossed as unambiguously presented or manifest form. The existence and character of a given form may be a wholly mind-independent affair, but to speak of its presentation implies actual or possible knowers. Furthermore whether something is unambiguous or clear is in part a function of the cognitive powers and accomplishments of the actual or imagined subject. So to say that something is beautiful if the perfection of its form is clearly presented indicates that, of necessity, beauty is something which involves a spectator. It is also apparent both from what Aquinas says and from the logic of his position that the spectators in question require the sort of intellectual capacity which there is little reason to think is possessed by any creature other than man. In short, natural beauty is *constitutively* tied to human experience.

Second, on Aquinas's view there is an equivalence between goodness and beauty – known as the 'convertibility of the transcendentals'. What this means is that in thinking or speaking of these attributes one is referring to the same feature of reality, viz., the condition of the natural form that constitutes an item's essential nature. Thus a thing is good and beautiful to the extent that its form is perfected. This is an interesting thesis, and on reflection a plausible one with relevance for environmental philosophy. But it has a corollary that moves aesthetics deeper into the territory of humanistic ecology. If the referents of 'good' and 'beautiful' are one and the same how do the terms differ? Aquinas answers that each expresses a distinct kind of interest in, or concern with, the forms of things.

> The beautiful is the same as the good, and they differ in aspect only. For since good is what all seek, the notion of good is that which calms the desire; while the notion of the beautiful is that which calms the desire by being seen or known. Consequently those senses chiefly regard the beautiful which are the most cognitive, viz., sight and hearing, as ministering to reason; for we speak of beautiful sights and beautiful sounds....Thus it is evident that beauty adds to goodness a relation to the cognitive faculty: so that *good* means that which simply pleases the appetite; while the *beautiful* is something pleasant to apprehend.[8]

Thus although Aquinas roots his account of beauty in objective fact, the existence of aesthetic objects and values involves human subjects taking delight in perceptually and intellectually discernible structures. His view should be congenial to those concerned with environmental axiology in general and with aesthetic values in particular. It accords a major role to natural forms and can accommodate within this classification entities more extensive than individual organisms, such as species and even ecosystems. Further, unlike the aesthetics of the scenic it need not confine itself to the 'visible surface' of the world. It can, for example, allow the aesthetic relevance of ecological history and of the sorts of environmental structures to which Aldo Leopold's *A Sand County Almanac* did much to draw attention. In 'Marshland Elegy' Leopold writes:

> Our ability to perceive quality in nature begins, as in art, with the pretty. It expands through successive stages of the beautiful to values as yet uncaptured by language. The quality of cranes, lies, I think, in this higher gamut, as yet beyond the reach of words.
>
> This much though can be said: our appreciation of the crane grows with the slow unravelling of earthly history. His tribe, we now know, stems out of the remote Ecocene. The other members of the fauna in which he originated are long since entombed within the hills. When we hear his call we hear no mere bird. We hear the trumpet in the orchestra of evolution. He is the symbol of our untamable past, of that incredible sweep of millennia which underlies and conditions the daily affairs of birds and men.[9]

It should be clear, however, that like the earlier attempt to conceive an aesthetics of the natural environment along the lines of a philosophy of art, an element of which is also present in Leopold's thinking, Aquinas's theory of natural beauty has an ineliminable subjective aspect.

Conclusion

We have come a long way from Petrarch's revulsion at his own delight, but we do not as yet have a clear and complete account of the nature and value of the aesthetics of environment. The task that remains, therefore, promises both theoretical and practical rewards. My general conclusion, however, is that whichever side of the diagram one starts from – focusing on the aesthetic attitude or the aesthetic object – one should be led to think that human experience plays a constitutive role in environmental aesthetics.

Notes

1 Petrarch 1956 (1336), p. 44.
2 Hopkins 1970, p. 66.
3 Johnson 1944 (1773), pp. 34–5. It is interesting to compare these remarks with those of Thomas Gray: 'I am returned from Scotland, charmed with my expedition: it is of the Highlands I speak: the Lowlands are worth seeing once, but the mountains are ecstatic and ought to be visited in pilgrimage once a year. None but those monstrous

creatures of God know how to join so much beauty with so much horror. A fig for your poets, painters, gardeners and clergymen, that have not been among them, their imagination can be made up of nothing but bowling greens, flowering shrubs, horse ponds, Fleet ditches, shell grottoes and Chinese rails. Then I had so beautiful an Autumn. Italy could hardly produce a nobler scene, and this so sweetly contrasted with that perfection of nastiness and total want of accommodation that only Scotland can supply.' Letter of 1765, Gray 1935, p. 899. I am indebted to Christopher Smout for this quotation. He uses it to introduce a fascinating discussion of attitudes to Scottish landscape; see Smout 1990.

4 For a discussion of the way in which ethical concerns may constrain aesthetic appreciation, see Foster 1992.

5 The first philosophical use of the term 'aesthetics' to identify a (more or less) autonomous field of experience is to be found in Baumgarten 1974 (1734). Baumgarten claims that the subject is the science of sensitive knowledge, *'scientia cognitionis sensitivae'*.

6 This in effect is the position advanced by Hume in his classic essay 'Of the Standard of Taste', see Hume 1965 (1757).

7 Aquinas 1914 (*c.*1270), Ia, q. 39, a. 8. For a brief account of Aquinas's view and of related ways of thinking see Haldane 1993.

8 Aquinas 1914 (*c.*1270), IaIIae, q. 17, a. 1, ad. 3.

9 Leopold 1989 (1949), p. 96. For an account of the aesthetic dimension of Leopold's writings see Callicot 1983.

References

Aquinas, T. 1914 (*c.*1270) *Summa Theologiae*, trans. Fathers of the English Dominican Province (London: Washbourne).

Baumgarten, Alexander 1974 (1734) *Reflections on Poetry*, trans. K. Aschenbrenner and W. Holther (Berkeley, Calif.: University of California Press).

Callicot, J. Baird 1983 'Leopold's Land Aesthetic', *Journal of Soil and Water Conservation*; reprinted in J. Baird Callicot, *In Defense of the Land Ethic: Essays in Environmental Philosophy* (Albany, NY: SUNY Press, 1989).

Foster, C. 1992 'Aesthetic Disillusionment: Environment, Ethics, Art', *Environmental Values* 1.3, pp. 205–15.

Gray, T. 1935 (1765) *Correspondence of Thomas Gray*, ed. P. Toynbee and L. Whibley (Oxford: Clarendon Press, vol. 2: *1756–65*, p. 899.

Haldane, J. 1987 'Aesthetic Naturalism and the Decline of Architecture, Part 1: Architecture and Aesthetic Perception', *International Journal of Moral and Social Studies* 2.3, pp. 210–24.

Haldane, J. 1988 'Aesthetic Naturalism and the Decline of Architecture, Part 2: Form, Matter and Understanding', *International Journal of Moral and Social Studies* 3.2, pp. 173–90.

Haldane, J. 1990a 'Philosophy and Environmental Issues', *International Journal of Moral and Social Studies* 5.1, pp. 79–91.

Haldane, J. 1990b 'Architecture, Philosophy and the Public World', *British Journal of Aesthetics* 30, pp. 203–17.

Haldane, J. 1993 'Aquinas' and 'Medieval and Renaissance Aesthetics', in D. Cooper (ed.), *A Companion to Aesthetics* (Oxford: Blackwell).

Hopkins, G.M. 1970 *The Poems of Gerard Manley Hopkins*, ed. W.H. Gardner and N.H. MacKenzie (Oxford: Oxford University Press).

Hume, D. 1965 (1757) *Of the Standard of Taste and Other Essays*, ed. John W. Lenz (Indianapolis, Ind.: Bobbs-Merrill), pp. 3–24.

Johnson, S. 1944 (1773) *A Journey to the Western Islands*, ed. R.W. Chapman (London: Oxford University Press).

Leopold, Aldo 1989 (1949) *A Sand County Almanac* (New York: Oxford University Press).

Petrarch, 1956 (1336) *The Ascent of Mont Ventoux*, in *The Renaissance Philosophy of Man*, ed. E. Cassirer, P.O. Kristeller and J.H. Randall (Chicago, Ill.: University of Chicago Press), pp. 36–46.

Smout, C. 1990 'The Highlands and the Roots of Green Consciousness, 1750–1990', Raleigh Lecture, *Proceedings of the British Academy*.

Chapter 20

De Consolatione Philosophiae

I

> While I was quietly thinking these thoughts [about misfortune] over to myself and giving vent to my sorrow with the help of my pen, I became aware of a woman standing over me. She was of awe-inspiring appearance, her eyes burning and keen beyond the usual power of men. She was so full of years that I could hardly think of her as of my own generation, and yet she possessed a vivid colour and undiminished vigour....Her clothes were made of imperishable material, of the finest thread woven with the most delicate skill....On the bottom hem could be read the embroidered Greek letter *Pi*, and on the top hem the Greek letter *Theta*. Between the two a ladder of steps rose from the lower to the higher letter. Her dress had been torn by the hands of marauders who had each carried off such pieces as he could get. There were some books in her right hand and in her left hand she held a sceptre....As she spoke she gathered her dress into a fold and wiped from my eyes the tears that filled them...the clouds of my grief dissolved and I drank in the light.[1]

So begins the famous work by Boethius from which I have taken my title: a work which, according to one of its earliest translators, King Alfred, is 'among the books most necessary for all men to know'. The woman of Boethius's vision is, of course, *Philosophy* – 'the nurse in whose house I had been cared for since my youth'.

That this general style of writing is not one favoured by present-day academic philosophers may seem to be a relatively insignificant fact connected with changing literary traditions. After all, in the course of the work Boethius presents or presupposes views on such perennial matters as the mind/body problem, knowledge, free-will, general ontology and time. I am sure, however, that the marked stylistic contrast also betokens a difference of belief about the nature and role of philosophy. Boethius's literary form is shaped by, and gives further shape to, an ancient conception of philosophy according to which its *telos* is the attainment of wisdom, philosophical enquiry being the discernment of, and progression along, a pathway leading to enlightenment, and *ipso facto* to what St Augustine termed *gaudium de veritate* – delight in the attainment of truth.

Viewing things in this way it also becomes clear why there is a problem in marking a sharp distinction within the writings of antiquity and the medieval period between philosophical texts and works of spiritual counsel. That we have no difficulty applying such a distinction to contemporary writings reveals much about the shared self-conception of present-day professional philosophers. What I have to say here may reflect some light upon the source of this difference. However, my ultimate concern is with a philosophical issue rather than with historical or interpretative ones, though those will feature along the way. More precisely, I want to raise two questions: first, can any interesting sense be made of the claim that philosophy might be a source of comfort or consolation? and second, is there reason to believe this claim to be true?

Let me add straight away that, so far as I am concerned, these questions introduce a genuinely open inquiry. I do not have any settled conviction on the matter, but equally, I should not be troubling to consider these issues if I did not think that the questions might be answered positively, and believe that it is important that we should know whether this is indeed so. There is, I believe, no single correct answer to the prior question *What is philosophy?* but if one of the things it *cannot* be is a source of reasoned comfort in circumstances where experience and reason itself lead us to be troubled about the human condition, its contingency and its evils, then this is something that needs to be demonstrated, appreciated and proclaimed – perhaps in the style of Quine who writes of even aesthetics and moral philosophy as 'being apt to offer little in the way of inspiration or consolation' (1981, p. 193).

II

Although I am not principally concerned with exegesis of Boethius's text, I want to consider certain ideas to be found there and in other of his writings, and to relate these to questions concerning the interpretation of a broad class of thoughtful experiences of nature and of art. It is a matter for some doubt, however, whether Boethius's ideas constitute a coherent whole. One may reasonably question whether what he has to say in *De Consolatione* is compatible with the sort of metaphysics he explores in *De Trinitate* and in his second commentary on Porphyry's *Isagoge* (an introduction to Aristotle's *Categories*). What I have in mind in saying this is that in the first and third of these works he offers a version of Neoplatonism in which the forms of things subsist in the mind of God, independently of and prior to their empirical instances; whereas in his commentary on Porphyry he sets up the problem of universals as being that of how natures can be both many and one, and then rehearses (and commends – though perhaps without endorsing) a recognizably Aristotelian solution: members of a kind have numerically distinct sensible natures but when they are brought under conceptual investigation a common universal nature is discerned by the intellect. I mention this instance of philosophical tension not just by way of example but because I shall have particular reason to return to it later. For now, however, I need to say more about the central theme of Boethius's essay and his treatment of it.

De Consolatione is a complex work almost every aspect of which presents interpretative questions. It was written in the period prior to his execution for treason, and the historical background, at least, is fairly straightforward. Boethius was born sometime after 480 into an aristocratic Christian Roman family. His father, who was a prefect of Rome and a consul, died when Boethius was a boy, and this led to his being adopted by Quintus Symmachus. His new family was even more eminent than his native one, and thereby Boethius was confirmed as a member of the highest Patrician class in a period when the loyalties and virtues of that group were tested by service to Gothic rulers in Rome and by divisions within the Western and Eastern branches of the Church. He was evidently a juvenile prodigy, exhibiting talents for scholarship and administration. The latter skill drew him to the attention of King Theodoric the Ostrogoth, who quickly promoted him a consul and thereafter gave him the offices of *magister officiorum* and *magister dignitatis* – in effect, head of the civil service and of the royal court.

During his youth and the period of his early political career Boethius studied the available works of Plato, Aristotle, Cicero, Porphyry and Augustine (hence his remark about having been 'cared for in the house of philosophy'). Perhaps in recognition of impending cultural disaster he set himself the task of translating and writing commentaries on the major Greek philosophical texts; but a further, and presumably more important, motive for this work was his belief that the central ideas of Plato and Aristotle are mutually compatible sets of truths which provide the philosophical means for articulating Christian doctrine.

Following political and religious difficulties between the western and eastern branches of the Empire, Boethius was accused of treason, exiled and imprisoned in Pavia (in northern Italy), where he was brutally tortured and beaten to death in 524. It was during the period of his exile that he composed *De Consolatione*. This is largely in dialogue form, being divided into five books each of which is subdivided into sections containing prose and poetry. The work begins with Boethius bemoaning this wretched fate in muse-inspired verse:

> I who once composed with eager zest
> Am driven by grief to shelter in sad songs;
> All torn the Muses' cheeks who spell the words
> For elegies that wet my face with tears
> No terror could discourage them at least
> From coming with me on my way.
> They were the glory of my happy youth
> And still they comfort me in hapless age.[2]

As he reflects on what he has written, however, he becomes aware of the figure of a woman – the *Lady Philosophy* – and there then follows the description of her with which I began. Like the entire work, this description is rich in allusion: the Lady is aged but of 'undiminished vigour' (perennial wisdom), wearing a self-woven garment of imperishable cloth (incorruptible and auto-nomous) with an embroidered ladder leading from *Pi* to *Theta* (the continuous ascent from practical to theoretical philosophy), but showing signs of abuse (schism within philosophy itself).

Philosophy's first words concern the Muses from whom Boethius had been taking comfort:

> Who are these hysterical sluts to approach this sick man's bedside? . . . . These are the very women who kill the rich and fruitful harvest of Reason with the barren thorns of Passion. They habituate men to their sickness of mind instead of curing them . . . be gone, and leave him for my own Muses to heal and cure.[3]

These harsh words recall something of Socrates's criticisms of Homer,[4] and they are shortly followed by a direct reference to the dialogues in which Boethius's innocent predicament is likened to that of Socrates and, perhaps (through the use of the phrase 'a victorious death'), to that of Christ also.[5] So the healing cure begins. Following his rehearsal of his troubles and misery, Boethius is urged to recall that his nature transcends that of a rational mortal animal, and likewise that the ultimate reality is not the empirical order but the beginning and end (i.e. goal) of its existence, viz., God. Thus misery at worldly misfortune involves a double error: identifying the self with the embodying organism, and reality with the sensible world. Whereas the states of mind induced by the arts encourage this mis-identification, by directing attention towards sensuous forms, the effect of philosophy is to encourage composure and detachment by remind-ing the soul of its true nature and origins.

III

There are scarcely any present-day philosophical discussions of the stated theme of *De Consolatione*.[6] But an article has been published by Andrew Belsey in which he discusses various ironic aspects of the work and addresses the question of what view of the philosopher's vocation emerges from it (1991, pp. 1–15). Belsey brings certain broadly political interests to his reading of Boethius and worries at the apparent encouragement of retreat into phil-osophical contemplation. Throughout the work, however, he discerns various levels of irony in the public recommendation of private detachment, and so finds it possible at least to qualify the charge of self-indulgent Stoicism in the face of evil:

What was said in the act of saying, even if not in the saying itself, was true philosophy – the transcending of disengagement, the metamorphosing of private consolation into political action. Far from being a turncoat, Boethius would be a beacon illuminating the true philosophical path.

(1991, p. 14)

Belsey is properly alert to the likelihood of literary subtleties and paradoxes in the text, but I think there are philosophical complexities from which his attention is distracted by his moral-cum-political interest. As regards the question of whether Boethius is offering a basically contemplative solution to what I shall just call 'the problem of life', I think the answer is 'yes', but not in the form in which contemplation is first introduced (as a form of Stoical detachment), which is where Belsey focuses a good deal of his interest. Moreover, I think that if anything can be made of the idea of a philosophical solution to 'the problem', it will require a metaphysical outlook that is at once *more substantial* than the gaze of 'calm indifference' which Belsey finally allows – so long as it is accompanied by combat with 'the gross and contemptible evils of worldly power' (1991, p. 15) – but also *less substantial* than that endorsed by Boethius himself.

The dialogue is presented as the record of a course of treatment in which Boethius is given a series of increasingly more powerful cures. At each stage the condition of his soul is revealed by the character of his complaints against the order of things, and a cure is administered relative to that condition. There are, then, several forms of philosophical consolation, and it is important to see that while these overlap (to some extent), they also draw upon two distinct traditions, *Stoicism* and *Neoplatonism*, and differ in their metaphysical commitments and practical implications.

In *Book II*, Boethius is reminded that he has been as much the beneficiary of Fortune as her victim, and therefore has no grounds for complaint that she has dealt him an unwarranted blow. Nothing is deserved and no objection or resentment is in order when life takes an unwelcome turn. Knowing this, one should bear one's gains and losses with equanimity and hold fast to the only enduring goods: self-possession of one's soul, the knowledge that the course of events is under the direction of a cosmic force, and the love of true friends:

> The world in constant change
> Maintains a harmony,
> And elements keep peace
> Whose nature is to clash...
> If Love relaxed the reins
> All things that now keep peace
> Would wage continual war
> The fabric to destroy
> Which unity has formed
> With motions beautiful.

Love, too, holds peoples joined
By sacred bond of treaty...
O happy race of men
If Love who rules the sky
Could rule your hearts as well![7]

Although in his survey of the text Belsey notes other elements of consolation, the attitude he focuses upon is that induced by this phase of the treatment, namely Stoical 'enlightened acceptance'. But immediately following the verses quoted above, *Philosophy* passes on to the next stage of treatment, saying 'the remedies still to come are, in fact, of such a kind that they taste bitter to the tongue, but grow sweet once they are absorbed'.[8] This introduces a discussion of the varieties of happiness and a specification of the 'true form' which the soul has the power to attain by means of philosophy – again Augustine's *gaudium de veritate*. Two ideas appear early on in this *Book* which signal the development of a Neoplatonic and non-Stoic form of consolation. These are the doctrine of knowledge as recollection (*anamnesis*) and the notion that earthly unhappiness is a result of the soul's embodiment – like a captured song-bird reduced to whispered airs of longing for the woodland home.

From that point onwards the treatment accelerates with ever-more potent cures. It is argued that certain qualities are pre-eminent values, and that they are extensionally equivalent: 'sufficiency, power, glory, reverence and happiness differ in name but not in substance'.[9] There is then a prefiguring of Anselm's onto-logical proofs for the existence of a maximally great being, i.e. one possessed of these 'different but identical' qualities in their highest degree of perfection. Since what all things desire is their happiness, and perfect happiness is to be found in God, the task of philosophy becomes that of launching the soul into flight towards the still point of the turning worlds. There, at the invisible centre, is a divinity from out of whose intellect emerged all things corporeal and incorporeal. Since the soul is (or, more strictly, contains) intellect it has a co-natural affinity with the source of its being, and to the extent that it comes to be possessed of the same perfections as constitute both the divine essence and what that essence (in its guise as *Intellect*) contemplates, i.e. ideal forms, it is to that degree itself divine: 'Each happy individual is therefore divine. While only God is so by nature, as many as you like may become so by participation.'[10]

Philosophy has more to say in reply to Boethius's questions about fate and the existence of evil in a world ordained by Providence. Basically, the story is that fate is the working out of the divine order through the causal nexus, and it is an aspect of divine activity which enlightened intellects stand on the far side of, viewing it with satisfaction and not, as do the ignorant, with resentment. The effects of providence are only fate for those who do not or cannot understand them. Likewise, the appearance of evil is an illusion, everything that happens has point and works ultimately for the greater glory of *Nous*, or, as Boethius might more aptly have said, *ad maiorem dei gloriam*:

If you desire to see and understand
In purity of mind the laws of God,
Your sight must on the highest point of heaven rest
Where through the lawful covenant of things
The wandering stars preserve their ancient peace:...
Those things which stable order now protects,
Divorced from their true source would fall apart.
This is the love of which all things partake,
The end of good their chosen goal and close:
No other way can they expect to last,
Unless with love for love repaid they turn
And seek again the cause that gave them birth.[11]

What has now been reached is far from a Stoical philosophy of passive reconciliation. While it suggests that the philosophical life will be an active one, Belsey is right to imply that what Boethius commends is not his own preferred form of engagement, i.e. combatting 'the gross and contemptible evils of worldly power'. But nor, I think, is it quite that which Belsey actually attributes to Boethius in writing *De Consolatione*, i.e. a combination of metaphysics with 'the transcending of disengagement, the metamorphosing of private consolation into political action...[and] the continuation of engagement even to the tragic end'. For Boethius, the essence of *philosophy* consists in the perfecting of one's intellect, thereby participating in the eternal contemplative life of God. That is its consolation: the perfect quality of its object, and *ipso facto* of itself and of its accomplished practitioner. As Socrates has it, reason is best because its objects are most noble.[12] What this account involves are several decidedly Platonistic elements and processes. Some of these have already been indicated, but another which it is relevant to mention is the idea that our general concepts of things, such as those of cats, bats and rats, are not only innate but *could not* have been acquired from empirical experience of instances of these natures, since, strictly speaking, there are no such instances but only 'images' of natures:

[F]rom those forms which are outside matter come the forms which are in matter and produce bodies. We misname the entitles that reside in bodies when we call them forms; they are mere images; they only resemble those forms which are not incorporate in matter.[13]

IV

What, then, is to be made of Boethius as a source of consolation? Compounding my earlier questions, has he an intelligible and plausible view? If this means to ask whether someone who was troubled by 'the problem of life' might reasonably take comfort from words spoken by the *Lady Philosophy*, then I think the answer is 'yes'. The work contains much enduringly good spiritual guidance of a mundane sort about recognizing contingencies, not exaggerating one's misfortune, counting one's blessings and discounting trivial goods. Also, notwithstanding the Platonic demotion of the sensible world to the domain of images and the banishment of the Muses, there are some striking poetic reminders of natural beauty which prefigure Hopkins in both their style and spirituality:

> The flower-bearing year will breathe sweet scent,
> In summer torrid days will dry the corn,
> Ripe autumn will return with fruit endowed,
> And falling rains will moisten wintry days.
> This mixture brings to birth and nourishes
> All things submerged in death's finality.
> Meanwhile there sits on high the Lord of things,
> Who rules and guides the reins of all that's made,
> Their king and lord, their fount and origin,
> Their law and judge of what is right and due.[14]

None of this, however, amounts to a *consolation of philosophy* – as opposed to wise and welcome words from a philosopher. If one looks then to the Boethian philosophy itself, I think it may be intelligible that one should regard the possibility of participation in the life of a divine intellect not merely as comforting but as an all-consuming purpose of existence which would exclude the very possibility of knowledgeable misery. But while it may be coherent, it barely registers on the credibility measure. It is, at best, an intelligible but implausible hypothesis. Moreover, it is even unclear what would count as phenomenological evidence in its favour. What, if anything, would it be like to intuit the essence of catness? or more generally to comprehend being as such? And if the answer is that there is nothing it is experientially 'like' for one's intellect to grasp ideas in the mind of God, then I think the problem arises of how, even if this were a possibility, *we* – as we find ourselves in the coloured, flavoured, textured grain of life – could make sense of it, let alone find it worth striving after.

V

However, this is not the end of the story. I mentioned that in his commentary on Porphyry's introduction to Aristotle's *Categories* (philosopher's philosophy with a vengeance!) Boethius sets out a quite different ontology of forms; and it was this, rather than the Platonism of *De Trinitate* and *De Consolatione*, that so greatly influenced philosophers of the thirteenth-century Aristotelian revival, such as Albert the Great and Thomas Aquinas.

Abstracting from details and differences, the general metaphysical view is that what makes an empirical object to be the thing it is, is not the *stuff* out of which it is made (*materia*) but its nature or *form* (*forma rei*). The pen which I am holding as I write this, is what it is as a metaphysically necessary consequence of having the *form* it possesses (i.e. its shape, construction and causal powers) and not in virtue of being a quantity of bakelite. This form is something we become aware of by studying the individual object. It is not something purely sensible, since, for example, function, and causal powers more generally, go beyond anything given in actual experience and warrant counterfactual claims. Still, by the exercise of reason and imagination in co-operation with sense-experience, we can say that in a broad sense the forms of things can be 'perceived'. This claim has two important aspects: first, the objects of such attention are individuals not universals; and second, they are objects of embodied experience not pure intellection.

It is not excluded by this view that there might also be the intellectual grasp of general natures abstracted from observation of individuals, but that is a further matter. According to one interpretation, what this involves is the intellect acquiring a nature identical to that of the abstracted form. Thus, for catness to exist as a universal nature apart from any actual cat's nature is just for some intellect to be informed by, and hence to be thinking of, the species-form catness. In the scholastic terminology of Aquinas, the actualization of the form is *one and the same thing as* the relevant actualization of the intellect thinking of it – *intelligibile in actu est intellectus in actu.*[15]

The relevant upshot is that a less extravagant version of Boethius's idea of philosophical consolation may now be available. We may say that human beings have the capacity to comprehend the natures of things, both individual and universal forms, and that the actualization of this capacity is a mode of self-realization through the exercise of our higher powers. Then, for reasons parallel to those given by Boethius, we may find it intelligible to say that this form of activity constitutes *a* purpose in life which renders it valuable and which eases or even eliminates 'the problem'. Assuming that the metaphysics of this view is intelligible and even plausible (and I believe it to be both), the questions remain of whether there is real reason to think that the contemplation of 'Aristotelian' forms is any more credible as philosophical consolation than Boethius's alternative, and whether there is any phenomenological basis for it. I shall end on what has to be a fairly brief consideration of these questions.

VI

Earlier, I mentioned the interpretation of a type of thoughtful experience associated with the observation of art and nature. The sort of thing I have in mind stands in need of philosophical investigation anyhow, and it would be a welcome outcome if the question of its nature and that of whether there is a form of philosophical consolation could be brought into complementary resolution. Here it will be best to proceed by example, and for reasons of personal familiarity but also because, as Aquinas says, visual perception is one of the most cognitive forms of experience,[16] I shall take my examples from painting and sculpture.

In the history of art an important growth point is marked by the career of Giotto – it is interesting and no accident that this was roughly contemporary with that of Aquinas.[17] In painting of the earlier Byzantine tradition subjects are treated in an apparently stylized iconographic fashion. This is not so much due to the loss of knowledge, formerly possessed by the Romans, of how to paint naturalistically, as to the Neoplatonic metaphysics that informed the Eastern Church Fathers who, in turn, shaped the theology of Christian culture. The Byzantine treatment of religious themes such as the crucifixion involves a timeless, 'viewpointless' presentation of the subject which is designed to suggest to the spectator the appearance of a transcendental realm. With Giotto, however, the depicted forms assume their natural embodiment. Figures possess the solidity and mobility of incarnate beings, are seen to occupy an environment of earth and air and are caressed by a light whose 'temperature' is almost sensible.

So began a tradition of aesthetic naturalism that was developed in a range of ways over the next six hundred years. Within this history, though, is a particular strand of pictorial treatment of material forms that is difficult to describe but easy to recognize once one is attuned to it. As well as Giotto, painters in this 'tradition' include Masaccio, Fra Angelico, Piero Della Francesca, Bellini, Vermeer, Chardin and Morandi. The domination by Italian artists may be significant, since part of what defines this group is the quality of the light which passes around and between the objects depicted and also spreads over them. The light, the geometry of apparently simple forms and the softly glowing or crumbling colours create an atmosphere that beckons and reassures the viewer that therein all is for the best. The values realized are those of simplicity, humility, serenity, dignity and, one might now add in echo of Boethius, of sufficiency, reverence and goodness. Consider two responses to Chardin's still-lives:

> Here you are again, you great magician, with your silent compositions! How eloquently they speak to the artist!…how the air circulates among these objects, and sunlight itself does not better reduce the disparities between the things it falls upon. For you there are neither matching nor clashing colours…[18]

> The miracle in Chardin's paintings is this: modelled in their own mass and shape, drawn with their own light, created so to speak from the soul of their colour, the objects seem to detach themselves from the canvas and become alive…[19]

These judgements are immediately intelligible and single out authentic features of the 'tradition', but they do not hit upon the particular, almost mystical quality that inheres in a few Chardins but is more clearly and more often present in the work of others of the group. The most telling of the later members is Morandi. Born in 1890, he was a near contemporary of de Chirico, with whom he was an associate in the *Pittura Metaphysica* group of the last years of the First World War. But while the association with de Chirico under the 'metaphysical painting' description is intelligible it is also quite misleading. For when one considers relevant work by the two painters it is clear that the mysterious qualities in their canvases are quite different in each case.

What de Chirico achieves by his vacant neo-classical city-squares and shadow-hung cloisters is a sense of absence, as if the reality lies elsewhere and what we see is intended to question whether the normal course of experience is not itself a dream or a fantasy. In this he shares the challenging spirit of the surrealists. But apart from some early pieces that resemble de Chirico's works of the same period, Morandi's paintings have about them a quite different air of mystery. They do not challenge one's sense of reality but rather provide a kind of ontological reassurance. Things are what and how they are, and the contemplative grasp of this realizes a need to place oneself philosophically within the world. It is a great tribute to de Chirico, I think, that he recognized the special quality of Morandi's vision:

> Giorgio Morandi searches and creates in solitude....He looks at a collection of objects on a table with the same emotions that stirred the heart of the traveller in ancient Greece when he gazed on the woods and valleys and mountains reputed to be the dwelling places of the most beautiful and marvellous deities.
>
> These objects are dead for us because they are immobile. But he looks at them with belief, he finds comfort in their inner structure – *their eternal aspect.*
>
> In this way he has contributed to the lyricism of the last important movement in European art: *the metaphysics of the common object.* However much we may be aware that appearances deceive, we often look at familiar things with the eyes of one who *sees and does not know.*[20]

In conclusion, then, the thought which I wish to propose for further consideration is that there is a mode of thinking of the nature of things which is contemplative but which does not seek to transcend the realm of numerically distinct empirical forms. When it comprehends those forms for what they are, and *ipso facto* comprehends the immanent principles of being of individual objects, it is satisfied at having engaged with reality and thereby having realized itself. This is the consolation Boethius believed he had found, that of uniting oneself with the real, of coming to be at one with things – not, as mystics have often claimed, at one with everything, the totality itself being conceived of, in Parmenidean style, as a unity, but united with each thing as one contemplates it for what it is.

Unlike Boethius's Platonic version, this account is believable and may be confirmed in the experience of a kind of art that defines itself in terms of the possibility of developing and communicating a sense of the being of things. If this account of the phenomenology of such works is correct, then the complementary resolution of which I spoke earlier has been achieved. The experience of a Morandi provides an entry into a perceptual mode of contemplative thought which constitutes one interpretation of the consolation of philosophy, and the consolation of philosophy answers the question: What explains the feeling one has, on seeing a Morandi, that in some sense all is well?

Let me add one final note by way of further evidence of a near equivalence between a certain kind of thoughtful art and a mode of philosophical reflection. In describing the relevant artistic tradition I spoke of pictorial treatments of objects, and I have thus far only discussed the work of painters. Among our contemporaries, however, are a number of sculptors who have sometimes achieved, and succeeded in communicating, the consoling vision of things as they are. Among these I would include Richard Long and Tony Cragg. While the characters and sensibilities of these artists differ markedly, at its best their work contributes a distinctive late-twentieth-century element to the 'tradition'. Why that should be is suggested by the following remarks of each discussing their work. First Long:

> I like simple, practical, emotional
> quiet vigorous art.
> I like the simplicity of walking,
> the simplicity of stones.
> I like common materials, whatever is to hand,
> but especially stones, I like the idea that stones
> are what the world is made of.
> I like common means given the
> simple twist of art.
> I like sensibility without technique.
>
> (1980)

Then Cragg:

> The need to know both objectively and subjectively more about the subtle fragile relationships between us, objects, images and essential natural processes and conditions is becoming critical. It is very important to have first order experiences – seeing touching smelling, hearing – with objects/images *and to let that experience register.*
>
> (1982, p. 340)

Finally, the idea that a kind of spiritual enlightenment consists in experiencing the real for what it is, and being consoled by it, also finds eloquent expression in the following words put into the mouth of Kim by Rudyard Kipling:

> Then he looked upon the trees and the broad fields, with the thatched huts hidden among crops – looked with strange eyes unable to take up the size

and proportion and use of things – stared for a still half-hour. All that while he felt, though he could not put it into words, that his soul was out of gear with its surroundings – a cog wheel unconnected with any machinery...

He did not want to cry – had never felt less like crying in his life – but of a sudden easy, stupid tears trickled down his nose, and with an almost audible click he felt the wheels of his being lock up anew on the world without. Things that rode meaningless on the eyeball an instant before slid into proper proportion. Roads were meant to be walked upon, houses to be lived in, cattle to be driven, fields to be tilled, and men and women to be talked to. They were all real and true – solidly planted upon the feet – perfectly comprehensible – clay of his clay, neither more nor less.

(1901)

In Boethius's figurative rendering, as *Philosophy* approached, 'the clouds of my grief dissolved and I drank in the light'.

Notes

1 Boethius, *Consolation*, I, prose 1 and 3, pp. 35–9.
2 Ibid., I, poem 1, p. 35.
3 Ibid., I, prose 1, p. 36.
4 Plato, *Republic* 595b9–c3 and 607c3–8. Also St Augustine, see *De Doctrina Christiana*, ii, 18, 28.
5 Boethius, *Consolation*, I, prose 3, p. 39. The parallel with Christ is suggested in passing by Henry Chadwick in his excellent book *Boethius: The Consolations of Music, Logic, Theology and Philosophy* (Oxford: Clarendon, 1981).
6 I mean by this to exclude the literature on Boethius's discussions of divine fore-knowledge and human freedom.
7 Boethius, *Consolation*, II, poem 8, p. 77.
8 Ibid., III, prose 1, p. 78.
9 Ibid., III, prose 9, p. 95.
10 Ibid., III, prose 10, p. 102.
11 Ibid., IV, poem 6, pp. 141–2.
12 Plato, *Republic*, 509d6–511e5.
13 Boethius, *De Trinitate*, II, as translated by H. Stewart and E. Rand, *The Theological Tracts*, Loeb Classical Library, *Boethius* (London: Heinemann, 1926).
14 Boethius, *Consolation*, IV, poem 6, p. 142. Compare this with, for example, Hopkins's poem 'God's Grandeur' (in particular the second stanza): The world is charged with the grandeur of God./It will flame out, like shining from shook foil;/It gathers to a greatness, like the ooze of oil/Crushed. Why do men then now not reck his rod?/Generations have trod, have trod, have trod;/And all is seared with trade; bleared, smeared with toil;/And wears man's smudge and shares man's smell: the soil/Is bare now, nor can foot feel, being shod./And for all this, nature is never spent;/There lives the dearest freshness deep down things;/and though the last lights off the black West went/Oh morning, at the brown brink eastward, springs – /Because the Holy Ghost over the bent/World broods with warm breast and ah! bright wings. *The Poems of Gerard Manley Hopkins*, ed. W.H. Gardner and N.H. MacKenzie, 4th edn (Oxford: Clarendon, 1970), p. 66.
15 Aquinas, *Summa Theologiae*, I, q. 14, a. 2.

16 Ibid., I-II, q. 27, a. 1.
17 For brief discussions of related matters see J. Haldane, 'Aquinas', 'Mediaeval and Renaissance Aesthetics' and 'Plotinus', in D. Cooper (ed.), *A Companion to Aesthetics* (Oxford: Blackwell, 1992).
18 Diderot, Review of the Paris Salon of 1765, quoted in P. Rosenberg, *Chardin* (Lausanne: Skira, 1963), p. 96.
19 E. and J. de Goncourt, *Gazette des Beaux Arts*, 1863–64, in Rosenberg, *Chardin*, p. 101.
20 G. de Chirico, 'Giorgio Morandi', from *La Fiorentina Primaverile* (1922), republished in *Giorgio Morandi* (London: Arts Council, 1970), p. 6.

References

Belsey, A. (1991) 'Boethius and the Consolation of Philosophy, or How to be a Good Philosopher', *Ratio* (New Series) 4.
Boethius (1987) *The Consolation of Philosophy*, trans. V.E. Watts (London: Penguin).
Chadwick, H. (1981) *Boethius: The Consolations of Music, Logic, Theology and Philosophy* (Oxford: Clarendon).
Cragg, T. (1982) 'Statement', *Documenta 7*.
Kipling, R. (1901) *Kim* (London: Macmillan).
Long, R. (1980) *Words After the Fact* (London: Anthony d'Offay).
Quine, W.V. (1981) 'Has Philosophy Lost Contact with People?', in *Theories and Things* (Cambridge, Mass.: Belknap Press).
Stewart, H. and Rand, E. (1926) *The Theological Tracts*, Loeb Classical Library. *Boethius* (London: Heinemann).

Index

Abelard, Peter 122–3
abortion 145–6, 174–5, 179, 232
abstraction 192–5, 238
action, costs of 140–1, 143, 149; theory necessary for 45, 225–6
Acton, Lord 60–1
aesthetic: delight 256–7; experience 238, 245, 248, 258–9, 263, 274; objects 238, 244, 248, 252–3, 258–9, 275; objects, identity of 259–61; value 259
aesthetics, history of 237–42; of common things 275–8; of environment 253, 256–63
Albert the Great 4, 123, 240, 273
Alberti, Leon Battista 241, 244, 246
Alcuin of York 95–6, 100
Alfred, King 266
analytical philosophy xii, 11–14, 75, 152–3, 186; defects of 12–13
Analytical Roman ARCIC 33
analytical Thomism x–xii, 10–11, 14
Anderson, John 187
Anglican-Roman ARCIC 33, 59–60, 108
Anscombe, Elizabeth xii, 10, 12, 16–18, 137–8, 222
Anselm 3–4, 121–3, 156, 237, 271
Apostles 97, 216, 224
Aquinas, Thomas x, xii–xiv, 3, 123, 126, 186, 227, 240; 'Angelic Doctor' 6; and Aristotle 3–4, 124, 191; on beauty 247–8, 252–3, 261–3; canonized 5; life of 4; on capacities 193–4; on form and matter 89–90, 108, 153, 158–60, 191–2, 247–8, 273–4; on future life 103; on human form 54, 81–2, 108, 124, 141, 156, 158, 167, 193–4, 196; on mind x–xi, 193; on moral knowledge 117; on moral law 123–4,

137; on ontology xi, xiv; on potential and actual 89–90; on practical reasoning xiv, 131, 140, 223–4, 232; on preconditions of learning 20, 190–5; on pursuit of good 117, 120, 136, 142, 193; on right reason 123–5; on social human nature 141–2, 167–8, 173, 195, 218; on substance/attribute 89–90; realism of 24, 27–8
architecture 243–53; and culture 250–1; as design 244–5; essentially functional 243, 245, 250, 253; universal principles of? 243; vernacular 251
argument to consistency 143
argumentum ex convenientia 96
Aristotle xiii, 124–6, 136, 139, 141, 239–40, 268, 273, on capacities 193; on form and matter 39, 88–9, 129, 267; on natural justice 130; on practical reasoning 223–4, 232; on right reasoning 116; on substance/attribute 89, 191; *see also* virtue, Aristotelian theory of
art, and craft 243–5; and mathematics 239–41; non-naturalistic 240, 275; techniques of 240–2, 275
aspect-involving 83–6, 92
Assumption 46, 67, 94–5; coherent possibility? 94, 96–7, 100–1, 105, 108; early celebration of 97–9, 107–8; evidence for 94–7; nature of 101–9; ought implies did 95–6, 100, 107; sources for 97–9, 107–8
Augustine 3–4, 76, 122, 256–7, 267, 271; on conscience 117–18, 120; on heaven 103; on merit 120
Austin, J.L. 12
Ayer, A.J. 12